Genetic Engineering

DREAM OR NIGHTMARE?

Turning the Tide on the Brave New World
of Bad Science and Big Business

Mae-Wan Ho

Second Edition Revised and Updated

D1270463

Continuum • New York

2000

The Continuum Publishing Company
370 Lexington Avenue
New York, NY 10017 6503

First published by Gateway 1998
Revised edition 1999
© 1998, 1999 Mae-Wan Ho and Third World Network

Printed by ColourBooks Ltd, Dublin, Ireland

Library of Congress Cataloging-in-Publication Data

Ho, Mae-Wan
    Genetic engineering : dream or nightmare? : turning the tide on the
brave new world of bad science and big business / Mae-Wan Ho. —
2nd ed. rev. and upated.
    p.cm.
Includes bibliographical references and index.
ISBN 0-8264-1257-2
    1. Genetic engineering–Moral and ethical aspects. 2.
Biotechnology–Moral and ethical aspects. I. Title.
QH442.H6 2000
174'.966—dc21   99-086899

CONTENTS

PREFACE TO THE FIRST EDITION

In July, 1994, I attended a meeting that changed my life. It was a conference in Penang, Malaysia, with the enigmatic title, Redefining the Life Sciences, and had been organised by Vandana Shiva, Martin Khor, Tewolde Egziabher and my colleague at the Open University, Brian Goodwin.

I was invited, along with fifty other participants, consisting of scientists, social scientists, policy-makers and political activists, and drawn from fifteen countries. I learned how the dominant reductionist scientific world view of the West was destroying the earth, creating poverty and suffering for vast numbers of people. At the same time, I learned how those same people were regenerating the land and their livelihoods with indigenous wisdom accumulated and passed down through the ages. Within a day, we felt like friends who had lost touch for a hundred years. We drafted a Scientists' Statement on the Need for Greater Regulation and Control of Genetic Engineering which was published by the Third World Network and widely distributed.

As a result of that inspiring meeting, I began to realise how much science matters in the affairs of the real world, not just in terms of practical inventions like genetic engineering, but in how that scientific world view takes hold of people's unconscious, making them act, unthinkingly, to shape the world to the detriment of human beings, how that science is used, often without conscious intent, to intimidate and control, how it is used to obfuscate, to exploit and oppress. I began to see how that dominant world view generates a selective blindness in scientists themselves, making them ignore scientific evidence, or fail to interpret correctly. I have felt obliged, ever since, to tell the other side of the story, in the interest of promoting real public understanding of science in general, and of genetic engineering biotechnology in particular. Earlier this year, Martin Khor finally convinced me to write this book, by skilfully sketching out its structure for me.

This book argues the case against genetic engineering biotechnology as bad science working together with big business for quick profit, against the public good, against public will and aspirations, against the moral values of society and the world community. I show how bad science, in the form of genetic determinism, is at odds with the reality of scientific findings. How it gives rise to misguided practices and to projects in genetic engineering biotechnology that are unethical and exploitative. I show how the very failures of genetic engineering biotechnology stem from the inability (of reductionist thinking) to take account of complexity, interconnectedness and wholeness. Most of all, it reveals how that same genetic determinist mindset leads scientists to ignore or misread existing scientific evidence already strongly suggesting that genetic engineering biotechnology is inherently hazardous to human and animal health and to the ecological environment.

It is a matter of urgency that an immediate moratorium should be imposed on any further release or marketing of genetically engineered products, pending an independent public enquiry into the hazards and risks of genetic engineering biotechnology which takes into proper account the most comprehensive body of scientific findings, as well as the social and moral implications.

This book owes its existence to so many of my friends that I hope they will forgive me if I fail to mention all of their names. Edward Goldsmith and Peter Bunyard initiated me to Gaia and global ecology and gave me the benefit of their extensive knowledge. Martin Khor, Vandana Shiva, Chee Yoke Ling, Tewolde Egziabher and Gurdial Nijar of the Third World Network all taught me a great deal about world politics and inspired me with their spirited, selfless dedication to the defence of freedom, equity, democracy, justice, and all the other noble qualities that make us human. I shared many seminars and workshops with Beatrix Tappeser, Christine von Weizsäcker, Elaine Ingham and Beth

Burrows, who also provided a substantial amount of the material that appears in this book. Sue Mayer, Isobel Meister, David King, Ricarda Steinbrecher, Liz Hoskens, Helena Paul, Kristin Dawkins, Doug Parr, Philip Bereano, Jaan Suurkula and Jan Storms have kept me informed of their campaigns, and sent me valuable material besides, via the Internet.

This book is a tribute to the many public interest organisations from all over the world, as well as the official UN delegates from many countries. I would like to mention, in particular, Kalemani Joe Mulongoy, for his efforts in ensuring public participation in the democratic process while he was a member of the Secretariat of the Biological Diversity Convention in charge of Biotechnology and Biosafety, for insisting that all sides of the biotechnology debate should be heard by policy-makers while he was Director of the Programme on Biotechnology and Biosafety at the International Academy of the Environment in Geneva and, most of all, for his integrity and the sacrifice he has had to endure in the interest of bringing transparency and equity to the world.

Many thanks are due to Vandana Shiva, Brian Goodwin, Peter Schei, Richard Strohman, Harry Rubin, Jaan Suurkula, Joe Cummins, Edward Goldsmith, David Korten, Eric Schneider, Helena Paul, Christine von Weizsäcker, Giles Maynard, Alick Bartholomew, Busca Mileusnic, Steven Rose and, especially, Charles Jencks, for reading and commenting on earlier versions of the manuscript.

I would like to stress that this book is not a personal attack on genetic engineers or molecular geneticists. Among the latter, I wish to express my indebtedness to Sue Povey and Dallas Swallow, with whom I had ventured into molecular genetics in the early 1980s, and who taught me most of what I know about genetic engineering biosafety. Jeff Pollard and Ted Steele have taught me a lot about the fluid genome, and continue to keep me in touch with their work. Thanks are also due to Peter Lund, David Heaf and others of the Ifgene group, with whom I have had many discussions on genetics and ethics.

Julian Haffegee not only assisted me in preparing this book, but kept the research in our laboratory going while I was fully occupied in writing. Christine Randall, my secretary, helped in organising my work and creating extra time for me in a hundred different ways. Last, but by no means least, I have benefited immensely from discussing many of the ideas in this book with Peter Saunders and Brian Goodwin, both of whom are involved in different aspects of the new science of organic complexity. Without their constant support and encouragement this book may well never have been finished.

Finally, I emphasise that none of those mentioned should be held responsible for the defects in my presentation, nor for the views expressed.

August 1997

PREFACE TO THE SECOND EDITION

In the eighteen months since the first edition of this book appeared there has been an extraordinary groundswell of opposition to genetic-engineering agriculture in Britain, which is now spreading like a shock wave throughout the world. Local action and campaigning groups mushroomed, from remote villages to the metropolis, their membership spanning the social spectrum and bridging all age gaps. Never before has civil society been so united. A resounding chorus of 'No to GMO!' has come from consumers, retailers, wholesalers, food and wine writers, and restaurateurs. The two biggest food giants in the world, Unilever and Nestlé, have joined in. Record numbers of farmers are converting to organic methods, as demand for organic produce is outstripping supply. Britain is among the seven European countries now operating bans on transgenic crops or a moratorium. Greece and five other EU countries have officially called for a moratorium throughout Europe.

It has been a truly inspiring year, thanks in large measure to the tireless efforts of citizens in local communities organising public debates, discussions, demonstrations, and other actions. And no-one should underestimate the power of the barrage of letters sent to members of Parliament and to local supermarkets. This is a critical moment in the history of our planet, when civil society is recapturing the agenda for the next millennium.

The debate on the future of agriculture has begun in earnest, but the one on health has yet to take place. We decided on a new edition of this book to update it with regard to events and, in particular, to take in the latest scientific findings, which strengthen the case argued: that genetic-engineering biotechnology is an extremely dangerous diversion from the real tasks of providing food, security and health care for all. We have also improved the clarity and style of presentation, and corrected typographical and other errors. A brief guideline on 'How to read this book' is added to help different readers find their way more easily.

The continuing support of those mentioned in the first edition has been crucial for this one. In addition I owe a lot to new friends and acquaintances acquired since then. Terje Traavik, a virologist from the University of Tromsø, Norway, and Vyvyan Howard, a toxicologist from the University of Liverpool, became my co-authors in an important publication on the contribution of genetic-engineering biotechnology to the recent resurgence of infectious diseases. Terje taught me a lot about the dangers of naked DNA. We had great fun sharing a people's biotechnology road-show in Canada, Switzerland, India, and Cameroon. Vyvyan got me thinking on the effects of environmental pollutants on horizontal gene transfer and is himself vigorously arguing the case for a moratorium.

Joe Cummins, emeritus professor of genetics in the University of Western Ontario, and Harmut Meyer of Friends of the Earth, Germany, also became my co-authors in another publication on the 'biotechnology bubble', in both the financial and technological sense of the term. Joe is the most knowledgeable geneticist I have ever met, and among the first to warn of the hazards of genetic engineering. I continue to benefit enormously from the essential service he provides in monitoring the dense scientific literature for the latest developments and transmitting them in a pre-digested form.

I have had the pleasure and privilege of sharing platforms with Michael Antoniou, who for a long time was the only practising molecular geneticist in Britain to speak openly on the hazards of genetic-engineering agriculture. His eloquence and integrity are an inspiration to all.

I also met great campaigners all over the world: Farhad Mazhar of Naya Krishi Andolan and Farida Akhtar of UBINIG from Bangladesh, who successfully fought the attempt by Monsanto to use the microcredit scheme to introduce transgenic agriculture into their country; Étienne Vernet of Ecoropa, France, who mobilised French scientists to openly question the safety of transgenic agriculture, and French farmers to revolt against the introduction of Novartis's transgenic maize; Florianne Koechlin and Pierre Lehmann, who campaigned for the Swiss referendum on banning transgenic agriculture and 'patents on life'; Isabel Bermejo, who first alerted the Spanish NGOs to the hazards of genetic-engineering biotechnology; Clare Watson and Quentin Gargan of Genetic Concern in Ireland, who mounted the first legal challenge against the Irish Government for approving field trials of trans-genic crops; and in Britain, Malcolm Walker of Iceland Foods, the first retailer to reject transgenic produce, Patrick Holden of the Soil Association, who put organic agriculture firmly into the bio-technology debate, and Peter Melchett of Greenpeace UK, who organised, among other things, the boycott of genetically engineered foods by hundreds of food and wine writers.

The electronic mail-outs of numerous campaigning groups and networks have been invaluable: the Genetic Engineering Network (Jacklyn Sheedy and others), the Wessex Natural Law Party (Mark Griffiths), Food Bytes (Ronnie Cummins). Diverse Women for Diversity (Beth Burrows), Biotech Activists (Mark Ritchie), FoE Mailout (Dan Leskien), and Greenpeace International (Benedikt Haerlin). Excellent papers, reports and analyses were provided in particular by Rachel's Environmental Weekly (Peter Montaigue).

It's a pleasure to acknowledge Alick and Mari Bartholomew, Tina Currie, Kevin Redpath and Barbara Pinto for their enthusiasm and good will, which were crucial to the success of the first edition. Angela Ryan and Julian Haffegee provided much-needed intellectual and technical support for the preparation of this new edition.

I would like to thank all who have collected signatures for the State of the World Statement on our behalf, or have sent in their own signatures, often accompanied by encouraging letters. I am also grateful to everyone who has commented to me on the book, personally, by letter, or e-mail, or has reviewed it in publications.

I am especially indebted to Moyra Bremner, who staunchly and eloquently defended me against an unfair critic and gave me plenty of good advice on how to improve the book. I apologise for failing to reply to everyone personally, because of intolerable pressures of speaking and other engagements; but I have taken all praises and criticisms equally to heart in preparing this edition.

How to read this book

This book aims to provide genuine understanding of the science underlying genetic-engineering biotechnology to the full spectrum of general readers who may not have any training in biology or genetics. I have in mind consumers, farmers and food retailers who want to decide whether to accept genetically engineered foods; health practitioners, insurers and people with disabling conditions looking for an informed perspective on genetic diagnosis and gene therapy; ordinary citizens concerned about the ethical implications of genetic discrimination, eugenics, human cloning, patents on organisms and genes, and effects on the Third World; and finally, activists and policy-makers seeking a global picture of how genetic-engineering biotechnology is shaping world politics and economics, as well as a deeper understanding of the science involved, in order to guide policy decisions.

The book is structured with this mixed readership in mind, and for this reason each chapter starts with a short synopsis. Chapter 1 is essentially self-contained and outlines the main arguments and themes covered in more detail in the rest of the book. You may wish to stop or pause here; but it will be rewarding to proceed at least to the next two chapters, each of which is also self-contained. Chapter 2 gives a more clearly defined picture of how genetic determinism drives and promotes the applications of genetic engineering and its social impacts; how it legitimises patents on organisms, including human beings and their genes; and how it justifies the lack of regulation and shapes world politics. Chapter 3 describes how genetic determinism has failed the reality test, even by the criteria of science itself. This not only accounts for the problems experienced with many of the applications but also explains why the technology is hit-or-miss and inherently hazardous.

To proceed, read chapter 8 on genetic engineering in agriculture, which will tell you what you need to know about genetically engineered foods and why genetic engineering does not feed the world. Chapter 10 explains the science behind the Dolly phenomenon and also deals with cloning and transgenic animals in general. To round off, read chapter 13 for a glimpse of the holistic perspective towards which the new genetics and other developments in contemporary Western science are leading us.

If your appetite for further knowledge and understanding is whetted after that, please read the rest. Chapters 4, 5 and 6 give a unique perspective of how genetic determinism emerged from a particular social and political situation and serves to reinforce the prejudices and falsehoods that gave birth to it. Chapter 7 is meant for those who want to know more about the fascinating findings of the new genetics and how it overturned every assumption of genetic determinism. Chapter 9 examines the possible links between genetic-engineering biotechnology and the resurgence of drug-resistant and antibiotic-resistant infectious diseases, which is precipitating a public health crisis throughout the world. Chapters 11 and 12 deal with the fallacies, pitfalls and hazards in the application of genetic-engineering biotechnology to human genetics and health.

Throughout these chapters I have explained as much of the science as is required for readers to be able to judge for themselves whether the arguments presented are valid. Personally, I have never taken 'expert opinion' simply on trust without understanding and questioning it; I hope my readers will do likewise.

We desperately need a wide-ranging, open and informed debate on all aspects of genetic-engineering biotechnology, and this book is a contribution towards that end.

One

THE UNHOLY ALLIANCE

Genetic-engineering biotechnology is an unprecedented intimate alliance between bad science and big business, which will spell the end of humanity as we know it, and of the world at large. Genetic-engineering biotechnology is inherently hazardous; but the genetic-determinist mentality that misinforms both practitioners and the public takes hold of people's consciousness, making them act unquestioningly to shape the world to the detriment of human beings and all its other inhabitants.

The Brave New World dawns

As the twentieth century draws to a close, people are waking up to the realisation that genetic-engineering biotechnology is threatening to take over every aspect of their lives. They have been caught unprepared for the avalanche of products arriving, or soon to arrive, in their supermarkets: rapeseed oil, soybean, maize, sugar beet, squash, cucumber …

It started as a mere trickle less than five years ago. First came the BST milk from cows injected with genetically engineered bovine growth hormone to boost milk yield; then the tomato genetically engineered to prolong shelf life. These products provoked much debate and opposition, as did the genetic screening tests for an increasing number of diseases. Surely, we thought, we wouldn't, and shouldn't, be rushed headlong into this Brave New World.

To quell our anxiety, a series of highly publicised consensus conferences and public consultations were held. Committees were set up by many European governments to consider the risks and the ethics; and the debates continued. The public were dimly aware of critics who deplored the idea of tampering with nature and scrambling the genetic information of species by introducing human genes into animals, and animal genes into vegetables. These critics warned of unexpected effects on agriculture and biodiversity, of the dangers of genetic pollution that could not be reversed. (*Biodiversity* is the diversity of living organisms in an ecosystem, defined as the total number of species or higher taxonomic categories.) They warned of genetic discrimination and the return of eugenics as genetic screening and prenatal diagnosis became widely available. They condemned the immorality of the 'patents on life', which include transgenic animals, plants and seeds taken from the Third World, as well as human genes and cell lines taken from indigenous peoples.

But by and large the public were lulled into a false sense of security, in the belief that the best scientists in the world and the new breed of 'bio-ethicists' were busy considering the risks associated with the new biotechnology and the ethical issues raised. Simultaneously, attractive pamphlets and reports were widely distributed by the biotech industries and their friends, and even by the government's own research councils. Their aim was to promote public understanding of 'genetic modification' (the term 'engineering' having been banished by the promoters, on the grounds that it sounded too unfriendly and frightening). Genetic modification, we were told, was simply the latest in a seamless continuum of biotechnologies practised by human beings since the dawn of civilisation, from the making of bread and wine to selective breeding. The significant advantage of genetic modification was that it was much more precise, as genes could be individually isolated and transferred as desired.

In this way, it was suggested, the possible benefits to humankind were limitless. There was something to satisfy everyone. For those morally concerned about inequality and human suffering, the technology promised to feed the hungry by genetically modifying crops so as to resist pests and diseases and to increase yield. For those who despaired of the present global environmental deterioration it promised to modify strains of bacteria and higher plants so that they could degrade toxic wastes or mop up heavy metals to clean up the environment. For those hankering after sustainable agriculture it promised to develop greener, more environmentally responsible transgenic crops, which would reduce the use of pesticides, herbicides, and fertilisers.

That was not all. It was in the realm of human genetics that the real revolution would be wrought. This was dedicated to uncovering the genetic blueprint of the human being; it would eventually enable geneticists to diagnose, in advance, all the diseases that a person would suffer in his or her lifetime, even before that person was born, or even as the egg was fertilised *in vitro*. A whole gamut of specific drugs could then be designed to cure all diseases, tailored to individual genetic needs. Even the possibility of immortality was dangling on the horizon as the claim was made that a 'longevity gene' had been isolated.

There were problems, of course, as there would be in any new technology. The ethical issues had to be decided by the public (by implication, the *science* was separate and not open to question). The risks had to be minimised (again, by implication, the risks had nothing to do with the science). After all, nothing in life is without risk; one takes risks simply by crossing the street. The new biotechnology (that is, genetic-engineering biotechnology) was under very strict government regulation, and the government's scientists and other experts would see to it that neither the consumer nor the environment would be unduly harmed.

Then came the relaxation of regulation on genetically modified products, especially in the United States, on the grounds that over-regulation was compromising the 'competitiveness' of the industry, and that hundreds of field trials had demonstrated the new biotechnology to be safe. And in any case, it was argued, there was no essential difference between transgenic plants produced by the new biotechnology and those produced by conventional breeding methods. (During a public debate with me, Henry Miller, a prominent spokesperson for the industry in the United States, went as far as to refer to the varieties produced by conventional breeding methods, *retrospectively,* as 'transgenics'.)[1] This was followed a year later by an avalanche of products, approved or seeking approval for the market, for which neither segregation from produce that was not genetically engineered nor special labelling was required. One was left to wonder why, if the products were as safe and as wonderful as claimed, they could not be segregated, as organic produce has been for years, giving consumers the choice of buying what they want.

Almost immediately, as though acting on cue, the Association of British Insurers announced that, in future, people applying for life insurance policies would have to divulge the results of any genetic tests they had taken. This was seen by many as a definite move towards open genetic discrimination. A few days later a scientist at the Roslin Institute near Edinburgh, Ian Wilmut, announced that the institute had successfully 'cloned' a sheep from a cell taken from the mammary gland of an adult animal. Dolly, the cloned lamb, was born.[2] The popular media went wild, with, at one extreme, heroic enthusiasm and, at the other, a Frankenstein-like horror. Of course it took nearly three hundred trials to get one success, but no mention was made of the huge majority of the embryos that failed. Why, I wonder, has this work only come to public attention now, when the research has been going on for at least ten years? Was that ethical? If it could be done in sheep, did it mean it could be done in other mammals? Are we now nearer to cloning human beings?

Before a year had elapsed a scientist in Chicago, Richard Seed, announced that he would begin work on cloning humans. President Clinton reacted swiftly, calling for legislation to ban human cloning, as did thirteen European countries. Among those who have objected are the House of Commons Science and Technology Committee, which has said it wants British law to be amended to make sure that human cloning is illegal. President Chirac of France and the German Minister for Research, Jürgen Rüttgers, have both also called for an international ban on human cloning. There is virtual unanimity among doctors and scientists that the technique is 'untested and unsafe and morally unacceptable.'[3] Seed scoffs at his detractors, saying that what is feared now will be tolerated and, eventually, enthusiastically endorsed.

A report appeared the following day in the Norwegian daily newspaper *Dagbladet* claiming that Dolly was eating herself to death and could not stop eating, even though she was more than twice the size of her litter-mates. (It later transpired that Dolly was pregnant.) Professor Kjetill Jacobsen, a developmental biologist at the University of Oslo, was quoted as saying that the cloning process that created Dolly did not involve fertilisation of the eggs by the sperm, which may be crucial in establishing metabolic regulation.

Members of the public were completely unprepared, as they were about to be plunged headlong, against their will, into a new genetically engineered world, in which faceless multinational corporations will control every aspect of their lives, from the food they eat to the baby they might conceive and give birth to.

But not yet ...

But, many have asked, isn't it a bit too late in the day to tell us that? Yes and no. Yes, because I, who should perhaps have known better, was caught unprepared like the rest. And no, because there are so many people who have been warning us of this eventuality, people who have campaigned tirelessly on our behalf, some of them from the earliest days of genetic engineering in the nineteen-seventies, though we may have paid them little heed. And no, it is not too late, if only because that was precisely what we were being encouraged to believe. A certain climate was created, that of being rapidly overtaken by events, which reinforced the feeling that the tidal wave of progress brought on by the new biotechnology is impossible to stem, so that ordinary people may be paralysed into accepting the inevitable.

And no, it is not too late, because we will not give up. For the consequence of giving up will be the dawning of a Brave New World, and soon after that there may be no world at all. The gene genie is fast getting out of control. The practitioners of genetic-engineering biotechnology, regulators and critics alike, have all underestimated the risks involved, which are *inherent* in genetic-engineering biotechnology, particularly when it is misguided by an outmoded and erroneous world view that stems from bad science.

Today, millions of people are calling for an outright ban on transgenic agriculture, or at least for an immediate moratorium on further releases of genetically engineered crops. Many are also calling for an independent public inquiry into the risks and hazards involved, taking into account the most comprehensive scientific knowledge available, and the social and moral implications. Public opposition to genetic-engineering biotechnology has been gaining momentum throughout the world, and has grown exponentially over the past two years.

Austria led the way in Europe. A record 1.2 million citizens, representing 20 per cent of the electorate, signed a people's petition in 1997 for the banning of genetically engineered foods, the deliberate release of genetically modified organisms, and the patenting of life. Genetically modified foods were earlier rejected also by a lay people's consultation in Norway, and by 95 per cent of consumers in Germany.

In Switzerland 100,000 citizens signed a petition for a referendum on an initiative banning genetic-engineering agriculture, transgenic animals, and patents on life. A massive counter-campaign mounted by the Swiss biotech giant Novartis led to the defeat of the initiative by 67 per cent in June 1998; but the opposition has by no means disappeared. Norway is banning the import of a range of transgenic crops and transgenic vaccines, and has legislated to reject the planting of transgenic crops unless it is proved to be safe *and beneficial*. In France, angry farmers destroyed the entire stock of Novartis's transgenic maize seeds intended for planting, while 200,000 citizens signed a petition for a moratorium, which went into effect for two years from July 1998. Opposition to transgenic crops has risen sharply in Britain within the past eighteen months and is now spreading like a shock wave across the world. Much of the initiative came directly from the grass roots. Local action and campaigning groups mushroomed, from the most remote villages to the metropolis, their membership spanning the social spectrum and all age groups. Demonstrations took place outside supermarkets and laboratories.

Field trials of transgenic crops were destroyed in open civil disobedience actions all over Britain and Ireland, where professionals such as university lecturers, lawyers and journalists participated along with young protesters. One such activist, John Seymour, an 84-year old author and organic farmer, compares the invasion of Ireland by Monsanto's 'genetically mutilated' crops to the Norman invasion and sees it as his duty to defend his country, even to the extent of going to prison. Fortunately, he and his co-defendants were let off on probation, the presiding judge acknowledging that they had real concerns to protect the public from the perceived dangers of the transgenic sugar beet planted.

A similar case involving two British activists was dropped by the government just before it was due to be heard in front of a jury. This reflects the extent to which the British government is unsure of itself with a public that overwhelmingly share the concerns of the activists. The government's Chief Scientific Adviser and Chief Medical Officer have recommended that a health monitoring unit be set up for genetically engineered foods, similar to the one monitoring Creutzfeldt-Jakob disease (CJD), the human variant of 'mad cow disease' (BSE). Its remit is to examine potential health effects, including 'foetal abnormalities, new cancers, and effects on the immune system.'[4]

The scientific debate, and to some extent the social and ethical implications, have received widespread coverage in the media. The results have been most heartening. Never before has civil society been so united over a single issue. A resounding chorus of 'No to GMO!' has come from consumers, retailers, wholesalers, food and wine writers, and restaurateurs. Record numbers of farmers are converting to organic, as demand for organic produce outstrips supply. Evidence for the efficacy and benefits of organic agriculture is mounting as the promises of genetic-engineering agriculture are fading. The British government finally opted for a moratorium on commercial planting, though not on field trials. As some of the field trials planned are large enough to overlap with commercial-scale planting, the moratorium may be little more than window-dressing, Nevertheless, Britain is among the seven European countries that are imposing a moratorium or selective ban on transgenic crops; the others are Austria, Luxembourg, France, Denmark, Norway, and Greece (which has called for a moratorium throughout Europe). The European Union has rejected all new applications for genetically engineered products since April 1998.

A series of legal actions has been taken by private citizens against their governments for approving legal action against field trials of transgenic crops, beginning in Ireland, then in the Netherlands, Germany, and Britain. Organic farmers in particular are concerned about genetic pollution of organic produce by transgenic crops. In May 1998 a coalition of scientists, health professionals, religious leaders and chefs began legal action in the United States challenging the policy of the Food and Drug Administration of approving the marketing of genetically engineered foods, demanding adequate safety testing and mandatory labelling. The European Council of Ministers adopted a directive that requires those products to be labelled only if they contain genetically engineered protein or DNA, and food additives and enzymes are exempt. Such a labelling scheme cannot be enforced in practice and does not protect consumers against unexpected toxins and allergens.

Nevertheless, by the end of April 1999 consumer pressure has caused all the main supermarket chains, as well as the world's two biggest food manufacturers, Nestlé and Unilever, to announce a total ban on genetically engineered products.

While opposition was building up in Europe, the biotech companies have chosen the Third World in which to develop markets for their genetically engineered crops. I met angry farmers in India in March calling for an outright ban on transgenic crops. Monsanto bought up an Indian seed company last year and proceeded to carry out field trials, without telling the state governments. Farmers burnt the field trials in a 'cremate Monsanto' campaign, followed by a 'Monsanto quit India' campaign.

In southern Asia a coalition of non-governmental organisations working with millions of farmers launched a two-pronged attack: a resistance campaign directed against all genetic engineering giants, such as Monsanto, and a campaign to preserve and save traditional seeds, which alone can truly feed the hungry people in the region.

Similar campaigns are taking place elsewhere. Dr Tewolde Egziabher of Ethiopia, a leading spokesperson of the African region, rejected the technology as 'neither safe, environmentally friendly, nor economically beneficial.' A coalition of Latin American NGOs has declared that they will not accept transgenic crops. In April, Brazil's most important agricultural state, Rio Grande do Sul, announced a ban on Monsanto's transgenic soya; a month later all twenty-seven states voted unanimously for a moratorium. At the same time the Brazilian government's Environmental Protection Agency and the NGOs Greenpeace and Consumer Defence Institute are locked in an unprecedented legal battle against the government and Monsanto over the commercial approval of Monsanto's transgenic soya. Eventually the federal court banned the transgenic soya until environment impacts have been studied. The international trade in transgenic crops has collapsed, and with it all American agricultural produce, because of the refusal to segregate transgenic from non-transgenic shipments. And resistance is still spreading.

Like other critics before me,[5] I do not think there is necessarily a grand conspiracy afoot—though I do believe that there are many forces shaping convergence towards a single terrible end. As the environmentalist Susan George has pointed out, 'they don't have to conspire if they have the same world view, aspire to similar goals and take concerted steps to attain them.'[6] I don't even think that 'they'—those who are actively pushing genetic-engineering biotechnology, or merely being swept along in the process—are necessarily aspiring to any goals, or taking rational, concerted steps to attain them: instead they are simply converging involuntarily, like sleep-walkers, under the insidious influence of a certain world view, without conscious knowledge, towards the brink of oblivion.

> I am concerned to reveal the links between global economics, biotechnology, runaway diseases, and the possibility of impending genetic catastrophe, unless we consciously will ourselves to break those links.

Make no mistake, however. There is a pattern to the madness that has gripped the industrialised world at the end of the twentieth century. The present global crisis of new and re-emergent infectious diseases, such as AIDS, Ebola, cholera, and TB, and of multi-drug-resistant strains of pathogens, is related to the reductionist scientific world view that in turn underpins both the genetic determinism that has dominated biology since Mendel and Darwin and the prevailing *laissez-faire* global economic system, with its image of the 'economic man'. I am not out to *prove* a deterministic connection between economic and genetic reductionism: that would be to fall prey to the crude mechanistic framework that is best left behind; I am, however, concerned to reveal the links between global economics, biotechnology, runaway diseases, and the possibility of impending genetic catastrophe, *unless we consciously will ourselves to break those links.*

Science is not bad, but there is bad science

I have said that perhaps I should have known better. I am one of those scientists who have long been critical of the mainstream reductionist scientific world view, and I have begun to work towards a radically different approach towards understanding nature.[7] But for a long time I was unable to see how much science really matters in the affairs of the world, not just in the form of practical inventions such as genetic engineering but in how a scientific world view can take hold of people's consciousness, leading them to act involuntarily, unquestioningly, to shape the world to the detriment of themselves. I was so little aware of how science may be used, without conscious intention, to intimidate and control, to obscure, to exploit and oppress. I failed to recognise how the dominant world view generates a selective blindness, to make scientists themselves ignore or misread scientific evidence. No wonder there is so much anti-science sentiment abroad.

The point, however, is not that *science* is bad (a charge that is too often made by the Green movement and by journalists in the popular media) but that there can be *bad science,* which ill serves humanity. Science can often be wrong. The history of science can just as well be written to show the mistakes it has made as the series of triumphs with which it is usually credited. Science is no more and no less than a system of concepts for understanding nature and for obtaining reliable knowledge that enables us to live sustainably with nature. In that sense, one can ill afford to give up science, for it is through our proper understanding and knowledge of nature that we can live a satisfying life and ultimately learn to distinguish the good science, which serves humanity, from the bad science, which does not. In this view, science is imbued with moral values from the start, and cannot be disentangled from them. It is therefore bad science that purports to be 'neutral' and divorced from moral values, as much as it is bad science that ignores scientific evidence.

> Ethical committees, by not questioning the science, will end up making the unacceptable acceptable.

It is clear that I part company with perhaps a majority of my colleagues in mainstream science who believe that science can never be wrong, though it can be misused. Or else, like Professor Lewis Wolpert, a prominent member of the Committee for the Public Understanding of Science in Britain, they carefully distinguish between 'science'—neutral and value-free—and its application, 'technology'—which can do harm or good.[8] This distinction between science and technology is spurious, especially in the case of an experimental science such as genetics, and almost all of biology, where the techniques determine what sort of questions are asked and therefore the range of answers that are important, and relevant to the science. Where would molecular genetics be without the tools that enable practitioners to recombine and manipulate genetic material from different sources? And, having manipulated the genetic material and noted the significant, triumphant results, it is then all too easy to see the world from a genetic-determinist viewpoint: that genes determine our destiny, and so, by manipulating our genes, we may also manipulate our destiny. It is an irresistibly heroic view—except that it is completely wrong and misguided.

It is also meaningless, therefore, to set up ethical committees that do not question the basic scientific assumptions behind genetic-engineering biotechnology. Their brief is severely limited, often verging on the trivial and banal—such as whether a pork gene transferred to food plants might run counter to certain religious beliefs—in comparison with the much more fundamental questions involved regarding eugenics, genetic discrimination, and indeed whether gene transfers should be carried out at all. These committees can do no more than make the unacceptable acceptable to the public.

The debate on genetic-engineering biotechnology is dogged by the artificial separation of 'pure' science from the issues it gives rise to. Ethics is deemed to be socially determined, and therefore negotiable, while science is seen to be beyond reproach, as it follows the 'laws' of nature. The same goes for the distinction between science and technology. Risk assessments are applied to the technology, leaving the science untouched. In this book I show why science cannot be separated from moral values or from the technology that shapes our society. In other words, bad science is unquestionably bad for one's health and well-being, and should be avoided at all costs. Science is, above all, fallible and negotiable, because we have the choice to do or not to do. It should be negotiated for the public good. That is the only ethical position one can take with regard to science. Otherwise we are in danger of turning science into the most fundamentalist of religions; and that, working hand in hand with corporate interests, will surely usher in the Brave New World.

Bad science and big business

What makes genetic-engineering biotechnology dangerous in the first instance is that it is an unprecedented alliance between two great powers that can make or break the world: science and commerce. Practically all established molecular geneticists have some direct or indirect connection with industry. This inevitably sets limits on what scientists can and will do research on, not to mention the possibility that it may compromise their integrity as independent scientists.[9]

The worst aspect of this alliance is that it has been formed between science at its most reductionist and monopolistic industry at its most aggressive and exploitative. This was brought home to me during a one-week course I attended on globalisation and economics taught by Martin Khor, an economist from Malaysia, who heads the Third World Network. The TWN, established in the nineteen-eighties, is a public interest organisation based in Penang, which has been in the front line of the struggle against the unequal relationships imposed by the industrialised North on the developing countries of the South. Martin Khor has very impressive ideas, which he is able to put across to advantage with his panoramic grasp of world politics. He is one of those who, very early on, identified genetic-engineering biotechnology as having a pivotal role to play in deepening the inequalities between North and South, as well as between the rich and poor everywhere else on earth. During his lectures it dawned on me that genetic-engineering technology is really bad science working hand in glove with big business for quick profit, aided and abetted by our governments for the banal reason, as Martin Khor says, that governments wish to be re-elected to remain in power.[10]

When I say 'bad science' I am not launching a personal attack on molecular geneticists, many of whom may be skilled and conscientious scientists working within a flawed conceptual framework. Speaking as a scientist who loves and believes in science, I have to say it is bad science that has let the world down and caused the serious problems we now face, not least of which is the promotion and legitimising of a particular world view. This world view is reductionist, manipulative, and exploitative. It is reductionist because it sees the world as bits and pieces and denies that there are organic wholes such as organisms, ecosystems, communities, and nations. It is manipulative and exploitative because it regards nature and human beings as so many objects to be used and abused for gain, life being a Darwinian struggle for survival of the fittest.

> Only forty-nine of the world's hundred largest economies are countries: multinational corporations now account for fifty-one of them.

It is by no means coincidental that the economic theory now dominating the world is rooted in that same *laissez-faire* capitalist ideology that gave rise to Darwinism. It acknowledges no values other than self-interest, competitiveness, and the accumulation of wealth—at which the industrialised countries have been very successful. Already, according to the report of the United Nations Development Programme (UNDP) for 1992, the richest fifth of the world's population has amassed 85 per cent of its wealth, while the poorest fifth gets a miserable $1\frac{1}{2}$ per cent. To put it another way, there are now 477 billionaires in the world, whose combined assets are roughly equal to the combined annual income of the poorer half of humanity—2.8 billion people.[11] Do we need to be more 'competitive' still to take from the poorest their remaining pittance?

Representatives of the governments of the superpowers are pushing for a globalised economy under trade agreements that erase all economic borders. 'Together, the processes of de-regulation and globalisation are undermining the power of both unions and governments and placing the power of global corporations and finance beyond the reach of public account-ability.'[12] The largest companies continue to consolidate that power through mergers, acquisitions, and strategic alliances. Many small biotech companies have been wiped out since the eighties, and a mere handful are left. These companies control not only agriculture and food but also health and reproductive technologies—in other words, our entire life support system.

Member-countries of the Organisation for Economic Co-operation and Development (OECD) have worked in secret on the Multilateral Agreements on Investment (MAI), which are written by and for companies, to prohibit any government from establishing performance or accountability standards for foreign investors. Vigorous campaigning by NGOs all over the world eventually blocked the negotiations in the latter part of 1998. Undaunted, the OECD countries are planning to transfer the MAI to the World Trade Organisation (WTO). There a member of the European Commission, Sir Leon Britten, is negotiating on behalf of the European Union to ensure that no barriers of any kind will remain in the South to dampen exploitation by the North, and at the same time to protect the deeply unethical 'patents on life' through agreements on 'trade-related intellectual property rights' (TRIPS).[13] In this way, in addition to gaining control of the food supply of the South through exclusive rights to genetically engineered seeds, the food giants of the North can asset-strip the South's genetic and intellectual resources with impunity, up to and including the genes and cell-lines of indigenous peoples.

There is no question that the mentality leading up to and validating genetic engineering is *genetic determinism*—the idea that organisms are determined solely by their genetic make-up. Genetic determinism derives from the marriage of Darwinism and Mendelian genetics (of which I say more in later chapters). Essentially it believes that the principal problems of the world can be solved simply by identifying and manipulating genes, for genes determine the characters of organisms. So, by identifying a gene we can predict a desirable or undesirable trait; by changing a gene we can change the trait; and by transferring a gene we can transfer the corresponding trait.

The Human Genome Project was inspired by the same genetic determinism that places the 'blueprint' for constructing the human being in the human genome. This may have been a brilliant political move to capture research funds and at the same time to revive a flagging pharmaceutical industry, but its scientific content was suspect from the first. While I do not doubt that many individual geneticists working on the Human Genome Project are motivated by the prospect of pure scientific discovery, or of benefiting humanity, they must realise that genetic discrimination and eugenics are both logical consequences of the ideology that provided the primary motivating force for the project.

Genetic-engineering biotechnology promises to work for the benefit of humankind. The reality is somewhat different.

- It is making products that, by and large, nobody needs and certainly not everybody wants but that are forced on consumers anyway, by the lack of segregation and labelling.
- It displaces and marginalises all alternative approaches that tackle the social and environmental causes of malnutrition and ill-health, such as poverty and unemployment, and the need for a sustainable agriculture that could regenerate the environment, guarantee long-term food security, and at the same time conserve indigenous biodiversity.
- It claims to solve problems that reductionist science and industry have created in the first place: widespread environmental deterioration from the intensive, high-input agriculture of the 'Green Revolution' and the accumulation of toxic wastes from chemical industries. What's on offer is more of the same, except with new problems attached.
- It leads to discriminatory and other unethical practices that are against the moral values of societies and nations.
- Worst of all, it is pushing a technology that is untried and, *according to existing knowledge, inherently hazardous to health and biodiversity.*

I am told there is a tradition in social law that questions inherently dangerous activities, that is, things that are not safe for citizens beyond a reasonable doubt. I shall make the case that genetic-engineering biotechnology falls squarely into this category. To proceed beyond this point is to subject the public to unacceptable risks; it is to break a fundamental, well-established legal and ethical norm.

> Practitioners, regulators and many critics of genetic-engineering biotechnology have displayed a certain blindness to concrete scientific evidence in their conscious or unconscious commitment to an old, discredited paradigm.

Let me elaborate on why the technology is inherently hazardous, an aspect that I believe has been underestimated, if not entirely overlooked, by practitioners, regulators and many critics of genetic-engineering biotechnology. The most immediate hazards are likely to be in public health—which has already reached a global crisis, attesting to the failure of decades of reductionist medical practices; though the hazards to biodiversity will not be far behind.

Genetic-engineering biotechnology is inherently hazardous

According to the report of the World Health Organisation for 1996, at least thirty new diseases, including AIDS, Ebola, and hepatitis C, have emerged over the past twenty years, while old infectious diseases, such as TB, cholera, malaria, and diphtheria, are coming back throughout the world. Almost every month now in Britain there are fresh outbreaks: *Streptococcus,* meningitis, *E. coli.* Practically all the pathogens are resistant to antibiotics, many to multiple antibiotics. Two strains of *Escherichia coli* isolated in a transplant ward outside Cambridge in 1993 were found to be resistant to twenty-one out of twenty-two common antibiotics.[14] A strain of *Staphylococcus* isolated in Australia in 1990 was found to be resistant to thirty-one different drugs.[15] Infections with these and other strains are becoming completely immune to treatment. Scientists in Japan have already isolated a strain of *Staphylococcus aureus* that is resistant even to the antibiotic of last resort, vancomycin. Since May 1998 strains in three other dangerous bacteria, including the one that causes TB, are also resistant to all known antibiotics, and therefore untreatable.[16]

> Genetic engineering is a technology designed specifically to transfer genes horizontally between species that do not interbreed, and to break down the species' defence mechanisms.

Geneticists have now linked the emergence of pathogenic bacteria and antibiotic-resistance to *horizontal gene transfer*—the transfer of genes to unrelated species through viruses and other infectious agents, acting as *vectors,* or carriers of genes. These infectious agents are passed from cell to cell, from organism to organism. The genes hitchhike, as it were, in the infectious agents and are smuggled into the cell, which would otherwise exclude them. Once in the cell, the genes can recombine with other genes present in the cell—belonging either to the cell itself or to other infectious agents present—and generate new combinations that may cause diseases. Horizontal gene transfer and subsequent genetic recombination generated the bacterial strains responsible for the cholera outbreak in India in 1992[17] and the *Streptococcus* epidemic in Tayside, Scotland, in 1993.[18] The *E. coli* O157 strain involved in recent outbreaks in Scotland is believed to have originated from horizontal gene transfer from the pathogen *Shigella.*[19]

Many unrelated bacterial pathogens, causing diseases from tree blight to bubonic plague, are found to share an entire set of genes for invading cells that have spread by horizontal gene transfer.[20] Similarly, genes for antibiotic-resistance have spread horizontally and recombined with one another to generate multi-antibiotic-resistance throughout the bacterial populations.[21] Antibiotic-resistant genes spread readily by contact between human beings, and from bacteria inhabiting the gut of farm animals to those in human beings.[22] Multi-antibiotic-resistant strains of pathogens have been endemic in many hospitals for years.[23]

What is the connection between horizontal gene transfer and genetic engineering? Genetic engineering is a technology designed for transferring genes horizontally between species that do not interbreed. (Breeding by normal reproduction transfers genes vertically from parents to offspring.) It is designed to break down the species barriers and, increasingly, to overcome the species' defence mechanisms, which normally degrade or inactivate foreign genes.[24] For the purposes of manipulating, replicating and transferring genes, genetic engineers make use of artificial vectors, which are made from viruses and other infectious agents that also cause diseases, including cancers, and spread genes for virulence and antibiotic-resistance. While natural vectors are limited by species barriers—so that pig viruses do not generally attack human beings, and tomato viruses will not affect cauliflowers— the artificial vectors made by genetic engineers are *designed* to cross species barriers. The technology will increase the horizontal transfer of precisely those genes that are responsible for virulence and antibiotic-resistance, allowing them to recombine to generate new pathogens.

What is even more disturbing is that geneticists have now found evidence that the presence of antibiotics typically increases the frequency of horizontal gene transfer 10 to 10,000-fold, possibly because the antibiotic acts like a sex hormone for the bacteria, enhancing mating and the exchange of genes between unrelated species.[25] Antibiotic-resistance and multi-antibiotic-resistance therefore cannot be overcome simply by making new antibiotics, for *antibiotics create the very conditions that facilitate the spread of resistance.* The continuing profligate use of antibiotics in intensive farming and in medicine, in combination with the commercial-scale practice of genetic engineering, may already be major contributing factors to the accelerated spread of multi-antibiotic-resistance among new and old pathogens that the WHO report of 1996 has identified within the past twenty years. For example, there has been a dramatic increase in both the incidence and the severity of infections by *Salmonella*,[26] with some countries in Europe witnessing a staggering twenty-fold increase in incidence since 1980.

That is not all. One by one those assumptions on which geneticists and regulatory committees have based their assessment of genetically engineered products as 'safe' have fallen by the wayside, especially in the light of evidence emerging within the past five years.

The prevalence of horizontal gene transfer

We have been told that horizontal gene transfer is confined to bacteria. This is not so. It is now known to involve practically all species of animals, plants, and fungi. It is possible for any gene in any species to spread to any other species, especially if the gene is carried on genetically engineered gene-transfer vectors. *Transgenes* and antibiotic-resistant *marker genes* from transgenic plants have been shown to end up in soil fungi and bacteria.[27] The microbial populations in the environment serve as the gene-transfer highway and reservoir, supporting the replication of the genes and allowing them to spread and recombine with other genes to generate new pathogens.[28]

Survival of 'crippled' laboratory strains of bacteria

We have been assured that 'crippled' laboratory strains of bacteria and viruses—those requiring special nutrients or special conditions to grow—do not survive when released into the environment. This is not true. There is now abundant evidence that the bacteria can either survive quite well and multiply or can go dormant and reappear after having acquired genes from other bacteria to enable them to multiply.[29] Bacteria co-operate much more than they compete. They share their most valuable assets for survival.

The persistence of DNA

We have been told that the genetic material DNA is easily broken down in the environment. This is not so. DNA can remain in the environment, where it can be picked up by bacteria and incorporated in their genome.[30] DNA is in fact one of the toughest molecules. Biochemists jumped with joy when they realised they no longer had to work with proteins, which lose their activity very readily; by contrast, DNA survives rigorous boiling. So when processed foods are approved on the grounds that there can be no DNA left in them, one should ask exactly how the processing is done, and whether the appropriate tests for the presence of DNA have been carried out.

The survival of 'crippled' laboratory strains of bacteria and viruses and the persistence of DNA in the environment are of particular relevance to the so-called 'contained' users producing transgenic pharmaceuticals, enzymes, and food additives. 'Tolerated' releases and transgenic wastes from such users may already have contributed large amounts of transgenic bacteria and viruses, as well as manipulated DNA, to the environment since the early eighties, when commercial genetic-engineering bio-technology began.

We are told that DNA is easily digested by enzymes in our gut. This is not true. The DNA of a virus has been found to survive passage through the gut of mice; furthermore, it readily finds its way into the bloodstream and into leukocytes (white blood cells), liver cells, and spleen cells, where the viral DNA becomes inserted into the mouse cell genome. And when the viral DNA is fed to pregnant mice it ends up in the cells of the fetus and the new-born.[31] The insertion of viral DNA into the cell's genome can create all manner of genetic disturbances, including cancer.[32]

The emergence of new viruses

There are further findings pointing to the potential for generating new disease-causing viruses through genetic recombination between artificial vectors containing viral genes and other viruses in the environment. The viruses generated in this way will have increased host ranges, infecting and causing diseases in more than one species, and therefore will be very difficult to eradicate. We are already seeing such viruses emerging.

- Monkeypox, a previously rare and potentially fatal virus caught from rodents, is spreading through central Congo (Kinshasa).[33] Between 1981 and 1986 only 37 cases were known; there have been at least 163 cases in one province alone since July 1995. For the first time, humans are transmitting the disease directly to one another.

- An outbreak of hantavirus infection that hit southern Argentina in December 1996 was the first in which the virus was transmitted from person to person.[34] Previously the virus was spread by breathing in the *aerosols* (fine airborne particles) from rodent excrement or urine.

- New highly virulent strains of infectious bursal disease virus (IBDV) have spread rapidly throughout most of the poultry industry in the northern hemisphere. They are now infecting Antarctic penguins and are suspected of causing mass mortality.[35]

- New strains of distemper and rabies viruses are spilling out from towns and villages to plague some of the world's rarest wild animals in Africa: lions, panthers, wild dogs, and giant otters.[36]

- Malaysia has been in the grip of an epidemic involving a new Hendra-like virus, which may have crossed from fruit bats to humans via pigs, resulting in over a hundred deaths since October 1998. More than 1 million pigs have been slaughtered in an attempt to control the epidemic.[37]

None of this plethora of new findings has been seriously taken into account by the regulatory bodies.[38] On the contrary, safety regulations have been relaxed. Members of the public are being used, against their will, as guinea pigs for genetically engineered products, while new viruses and bacterial pathogens may be created by the technology with every day that passes.

The present situation is reminiscent of the development of nuclear energy, which gave us the nuclear power stations that we now know to be hazardous to health and environmentally unsustainable because of the long-lasting radioactive wastes they produce. Joseph Rotblat, a British physicist who won the Nobel Prize in 1995 after years of battling against nuclear weapons, has said: 'My worry is that other advances in science may result in other means of mass destruction, perhaps more readily available even than nuclear weapons. Genetic engineering is quite a possible area, because of these dreadful developments that are taking place there.'[39]

The large-scale release of transgenic organisms is much worse than nuclear weapons or radioactive nuclear wastes, as genes can replicate indefinitely, spread, and recombine. There may yet be time to stop the dreams turning into nightmares if we act now, before the critical genetic melt-down is reached.

Two

GENETIC-ENGINEERING BIOTECHNOLOGY NOW

The commercialisation of science in genetic-engineering biotechnology has compromised the integrity of scientists; reduced organisms, including human beings, to commodities; intensified the exploitation and oppression of the Third World; and threatened human and animal health and biodiversity. It fuels the resurgence of eugenics and genetic discrimination against non-white populations, minority groups, and all the politically dispossessed peoples of the world. It results in a monolithic wasteland of the genetic-determinist mentality that is the beginning of the Brave New World.

Genetic engineering then and now

Genetic engineering is a set of techniques for isolating, modifying, multiplying and recombining genes from different organisms. It enables geneticists to transfer genes between species belonging to different kingdoms that would never interbreed in nature. A fish gene can be transferred to tomatoes; human genes can be transferred to sheep, to pigs, or to the bacterium *Escherichia coli* that inhabits the gut of all mammals.

Genetic engineering originated in the nineteen-seventies from the discovery of several important techniques (see chapter 3). Soon afterwards the molecular geneticists who discovered the techniques, or were in the forefront of developing and using genetic engineering, became aware of the dangers of opening a Pandora's box. They saw the distinct possibility of inadvertently (or intentionally) creating pathogenic strains of viruses or bacteria by recombining genes in the laboratory. This led to the Asilomar Declaration, which called for a moratorium on genetic engineering until appropriate regulatory guidelines had been established.[1]

I had the experience of setting up a genetic engineering laboratory in my university in the nineteen-eighties, when experimenters were taught to take great care to ensure that the microorganisms and genes we were manipulating remained in the laboratory. We had to work in special flow hoods; nothing got flushed down the sink; and accidental spills had to be wiped down immediately and thoroughly with antiseptics. Wastes were autoclaved before disposal, or incinerated. There was no question that we were to think it safe to release genetically engineered organisms into the environment, even though the strains we dealt with were genetically 'crippled', or handicapped in some way so that they would not have been expected to survive if they were accidentally released. (In fact that assumption has now been proved wrong, so it was just as well that we operated on the precautionary principle.)

> Many of the leading molecular geneticists today either own biotech companies or are collaborating with such companies.

I went into genetic engineering as someone interested in evolution, to learn about genetic processes that could respond, in a repeatable and non-random way, to the environment and so influence the course of development and evolution. Essentially I did not accept the conventional simplistic view that evolution occurs mainly by the natural selection of random genetic mutations. I left the field in the late eighties, satisfied that genetic determinism had been invalidated by the findings of the new molecular genetics, which indicated, among other things, that genes and genomes were able to respond in non-random ways to the environment. This left me free to begin research into the biophysics of self-organisation: how it is that organisms function as coherent wholes

and not just as collections of genes.[2] Unfortunately, well into the
nineties those research findings in molecular genetics still have not
been taken into account, and the outlook of mainstream science
has not changed; if anything, it has become worse. Genetic
determinism is rife, not least because it is perfect for promoting
genetic-engineering biotechnology.

Now the risks from genetic manipulation have become far
greater. Genetic engineering techniques are at least ten times faster
and more powerful than before. The new breed of genetically
engineered organisms (or 'transgenics') that are deliberately
released on a large scale are designed to be ecologically vigorous,
and therefore are potentially much more hazardous, than the
genetically crippled micro-organisms that were engineered for
contained use in the laboratory in the seventies.[3] Where is the
voice of science now? The scientists say it is for the politicians and
the public to decide. Of course the public should decide; but that
does not absolve scientists from their special responsibility as both
citizens and scientists. As C. P. Snow wrote on scientists' responsibility with regard to making the nuclear bomb, 'it is not enough
to say that scientists have a responsibility as citizens. They have a
much greater one than that, and one different in kind. For
scientists have a moral imperative to say what they know.'[4]

Though an increasing number of scientists are critical of
genetic-engineering biotechnology, there has been no equivalent
of the Asilomar Declaration from molecular geneticists in the
nineties calling for a moratorium. As the biologist Ruth Hubbard
of Harvard University notes,[5] many of the present-day leading
molecular geneticists either own biotech companies or are
collaborating with or working for such companies. Genetic-
engineering biotechnology is the commercialisation of science on
an unprecedented scale. 'Scientists are increasingly being forced
to get into bed with big business … Where research was once
mostly neutral, it now has an array of paymasters to please. In
place of impartiality, research results are being discreetly managed
and massaged, or even locked away if they don't serve the right
interests … More pernicious, according to "The Sci Files", a new

BBC TV series … is the slide into self-censorship in an attempt to ensure that the contracts keep coming.[6] We have moved far away indeed from the world of C. P. Snow.

The change is partly out of necessity, as over the past decade the British government has cut more than £1 billion from research funding, and partly because people believe there is money to be made from science. Even what remains of government research support is strongly committed to a closer link with industry, as was made clear by a white paper on science in 1993. It emphasised the need to concentrate on research that would help the economy; and genetic-engineering biotechnology is clearly seen to be the prime candidate.

> The Government is committed to ensuring that the United Kingdom can remain a leading developer and producer of biotechnology … World markets for biotechnology products have been estimated to exceed £70 billion [$100 billion] by the year 2000, growing at some 30 per cent a year, and as one of the most active European countries in the field, the United Kingdom's share of sales dependent on biotechnology could rise from £4 billion to £9 billion by 2000 …[7]

That turned out to be an extreme overestimate. The figure of $100 billion for the world market was revised downwards to $48 billion in 1998, of which only $1 billion would be in food and agriculture.[8] By the end of April 1999 the international market for transgenic food products has collapsed, as all the big supermarket chains in Britain and other European countries, as well as two of the world's biggest food companies, Unilever and Nestlé, announced bans on genetically engineered products.[9] And resistance is still spreading in south-east Asia, Latin America, and eastern Europe.

The 'patenting of life'

The commercialisation of genetic engineering has been growing steadily since the nineteen-seventies. The first company, Genentech, was formed—even as a moratorium was being debated in 1976—by a molecular geneticist, Paul Berg, who had signed the

Asilomar Declaration a year earlier. The next milestone was the US Supreme Court ruling in 1980 that genetically engineered micro-organisms could be patented. Then came the $3 billion Human Genome Initiative, financed by the US government,[10] which opened the floodgates to 'patents on life'. A long list of patents have already been granted, and many more are pending, on controversial 'inventions' such as

- transgenic organisms, human genes, and gene fragments;
- a human cell line established from the spleen of a patient removed as part of cancer therapy;[11]
- cell lines from indigenous peoples obtained—without informed consent—ostensibly for the study of human diversity;
- seeds and plant varieties taken by Northern 'bio-prospectors' from indigenous communities in the Third World, who freely provided the material as well as their knowledge.

These patents go to feed the mushrooming biotech industry, greedy for products and quick profit.

To facilitate patenting for commercial exploitation, the Trade-Related Intellectual Property Rights (TRIPS) treaty was introduced in the draft final act of the General Agreement on Tariffs and Trade (GATT), before that organisation was dissolved and replaced by the World Trade Organisation (WTO). The TRIPS treaty 'effectively excludes all kinds of knowledge, ideas and innovations [for patenting]—that take place in the "intellectual common"—in villages among farmers, in forests among tribals.'[12] It regards as invention, and therefore patentable, only those acts carried out within the framework of Western science. Science is here working hand in glove with corporate interests to define what is scientific and what is not, and therefore what qualifies as a real invention for the purpose of financial reward.

Patenting plant varieties from Third World countries robs farmers of their livelihood, and can have widespread re-percussions. The neem plant in India, for example, whose seed oil possesses insecticidal and many medicinal properties, has been freely available for millennia, so much so that the health care system of the whole of India is dependent on it. As soon as it was 'discovered' and patented by the American company W. R. Grace it became a scarce commodity. Its market value shot up to a hundred times its value within two years, to put it far beyond the means of most ordinary people. A national health system has thereby been seriously undermined.

Intellectual property rights over genetic resources are emerging as a major North-South issue. It began with the enactment of an international convention in the early sixties, the Union for the Protection of New Varieties of Plant (UPOV), which gave property rights to plant breeders for varieties improved through human intervention. The source material, obtained freely from the biodiverse countries of the South, was considered the 'common heritage of mankind' and therefore not subject to private ownership. This gave free access to corporate interests to 'bio-prospect' in the South and started the process of the increasingly arbitrary categorising of 'innovation' by Northern companies, while the real innovative contributions of local communities were denied.[13] Under this unfair convention, Northern countries are allowed to take freely from the South, as 'common heritage', genetic resources that are then returned to them as priced commodities.

Strong protests from Third World countries led to a meeting in 1987 of the Commission on Plant Genetic Resources of the Food and Agriculture Organisation of the United Nations (FAO), which recognised the contribution of traditional farmers in developing the neem plant, and therefore their right to ownership. But that right was not vested in individual farmers; instead it accrued to the farmers' governments to receive assistance in maintaining the genetic resources. In other words, the North is 'obliged' to help the South, tied in to the concept of aid and dependence that has for centuries allowed the North to exploit the South. An international gene fund was set up to establish the farmers' rights, but the lack of contributions from Northern companies and their governments made this fund inoperative. The TRIPS proposal is generally seen as the latest attempt to formalise the continuing piracy of Third World genetic resources by Northern biotech companies, sanctioned by the science driving genetic engineering.

The UN Convention on Biological Diversity, signed in Rio de Janeiro in June 1992, is intended to conserve biological diversity in an equitable way. As the main genetic diversity is in the poorer, less industrialised countries, and as this is the material that the genetic engineering industry wishes to use, the convention will play an important role in determining the socio-economic impacts of the technology.

Dr Tewolde Egziabher, an agronomist and UN delegate from Ethiopia, has emerged as an important spokesperson for the entire African group of countries. He works closely with the Third World Network; he was one of the prime movers in putting the International Biosafety Protocol on the agenda of the CBD as it was signed in 1992, and has been responsible for major contributions to the protocol ever since. He has always insisted that the socio-economic impacts of genetic-engineering biotechnology should be included as part of the biosafety risk assessment. One of the main reasons is that the CBD has done nothing to stem the drain of natural resources of the South to the North. On the contrary, the very basis of the sustainability and long-term food security of the South is now threatened as the result of genetic-engineering agricultural biotechnology promoted under the convention.[14]

> The strongest objection to the 'patenting of life' is that it has turned organisms, including human parts, into saleable commodities.

The CBD has been hailed as 'the culmination of two decades of arduous international efforts in which the conservation of biological diversity is being recognised as a common concern of humankind, and considered an integral part of the development process ... [It will] reconcile the need for conservation with the concerns for development based on justice and equity.'[15] But instead the pilfering of biological diversity has intensified, as agricultural biotechnology drives 'gene-hunters' to prospect for commercially lucrative genetic resources in the South, under the aegis of intellectual property rights that allow the patenting of living organisms and their genes.

To make things worse, large proportions of the biological diversity of the South are already held in 'gene banks' as *ex situ* collections in the North—and the North is insisting that such collections be excluded from the convention, with the result that they will be freely available for exploitation by biotech interests. While negotiations are still going on, European botanical gardens and other collections of tropical plants have already been approached by a representative of Phytera, an American biotech company specialising in pharmaceuticals, to gain access to items in their collections. A small initial fee would be paid on the delivery of each item, and in the event of the successful introduction to the market of a product derived from the item, a small proportion of the profit would be returned to the garden or herbarium.[16]

Life as commodity

The strongest objection to the 'patenting of life', however, is that it has turned organisms, including parts of human beings, into saleable commodities. This is morally repugnant, especially to many indigenous cultures in the Third World, and has also united diverse groups in the North: these include environmental activists and religious organisations as well as ordinary citizens who feel that the final frontier of human decency has been breached in the name of free enterprise.

As a result of worldwide opposition, a number of patents have been revoked or retracted by the claimants.[17] At the end of 1995 the Center for Disease Control in the United States dropped its patent claim on a cell line from a Guaymi woman from Panama after protests from the World Council of Indigenous Peoples and the Guaymi General Congress. At the same time UNESCO's International Bioethics Committee, rather than endorsing the Human Genome Diversity Project (part of the Human Genome

Project, set up ostensibly to document and preserve genes from indigenous peoples before they become extinct), endorsed the criticisms of the project raised by indigenous peoples and their governments. In 1994 the US Patent and Trademark Office provisionally revoked the patent of a company called Agracetus on all genetically engineered cotton, and the Indian government revoked the same company's application for a patent in India on genetically engineered cotton. Many legal oppositions were submitted to the European Patent Office against the patent of the 'onco-mouse'—a transgenic mouse designed to be prone to cancer. That has blocked more than three hundred other applications for patents on animals, pending the outcome of the onco-mouse case.

The European Parliament, responding to public opposition, voted to reject the European Commission's Draft Directive on the Protection of Biotechnological Investigations in its first round in March 1995. By the end of 1995 the Commission published a revised draft directive; but the changes were cosmetic and the wording ambiguous, to say the least. It allows the patenting of any micro-organisms, any plant or animal derived from 'a micro-biological process', and any isolated human gene sequence, of whatever known or unknown function. In short, it would give biotech companies patent protection for products of genetic engineering over and above any other real invention covered by existing patent laws. It therefore requires no act of invention. This in effect grants unprecedented monopolistic rights to corporate patent-holders that not only prevent competitors from developing related products but also impede scientific research. As a group of scientists writing in the correspondence pages of *Nature* point out,

> advances in biotechnology are already patentable under European patent law. What is at issue is whether these patents should be very much broader in scope than those in other fields, and in particular, whether someone who isolates and characterises natural material should be able to patent not just the method by which this was done but also the material itself. If this principle had been applied in chemistry, the elements would have been patented, and indeed, the directive does refer to 'elements of plants and animals'.[18]

A controversial patent, granted in both the United States and Europe to a company called Biocyte, covers all human blood cells from the umbilical cord of newborn babies.[19] These cells are routinely used for therapeutic bone-marrow transplants, without cost and in the time-honoured tradition of offering the gift of life to those in need. This patent has now been revoked, both in the United States and the European Union, as a result of strong protest by public-interest organisations.

The political repercussions of agreements on intellectual property rights on living organisms are far-reaching.[20] In April 1997 the US State Department objected to the Thai government's draft legislation allowing Thai doctors to register traditional medicines, on the grounds that it could constitute 'a possible violation of TRIPS and hamper medical research into these compounds.' In fact Thailand is not obliged to comply with TRIPS until at least the year 2000; and medical practices may be exempted. The United States had already threatened the Ecuadorian government with the cancellation of trade preferences if Ecuador did not ratify a bilateral agreement on intellectual property rights; and Ethiopia, Panama and Paraguay have been added to the list of countries that limit American commercial interests. The United States unilaterally cancelled half of Argentina's trade benefits, valued at $260 million, on the grounds that Argentina's intellectual property laws did not comply with 'international standards'. In June 1997 the US ambassador to India announced that 'certain areas of research and training will be closed to co-operation' if India failed to amend its patent laws, threatening some 130 scientific projects at present supported by the US-India fund. The United States has also lodged formal complaints with the WTO against India and Pakistan regarding their national patent laws governing pharmaceutical and agricultural chemical products. The same complaints have been lodged against the Danish government.

On 16 July 1997 the European Parliament succumbed to commercial pressures and voted to accept the revised directive on patenting. One hopeful sign is that a year later, the Netherlands and Italy are challenging the legality of that directive.

The question of 'safety'

The *Convention on Biological Diversity: Agenda 21* contains a chapter (chapter 16) entitled 'Environmentally sound management of biotechnology', which recommends that some billions of dollars of the UN budget be committed to genetic-engineering biotechnology so as to increase food yield to feed the hungry, to improve human health and control population, to purify water, clean up the environment, reforest wasteland—in short, to solve all the problems of the Third World. At the same time the impacts and the hazards of the new technology are consistently glossed over by the use of some of the verbal ploys we have already seen, for instance emphasising the supposed continuity between conventional biotechnology (such as wine-making) and 'modern biotechnology' (that is, genetic engineering); the claim that years of experience have demonstrated modern biotechnology to be safe; and the substitution of the less emotive term 'genetic modification' for 'genetic engineering'. (It is remarkable how much of the same propaganda material eventually finds its way into the literature promoting 'public understanding' of genetic-engineering biotechnology, and is echoed by all the spokespersons of the industry, including many scientists who should know better.)[21] This comes at a time when no other UN project is being financed under the Commission for Sustainable Development. Chapter 16 of the convention is generally regarded as a thinly veiled attempt to promote and subsidise the biotech industry. This would not be surprising, given the openly partisan view expressed by the British government in favour of the industry, which is not atypical of governments in other industrialised countries—with a few notable exceptions, such as Austria, Denmark, Norway, and Sweden.

> 'Unexpected' toxins and allergens have already been associated with genetically engineered foods.

Moreover, as opposition to genetic-engineering biotechnology has been gathering momentum in developed countries, the industry is selecting the Third World for test sites as well as for markets.

Critics are concerned about the uncontrolled release of transgenic organisms in the Third World, and about people being used as human guinea-pigs for testing genetically engineered drugs and vaccines. By 1994 there had already been at least ninety releases of transgenic crops in non-OECD countries and Mexico, a third of which were by multinational corporations such as the American companies Monsanto and Calgene (later bought by Monsanto) and the Swiss company Ciba Geigy (now part of Novartis).[22] A rabies vaccine containing a live virus was tested on cattle in Argentina without authorisation, and farm workers, who were not informed of the experiment, were later found to be infected with the virus.[23]

Most Third World countries have neither the legal framework nor the capacity to regulate genetic engineering. The same is true, surprisingly, of industrialised countries. There is at present no legal control over genetically engineered versions of drugs and chemicals already approved for the market, nor in the United States is there any legal requirement that they be labelled as such. The same goes for transgenic crop plants and other products where 'substantial equivalence' is claimed. As there is no clear definition of what constitutes 'substantial equivalence', a gaping loophole is left in safety assessment.[24]

There have already been serious indications of what can happen when safety is ignored. 'Unexpected' toxins and allergens have been associated with genetically engineered foods. The first case was in 1989, when trace contaminants in the amino acid tryptophan, produced by a Japanese biotech company using a genetically engineered micro-organism, were implicated in an outbreak of a mysterious illness, eosinophilia-myalgia syndrome (EMS), which led to thirty-seven deaths and more than 1,500 other people being affected, some remaining seriously ill to this day.[25] Since then soya bean genetically engineered with a brazil nut gene was found to be allergenic to people sensitive to brazil nuts,[26] while a strain of yeast engineered to ferment faster accumulated a metabolite at mutagenic levels.[27] As portents of the ecological hazards of transgenic crops, field trials have shown that herbicide-resistance in transgenic potato[28] and transgenic oil-seed rape[29] have spread to weedy relatives within a single growing season, thereby creating herbicide-resistant 'superweeds'. A genetically engineered soil bacterium, thought to be quite harmless, turned out to drastically inhibit the growth of wheat seedlings.[30]

By 1995, therefore, there were already widespread concerns about the health hazards and ecological impact, as well as the socio-economic implications, of genetic-engineering biotechnology that would arise from the erosion of farmers' rights—displacing small local farmers and making them liable for royalties on patented seeds—or from the replacement of indigenous crops with transgenic organisms grown in the laboratory. This convinced all Third World countries (the 'Group of 77' and China), eastern European and most western European countries that a legally binding international biosafety protocol for the use and transfer of genetically engineered organisms should be established as a matter of urgency. This was openly opposed by the United States (which has so far failed to ratify the Convention on Biological Diversity), on the grounds that it would reduce American 'competitiveness'. The United States was supported at first by Britain, Australia, Germany, the Netherlands, and representatives of the biotech industry, who have consistently rejected a legally binding biosafety protocol, calling instead for 'voluntary guidelines'.

At the time that I became involved in biosafety issues, the list of hazards from the products of genetic-engineering bio-technology was growing, but the official UN panel of biosafety experts remained unmoved. Its report in May 1995 still maintained that there was no difference between conventional and modern biotechnology,[31] and that years of experience had shown modern biotechnology to be safe. It even proposed a *relaxation* of the voluntary guidelines drawn up by Britain and the Netherlands and already considered inadequate by many scientists. The Third World Network, represented by Martin Khor, Chee Yoke Ling and Nijar Gurdial, together with the Edmonds Institute in the United States (run single-handedly by the incredible Beth Burrows), began bringing scientists to UN conferences. These activists were kept busy organising workshops and seminars during the lunch hours, issuing briefing papers and daily bulletins produced by Beth Burrows and members of other NGOs. These were eagerly awaited and snapped up by the delegates, especially those from Third World countries.

The seminars and workshops were a significant part of the process. One regular member of our group was Christine von Weizsäcker of Ecoropa. She has the advantage of having been trained in both biology and philosophy, and always added an extra analytical dimension to our seminars, which were typically inter-disciplinary, dealing with all aspects of biosafety: the scientific, the legal, and the socio-economic. You will be meeting other members of our 'independent panel' later; but Vandana Shiva, already well known for her writings and political activism, is without doubt the star speaker. Not only is she well versed in the scientific details of genetic engineering, which she has picked up in no time at all, but she is incredibly well informed on all the relevant issues of the day, and a top debater to boot.

Seminars and workshops were not enough. Martin Khor organised a group of scientists and legal experts from many countries, both North and South, to draft an alternative, independent report on biosafety, based on the most up-to-date scientific findings, spelling out the hazards and calling for tighter monitoring and control.[32] (In retrospect, we should have called for a moratorium there and then.) This document was published by the TWN and circulated to the UN delegates at every opportunity.[33]

Our legal experts include Chee Yoke Ling and Nijar Gurdial. Yoke Ling trained in law at the University of Cambridge but gave up the possibility of a lucrative practice in Hong Kong to work for the TWN. Nijar Gurdial did give up his practice to work for the TWN, despite having a serious heart condition. He recognised the implications of the new genetics for biosafety almost immediately and worked them into our Biosafety Report. Gurdial and Yoke Ling have both been involved in intellectual property rights and biosafety issues since 1992. Yoke Ling in particular knows a great deal about the history of biosafety and what goes on behind the scenes.

The biotech industry's vehement opposition to a biosafety protocol was a major factor preventing the Bush administration from signing the convention; and even when Clinton signed it the Congress refused to ratify it. When a protocol was finally agreed by an overwhelming majority of the countries in July 1995, the biotech industry, together with the Clinton administration, began to work hard to undermine it. In particular they insisted on excluding not only liabilities and compensation but also the socio-economic impacts. Experience with the 'Green Revolution' has taught many countries to be wary of the new biotechnology, with its possible impact on the environment, agricultural and natural biodiversity, and the livelihood of small farmers.

Before a subsequent meeting on biosafety in Århus, Denmark, in July 1996, the US government sent messages to relevant government departments in developing countries asking for their position on biosafety. The messages carried underlying threats that a 'badly drafted protocol' would deny developing countries the benefits of genetic engineering and might even be illegal under the trading rules of the WTO.[34]

Science has become enmeshed in the tangle of trade, technology, perceived risks or lack thereof, and international intrigue. It provides the ideological backdrop, the material substance and the terms in which an exploitative, unequal trade relationship can be defined between North and South. The North is given sole recognition of its science, in the concrete form of intellectual property rights, while the South is deprived not only of its own science but of its right to exclude the encroaching science of the North and to prevent the North's usurping of the sciences of the South as its own in widespread acts of bio-piracy. The same science claims to override any possible objections from the European Union to imports of genetically engineered foods, and any requirement for segregation and labelling.

In June 1997 the biotech industries wrote to President Clinton in preparation for the forthcoming meeting of the 'Group of Eight'.[35]

Because trade is so important to American agriculture and the US food industry, it is imperative that policy and regulations governing international commerce of genetically modified food and agricultural products are based on sound science and not just emotion which often turns into pure hyperbole. It is also important to note that segregation of bulk commodities is not scientifically justified and is economically unrealistic.

Some officials of the EU advocate requirements that could be considered non-tariff trade barriers to the US and other countries exporting to the EU. It is critical [that] the EU understand at the highest level that the US would consider any trade barrier of genetically modified agricultural products, be it discriminatory labelling or segregation, unacceptable and subject to challenge in the World Trade Organisation (WTO).

> A 'science war' is going on in the real world that is far more important than the skirmish in academia between the 'relativists' in sociology, who say science is a pure social construct, and the 'absolutists' of the scientific mainstream, who regard science as the ineluctable, eternal laws of nature.

The US government took a correspondingly firm stand. The Secretary for Agriculture, Dan Glickman, told a conference of the International Grains Council in London that it would not tolerate segregation or labelling. 'Sound science ought to be the only arbiter. The greatest threat to free trade is bad and phoney science … We know that biotechnology holds out our greatest hope of dramatically increasing yields.' This makes it all too clear that 'sound science' is that which sanctions free trade and protects biotech interests at the expense of any safety considerations.

The Biosafety Protocol was due to be completed in Cartagena, Colombia, in February 1999, but it was blocked by the United States and five other countries, representing biotech interests and acting against the overwhelming majority of the world's countries. The corporations will stop at nothing to force genetically engineered crops and products on the world; but civil society is fighting back, and science is playing a central role.

A 'science war' is going on in the real world that is far more important than the skirmish in academia between the 'relativists' in sociology, who say science is a pure social construct, and the 'absolutists' of the scientific mainstream, including Lewis Wolpert and others, who regard science as the ineluctable, eternal laws of nature. They are both wrong and both irrelevant. This science war is real. It is what makes former ivory-tower academics like myself take to the streets.

Official disinformation on safety

The official position of the United States on biosafety comes from a report of the National Research Council, *Field Testing Genetically Modified Organisms: Framework for Decisions,* which states *a priori* that 'no conceptual distinction exists between genetic modification of plants and micro-organisms by classical methods or by molecular techniques that modify DNA and transfer genes.' (Similar statements have made their way into chapter 16 of *Agenda 21* and many other UN documents on biosafety. It is no coincidence that this is also the position adopted by the biotech industry, and by scientists defending the industry.) This statement is clearly untrue (as I shall show in the next chapter). But the *a priori* assumption that there is no difference between genetically engineered varieties and those made by traditional breeding methods has meant that field tests are both inadequately designed and inadequately monitored for safety. It is on the basis of such inadequate field tests that transgenic crops have been approved as safe for human and animal consumption, without any legal requirement for appropriate tests for safety to be carried out.

> The *a priori* assumption that there is no difference between genetically engineered varieties and those made by traditional breeding methods has meant that field tests are both inadequately designed and inadequately monitored for safety.

In 1995 scientists from the US Environmental Protection Agency issued a report charging their own agency with failing to assess the risks associated with the massive release of a new living organism that could not be contained or eradicated.[36] The organism was a *Rhizobium*—a bacterium that normally lives as a nitrogen-fixing symbiont in the roots of legumes—engineered with, among other things, an antibiotic-resistant marker gene from the pathogen *Shigella,* which causes dysentery and infantile gastro-enteritis. Among the risks not assessed were the potential transfer of antibiotic-resistance to other pathogens and the subsequent creation of drug-resistant diseases in humans, livestock, and wildlife, toxicity to humans, and hazards to the ecological environment. (Incidentally, no data was produced on whether the genetically engineered *Rhizobium* was effective in improving the yield of crop plants.)

The Union of Concerned Scientists in the United States has evaluated the data in field trials to see whether it supports the conclusion of safety. Margaret Mellon and Jane Rissler have this to say: 'Care should be taken in citing the field test record as strong evidence for the safety of genetically engineered crops. It is not. Unless they are redesigned to collect environmental data, the field tests do not provide a track record of safety, but a case of "don't look, don't find."'[37] To this, Henry Miller (the same defender of genetic-engineering biotechnology mentioned in chapter 1) retorted that, as there was no essential difference between genetically engineered organisms and the strains obtained by conventional methods, field trials were done on a 'don't need, don't look' basis.[38] That is a strong admission that the scientific framework is used to legitimise the culpable lack of adherence to regulation on the part of the scientists, as well as the lack of real regulation imposed by the regulatory bodies. And the biotech industry in the United States is asking for even less regulation than exists at present for traditional approaches.[39]

I have examined Monsanto's application to release transgenic sugar beet in Britain between 1997 and 1999. Crucial information is concealed as 'confidential business information', and no actual scientific data is supplied anywhere in the application, only a series of unsupported assertions and statements. I was no wiser afterwards about the nature of the transgenic organism to be released. In addition, it confirmed my worst fears about the inadequacy of the information for a proper risk assessment. I wrote to the Department of the Environment about my concerns and received a very inadequate reply, which failed to deal with most of the points I raised.[40]

There is, up to now, no evidence to support the assertion of the biotech industry and the regulatory bodies that genetic-engineering biotechnology and its products are safe. Tests for the toxicity and allergenicity of food products, where they have been carried out at all, are solely aimed at known allergens and toxins and are not designed to reveal unexpected products resulting from the genetic engineering.[41] Not only are field trials inadequately designed and monitored but the regulation is perfunctory. Horizontal gene transfer has never been monitored in field tests, nor is it required by regulations. The departments concerned are not equipped to cope with the flood of applications for approval. Yet even these weak regulations have been further relaxed.

From the beginning, the scope of the risk assessment has been restricted. It has not taken account of all the scientific findings— the absence of evidence is too often taken to be evidence of absence. Moreover, risk assessment takes place in a social vacuum. Socio-economic impacts and ethics are consistently excluded from consideration. At such times, expert panel members insist that they will consider only scientific evidence, while it is clear that they do not consider *all* the scientific evidence. Once again science is being used to legitimise and exclude.

Let us look at some of the socio-economic impacts that are already in evidence.

The human genomania

The title of this section is taken from a paper by Ruth Hubbard, a politically concerned scientist and a critic of genetic determinism since the nineteen-seventies, when genetic engineering began.[42] She points out that, even before the Human Genome Project got under way, the diagnosis of genetic disease, such as sickle-cell anaemia, which predominantly affects Afro-Caribbeans, has resulted in people being discriminated against in health insurance and in employment in the United States. The diagnosis of diseases for which no cure is forthcoming is of questionable value, as even for many so-called 'single-gene' diseases the clinical prognosis can vary widely from one person to another, simply because genes do not function in isolation from all other genes and so will differ considerably in interaction from person to person.

> Identifying health disorders as 'genetic predispositions' places the blame for society's ills on people's genes, whereas the overwhelming causes of ill-health are environmental and social.

Nonetheless, geneticists are now attempting to identify 'genetic predispositions' and 'genetic propensities' for disorders such as cancer, diabetes, schizophrenia, and, worse, for conditions such as alcoholism, homosexuality and criminality that, over-whelmingly, come under the influence of environmental and social factors. This not only diverts attention from the real causes but also stigmatises people by placing the blame for society's ills on people's genes[43] and through the arbitrary categorisation of 'normal' versus 'abnormal'. The International League of Societies of Mentally Handicapped Persons gave evidence to the International Bioethics Committee of UNESCO pointing to the invisible social, legal and financial pressures already forcing women to abort disabled fetuses, and to the fact that genome research could 'geneticise' social policies and reduce financial support for dis-abled people.[44] So-called 'therapeutic' abortions of affected fetuses and the contemplation of germ-line gene therapy and genetic manipulation are negative and positive eugenic practices, respectively, which have now been privatised by industry.[45]

Eugenic movements have played a prominent role in the politics and history of much of the present century. They justified the devastation of indigenous populations by colonising Europeans, the introduction of apartheid in South Africa, and the genocide of Jews in Nazi Germany. Hundreds of thousands of

American citizens, declared 'feeble-minded', were forcibly sterilised between 1924 and 1974; and the scheme was planned and supported by scientists.[46] Concerns about population increase are consistently directed at populations that are non-white, whereas the real issue is the unequal distribution of resources, of which the well-to-do in predominantly white industrialised countries are consuming a disproportionate share. Finally, one cannot be complacent about the dangers of state-sanctioned eugenic practices even today. In 1996 China legislated for the compulsory termination of pregnancies diagnosed positive for genetic diseases.

Enclosing the 'intellectual commons'[47]

There are yet other repercussions of the present pre-eminence of genetic-engineering biotechnology. By defining innovation—for the purpose of financial reward through patenting—as something done within the dominant scientific tradition of northern Europe, the TRIPS proposal in effect excludes all other knowledge systems, especially those in the Third World as well as indigenous or folk wisdom in the North. It also marginalises any other alternative framework. Public funding for scientific research since the early nineties in most developed countries has been disproportionately biased in favour of product-oriented genetic-engineering biotechnology.

While funds are no longer made available to many areas of basic science, disciplines ranging from embryology and ecology to psychology and anthropology have one by one succumbed to the dominant reductionist mentality of genetic determinism. The pluralistic open inquiry that has long been the ideal of science is fast becoming obsolete. Some molecular geneticists have privately told me that they have become increasingly disillusioned with a system that judges excellence on the number of patents owned rather than on the genuine advancement of science. At the same time there has not been a single wide-ranging and open debate on genetic-engineering biotechnology within our academic institutions that has been organised by the academic staff; where such debates have taken place, the initiative has come invariably from a small minority of the students. Genetic-engineering bio-technology has in effect reduced the life sciences to a monolithic intellectual wasteland of genetic determinism. It is a 'de-intellectualisation of civil society, so that the mind becomes [subjugated to] a corporate monopoly.'[48]

This is the real beginning of the Brave New World, where ideological control is diffuse yet automatic and complete. That it is all done under the guise of freedom and democracy and in the name of scientific progress, within 'free' economies constituting the global free-trade regime of the WTO, makes it all the more sinister, and all the more difficult to grasp hold of and resist. As distinct from openly totalitarian regimes, there is no dictator in charge, there is no-one really making decisions, rational or otherwise; instead there are merely automatons driven by a sense of anxiety, isolated individuals driven by a need to amass wealth today, and governments driven by the need to remain in power against the insecurities of the morrow. No-one is apparently in charge, especially not those running the big companies, which they do not own, who are accountable to no-one except the share-holders, who by and large care nothing about their companies except the share price of their holdings. There are no responsible bosses on whom to lay the blame, only faceless managers who have no real stake in society. In such a system each person is a piece of flotsam, swept on by the tide of events, until the moment of oblivion.

'Monocultures of the mind'

The failure of the 'Green Revolution' is now generally acknow-ledged. Large-scale monoculture crops and the accompanying use of agrochemicals led to the erosion of indigenous biodiversity, to environmental destruction, the displacement of indigenous farmers, and widespread poverty. Many Third World countries have since devoted great efforts to restoring the environment and to regenerating indigenous biodiversity. They are doing this through a revival of traditional organic farming, whose methods are proving both to be sustainable and to provide much greater productivity than Western monoculture technologies.[49] With the benefit of hindsight into the failures of the 'Green Revolution', why is so much hope pinned on gene biotechnology? It is an even more reductionist ideology, producing even more genetically uniform monocultures requiring the use of agrochemicals. The significant difference lies in the additional danger of genetic pollution, which, unlike chemical pollution, is a self-perpetuating, self-amplifying process that will be impossible to recall.

Sustainable agriculture is also increasingly practised in Northern countries as decades of mechanisation and heavy dependence on agrochemicals have led to declining soil productivity, deteriorating environmental quality, reduced profits, and threats to human and animal health. The 1989 report of the National Research Council of the US Academy of Sciences emphasised the development and use of alternative farming systems as a means of increasing productivity and decreasing environmental damage. It is estimated that the use of pesticide could be reduced by 75 per cent in ten years without loss of productivity.

There are many forms of sustainable agriculture, using a combination of modern and traditional methods, all characterised by a holistic 'system-level approach to understanding the complex interactions within agricultural ecologies.' Recent surveys suggest that sustainable agriculture not only overcomes all the problems of conventional mechanised farming but is also 22 per cent more profitable.[50] As the ecologist Liebe Cavalieri, an opponent of genetic-engineering biotechnology since the seventies, concludes, 'sustainable agriculture is an essential goal for a viable future. It's time to put the emphasis on the real means that will get us there.'[51] Despite this, the US Department of Agriculture provided less than $5 million to research on sustainable agriculture in 1994, compared with $90 million allocated to gene biotechnology. There has been little improvement since.

Vandana Shiva, theoretical physicist turned political activist, has been in the forefront of the Third World's struggle against the exploitative and destructive policies of the North. In the process she came to realise the pervasive influence of the reductionist ideology—'monocultures of the mind'[52]—in shaping the policies of the North. In particular, she sees redefining the life sciences as an important part of the struggle. I have come to realise just how much I agree.

Three

THE SCIENCE THAT FAILS THE REALITY TEST

Reductionist science has failed the reality test, because it has been shown not to work in so many cases. Genetic determinism, the most insidious form of reductionist science, fails the reality test also on the basis of scientific evidence. But mainstream scientists have obfuscated and misread the evidence to serve industry and the status quo. The dangers of the mismatch between a powerful set of techniques and an outmoded, discredited ideology guiding its practice should not be underestimated.

Reductionist science has failed to work

In a sense, reductionist science has already failed the reality test, simply because it has been shown not to work in so many cases. The list includes the 'Green Revolution', eugenics, and nuclear energy; to these we can add the failure to recognise links between BSE ('mad cow disease') and the human neuropathy Creutzfeldt-Jakob disease (CJD), between severe pesticide poisoning and organophosphates, and between chlorofluoro-carbons (CFCs) and the loss of the ozone layer. And many of us still recall the horror of thalidomide, rushed onto the market without adequate tests as a sedative for pregnant women and eventually withdrawn in 1961 after eight thousand babies had been born with severely truncated limbs.

I do not deny that reductionist science has worked, and worked well, in solving problems in isolation. What it is notoriously bad at is taking proper account of the organic interconnections, the ecological and social relationships, that sustain the living system as a whole.

What I want to show is that genetic determinism, the most insidious form of reductionist science, has failed the reality test also on the basis of scientific findings: it has been proved wrong by the criteria of science itself. This would be entirely obvious were it not that there has always been an establishment of main-stream scientists purporting to speak for all scientists, in effect excluding all dissenting views and always appearing to favour the status quo, much to the comfort of the powers that be. In every one of the failures of science listed above it was the other scientists who provided the evidence, as well as the counter-arguments, that ultimately proved the orthodox opinion wrong. That is why the blanket condemnations of science and scientists that increasingly appear in the popular media are misdirected. Journalists in the popular media ought to work harder to find scientists with dissenting views and to encourage open debate, rather than promoting indiscriminate anti-science sentiments.

I shall show how genetic determinism fails the reality test within science itself. But first let us examine what genetic engineering entails.

The genetic engineering revolution

Genetic engineering is a set of techniques for modifying and recombining genes from different organisms; it is also referred to as recombinant (rDNA) technology.

The first genetic engineering technique to be developed, DNA sequencing, allows the sequence of bases in any stretch of DNA to be determined. The second technique is making recombinant DNA (rDNA) in the test-tube, using enzymes isolated from micro-organisms to cut and join pieces of DNA together. This enables geneticists to put foreign genes into viruses, plasmids, or mobile genetic elements, all of which are pieces of parasitic DNA that can infect cells and multiply in them, or insert themselves into their chromosome and replicate with the host cell. By cutting and joining bits of viruses, plasmids and mobile genetic elements together, scientists can make appropriate 'vectors' for transferring genes from a donor species to a recipient species that does not naturally interbreed with it.

The structure of DNA

DNA is a very long chain-like polymer made up of many thousands of simpler units joined end to end. The units differ in the organic bases they contain, of which there are four: adenine (A), thymine (T), cytosine (C), and guanine (G). The sequence in which the bases occur differs for each DNA molecule; this accounts for the specificity of the genetic 'message' it encodes. As we shall see later, the bases are like the alphabet of a language that can be composed into words, and the words in turn strung into a sentence. Each DNA molecule is packaged into a linear structure, a *chromosome*. Each cell can have one or more chromosomes: for example, a bacterial cell has one chromosome, whereas the human cell has twenty-three pairs of chromosomes. A gene is a stretch of DNA on the chromosome, usually thousands of units in length, which has a defined function. It might code for one of the thousands of proteins present in our cells, or it might work as a signal for making that protein. (We shall see in chapter 8 why this is a simplistic view of the gene, but it will suffice for the moment.)

The third technique is the chemical synthesis of DNA of any desired base sequence. A fourth technique, the polymerase chain reaction (PCR), discovered in 1988, allows specific gene sequences in a mixture to be rapidly replicated many tens of thousands or hundreds of thousands of times; this is extensively used in 'DNA fingerprinting'.

I should dispel right away the myth that genetic engineering is just like conventional breeding techniques. It is not.[1] Genetic engineering is a new departure from conventional breeding technologies. It makes novel combinations of genes, or gene constructs, that do not occur in nature. It bypasses conventional breeding by using the artificially constructed vectors to multiply copies of the gene constructs and to carry and smuggle them into cells that would otherwise reject them. Once inside cells, these vectors slot themselves into the host genome. In this way, transgenic organisms are made that have incorporated the desired transgenes. The insertion of foreign genes into the host genome is random and has long been known to have many harmful and fatal effects, including cancer; and this is borne out by the low success rate in creating desired transgenic organisms. Typically, a large number of eggs or embryos have to be injected or infected with the vector to obtain a few organisms that successfully express the transgene (see chapter 10).

> Genetic engineering is a new departure from conventional breeding technologies. It bypasses conventional breeding by using artificially constructed vectors to multiply copies of genes and to transfer genes.

The most common artificial vectors used are a chimeric re-combination of natural genetic parasites from different sources, including viruses that cause cancers and other diseases in animals and plants, with their pathogenic functions 'crippled'. These are tagged with one or more antibiotic-resistance 'marker' genes, so that cells transformed with the vector can be selected. For example, the vector most widely used in plant genetic engineering is derived from a plasmid that induces tumours in plants, carried by the soil bacterium *Agrobacterium tumefaciens*. In animals, vectors are constructed from retroviruses causing cancers and other diseases. A vector now used in fish has a framework from the Moloney murine leukaemic virus, which causes leukaemia in mice but can infect all mammalian cells. It has bits from the Rous sarcoma virus, which causes sarcomas in domestic fowl, and from the vesicular stomatitis virus, which causes oral lesions in cattle, horses, pigs, and humans.[2] Such mosaic vectors are common and are particularly hazardous. Unlike natural parasitic genetic elements, which have various degrees of host-specificity, vectors used in genetic engineering have—partly by design and partly because of their mosaic character—the ability to overcome species barriers and to infect a wide range of species.

Another obstacle to genetic engineering is the fact that all organisms and cells have natural defence mechanisms, which enable them to destroy or inactivate foreign genes; and transgene instability is a big problem for the industry (as we shall see in more detail in chapters 7, 8, and 9). Vectors are increasingly constructed to overcome those mechanisms that maintain the integrity of species; the result is that the artificially constructed vectors are especially good at carrying out successful horizontal gene transfer (see chapter 9).

Genetic engineering not only makes it possible for geneticists to manipulate genes but also happens to be a powerful research tool that enables geneticists to study the genome of organisms in ways that were not possible before. The scientific community were completely unprepared for the plethora of new findings that came to light, which sent shock waves through the foundations of classical genetics. Just as quantum physics replaced the classical Newtonian framework at the beginning of the present century, the 'new genetics' that came in the wake of genetic engineering overturned every preconceived notion of the old genetic paradigm.

Paradoxical as it may seem, genetic engineering is possible precisely because the paradigm of genetic determinism is invalid. Many of the promises of genetic-engineering biotechnology can never be fulfilled, because the paradigm is an erroneous, reductionist representation of organic wholeness and complexity. The numerous problems that have arisen with genetic-engineering biotechnology are indicative of that fundamental error in judgment on the part of those who see it as the solution to all the problems that humanity faces today. When biotech stocks fell into the doldrums in 1994, *Business Week* reported: 'The industry is still peddling dreams ...' From Wall Street's perspective, 'the industry hasn't worked, and the likelihood of success is lower ... A long list of products has failed clinical trials; even the remaining handful that got through are not without problems.'[3]

Genetic engineering differs radically from conventional breeding

- Genetic engineering makes novel combinations of genetic material in the laboratory between species that do not interbreed in nature.

- While conventional breeding methods shuffle different forms (*alleles*) of the same genes, genetic engineering enables completely new (*exotic*) genes to be introduced, with unpredictable effects on the physiology and biochemistry of the resulting transgenic organism.

- Gene multiplications and a high proportion of gene transfers are mediated by artificial vectors derived from viruses, plasmids, and mobile genetic elements—all of them genetic parasites that have the ability to invade cells and insert themselves into the cell's genome, causing genetic damage.

- The artificial vectors are designed to break down species barriers so that they can shuttle genes between a wide range of species. Their wide host range means they can infect many animals and plants, and in the process pick up genes from viruses of all these species to create new pathogens.

- The artificial vectors routinely carry marker genes for antibiotic-resistance, which is already a big public health problem.

- The artificial vectors are increasingly constructed to overcome the recipient species' defence mechanisms that break down or inactivate foreign DNA.

- The insertion of foreign genes into the recipient organism's genome is random, giving rise to correspondingly random genetic effects, including cancer in mammalian cells.

This remains true today. 'Overall the industry has been so consistently disappointing that laymen should stay away lest they get fleeced … And until the gene-bending gods can separate the hype from the glory, they're not getting any of my savings.'[4] One British company, British Biotech, collapsed in April 1998. Shares had plummeted within a year from 270p to 59p just before it sacked its chief scientist for exposing the company's hype about cancer and pancreatitis drugs. At least two managers and one scientist, no longer working with the company, had made millions in share deals.[5] The industry is still peddling dreams: cure for cancer, designer babies, cloning, and other means to immortality. It is preying on the very illness and anxieties inherent in a society dominated by reductionist science.

> The biotech industry is still peddling dreams: cure for cancer, designer babies, cloning, and other means to immortality. It is preying on the very illness and anxieties generated by a society dominated by reductionist science.

I was involved in a debate on genetic-engineering bio-technology organised by the Society of the Chemical Industry at the University of Cambridge. At dinner afterwards I found myself sitting next to the chief executive officer of a biotech company. In an unguarded moment he confessed that he personally didn't feel happy about biotechnology, but what could he do? It was the system, and mortgages had to be paid. He was coping, he said, by practising transcendental meditation—unlike his colleagues, most of whom were on Prozac.

Financial ruin is a small price to pay when the future of the planet and all its inhabitants is at stake. The dangers of the mismatch between a powerful set of techniques and an outmoded, discredited ideology guiding its practice should not be underestimated. It also constitutes the main stumbling-block to a rational debate on genetic-engineering biotechnology and its legitimate spheres of application.

With this in mind, let us look at the paradigms of genetic determinism and of the new genetics.

The paradigm of genetic determinism

A *paradigm* is an outlook: it is a comprehensive system of thought and practice developed around a central idea. A scientific paradigm is obviously built around a scientific theory, but it can also be so pervasive as to spill over into all other disciplines and to permeate the popular culture. Genetic determinism is of this nature. It portrays genes as the most fundamental essence of organisms. It supposes that, while the environment can be moulded and re-shaped, biological nature in the form of genes is fixed and unchanging and can be separated from environmental influence. Further, it assumes that the function of each gene can be defined independently of every other. It is on such a basis that the Human Genome Project promises to unravel the 'genetic program' for making a human being. James Watson, the first director of the Human Genome Organisation (HUGO), set the tone. 'We used to think that our fate was in the stars. Now we know, in large measure, our fate is in our genes.'[6]

The twin pillars of genetic determinism are Darwin's theory of evolution and the gene theory of heredity, as developed by Mendel, Weismann, Johannsen, and others. Darwin proposed that evolution occurs by natural selection, in which nature in effect 'selects' the fittest in the same way that artificial selection practised by plant and animal breeders ensures that the best, or most desirable, characteristics are bred or preserved.[7] The ideology of natural selection is clear: those who do well and survive to reproduce are naturally favoured with superior qualities, which can be passed on, like a legacy, to the next generation; in the same way, those with inferior qualities are eliminated. Darwin's theory lacked a mechanism of heredity and variation. This was supplied by Mendel, who proposed that (Darwinian) qualities are inherent in constant factors (later called *genes*) determining the organism's characteristics, which are passed on to the next generation during reproduction, and that variations are generated by rare random mutations in those genes. (A *genetic mutation* is a change in the base sequence of the stretch of DNA that constitutes the gene.)

The combination of Mendelian genetics and Darwinian theory resulted in the 'neo-Darwinian synthesis'. But from the beginning these theories were built on abstraction and ideology, as well as a certain blindness to, and misreading of, scientific evidence. This has recurred again and again, and even outright fraud has been committed (as we shall see in later chapters) in the development of the genetic determinism that we have today.

The paradigm of genetic determinism today is neo-Darwinism writ large. Everything from IQ to criminality can be explained by invoking the genes responsible, which have been naturally selected for or against. And so they can be hunted down in the genome and, having been identified, can be selected for or against by human beings, thereby, we are told, extending our choice as human beings.

There are four basic assumptions in the genetic-determinist paradigm:

- Genes determine characteristics in a straightforward, additive (that is, non-interactive) way.
- Genes and genomes are stable and, except for rare random mutations, are passed on unchanged to the next generation.
- Genes and genomes cannot be changed directly in response to the environment.
- Acquired characteristics cannot be inherited.

One has to appreciate that these assumptions have been the bread and butter of mainstream biology for at least a hundred years, rather in the way that Newtonian mechanics had been the foundation of physics in the pre-quantum era. *All these assumptions have been contradicted by scientific findings.* Some of us have argued that they were untenable even before the recombinant DNA (rDNA) era; but none of us was prepared for the surprises that rDNA research has turned up within the past twenty years.

The first assumption is clearly contradicted by everything that has been known about metabolism and genetics for at least forty years, and no biologist would admit to believing in it. However, it is logically part and parcel of the genetic-determinist science on which the practice of commercial genetic engineering is based.

> So-called single-gene defects account for less than 2 per cent of all human diseases; and even these are now proving to be very complex. Many different mutations of the same gene or of different genes may give the same disease, or not, as the case may be. There is really no such thing as a single-gene disease.

Organisms, including human beings, have tens of thousands of genes in their genome. Each gene exists in multiple variants (we shall see exactly how many in chapter 11). One of the main functions of genes is to code for the thousands of enzymes catalysing thousands of metabolic reactions in the body that provide the energy to do everything that constitutes being alive. These metabolic reactions form an immensely complicated network in which the product of one enzyme is processed by one or more other enzymes. No enzyme (or gene), therefore, ever works in isolation. Consequently, the same gene will have different effects from individual to individual, because the other genes in the 'genetic background' are different.

So-called single-gene defects account for less than 2 per cent of all human diseases.[8] And even these are now proving to be very complex. Many different mutations of the same gene or of different genes may give the same disease, or not, as the case may be. This is so for sickle-cell anaemia, common in Africans and African-Americans; for cystic fibrosis, common among northern Europeans; and a conglomerate of cranio-facial syndromes, which includes achondroplastic dwarfism. It has provoked a geneticist to declare that there is 'no such thing as a single-gene disease.'[9]

Findings that have been steadily accumulating for the past twenty years reveal further undreamt-of complexity and dynamism in cellular and genic processes. Many of these processes destabilise and alter genomes within the lifetime of the organism.[10] This is in direct contrast to the static, linear conception of the central dogma of molecular biology that previously held sway. This states that the genetic material DNA makes RNA in a faithful copying process, called *transcription*. RNA is a nucleic acid like DNA except that the sugar is ribose instead of deoxyribose, and in place of the base thymine (T) it has uracil (U). The RNA then makes a protein by a process of decoding called *translation*. There is a strictly one-way 'information flow' from the genetic message coded in the DNA to RNA to protein, and no reverse information flow is possible (fig. 3.1*a*). In other words, proteins cannot determine or alter the transcribed message in RNA, and RNA cannot determine or alter the genetic message in DNA. We shall see that such a reverse information flow not only occurs—and in a wide variety of forms—but is a necessary part of how genes function within a metabolic-epigenetic super-network (fig. 3.1*b*).

a. The Central Dogma

DNA ⟶ RNA ⟶ Protein

b. The New Genetics

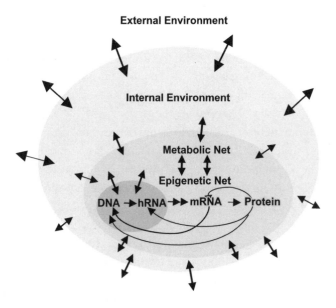

Fig. 3.1: Genetics old and new

The fluid genome of the new genetics

In place of the previous, simplistic model, the new genetics reveals a complicated network of feed-forward and feedback processes that has to be traversed just to 'express' one gene, that is, to make a single protein. Genes are found to exist in bits, and the bits must be appropriately joined together to make the messenger-RNA (mRNA). Numerous other proteins take part in making every single protein, chopping and changing, editing and recoding in an epigenetic network that interposes between the genes and the metabolic net and interlocks with it as an epigenetic-metabolic super-network. It becomes increasingly difficult therefore to define and delimit a gene, as the super-network ultimately connects the expression of each gene with that of every other.

The genome itself, embedded within the epigenetic-metabolic super-network, is far from stable or insulated from environmental exigencies. A large number of processes appear to be designed especially to destabilise genomes during the lifetime of all organisms, either as a part of normal development or in response to the environment—so much so that molecular geneticists have been inspired to coin the descriptive term 'fluid genome'. Base sequences can mutate; stretches of DNA can be inserted, deleted, or amplified thousands and tens of thousands of times. The sequences can be rearranged or recombined; genes can jump around from one site to another in the genome; and some genes can convert other genes to their own DNA sequences. These processes keep genomes in a constant state of flux in evolutionary time.[11] Genes are found to jump horizontally between species that do not interbreed, being carried by mobile genetic elements or viruses. A particular genetic element—the P-element—has spread to all species of fruit flies in the wild within a span of less than fifty years, probably carried by a parasitic mite that infects all the species.[12]

These fluid genome processes are by no means entirely random, accidental or meaningless but are subject to physiological and cellular regulation, which can be disrupted by gene transfers, as for example the insertion of retroviruses that can cause cancer. On the other hand, gene jumping, recombination and other alterations of the genome have been found also to be part of the normal physiological response to environmental stress or starvation in non-dividing cells that enables them to cope with new challenges.[13]

Most provocative of all, there is now abundant evidence of the previously forbidden reverse information flow in the genomes of all higher organisms.[14] Predictable and repeatable genetic changes have been found to occur simultaneously and uniformly in all the cells of the growing tips of plants exposed to different fertilisers.[15] Similarly, plants exposed to herbicides, insects exposed to insect-icides, cultured cells exposed to drugs, and bacteria exposed to antibiotics—all are capable of changing their genomes in a repeat-able way by mutations or gene amplifications that render them resistant to the noxious agent.[16] These genetic changes are readily passed on to the next generation. In other words, there is abundant evidence of the 'inheritance of acquired characteristics' in many different forms.

As a final blow to the classical genetic paradigm, starving bacteria and yeast cells are now known to respond directly to the presence of (initially) non-metabolisable substrates by mutational changes apparently so specific that they are referred to as 'directed mutations' or, even more provocatively, 'adaptive mutations'.[17] (You will have the opportunity to read about the fluid and adaptable genome in detail in chapter 7.)

Mismatch between mindset and reality

There is therefore a serious mismatch between the mindset of genetic-engineering biotechnology (with the projected benefits and wealth to be gained therefrom) and the reality of the new genetics. Genetic engineers essentially believe that by manipu-lating genes, all the major problems of the world may be solved. They reason that, as genes determine the characteristics of organisms, so, by changing the appropriate genes, they can engineer organisms to fulfil all our needs.

This can only be true if genes determine the characteristics of organisms in an uncomplicated way, so that by identifying a gene one can predict a desirable or undesirable trait; by changing the gene, one changes the trait; by transferring the gene, one transfers the corresponding trait, once and for all. In other words, *genetic-engineering biotechnology only makes sense if one believes in*

genetic determinism. No-one would regard it as a good investment if they did not believe in genetic determinism. More to the
point, no-one would think of it is a good investment if they did
not believe that everyone else thought genetic engineering
worked in the way it claims.

Genetic engineering mindset	Reality of scientific findings
Genes determine characteristics in linear causal chains; one gene gives one function.	Genes function in a complex network; causation is multi-dimensional, non-linear, and circular.
Genes and genomes are not subject to environmental influence.	Genes and genomes are subject to feedback regulation.
Genes and genomes are stable and unchanging.	Genes and genomes are dynamic and fluid, can change directly in response to the environment, and give 'adaptive' mutations to order.
Genes stay where they are put.	Genes can jump horizontally between unrelated species and recombine.

Fig. 3.2: Mindset versus reality

The mismatch between mindset and reality is ultimately why
genetic-engineering biotechnology not only cannot deliver its
promises but also poses such hazards. I shall refer to a few
symptoms here and leave the detailed diagnosis to later chapters.

Mismatch 1 leads to unrealistic assumptions about the
efficacy of gene transfers. Single-gene transfers have invariably led
to 'unexpected' changes in the recipient organism (unexpected
only because reductionists fail to take account of complexity and

interconnectedness). Toxins and allergens have arisen as so-called side effects in transgenic plants and micro-organisms, and very sick, monstrous transgenic animals have resulted from having a single gene introduced. This is unsafe for consumers, particularly as regulatory bodies see risk assessment from the same reductionist viewpoint, often concentrating exclusively on the genes and gene products introduced. It is also morally unacceptable to increase the suffering of animals, for which there is neither need nor good scientific justification.

Mismatch 2 leads to the unrealistic neglect of physiological and environmental feedback regulation. Calgene's 'Flavr-Savr' tomato, genetically engineered to improve shelf life and the very first *live* transgenic food to be introduced to our supermarkets, has now been withdrawn. Apparently, because it was developed in California, it does not grow properly in Florida.[18] Monsanto's *Bt*-cotton crop—engineered with a gene from *Bacillus thuringiensis,* a soil bacterium producing a toxin against insect pests—did not work properly when it was first planted commercially in Texas in 1996, because it was 'too hot.' Nor did it work properly in Australia—probably because it was 'too cold.'[19] The same company's herbicide-tolerant transgenic cotton also failed miserably the following year; it gave deformed cotton balls, which dropped off when they were sprayed with the herbicide Roundup.[20]

The instability of transgenic lines is a big problem for the biotech industry, though it is doing its best not to communicate such failures to the public. Monsanto took two varieties of geneti-cally engineered canola seeds off the Canadian market after testing revealed that at least one of the patented herbicide-tolerant transgenic varieties contained an 'unexpected' gene; this was after sixty thousand bags of the seeds had been sold throughout western Canada.[21] Once again it is the reductionist disregard for complexity and wholeness that is failing. It is unsafe and insupportable as a long-term investment. The industry has in fact produced little more than dreams. Monsanto's shares have plummeted with the collapse of the market for transgenic produce.

Mismatch 3 is particularly relevant to a large class of existing transgenic plants with built-in biopesticide, the *Bt*-toxins. Insects were found to develop resistance rapidly when exposed to the toxins. That was the other problem with the *Bt*-cotton crop in Texas. Classical neo-Darwinian theory puts this down to the natural selection of existing, rare 'random' mutations. However, the real story is that all cells and organisms have the physiological capability of developing resistance through a wide variety of genetic mechanisms, from multiplying particular genes thousands of times to generating new genes by recombinations or by *hyper-mutations*—mutations that are a million times faster than usual (see chapters 7 and 8). They can also acquire the genes needed from their friends, which include organisms from other species (see mismatch 4 below). Genes and genomes are inherently fluid and dynamic. Reductionist science fails to recognise that genetic stability is a property not of the gene transferred but of the eco-logical whole in which the organism is entangled (see chapter 13).

> 'Indeed, if one lesson has emerged from the spectacular failure of Western medicine to "eradicate" certain diseases, it is that diseases cannot be reduced to a single cause nor explained within the prevailing linear scientific method: complexity is their hallmark.'

Mismatch 4 is perhaps the most serious. It is the failure to recognise that genes do not remain static in the genome once and for all. They can also jump between species that do not normally interbreed, particularly when the conditions are favourable. The instability of the genome is due to a large extent to genetic para-sites, including mobile genetic elements, plasmids, and viruses, that can hop in and out of genomes, replicate, and infect other cells. As pointed out in chapter 1, genetic engineering is inherently hazardous, because it uses vectors constructed out of precisely these genetic parasites to facilitate horizontal gene transfer. And horizontal gene transfer is already known to be responsible for the emergence of new and old pathogens and of multi-antibiotic-resistance.

The failures of reductionist medicine

If we need more evidence that reductionist science has failed the reality test, it can be found in the area of public health. As is evident from the 1996 report of the World Health Organisation (WHO), diseases such as TB, malaria, cholera and yellow fever are still a major cause of death in many parts of the world—and are returning to regions where they were on the decline. New diseases also continue to emerge at unprecedented rates as a result of social conditions and environmental disturbances that enable pathogens to gain access to new host populations, or to become more virulent in immunologically weakened human hosts suffering from poverty and malnutrition. Many of the agents of infectious diseases rapidly develop resistance to drugs and chemicals, while new variants continue to arise that escape the protection of vaccines, as we would expect from what we know of the 'fluid genome'. The Harvard Working Group on New and Resurgent Diseases concludes: 'Disease cannot be understood in isolation from the social, ecological, epidemiological and evolutionary context in which it emerges and spreads. Indeed, if one lesson has emerged from the spectacular failure of Western medicine to "eradicate" certain diseases, it is that diseases cannot be reduced to a single cause nor explained within the prevailing linear scientific method: complexity is their hallmark.'[22]

Genetic-engineering biotechnology greatly exacerbates the problems of resurgent diseases by facilitating horizontal gene transfer. It is also diverting attention and resources away from the real causes of ill-health, which are overwhelmingly environmental and social. Agrochemicals, industrial waste and radioactive wastes are linked to many debilitating diseases, especially cancer.[23] Poverty and consequent malnutrition compromise people's immunological defence against infection. This and the lack of sanitation, proper housing and clean water supply are all conditions that promote the spread of infectious diseases.

The very same chemical and pharmaceutical industries that have flooded our environment with the toxic wastes that made us ill are profiting from ill-health by producing ever more exotic drugs, vaccines, and cures. Often these drugs cause side effects worse than the conditions they are supposed to treat. The history of the pharmaceutical industry is littered with failures of wonder-drugs. In the United States, *iatrogenic diseases* (diseases caused by prescription drugs) are estimated to result in 2 million people being admitted to hospital each year and 180,000 deaths.[24] Is it not time to stop profiting from ill-health, much of which has been created by the reductionist, 'magic-bullet' approach, leading to the overuse and abuse of drugs?

Implications of the new genetics for heredity

The genetic-determinist paradigm has collapsed under the weight of its own momentum in the findings of the new genetics. Genes are far from being the constant essence of organisms, whose effects can be neatly separated from one another or from the environment. There is, furthermore, no constant 'genetic program' or blueprint for making the organism, as the genes and the genome itself can also change during development. For an organism, being alive depends on a dynamic balance of feedback relationships between it and the environment, which extends through its entire physio-logical system to its genes. Heredity—the stability of reproducing the same life cycle—is the property not so much of the genes as of the whole system of the organism within its ecological environ-ment. All its parts are, ideally, maximally responsive and communicative with every other part[25] and must change as appropriate in the maintenance of the whole. Heredity, therefore, does not reside in our genes any more than it resides in the environment and cultural traditions that we have created and that are also passed on to future generations. Heredity is the whole way of life characteristic of the species. The biological and the socio-ecological are inextricably entangled. Consequently, our fate is written neither in the stars nor in our genes, for we are active participants in the evolutionary drama.[26] The new genetics that makes it possible to do genetic engineering belongs with a paradigm of organic wholeness and complexity emerging in many areas of contemporary research in the West, which is reaffirming the wisdom of traditional indigenous cultures all over the world.[27] We can therefore choose to shape the socio-ecological conditions for our biological health and well-being, rather than persist in futile and hazardous attempts to manipulate our genes and the genes of other species.

The struggle to reclaim holistic ways of life

The collapse of the genetic-determinist paradigm is both symptomatic and symbolic of the collapse of the reductionist world view. It is significant that, in opposition to the patenting of life, the French geneticist Daniel Cohen, a prominent figure in the Human Genome Project, made the first move to offer a wide range of DNA sequence data obtained in his laboratory to the United Nations as the property of humanity, to use freely for any appropriate purpose.[28]

The debate over gene technology is not about disembodied, objective, ivory-tower scientific knowledge. Knowledge is what people everywhere else in the world live by. The Western ideal of being objective is misplaced, for it implies that one must be a completely detached, unfeeling observer, outside nature. Within the participatory framework of all other knowledge systems, the ideal of objectivity in knowledge is to be maximally communicative and connected within the nature that is the object of our knowledge, which we, as both knower and actor, participate in shaping.[29] The present opposition to genetic-engineering biotechnology is therefore also a concerted struggle to reclaim holistic world views and holistic ways of life that are spontaneous, pluralistic, joyful, integrative, constructive, and life-sustaining.

Four

THE ORIGINS OF GENETIC DETERMINISM

Genetic determinism has a strong hold over the public imagination. Its ideological roots reach back, deep within the collective unconscious of our culture, to Darwin's theory of evolution by natural selection, which is itself a product of the socio-economic and political climate of nineteenth-century England. The belief in the constancy and fixity of genes replaced the belief in an immortal soul when science took the place of religion. Yet people started to forget the organism altogether by thinking of it as a mere collection of genes. They discount not only how genes can give rise to organisms (if indeed they can) but also how genes interact with one another and are absolutely dependent on the cellular and ecological contexts to guide their function.

Deconstructing the old

When I left molecular genetics ten years ago, I felt I was entering a wonderfully constructive period in science, when we would articulate a holistic world view *based on contemporary Western science*. I have since come to realise that our efforts at deconstructing the old paradigm were not good enough. Most of all, I now know how much it matters to the issues raised by genetic-engineering biotechnology and the way they will shape our lives—and how important it is that we exorcise the ghost of the old paradigm, to set ourselves free, before we can wholeheartedly accept the new.

Genetic determinism has a strong hold over the public imagination. That is because its ideological roots reach back, deep within the collective unconscious of our culture, to Darwin's theory of evolution by natural selection and beyond; for Darwin's theory is itself a product of the socio-economic and political climate of its time. Nineteenth-century England saw the rise of capitalism and the expansion of trade by imperial conquest. Its ruling class in particular believed in progress through competition in the free market or, more accurately, through the 'free market' created by military might. This was also the era of positivist philosophy, which believed in the triumph of mechanical materialism over both religion and other romantic ideas that there might be any 'purpose' to life.

The scholar and historian Jacques Barzun maintained that one of the great turning-points in modern history came in 1859, when Charles Darwin's *Origin of Species,* Karl Marx's *Critique of Political Economy* and Richard Wagner's *Tristan and Isolde* made their first appearance. Together they dominated the epoch, and their theories epitomised a century of thought that continues to the present day. 'Emerging out of an era of Romanticism and flowering in an age of "scientific thought", their "mechanical materialism" expresses the prevalent conception of matter as the source and substance of the universe. Feeling, beauty, and moral values are mere illusions in a world of fact, and the human will is powerless against the ineluctable laws of nature and society.'[1]

While it is true that mechanical materialism breeds alienation and a sense of powerlessness, particularly in those who do not possess the scientific knowledge, its explicit aim is otherwise: for it firmly believes in the power of abstraction and reduction to make sense of the untidy, intangible complexity of real processes, so that humankind might better control and dominate nature. Let us begin with the theory of evolution.

Lamarck, Darwin, and evolutionary theory

Evolution refers to the natural (as opposed to supernatural) origin and transformation of the living inhabitants of the planet Earth throughout its geological history to the present day. Many in the West have speculated on evolution since the time of the Greeks.

The ideas that have come down to us, however, originate in the European Enlightenment. That period saw the formulation of Newton's laws of mechanics and the flowering of mathematics and other modern Western scientific ideas, including John Ray's concept of species and Carl von Linné's system for classifying and naming organisms, still used today.

The first comprehensive theory of evolution was presented in the early nineteenth century by Jean-Baptiste de Monet de Lamarck, who was very much a product of the Enlightenment, both in his determination to offer a naturalistic explanation of evolution and in his systems approach. He dealt at length with physics, chemistry and geology before embarking on presenting evidence that biological evolution had occurred. He also suggested a mechanism of evolution, whereby new species could arise through changes in the relationship between the organism and its environment in pursuit of its basic needs, thereby producing new modifications in its characteristics, which become inherited after many generations.[2]

Lamarck's theory was widely misrepresented as merely the inheritance of acquired characteristics, or caricatured as changes resulting from the wish-fulfilment of the organism. Half a century later, however, Charles Darwin was to include a number of Lamarck's ideas in his own theory of evolution by natural selection, though without due attribution.

Darwin's theory of evolution by natural selection says that, given that organisms can reproduce more of their numbers than the environment can support, and that there are variations that are inherited, then within a population, individuals with the more favourable variations will survive to reproduce their kind, at the expense of those with less favourable variations. The ensuing competition and 'struggle for life' results in the 'survival of the fittest', so that the species becomes better adapted to its environment. And if the environment itself changes in time, there will be a gradual but definite change in the species.[3] In this way nature in effect 'selects' the fittest, in the same way that artificial selection practised by plant and animal breeders ensures that the best or the most desirable characteristics are bred or preserved, while those that are undesirable or 'unfit' are eliminated. In both cases, new varieties are created after some generations.

It is to Darwin's credit that he realised that natural selection could not explain everything; so, *in addition* to natural selection, he invoked the effects of use and disuse and the inheritance of acquired characteristics in the transmutation of species—both previously proposed by Lamarck. The effects of use and disuse simply mean that if the organism makes use of any part of its body habitually, that part will develop and work better; conversely, any part that is under-used will atrophy or shrivel away. People who train for the marathon will have strong muscles in their legs that do not fatigue easily;[4] conversely, astronauts cannot tolerate low-gravity conditions for very long before their muscles begin to suffer degeneration from disuse. The effects of use and disuse are now well documented; but whether those effects are inherited is not yet known. It is clear, however, that those Lamarckian ideas do not fit in to the theory of natural selection and are rejected by Darwin's followers, who regard the lack of a mechanism of heredity and variation as the weakest link in the argument for natural selection.

The epigenetic versus the genetic paradigm

History has a habit of creating heroes and anti-heroes; and so Darwin triumphed while Lamarck bore the brunt of ridicule and obscurity. The reason is that the theories of the two men are logically diametrically opposed. Darwin's theory is of natural selection, and selection entails a separation of the organism from its environment. The organism is thus conceptually closed off from its experience, leading logically to Weismann's barrier (see page 104) and the central dogma of molecular biology (chapter 6), which is reductionist both in intent and actuality. The life experiences of the organism and the organism itself are both negated, as only its genes are of any consequence in development, as in evolution. This fatalism is inherent in the genetic-determinist paradigm.

> Lamarck's theory requires a conception of the organism as an active, autonomous being, which is open to the environment. Its openness is inherently subversive of the status quo. No wonder it was suppressed.

Lamarck's theory, on the other hand, is of transformation arising from the organism's own activities and experience of its environment during *epigenesis* or development. This requires a conception of the organism as an active, autonomous being, which is open to the environment. Its openness is inherently subversive of the status quo. No wonder it was suppressed. It also invites us to examine the dynamics of transformation and the mechanisms whereby the transformation could become 'internalised' in the course of development and evolution. It is consistent with the epigenetic approach that has emerged as an alternative to neo-Darwinism since the late nineteen-seventies,[5] to which I have contributed and which is fully vindicated by the new genetics. The epigenetic approach is one that takes the organism's experience of the environment during development as central to the evolution of the organism. It is potentially always subversive of the status quo, which is why it is invariably vehemently denied by the present orthodoxy.

Mendel's contribution

It was Gregor Mendel who provided the missing link in Darwin's argument. Mendel published his work in the same year that Darwin's *Origin of Species* appeared. Yet, in direct contrast to the instant fame that Darwin's publication brought to its author, Mendel's theory, which conforms even more to the mechanical materialism model, languished in the archives for more than forty years before it was rediscovered at the beginning of the present century. By the time Mendel's work was rediscovered, the German biologist August Weismann had already identified the material basis of heredity as the 'germplasm' or germ cells (that is, reproductive cells), which became separate from the rest of the animal's body during early development. Weismann was inspired by the same zeal for mechanical materialism as Mendel. His explicit aim was to reduce heredity to its material, mechanical causes. He was studying the development of insects, the embryos of which form separate germ cells in the posterior pole very early in development. This gave Weismann the idea that hereditary influence— later to be equated with Mendelian genes—could be passed on unchanged from one generation to the next through the germ cells. Weismannism and its implied 'immortality of the germplasm' took on the symbolic significance of the persistence of the eternal soul, of order and stability in the face of change, and has had a strong and lasting influence on Western thought.

The gene theory of heredity

Mendel's gene theory of heredity attempts to explain how the characteristics of organisms are inherited in subsequent generations. It explains not only why organisms that are alike should 'breed true' when they reproduce among themselves but also why when organisms that differ in some characteristics are interbred their offspring may be intermediate between the parents or may resemble one or the other parent; furthermore, all the possibilities may be found in later generations. Within families, for example, children may resemble one or the other of their parents, or may resemble neither of them but resemble a grandparent or an aunt or a distant cousin instead.

It turns out that to account for all these possibilities in sexually reproducing organisms (as non-sexually reproducing organisms merely reproduce identical copies, or clones, of themselves), a *particulate* theory of inheritance is required. In other words, there must be factors that can remain separate and discrete, as opposed to those that mix and blend and lose their identity. It will help to summarise the elements of the theory in its fully developed form, that is, in the form in which it came to be accepted for the best part of the present century, up to at least the early nineteen-seventies. I shall point out later why it does not explain heredity except in a very trivial and limited way.

Elements of the gene theory

1. The characteristics of an organism are determined by stable unit factors called genes, each occurring twice—in two *alleles* (variants of a particular gene)—which may be the same as or different from each other.
2. Each organism carries a large number of genes.
3. The genes are passed on unchanged from parent to offspring by means of the germ cells.
4. Each germ cell contains a single copy of each gene, so that the precise combinations of genes will vary at random from one germ cell to the next.
5. When the germ cells unite at fertilisation, the resulting *zygote* (fertilised egg) will again have two alleles of every gene.
6. The separation of alleles and recombination between alleles of different genes during reproduction account for the resemblances and differences between successive generations.
7. The genetic constitution of an organism, its *genotype*, is to be distinguished from its expressed characteristics, the *phenotype*.
8. The action of one allele may be *dominant* or *recessive* to that of another, according to whether it is expressed or not in combination with the other allele.

From elements 1 to 6 of the gene theory one can see that it is entirely a matter of chance which combinations of genes are passed on from each parent, and this in turn will determine the characteristics of each of the offspring. If we concentrate on the father in a family, he would have had an equal contribution from each of his parents: one allele of every gene from his mother, and the other allele from his father. However, the sperm he produces may contain any combination of alleles: all from his father (*paternal contribution*), all from his mother (*maternal contribution*), or any possibility in between the two extremes. So, just by chance, a child he produces may have half its genetic make-up from one grandparent; and this may account for why it ends up resembling that grandparent.

But the two parents make an equal contribution to their children;[6] so why aren't the children intermediate in every respect between the two parents? Among families where one of the parents is fair-haired and the other dark-haired, for example, it may turn out that none of the children has intermediate hair colour: instead, either all of the children are dark-haired or half of them are fair-haired and the other half dark-haired. To explain this, the additional concepts of *dominance* and *recessivity* are required, as given in elements 7 and 8 of the gene theory. The allele for dark hair is dominant, while the allele for fair hair is recessive.

The questionable Mendelian ratios

Mendel's theory of particulate inheritance involving dominant and recessive characteristics was based on his experiments in crossing pea plants. However, the earliest cross-breeding experiments, described by Mendel's teacher, were pioneered by Joseph Kölreuter, professor of natural history in Karlsruhe in 1760, who carried out five hundred different hybridisations, involving 138 species, with parallel investigations into the mechanisms of pollination and fertilisation. His work lay neglected until it was repeated and confirmed by Carl von Gärtner in the twenty years between 1824 and 1844.[7]

> Mendelian heredity applies only to a restricted range of characteristics, observed over a limited number of generations under more or less unchanging environmental conditions, and only when the organisms within the same species, with the same number of chromosomes, are crossed.

Both Kölreuter and Gärtner were prodigious and diligent experimenters, and they had noticed that when two varieties were hybridised, the offspring, or first filial generation (F1), were uniformly alike, and intermediate between the parental varieties in many characteristics. When the F1 hybrids were crossed among themselves or self-pollinated, however, the resulting (F2) generation threw up a great many variations, and only some characteristics gave ratios approximating the 3:1 or 1:2:1 that Mendel later observed. Neither, however, succeeded in formalising the results as Mendel did. One important reason was that not all characteristics behaved in that way. This was also the case with Mendel's own experimental findings. We now know that Mendelian heredity applies only to a restricted range of characteristics, observed over a limited number of generations under more or less unchanging environmental conditions, and only when the organisms within the same species, with the same number of chromosomes, are cross-bred. In fact one of the characteristics Mendel studied, that of wrinkled peas, was brought about by a mobile genetic element or 'jumping gene' that had inserted itself into the normal wild-type allele for round peas—a definitely non-Mendelian process.[8]

Mendel's laws are a great simplification and idealisation. Furthermore, they did not come from his observations, or from the observation of his predecessors. Where did they come from?

The clue is to be found in one of Mendel's letters to the botanist Karl von Nägeli, in which he describes his own task as ascertaining the 'statistical relations' of the different forms among the offspring of the hybrids. Mendel had obtained a good knowledge of mathematics from his studies in physics. Christian Doppler and Andreas von Ettinghausen were his physics teachers, both of whom emphasised the mathematical approach. There was also correspondence between the abbot of the monastery in Brno where Mendel was a monk and Karl Friedrich Gauss, a founding father of probability theory and much else besides, who was concerned with the errors of measurements. The abbot took a great interest in Mendel's work, and in all probability Mendel knew what to look for in his experiments. In other words, he had proceeded deductively from general principles to specifics, with a mathematical theory already in mind, which he sought to confirm by experiments.

> Mendel has abstracted away the untidy complexities of living, experiencing organisms for ideal, eternal entities that behave in a simple, logical way.

The statistician Ronald Fisher, a prominent figure in the development of population genetics and neo-Darwinian theory of evolution, analysed Mendel's results statistically and concluded that the agreement with the 3:1 ratio was so perfect that ninety-five times out of a hundred the result could not have been obtained. In other words, the agreement with expectation based on the gene theory was too good to be true. Did Mendel fabricate his results? Not at all. As the historian of science Robert Olby points out, Mendel merely stopped scoring when he got the right numbers, because he knew what ratio he was looking for.[9] Who can blame him? Scoring peas is a tedious task, particularly if you know the answer already.

> People should not take scientific theories too seriously by treating them as 'laws' of nature, as though they had been laid down by God.

As we have seen, there were many characteristics that did not fit the neat pattern of Mendelian heredity. But Mendel concentrated only on those that did. The resulting theory therefore can give, at best, a very partial and idealised account of heredity. The parallel between Mendel's laws of heredity and Newton's laws of mechanics and statistical mechanics is more than coincidental: the one is modelled on the other. Each fixes on the essential variables—the ratio of phenotype classes in the case of genetics, different kinds of motion in the case of mechanics—and proposes to explain how they come about according to the behaviour of (invisible) controlling entities. In the case of Newton's laws it is force, or gravity; in the case of Mendel's laws it is the genes. In so doing, Newton has banished the vibrant world of colour and form, of light and music, replacing it with a silent universe of lifeless, immobile objects subject to the push and pull of external forces. In the same way, Mendel has abstracted away the untidy complexities of living, experiencing organisms for ideal, eternal entities that behave in a simple, logical way.

Newtonian mechanics was supplanted at the beginning of the present century by Einstein's theory of relativity on the large scale, and by quantum mechanics in the sub-microscopic domain. Mendelian genetics suffered a similar fate since the nineteen-seventies, but not before it had inspired a great number of discoveries, which culminated in the DNA double helix and the cracking of the genetic code.

One lesson to learn from this episode is the provisional nature of all scientific theories. More importantly, people should not take scientific theories too seriously by treating them as 'laws' of nature, as though they had been laid down by God. Scientific theories, and mathematics for that matter, are tools for helping us think more clearly in our effort to understand nature and in our quest for the poetry in nature that is ever beyond what words or theories can say.[10]

Appendix
Mendelian genetics explained

Historically, the concepts of dominance and recessivity preceded those of genotype and phenotype. Suppose we represent the dark-haired allele by *D* and the fair-haired allele by *d*: we can now explain the inheritance of hair colour by assuming that *D* (for dark hair) is dominant to *d* (for fair hair). What is the phenotype of individuals with the genotypes *dd*, *DD*, and *Dd*? The answer is fair (*dd*), dark (*DD*), and dark (*Dd*). The individuals carrying two identical alleles (*dd* and *DD*) are *homozygotes,* or are *homozygous* for the gene, whereas those carrying different alleles are *hetero-zygotes,* or are *heterozygous* for the gene.

Let us see what happens in a family where both parents are fair-haired, whose genotypes are therefore both *dd*. We can represent the process of reproduction by a diagram, as follows:

Genotype of parents:	*dd*	*dd*
Phenotype:	fair	fair
Genotype of gametes:	*d*	*d*
Genotype of children:	*dd*	
Phenotype:	fair	

This neatly explains why the offspring will always be fair-haired, like the parents. The same would apply to the dark-haired homozygotes, *DD*. Homozygotes, therefore, always 'breed true': they form so-called 'pure lines'. (Terms such as 'breeding true' and 'pure lines' are easily pressed into the service of calls for the preservation of 'racial purity' and other racist, eugenicist slogans. This is based on the mistaken assumption that pure lines actually exist. All human populations are genetically diverse, with several common alleles in most genes. For most sexually reproducing organisms it is impossible to obtain pure lines, which, by definition, would have to be homozygous in all their genes. When laboratory experiments are carried out to try to make lines that are homozygous in as many genes as possible by inbreeding, that is, mating genetically related individuals, such as siblings with one another or parents with offspring, they tend to die out rapidly from adverse effects, collectively referred to as *inbreeding depression*.)

What happens in families where both parents are heterozygous?

Genotype of parents:	*Dd*		*Dd*	
Phenotype:	dark		dark	
Genotype of gametes:	*D* *d*		*D* *d*	
Genotype of children:	*DD* *Dd*		*dD* *dd*	
Phenotype:	dark dark		dark fair	

Each heterozygous parent produces two types of gametes, carrying the allele *D* and *d,* respectively, with equal probability. A random combination of gametes from the two parents gives an equal probability of all possible combinations of genotypes: 1*DD* : 2*Dd* : 1*dd*. The result is the famous 3:1 Mendelian ratio of dark-haired to fair-haired phenotypes in the offspring. This is explained by saying that the dark allele, *D,* is dominant over the fair allele, *d*; or, alternatively, the fair allele is recessive to the dark allele. This 3:1 ratio holds only on average; it will be approximated more and more closely when a large number of children are produced, or when the children from a large number of similar families are counted. It is quite likely that some heterozygous matings will produce mostly fair-haired or dark-haired children just by chance. I leave it as an exercise for the reader to work out the possibilities in families where one parent is fair-haired and the other dark-haired. (Hint: there are two kinds of such families.)

What happens if neither of the alleles for hair colour is dominant or recessive? In that case they are referred to as *co-dominant*; the phenotype of the heterozygote will be intermediate, and the ratio of phenotypes will then be exactly the same as that of the genotypes: 1 dark (*DD*) : 2 brown (*Dd*) : 1 fair (*dd*).

We can already see that the relationship between genes and characteristics is not completely straightforward even in Mendelian genetics, as some genes can be dominant in expression to others.

To illustrate how the alleles are reshuffled at reproduction, let us bring in another gene, an allele of which is responsible for cystic fibrosis—by far the most common genetic disease among northern Europeans. It is estimated that approximately one in ten in the population is heterozygous, or a carrier of the disease who shows no adverse symptoms. This means that the allele giving rise to the disease is recessive to the majority 'normal', or wild-type, allele. It is conventional among geneticists to represent the recessive allele by a lower-case letter and the dominant allele by the corresponding capital letter; so let us call the cystic fibrosis allele *c* and the wild type *C*. Let us assume that both parents are heterozygous for the hair colour alleles as well as the cystic fibrosis alleles, and try to predict the result of their reproduction.

Genotypes of parents:	*CcDd*	*CcDd*
Phenotypes:	dark, normal	dark, normal
Genotypes of gametes:	*CD*　*Cd*	*cD*　*cd*

To predict the genotypes and phenotypes of the children, let us use a Punnett square (named after the geneticist who first used it). The possible gametes of one parent are represented in a row at the top, those of the other in a column on the left. All possible combinations are then filled in at the appropriate intersection of column and row, as follows:

	CD	*Cd*	*cD*	*cd*
CD	*CCDD*	*CCDd*	*CcDD*	*CcDd*
Cd	*CCDd*	*CCdd*	*CcDd*	*Ccdd*
cD	*CcDD*	*CcDd*	*ccDD*	*ccDd*
cd	*CcDd*	*Ccdd*	*ccDd*	*ccdd*

The ratios of the possible genotypes are:

1	2	2	4	2	1	2	1	1
CCDD	*CCDd*	*CcDD*	*CcDd*	*Ccdd*	*CCdd*	*ccDd*	*ccDD*	*ccdd*

The phenotypes, which you can verify for yourself, are:

9 normal, dark	3 normal, fair	3 cystic, dark	1 cystic, fair

You have now completed the basics of Mendelian genetics, and learnt much of the language besides. It is usually presented as the two 'laws': the law of segregation, referring to the separation between the alleles in the formation of gametes, and the law of independent assortment, referring to the random way in which the alleles of different genes are allotted to the germ cells.

Actually the second law is not accurate, as the genes are strung together linearly in groups, called *linkage groups,* later found to correspond to chromosomes. Humans have two sets of chromosomes, existing as twenty-three pairs, while germ cells have only one set. Alleles of genes in the same linkage group (that is, linked together on the same chromosome) tend to stay together more often than alleles of genes in different chromosomes. But even linked genes tend to be shuffled or *recombined,* as the chromosomes pair off and exchange parts in the formation of germ cells. So, if one of the chromosomes in the pair contains the sequence of genes *ABCDEFG* and its partner (the *homologue*) contains *abcdefg,* they may exchange parts to give *ABcdefg* and *abCDEFG,* or other possibilities, which usually (though not always) preserve the order in which the genes occur on the chromosome. The more closely linked two genes are, the less likely it is that the linkage will be disrupted. For example, A and B are linked right next to each other, so it is less likely that they will get unlinked than A and C, or A and D, and so on. Similarly, the linkage between a and b will be less likely to be disrupted than that between a and c, or between a and d. In fact by looking at the frequency with which linked alleles become unlinked or recombined it is possible to estimate how close they are to each other on the chromosome. As we shall see later (chapter 11), this is the basis of much of the gene-hunting that goes on today.

Five

NEO-DARWINISM: TRIUMPH OR TRAVESTY?

Neo-Darwinism is the marriage of Mendelian genetics and Darwinism. The theory of the gene was based on evidence that was directly in conflict with it; only the climate of biological opinion was favourable. Neo-Darwinism became established as a theory that purports to explain everything and is thereby in danger of explaining nothing. A theory that lacks content is easily pressed into the service of pernicious ideologies.

The theory that explains everything

The marriage of Mendelian genetics with Darwinism was not an immediately happy affair. In this chapter I briefly review the history of how neo-Darwinism became established as a dominant theory that purports to explain every aspect of the organism yet ends up obscuring the organism completely from view. It is important to examine in some detail the anatomy of a neo-Darwinian explanation to realise why the theory is so easily pressed into the service of pernicious ideologies.

Gradual evolution versus evolution in jumps

As soon as Darwin's theory of natural selection was proposed, argument began about whether small or large variations were important for evolution. On the whole, the Mendelians believed in the efficacy of large, discontinuous variations arising from mutations, or *sports*, whereas their opponents, the biometricians, believed that continuous variations were the stuff of evolution. Those who believed in gradual evolution concentrated on characteristics that vary continuously in the population, such as height, weight, milk yield, and so on. Others, who opted for large changes, concentrated on characteristics that vary discontinuously, that is, those that fall into a few discrete or non-overlapping classes, such as the colour or shape of flowers or the presence or absence of a structure.

> No explanation of evolution is complete without a theory of how Mendelian genes could produce the variation of biological form.

The question whether continuous variation or discontinuous variations are the stuff of evolution began with Darwin's insistence that *'natura non facit saltum'* (nature does not make jumps): natural selection acts on the 'insensibly fine gradations' of continuously varying characteristics. Under Darwin's theory of *pangenesis,* the influences of successive generations are continually being mixed and blended. However, this cannot account for discontinuous changes. Darwin remained firmly wedded to gradualism, even though his staunchest supporters, Thomas Huxley and Francis Galton, both pointed out that large, discontinuous variations could also be subject to natural selection and, if anything, made it easier to produce evolutionary change.

Discontinuity versus continuity[1]

William Bateson had been studying natural and artificially induced variations in plants and animals, which often fell into discrete, non-overlapping classes. Furthermore, many species showed parallel variations. Bateson was trying to work out how those characteristics were inherited when he discovered Mendel's paper. By that time he was already in dispute with the biometricians Karl Pearson and W. F. R. Weldon, who accepted Darwin's hypothesis of blending inheritance and believed that continuous variations were the raw material of natural selection. (Biometricians use mathematical techniques to study continuous variations in populations.) Their disagreement soon intensified into a full debate, in which others joined, with Mendelians on one side and biometricians on the other. This debate was eventually resolved by the birth of population genetics. At least that is how the story is told.

Pearson and Weldon, like Darwin's cousin Francis Galton before them, used statistical techniques to study continuous variations. They refined and corrected Galton's mathematical derivations, showing how, contrary to Galton's claims, natural selection could act on continuous variation if the extremes were selected for breeding, in which case the offspring would not regress to the mean of the parental generation.

In opposition to Pearson and Weldon, William Bateson insisted that discontinuous variations were indeed the stuff of evolution and, on discovering Mendel's work, believed that Mendel had provided a theory of the inheritance of discontinuous variation. But he was by no means satisfied by the explanation of evolution as the natural selection of Mendelian genes. It was his belief that no explanation of evolution is complete without a theory of how Mendelian genes could produce variation of biological form. It was clear to him that organisms do not vary at random but rather in accordance with certain 'laws' or regularities governing growth and variation. This, incidentally, forms much of the substance of the present-day alternative approaches to neo-Darwinism.[2]

> The question of the real causes of morphogenesis and evolution has never been settled or resolved in the exclusive emphasis on genes in mainstream evolutionary theory.

Bateson's debate with Pearson and Weldon was as much a conflict of personalities as a power struggle over the control of the 'Evolution Committee' of the Royal Society, the trend-setting society of mainstream scientists established in the seventeenth century and that has dominated British science up to the present day.

In my view, the important disagreement between Bateson and the biometricians was not over whether continuous or discontinuous variations are the stuff of evolution: it was over how evolution should be explained. Pearson and Weldon were content to explain evolution according to hereditary influences that pass from one generation to the next and that account for correlations between generations. The reason for concentrating on continuous variations was that they were mathematically tractable using the linear, additive models that allowed equations to be solved. Pearson and Weldon were not interested in the real biology of organisms. In contrast, Bateson was dissatisfied with explanations based on abstract hereditary influences or, for that matter, on Mendelian genes. In that respect he was not a Mendelian, for he was after a more fundamental explanation of biological forms and variations: of how they are *generated* during development. For example, he suggested that discontinuous variations correspond to points of stable equilibrium in a continuum of possible forms, and that repeated body parts or segments— common to many groups of organisms—are generated by physical mechanisms similar to standing waves or vibrations. These ideas are borne out by a large body of present-day work that attempts to understand *morphogenesis*—the development of shapely, differentiated organisms from a relatively formless egg—in accordance with non-linear physico-chemical, mathematical models.[3]

Eventually Mendelian genetics became united with biometrics to give biometrical and population genetics, in which continuous variations are interpreted as a result of *polygenes* or *multigenes* (that is, combinations of many genes), each giving a very small effect. This is usually said to be the resolution of the debate but is really a digression. The real causes of morphogenesis and evolution have been obscured in the exclusive emphasis on genes in mainstream evolutionary theory ever since.

The myth of 'pure lines' and the gene theory

A crucial step in the development of the gene theory was taken by the Danish botanist Wilhelm Johannsen (who coined the terms *gene, genotype,* and *phenotype*). He carried out 'pure line' experiments, which purported to show that a genetically uniform line bred true to the genes it carried (its genotype), and not to its observable characteristics (its phenotype). In a genetically uniform line of self-fertilising French beans, Johannsen bred from the smallest and the largest seeds and found that the offspring gave the same range of variation in seed size. In other words, there was no correlation or resemblance between the size of the parental seed and the size of the seeds in the offspring. In fact Johannsen found statistically significant correlation between parent and offspring,[4] which he chose to ignore; instead he *interpreted* his results in accordance with the German biologist August Weismann's theory of the germplasm.

Several other scientists soon followed suit in demonstrating how the selection of phenotype was ineffective in 'pure lines', all based on the *a priori* acceptance of Weismann's theory and not on experimental observations. This was eventually soundly criticised by the American biometrician J. Arthur Harris, who, on reviewing the entire body of work, pinpointed the real reason why the 'pure line' theory was so readily accepted, based on evidence that was directly in conflict with it: the climate of biological opinion was favourable to pure line theory.

The experimenters' reasoning had been circular. The continuity of the germplasm was assumed; they then observed that selection could not change the pure line. If it did, the line was not pure. And, on these grounds, it was concluded that phenotype selection had no effect on pure lines. As the genotype was, at that time, inaccessible to direct observation, there was no independent measure of genetic uniformity or heterogeneity. Similar circular reasoning soon became the established practice of the genetic-determinist paradigm, especially as the gene theory turned mathematical in population and biometrical genetics and took on the status of a rigorous science. This has misled generations of evolutionists to this day.

The mathematical gene theory

Mendel's theory already had a mathematical structure that lent itself to generalisation. It was only a matter of time, therefore, before it was extended to describe how genes behave in populations. This step was first taken in 1902 by Yule, who showed mathematically that the Mendelian ratios 1*AA* : 2*Aa* : 1*aa* in the second generation after hybridisation would remain unchanged in subsequent generations, *as long as individuals in the population mate at random*. This means purely according to chance, so that matings between the same or different genotypes are neither more nor less frequent than their proportion in the population would predict.

> The mathematical expression of Darwin's theory with regard to the natural selection of genes was the important turning-point for the general acceptance of the theory, for it accorded it a status equal to Newtonian mechanics. While the theory says a great deal about how genes behave in populations, it offers no real explanation of how organisms can develop or evolve.

Moreover, the frequency of both alleles would also remain constant in all subsequent generations. This was further generalised independently by the British mathematician Hardy and the German physician Weinberg, who showed that in large, randomly mating populations any frequencies of two alternative alleles of a gene, say *A* and *a,* will remain constant in the absence of selection. This is the 'Hardy-Weinberg law', which states that if the frequency of the *A* allele is p and that of the *a* allele is q, the proportion of genotypes *AA, Aa* and *aa* is given by the binomial expansion $(p + q)^2 = p^2 + 2pq + q^2$, and will so remain for all subsequent generations. In other words, it takes only one generation to reach an equilibrium—the *Hardy-Weinberg equilibrium*. (However, when there are more than two alleles segregating, it takes more than one generation to reach equilibrium, as Weinberg showed later on.) The Hardy-Weinberg law forms the basis of population genetics later developed by Fisher, Haldane, and Sewell Wright, though each of them emphasised different aspects.

The debate between the Mendelians and biometricians was, as I said, a distraction. As soon as particulate inheritance was accepted it was possible to interpret continuous variations as the result of the combination of many genes, each with a small additive effect.

By 1918 mathematical treatments of the effects of selection in Mendelian populations had already been done. The ground was prepared for Darwinism to be reinterpreted according to the gene theory in the 'neo-Darwinian synthesis' from around the nineteen-thirties up to the sixties.

The mathematical expression of Darwin's theory with regard to the natural selection of genes (determining characteristics) was the important turning-point for the general acceptance of the theory, for it accorded it a status equal to Newtonian mechanics, statistical mechanics, or the second law of thermodynamics. The mathematics glosses over the fact that, while the theory says a great deal about how genes behave in populations, it offers no real explanation of how organisms can develop or evolve.

> To invent a characteristic and, on top of that, a gene determining it is to commit the fallacy of *reification*—mistaking processes for things.

The link between genes and characteristics

A neo-Darwinian explanation typically starts by identifying a characteristic that is assumed to be controlled by a gene that confers a selective advantage or disadvantage, so that it is selected for, or against; and this explains why the organism does or does not possess the characteristic in question. In this way it is possible to 'explain' any and every characteristic that the organism is said to possess.

However, the link between genes and characteristics is in most cases not at all straightforward; and the problem has not been solved by identifying the genes that affect the characteristics. The most concrete thing that is known about genes (as we shall see in chapter 6) is that they code for proteins, or for signals that regulate the synthesis of different proteins. It is a big conceptual jump from that to the characteristics of organisms.

An immediate difficulty arises in the identification of the characteristic itself. It is one thing to name a characteristic, such as hair colour, or colour of eyes; it is quite another to say that there is a characteristic called 'aggression'. Animals may engage in aggressive acts, but that does not mean there is a *characteristic* called aggression; similarly, some humans may show preference for members of the same sex, but that does not mean there is a characteristic called homosexuality. Both are social acts carried out in certain contexts. To invent a characteristic and, on top of that, a gene determining it is to commit the fallacy of *reification*— mistaking processes for things. There may be many mutations in many genes that affect a person's ability to read or speak or remember things, but that does not mean there are genes for reading, speech, or memory. Even in the case of the bodily form of organisms—their morphology—there are no theoretical or conceptual grounds justifying the separation of a characteristic from the interconnected whole that is the organism. But this in effect is what is being done by geneticists who study development. They discover mutations in some gene that affect some aspects of development—the segmentation pattern of the body, say—and this gene becomes a 'gene for segmentation' or 'segmentation gene'.

> Neo-Darwinian explanations, in purporting to explain everything, ultimately explain nothing, because there is no independent verification of the 'adaptive story' that must be invented to 'explain' how the characteristic is selected for or against.

The second difficulty, which follows from the first, is the equally unrealistic assumption that there exist 'polygenes'—a group of genes that determine or influence the supposed characteristic, each acting in an additive way, that is, independently of the rest. For this goes against everything that is known about gene action and metabolism (see chapter 3). Genes are involved in the development of all aspects of the organism; but the individual genes cannot be extricated from the whole context of the organism in its eco-social environment.

Neo-Darwinian explanations, in purporting to explain everything, ultimately explain nothing, because there is no independent verification of the 'adaptive story' that must be invented to 'explain' how the characteristic is selected for or against. Nevertheless this completes the circle that validates and legitimises the hunt for the genes or genetic basis of every characteristic or condition in question. The inherent danger in this kind of reasoning is that it is all too easy to reinforce the prejudice with which one begins, giving rein to the worst excesses of eugenic and racist ideologies in the present century.

Let us look at a central concept in biometrical genetics: *heritability*. This continues to be misused by the genetic-determinists of our day in their attempt to lend credence to the existence of dubious genetic characteristics, such as intelligence or criminality, and then to use the supposed measure of such characteristics to stigmatise individuals, races, or social classes.

The heritability of IQ and other polygenic traits

The public are often told that there is a large genetic component in intelligence as measured by IQ, or in criminality as measured by some psychometric tests. It is often claimed that the genes are about 50 per cent responsible for such characteristics. These statements are based on an erroneous interpretation of estimates on heritability from biometrical genetics.

The first thing one has to realise about heritability is that, contrary to what is claimed, it does not tell us anything about the degree to which a characteristic is determined by the genes. Technically, it is measured as the proportion of the total (*phenotypic*) variation in a *population* that is due to genetic variation:

$$heritability = \frac{genetic\ variation}{total\ variation}$$

The total variation is assumed to be made up of those due to the genes plus those due to the environment; so:

$$heritability = \frac{genetic\ variation}{genetic\ variation + environmental\ variation}$$

Heritability is a population measure and says nothing about the individual.[5] Furthermore, it is specific to the population only of that particular *generation,* because the environmental conditions may differ for different generations. Estimates of heritability carried out on the same plant varieties have been found to vary widely in successive years. That alone should convince us that heritability is not a constant property of any trait whatever. It is pointless, therefore, to measure heritability unless the population is being bred continuously in an absolutely constant, controlled set of environmental conditions.

To measure heritabilities rigorously, a laborious breeding programme has to be set up. It goes like this. One has to extract a dozen or more 'pure' (genetically uniform) lines from the population by many successive generations of inbreeding, until, theoretically, no more genetic variation remains. If the lines survive the inbreeding—and many of them may not, because of inbreeding depression—they will then be homozygous in most, if not all, of their genes. Next, the lines have to be crossed in pairs to produce the F1 generations, which will all still be genetically uniform, though all individuals will be heterozygous for many of their genes, instead of being homozygous, as in the 'pure lines'. The variation of the characteristic in question can then be compared for the pure lines, the F1 hybrids and the original 'random mating' line in a suitably randomised experimental design, so that the range of environments experienced by each line is the same.

Now, according to the theory of biometrical genetics, the variance (a mathematical measure of variation) in each of the pure lines as well as the F1 hybrids is due to the environment alone, as there is no genetic variation between individuals. So the average of their variances gives an estimate of the environmental component of the variation. The variation in the random mating line, on the other hand, will consist of both the genetic and the environmental variation. The important point about this estimate is that the genes in question have to be randomised over all environments and over all genetic backgrounds. This means that the population needs to be very large and that mating has to take place strictly according to chance (that is, *randomly*) and not more or less frequently than that predicted from the frequencies of the genotypes.

> The most reasonable statement one could make with regard to all characteristics of the organism is that genetic and environmental factors are inextricably intertwined.

If the population is indeed randomly mating and very large, then some shortcuts are available. One can estimate heritabilities by how much offspring resemble their parents, or how much siblings resemble each other, or, ultimately, how much *monozygotic twins* (twins derived from a single egg and therefore identical in their genetic make-up) are alike. The difficulty is that human populations are far from random-mating, and the genes involved are therefore not at all randomised with respect to the genetic background. The stratification of the environment by class and other social factors also means that the genes are far from randomised over all environments. This makes heritability estimates of human poly-genic traits very unreliable, even in cases where one assumes it is meaningful to treat as 'traits' such measures as IQ scores. Much is made of the strong resemblance that is commonly found between identical twins who have been separated from birth; this is used to support the idea that certain traits have a very large 'genetic component'. These studies actually suffer most from the limit-ations of small samples, with highly non-random association of environments and of genetic backgrounds. (We shall look at the whole issue of IQ measurement in more detail in chapter 11.)

The most reasonable statement one could make with regard to all characteristics of the organism is that genetic and environ-mental factors are *inextricably intertwined.* This is borne out by everything we know about the molecular basis of gene function (see chapter 7). Should anyone think of attempting these classical breeding experiments to measure heritability: don't. They are pointless, for in fact it is impossible to derive really pure lines. 'Pure lines' are among the purest genetic fictions ever invented.

Anyone who has experience of keeping genetic stocks in the laboratory knows that they must be periodically 'purified', otherwise they become very variable. We now know that, because of the fluidity of the genome, new variations will keep arising in the different lines, even as they are being bred to be homozygous and uniform. Moreover, it is well known from classic genetic analyses that populations that are more genetically uniform tend to be phenotypically more variable. This is attributed to the failure of 'developmental homeostasis'—the totality of the regulatory mechanisms of the system that buffer it against perturbations, keeping it constant and stable.

Appendix
Population genetics

At the basis of the neo-Darwinian synthesis is the mathematical representation of genes in population by Ronald Fisher, J. B. S. Haldane, and Sewell Wright, all of whom were concerned to show that Mendelian genetics and Darwin's theory of natural selection were not in contradiction but could be unified into a single, rigorous mathematical theory. Fisher's approach was to concentrate on the selection of polygenes (many genes, each with a small effect on a particular characteristic) in large populations over long periods. This was closest to Darwin's original conception of gradual evolution. Fisher formalised this scheme as 'the fundamental theorem of natural selection,' which states that 'the rate of increase in fitness of any population is equal to the genetic variance (variation) in fitness.' This theorem assumes that genes have small, additive (non-interacting) effects on the characteristic under selection. In other words, it assumes that the genes act independently of one another. Operating within this model, Fisher worked out estimates concerning the *heritability* of traits, which refers to the proportion of the observed variability in a population that can be attributed to or associated with the underlying genetic variation. This is the estimate that is most frequently used today by biometrical geneticists in controversial studies on such measures as IQ scores.

Sewell Wright, by contrast, recognised at the very beginning of his career the importance of *epistasis* or interactions between genes through selection experiments on guinea-pigs in the laboratory of the biologist William Castle. He found that the inheritance of coat colour was controlled by a system of genes that interacted non-linearly with one another, rather than acting additively and independently. This convinced him that selection acted on whole *combinations* of genes and not on single genes. His picture of evolution involved selection acting on chance combinations of genes, giving large effects which are fixed in small populations, rather than on individual genes, with small effects in large populations. He recognised that the same genes will have different effects in different genetic backgrounds, and he developed the most rigorous mathematical theory of path coefficients, which enabled experimenters to make inferences concerning environmental versus genetic effects, as well as additive and non-additive, interactive effects. However, to perform analyses by path coefficients one has to have a huge amount of data as well as a knowledge of the breeding habits of the population, that is, whether mating occurs at random or whether inbreeding and other non-random matings are practised. These requirements are almost never satisfied except in controlled plant and animal breeding experiments.

J. B. S. Haldane's theory is intermediate between that of Sewell Wright and Fisher. Though he concentrated on the selection of single genes with large effects, he did occasionally recognise the importance of dominance and other interactions between genes. In general, his theory, like that of Fisher, fits the description of 'bean-bag genetics', a term of derision used by the biologist Ernst Mayr, who was extremely critical of mathematical approaches to evolution in general that did not take into account the non-linear interactions between combinations of genes. Indeed, genes are conceptualised as separate, non-interacting entities, like a collection of beans that are thrown, by pure chance, into different combinations. However, Mayr's own insistence that genes act together as 'co-adapted gene complexes' would seem to place him fairly close to Sewell Wright's position. The main difference seems to be that Mayr's co-adapted gene complexes are specifically selected for, so that they remain associated together more often than can be accounted for by chance. However, he never proposed any description of the mechanism whereby this could be achieved, given that linked genes are also recombined at random during reproduction, according to the theory.

Six

THE CENTRAL DOGMA OF GENETIC DETERMINISM

In the years following the discovery of the double helix, the organism has been completely eclipsed. It is seen as a collection of genes that control development according to a 'genetic program'. Evolution is said to occur by the natural selection of random mutations, ensuring that the fittest mutants survive to reproduce. The organism is therefore projected as a passive object, buffeted by selective forces over which it has no control. Its life experience is negated, as only the genes it carries are of any evolutionary consequence. It is no accident that a culture bent on promoting capitalism and free enterprise should be obsessed with things rather than processes. The notion of 'gene banks' and 'genetic resources' makes it plain that life, the process of being alive, as well as real organisms and diverse ecological communities, are all negated in favour of genes that can be grasped hold of, possessed, preserved and exploited as commodities.

_____

From theory to molecules

The neo-Darwinian synthesis was predominantly a theoretical exercise involving mathematicians dealing with abstract hereditary factors and experimenters who were primarily interested not in what genes were or what they did but in how breeding experiments could be conceptualised according to hereditary influences or factors. By contrast, molecular biology developed out of a deliberate search for the material basis of heredity, begun by August Weismann. Weismann was responsible for proposing the theory of the continuity of the 'germplasm', which, as we have seen, exerted a great influence over the neo-Darwinian synthesis.

The immortal germplasm and the soul

The theory of the 'germplasm' depended on two vital observations. First, Weismann found that in insect embryos the future germ cells became separated from the rest of the body very early in development. From this he deduced that germ cells are protected from environmental influences, so that the germplasm they carry retains its constancy and immortality. Second, he discovered in the fertilised egg of the roundworm, *Ascaris*, a pair of large chromosomes, whereas the unfertilised egg had only one of them. From this he deduced that the germplasm resides in chromosomes, whose number is halved in the germ cells, so that when male and female germ cells unite on fertilisation the original number is restored.

Weismann's theory of the continuity and immortality of the germplasm was idealism through and through. As many later commentators pointed out, the early separation of germ cells is peculiar to insects: it does not occur generally in mammals, and not at all in plants. Furthermore, *there is no evidence that the genetic material in germ cells is immune from environmental influence* (see chapter 7). Nevertheless, Weismann had correctly identified the chromosomes as the bearers of genetic material, which immediately narrowed the search for the material basis of entities that behaved like Mendelian genes.

The occurrence of chromosomes in pairs and their segregation in the germ cells exactly paralleled the segregation of Mendelian genes; moreover, chromosomes, just like genes, were subject to independent assortment in the formation of germ cells, so that each germ cell ended up with a different combination of maternally derived and paternally derived chromosomes (see chapter 4).

The chromosome theory of inheritance

Further advances were made from about 1910, when Thomas Hunt Morgan set up a laboratory devoted to the study of the chromosomal genetics of the fruit fly, *Drosophila melanogaster.* He and his colleagues eventually established that genes were linked together in linear arrays, each array corresponding to a chromosome. Each chromosome contained thousands, if not tens of thousands, of genes. To prove that genes are linked together in linear arrays on chromosomes, they produced large numbers of mutations by means of X-rays. Lines homozygous for different alleles in different genes were established and crossed with one another, so that the progeny could be analysed for the genes deviating from independent assortment. It was found that genes on different chromosomes would assort independently, whereas those on the same chromosome would not. And the closer together any two genes were on the same chromosome, the less likely it was that the linkage between them would be disrupted. In this way genes were assigned to chromosomes, and detailed genetic maps of chromosomes were produced. As microscopic techniques improved, impressive changes in chromosomes corresponding to various changes in the linkage maps of genes could also be identified. The resulting 'chromosome theory of inheritance' may be summarised as follows:

The chromosome theory of inheritance

- Genes occur in linear arrays on chromosomes.
- Different chromosomes contain different combinations of alleles of genes.
- Chromosomes occur in (homologous) pairs in sexually reproducing organisms (such as human beings).
- Only one of each pair of chromosomes is present in germ cells.
- In the formation of germ cells, homologous chromosomes exchange parts, so that the linked genes are recombined; the more closely together the genes occur on the chromosome, the less likely they are to be recombined.

Morgan began as a developmental biologist extremely sceptical of the chromosomal theory, for he regarded the process of heredity as inseparable from that of development. However, the success of the chromosome theory, together with Weismann's theory of the germplasm, split the two fields. The process of development was no longer considered important for the study of evolution, which consisted exclusively in the natural selection of random mutations. Morgan stated in 1916:

> If, through a mutation, a character appears that is neither advantageous nor disadvantageous, but indifferent, the chance that it may become established in the race … is extremely small … If, through a mutation, a character appears that has an injurious effect … it has practically no chance of becoming established.
>
> If, through a mutation, a character appears that has a beneficial influence on the individual, the chance that the individual will survive is increased, not only for itself, but for all of its descendants … It is this increase … that might have an influence on the course of evolution.[1]

This is essentially the 'bean-bag' theory of evolution, which most population geneticists came to embrace (see chapter 5, appendix).

The DNA double helix and the central dogma[2]

The chromosome theory established the material basis of genes. But what did the genes actually do? As long ago as 1902 the physician Archibald Garrod recognised that 'inborn errors of metabolism' in humans were metabolic blockages produced by defects in single genes. One of the main functions of genes, therefore, was to facilitate specific chemical reactions in metabolism. The detailed analysis was carried out by George Beadle and Edward Tatum in the bread mould *Neurospora crassa*. They showed that each gene is responsible for the synthesis of one enzyme, a protein that catalyses a specific metabolic reaction, and that a mutation in each enzyme leads to a specific metabolic blockage. For a long time there was a debate about whether the genes on chromosomes were actually the enzyme proteins themselves or the nucleic acid DNA, which was also known to be a chemical constituent of the chromosomes. This was resolved by Avery, MacLeod, and McCarty, who were studying the bacterium *Streptococcus pneumoniae,* frequently isolated from patients with pneumonia. The bacterium exists in two forms: a smooth form, which causes disease, and a less virulent rough form. The experimenters showed that when DNA was extracted from the smooth bacteria and added to cells of the rough type, a high proportion of the latter were *transformed* into the smooth type, thus demonstrating the role of DNA as the genetic material. Transformation by direct uptake of DNA is one of the regular routes whereby different bacteria can exchange genes. (We shall look more closely at gene transfer between micro-organisms in chapter 9.)

The structure of proteins

Proteins are long polymers made up of hundreds of simpler units called amino acids. There are twenty different amino acids, all of which have the general chemical formula NH_2–$CH(R)$–$COOH$, differing from one another in the group R (see fig. 6.1).

There is a great diversity of proteins, each of which has a specific sequence of amino acids. For example, a protein with 100 amino acids can have 20^{100} possible sequences.

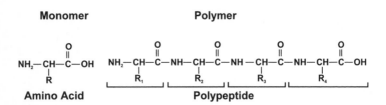

Fig. 6.1: The chemical structure of proteins

The structure of DNA

DNA was known to consist of very long polymers consisting of simpler units called *nucleotides* (fig. 6.2). Each nucleotide is made of a sugar, deoxyribose, to which is attached an inorganic phosphate group and an organic base. The nucleotides differ in the organic base they contain, of which there are only four: adenine (A), guanine (G), cytosine (C), and thymine (T). Another kind of nucleic acid that is abundant in the cell is RNA. This is very similar to DNA except that the sugar is ribose instead of deoxyribose, and the base uracil (U) replaces thymine. Each nucleic acid polymer is made up of many nucleotides joined together by phosphodiester bonds between the sugar of one nucleotide and the phosphate of the next, so that a backbone of alternating sugar and phosphate groups is formed, with the bases sticking out on the side.

Apart from this, little was known about the three-dimensional structure of DNA; this is important, as it holds the key to how DNA functions as genetic material.

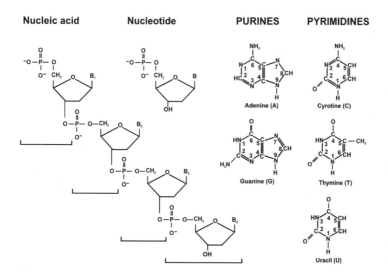

Fig. 6.2: The chemical structure of DNA and RNA

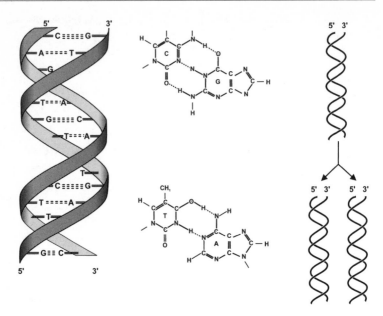

Fig. 6.3: The DNA double helix and how it can be faithfully copied

Linus Pauling had worked out the three-dimensional structure of proteins by X-ray diffraction, a new technique that uses very short-wavelength X-rays to resolve molecular structure, rather in the way a microscope enables one to resolve the structure of cells. Rosalind Franklin and Maurice Wilkins at King's College, London, were already using X-ray diffraction to look at DNA. Another clue came from Erwin Chargaff, who had separated and measured the amount of the four nucleic acid bases in DNA from various sources. He found that the amount of guanine always equalled that of cytosine, and the amount of adenine always equalled that of thymine; in other words, G = C, and A = T. By piecing together this information with the X-ray pictures, James Watson and Francis Crick built the first model of the DNA double helix. Essentially, each molecule consists of two polymeric chains wrapped around each other by pairing their bases: G to C and A to T. The sequence of bases in one strand will therefore be *complementary* to that in the other strand—rather like the positive and negative of a film.

So, a faithful copy of the complementary strand can always be obtained from one of the strands; and this was the basis of accurate reproduction of genetic information (see fig. 6.3).

The genetic code

From that original deduction, Francis Crick and Sidney Brenner set about analysing mutants of bacterial viruses in which different numbers of base pairs were deleted, in order to prove that it was indeed a triplet code. Successive triplets of bases on one of the DNA strands were read as an amino acid in a definite reading frame with no overlapping.

But how was the sequence of bases in DNA related to the sequence of amino acids in proteins? About the same time, Claude Shannon had produced a very influential 'theory of information' in connection with the transmission of messages by telegraph. The idea of a 'genetic code' naturally suggested itself. The proteins can be seen as the final messages that are transmitted to the cell. Each amino acid is like a word in the message, and words must be specified by an alphabet. We know that there are only four letters in the genetic alphabet, these being the four bases; the minimum number of letters needed to code for the twenty different amino acids is therefore three, which gives $4^3 = 64$ different *codons*.

But which triplets specified which amino acid? That was the problem of 'codon assignment'. Before it could be tackled, Francis Jacob and Jacques Monod showed that the code in DNA is not translated directly but goes through an intermediary or 'messenger RNA', transcribed from the gene, whose sequence is complementary to the DNA sequence of the gene. The messenger RNA is then transported outside the nucleus to the cytoplasm of the cell, where it is translated into protein. Marshall Nirenberg, Heinrich Matthaei and Severo Ochoa set to work on the genetic code. By adding synthetic messenger RNA of known base sequences to a cell-free system for making proteins in a test-tube and isolating and analysing the product, they were eventually able to make the complete assignment of codons by about 1966. Apart from codons for the amino acids there are also codons for stopping and starting. As there are sixty-four possible triplets, some amino acids have more than one codon.

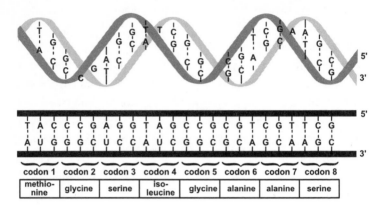

Fig. 6.4: The flow of information from DNA to RNA to protein in accordance with the central dogma of molecular biology

It was an immense effort on the part of many dedicated scientists to work out the full story of what genes do and how they do it. Crick, who played a leading role in uncovering the story of the gene, encapsulated it in the 'central dogma' of molecular biology: DNA makes RNA makes protein in a one-way information flow, and no reverse information flow is possible. The central dogma seems to be a direct vindication of Weismann's theory of the germplasm, which has since come to be known as 'Weismann's barrier'. This barrier is supposed to strictly prevent environmental influences, or any experience in the lifetime of the organism, from directly (that is, predictably) affecting its genes, particularly in the germ cells, and so 'acquired characteristics' will not be inherited.

> In the new orthodoxy, the organism has been completely eclipsed from view. It tends to be regarded as no more than a collection of genes and its development as the unfolding of a 'genetic program' encoded in the genome.

Many of the chief participants in the story of the gene were physicists who made a conscious decision to devote their time and effort to work on the science of life—some because they had become distressed and disillusioned with the nuclear bomb, which became a 'science of death', a few because they were genuinely inspired by the little book *What is Life?* by the quantum physicist Erwin Schrödinger, published in 1944. There is no doubt that the rapid advances in genetic science were made possible by the application of physical techniques such as X-ray mutagenesis and X-ray diffraction and by concepts from information theory. However, the physicists also reinforced the reductionist view that the story of life is just the story of the gene; and this attitude has dominated biology to the present day.

The 'selfish gene' and the vanishing organism

In the new orthodoxy that has reigned supreme over the twenty years following the discovery of the double helix, the organism has become eclipsed from view. It tends to be regarded as no more than a collection of genes and its development as the unfolding of a 'genetic program' encoded in the genome. The reasoning is that random mutations give rise to mutant characteristics, and natural selection allows the fittest mutants to survive and re-produce. Environmental changes provide new selective forces, and evolution is thereby guaranteed. The organism is therefore projected as a completely passive object, buffeted by selective forces in an environment over which it has no control. Its life experience is equally negated, as only the genes it carries are of any evolutionary consequence.

This ideology, which has underpinned the establishment of 'gene banks', supposes that as long as the genes or germplasm are preserved, it doesn't matter if the organisms become extinct. The rush to collect blood samples from indigenous peoples in the disreputable Human Genome Diversity Project, financed by governments in the industrialised North, was inspired by the same mentality, which decrees that one must preserve those valuable genetic resources as immortalised cell lines in the laboratory before the indigenous peoples become extinct. This is something that many geneticists regard as regrettable but inevitable. Have they ever asked themselves whether they have got their priorities right when they put the genes before the human beings to whom the genes belong? Should they not devote at least as much effort to helping those same indigenous people from extinction as they do to cheating them of their genes?

Richard Dawkins has pushed the reductionist trend of neo-Darwinism to its logical conclusion in proposing that organisms are nothing but automatons controlled by 'selfish genes', whose only imperative is to replicate, at the expense of other selfish genes.[4] E. O. Wilson extended neo-Darwinian theory to animal and human societies to define the new discipline of sociobiology, which purports to explain all social behaviour in animals, from ants to human beings, as the result of genes that have been selected in evolution. This has produced a veritable industry for many third-rate scientists with limited imagination who can think of nothing better to do than dream up selective advantages for putative characteristics controlled by putative genes, thereby becoming an instant success with their professors as well as the darlings of the equally simple-minded science journalists writing for the popular media.

In the opening pages of his book Wilson gives the game away by posing the 'fundamental' and paradoxical question of socio-biology (that is, paradoxical *within* neo-Darwinism): how could altruistic behaviour evolve, given that genes, and the behaviour they control, are fundamentally selfish?[5] The paradox disappears, of course, when one rejects the assumption that selfishness or competitiveness are fundamental to the living world. Animals engage in competitive or aggressive acts, but that does not mean there are inherent qualities of competitiveness or aggressiveness that can account for those acts. Furthermore, examples of co-operation among animals far outstrip those of competition. The Russian social anarchist Pyotr Alekseevich Kropotkin argued that co-operation, or mutual aid, was much more important than com-petition in the evolution of animals and of our own species.[6] He gave abundant evidence of the natural sociality of all animals, which is independent of genetic relatedness. Animals, including human beings, simply enjoy society for its own sake. One could easily invert Wilson's question and ask, why do animals compete, given their natural sociality?

> Darwin's theory is all of a piece with nineteenth-century English society's preoccupation with competition and the free market and with capitalist and imperialist exploitation.

This illustrates the social and political underpinnings of all scientific theories—my own being no exception. Perhaps the advantage of being a foreigner, a culturally dispossessed one at that and having to adopt a foreign culture as my own, is that I find I cannot take anything for granted. Perhaps that makes it easier to transcend the social and political underpinnings of the dominant culture. Darwin's theory is all of a piece with nineteenth-century English society's preoccupation with competition and the free market and with capitalist and imperialist exploitation. Unfortunately this same ideology is very much alive today and is being played out in the negotiations at present going on in the World Trade Organisation.

It is no accident that a culture bent on promoting capitalism and free enterprise should be obsessed with things rather than processes. The notions of 'gene banks' and 'genetic resources' make it plain that life, the process of being alive, as well as real organisms and diverse ecological communities, are all negated in favour of genes, which can be grasped hold of, possessed, preserved and exploited as commodities.

Seven

THE FLUID AND ADAPTABLE GENOME

Would anyone think of investing in genetic-engineering biotechnology if they knew how fluid and adaptable genes and genomes are? The notion of an isolatable, constant gene that can be patented as an invention for all the marvellous things it can do is the greatest reductionist myth ever perpetrated. Genes and genomes need to be fluid and adaptable in order to maintain stability on the one hand and to respond to environmental challenges on the other. That is the essence of organic stability, as opposed to mechanical stability. It is also becoming clear that the 'fluid genome' processes are a complex regulatory system for carrying out the 'natural genetic engineering' on which life depends.

Natural genetic engineering is nothing if not precise. The artificial genetic engineering done by human beings, by contrast, ends up being random, because it is controlled neither by the organism nor by the human being. It is also dangerous, because it attacks the very mechanisms that maintain the integrity and autonomy of living organisms, even as they are inextricably entangled with their ecological environment.

The end of mechanistic biology

The new genetics spells the end for mechanistic biology, which has dominated the world for at least a hundred years. To appreciate the profound conceptual change involved, let me remind you of the textbook genetics taught up to the early seventies and possibly beyond, which came straight out of the central dogma of molecular biology (see chapter 6), which reigned supreme from the fifties to the seventies.

Genes were supposed to determine proteins in a completely mechanical sequence, which is well illustrated by the sort of diagram given in fig. 6.4 in the previous chapter. There were a few complexities—for instance the fact that not all genes are expressed in all cells, so there must be other genes that control the genes being turned on and off. But what controls the genes that turn other genes on and off? This mechanical hierarchy of genes controlling genes controlling other genes soon gets into an infinite regression, which fails to explain how living organisms can become organised. But these are essentially the sort of explanations on offer to this day.

Since the early seventies all but the very first assumption of the central dogma have been overturned. The first assumption remains true only by definition, as it is well known that certain cellular states, or gene-expression states, are heritable quite independently of changes in DNA or RNA. The first crack appeared before rDNA research really got under way. This was the discovery by the American geneticists Howard Temin and David Baltimore of a viral enzyme, *reverse transcriptase,* that does the reverse of transcription: that is, it makes a copy of complementary DNA (cDNA) from an RNA sequence. The kind of viruses possessing reverse transcriptase are *retroviruses,* implicated in AIDS and many forms of cancer, which have RNA as their genomes.

Overlapping genes were first discovered in the bacteriophage φ174 (a virus of bacteria) when its complete base sequence was worked out by Sanger in 1977. The phage possesses at least one gene that codes for two separate proteins. The read-out for the second protein starts one base out of phase in the middle of the gene and continues to the end, so the second message gives a completely different protein. Overlapping genes have since been found in many other viruses.

The central dogma of molecular biology from the fifties to the seventies[1]

1. DNA (and, in some viruses, RNA) is the genetic material.
2. Genetic information flows from DNA to RNA to protein by way of a triplet genetic code.
3. The base sequence of the RNA transcribed, and later translated into a protein, is a faithful complementary copy of the DNA encoding the protein.
4. One protein is specified by one gene, which is a continuous sequence of DNA.
5. The sequence of bases in the gene corresponds exactly to the sequence of amino acids in the protein it encodes.
6. The genetic code is universal.
7. The sequence of base triplets in a gene is read in one direction, without overlapping, and only in one correct reading frame.
8. The DNA of most cells remains constant during development; only the genes expressed differ between different types of cells.
9. Environmentally induced modifications in the characteristics of somatic cells do not affect the DNA and cannot be inherited.

Then it was discovered that mitochondrial DNA (DNA inside the cellular organelles, where organic substrates derived from food are oxidised to provide energy for all kinds of vital activities) uses a genetic code that differs from the 'universal' code in several respects. Subsequently the ciliated protozoa (single-celled animals), such as *Paramecium* and *Tetrahymena,* were found to use yet another code. So the genetic code is by no means universal.

Surprising though those findings were, they could easily be dismissed as exceptions. By far the most significant picture to emerge is how dynamic and flexible genes and genomes are in both organisation and function. This is in striking contrast to the relatively static and mechanical conception that previously held sway.

> The first reductionist fallacy in the patenting of genes is that DNA by itself can specify anything at all, as DNA depends for its replication on the entire cell.

The case of the vanishing gene

In the mind of genetic engineers, the 'gene' is still very much the same as the one that molecular biology established between the nineteen-fifties and seventies: it is a continuous stretch of DNA with a specific base sequence (remaining unchanged except for extremely rare random mutations); it is in a definite position within the constant genome of the cell; and it determines the amino acid sequence of a corresponding protein. The amino acid sequence of a protein in turn determines its function in the organism. This notion of an isolatable gene specifying a function independent of the cellular and environmental context of the organism is also the one that validates the patenting of genes.

The first reductionist fallacy in the patenting of genes is that DNA by itself can specify anything at all, as DNA depends for its replication on the entire cell. What the findings of the new genetics also show is that the gene itself has no well-defined continuity or boundaries, the expression of each gene being ultimately dependent on, and entangled with, every other gene in the genome. There is certainly no one-way information flow proceeding from DNA to RNA to protein and the rest of the organism, as projected by the central dogma. Instead gene expression is subject to instructions, modifications, and adjustments, according to the environmental, physiological and cellular contexts. Moreover, the base sequence of DNA in genes and genomes is subject to small and large changes during normal development and as the result of environmental perturbations.

The period from approximately the mid-seventies to the mid-eighties was one of the most exciting and rewarding for biology. It was as though a hundred flowers were blossoming after the tyranny of the central dogma. Every week, it seemed, a new discovery was made that contradicted what had been accepted for decades. And it was a truly collective endeavour. Hundreds, if not thousands, of molecular geneticists in academic institutions all over Europe and the United States were involved, sharing information, exchanging researchers, collaborating and co-operating in any and every way possible. Though they probably had no time to reflect on it then, those researchers were building a new genetics paradigm. The notion of an isolatable, constant gene that could be patented as an invention for all the marvellous things it could do had never crossed their minds. And if it did, and if they had reflected on the implications of the totality of their discoveries, they would have recognised this notion for what it is: the greatest reductionist myth ever perpetrated, which flies in the face of all the scientific evidence.

> Those researchers were building a new genetics paradigm. The notion of an isolatable, constant gene that could be patented as an invention had never crossed their minds. And if it did, and if they had reflected on the implications of the totality of their discoveries, they would have recognised that notion for what it is: the greatest reductionist myth ever perpetrated, which flies in the face of all the scientific evidence.

Let me try to convey some of the excitement of that period, to include findings that continued to be made into the nineteen-nineties.

The interrupted gene

The discovery of the interrupted gene made headlines in the late seventies, as it was completely unexpected. The discovery was made possible by *gene cloning,* the technique of making many copies of a gene, isolating the gene, and identifying it. When a specific gene is isolated, its base sequence can be determined and compared with that of the mRNA transcribed from the gene, as well as the amino acid sequence of the protein translated from the mRNA. By carrying out these procedures, researchers found that the gene corresponding to the coding sequence in the genome is actually interrupted at intervals by long stretches of non-coding sequences. The coding regions came to be known as *exons* and the non-coding regions as *introns*. This structure is now found to be characteristic of most genes of higher organisms. The number and size of introns vary greatly, and they are often much longer than the coding sequences (we shall come across some human genes in chapter 12). During transcription, the complementary sequence of the entire gene is transferred to a precursor RNA or primary transcript, which is then further processed into the messenger RNA. Processing turns out to be very complicated and involves, among other things, splicing out the introns so that the complete coding sequence can be translated into a continuous protein chain. The gene sequence in the genome therefore does not at all correspond to that predicted from the amino acid sequence of the protein encoded.

> The gene is ultimately delocalised over the entire organism in its ecological setting.

Interrupted genes were a surprise; but it is really the discovery of the many layers of complexity involved in gene expression that gives rise to a more profound change to the status of the gene. The gene responsible for making a single protein is functionally, as well as structurally, ill-defined. It is delocalised throughout the genome, being entangled with all the other equally ill-defined genes. As the expression of the gene—the synthesis of the protein—is also sensitive to prevailing physiological and environmental conditions, the gene is ultimately delocalised over the entire organism in its ecological setting.

The delocalised, entangled gene

The DNA sequence by itself can do nothing, as it depends on enzymes and other proteins interacting with it to be replicated, and to be transcribed. Gene expression—the eventual appearance of the protein encoded—turns out to be an extremely complicated process. It depends on special 'regulatory' DNA sequences, which may be found in front of (5′ to) or behind (3′ to) the region of the (interrupted) gene, within the introns themselves, or sometimes very far away on the chromosome. These sequences interact with a host of regulatory proteins, or *transcription factors,* encoded by other genes scattered throughout the genome (on other chromosomes). Each of these genes will most probably possess a gene structure like the one they are regulating, and requiring other transcription factors for regulation. Each transcription factor recognises a special short-sequence *motif* within the regulatory region or regions. Transcription cannot start until the *transcription complex,* consisting of many transcription factors, is bound to one of the regulatory regions, the *promoter,* which marks the starting-site of transcription.

Some thirty or more transcription factors are common to all cell types and are essential for the transcription of many, if not all, genes; more than twice that number of other factors are cell-specific, or are activated by special stimuli, such as heat shocks, specific metabolites, or hormones, which are themselves subject to environmental modulation.[2]

Another illustration of the delocalised, mutual entanglement of gene functions is in the gene-protein relationship. According to the central dogma, one gene encodes one protein. In reality, all possible mappings exist between genes and proteins: one to one, one to many, many to one, and many to many. For example, alternative splicing of the primary transcript (to remove introns) gives rise to more than one protein from the same gene. This occurs in different tissues as well as in the same tissues. Splicing may even occur between transcripts of different genes to give a hybrid protein.[4] In some cases a large *polyprotein* encoded by one gene is split, after translation, into two or more proteins. More surprisingly, many genes can be joined together by DNA rearrangement in the genome, which is then transcribed and translated to give one protein. This occurs in the synthesis of the *immunoglobulins* or antibody proteins that bind specific foreign antigens, as the body mounts an immune response. By recombining different variants in multigene families of several different genes, a diversity of antibodies can be made that are specific for binding each of the thousands of different foreign antigens that the organism is likely to come across.

Finally, many genes can code for the same or similar proteins in so-called *multigene families*. These are families of genes that exist in multiple copies (from several copies to many thousands or hundreds of thousands of copies) in the genome. *Simple* multigene families have identical or nearly identical sequences that are arranged in one or more tandem arrays (continuous head-to-tail repeats). These function simultaneously to make large amounts of single proteins, such as the *histones,* which package DNA into chromosomes in cells of higher organisms, and ribosomal RNA, which is involved in translating mRNA into proteins. Complex multigene families, on the other hand, contain sequences that are not identical, though they are similar and serve related functions. Examples are the *haemoglobins,* the oxygen-carrier proteins of the *erythrocytes* (red blood cells), which exist in several embryonic, fetal and adult forms.

The gene that gets silenced

Though genes encode amino acid sequences of proteins, they may not become expressed, subject to 'instruction' from the cellular and physiological states. Approximately half of all genes in the eukaryotic genome have a large number of repeats of the dinucleotide CG at their front (5′) ends. The cytosine bases often have a methyl group, $-CH_3$, added to them. It turns out that when a lot of cystosine bases are methylated, the gene is no longer transcribed. This regulatory mechanism operates not only on normal genes in the genome but also on transgenes, much to the frustration of genetic engineers (see chapters 8 and 9), and on integrated viral sequences.

Another gene-silencing mechanism works after transcription; the transcripts are simply rapidly broken down before they can be translated.[5] These mechanisms can be triggered simply by introducing more copies of a gene that already exists in the genome and are part of the cell's defence against foreign, unwanted DNA that all organisms possess.

A major silencing or inactivation of genes has been known for a long time, though it is still not yet fully understood. It involves one or other of the two X chromosomes carried by the female of many species, including human beings, where the males have one X chromosome and a very much smaller Y chromosome, with only a very few genes. Inactivation of one of the two X chromosomes in the female starts at one end and spreads eventually to the entire chromosome, which ends up looking like a contracted round blob in the nucleus. The genes on the inactive X are all heavily methylated, except for a few that are still active. It seems entirely a matter of chance which X chromosome in any particular cell becomes inactivated, so heterozygotes will end up being a mosaic—a mixture of different cells in the body. One of the most common mosaics is the tortoiseshell cat, a female heterozygous for an X-linked gene, which gives either orange or black coat colour. Random X chromosome inactivation among the cells of the body gives an attractive patchwork of orange and black.

What is interesting about DNA methylation is that it is inherited, so that when the DNA is replicated the bases marked by methylation in the old strand are also methylated in the new strand. This so-called 'epigenetic' inheritance is at least partly responsible for the stability of the differentiated states of cells. When certain genes lose methylation patterns as a result of changes in cellular states, this is also passed on to the daughter cells. Both the acquisition and the loss of methylation are therefore examples of the 'inheritance of acquired characteristics' (which I shall deal with in more detail later).[6]

The gene that gets edited

Since the nineteen-seventies geneticists have uncovered more and more complications in the 'processing' of the primary RNA transcript into messenger RNA, which gets translated into protein. The most surprising of all is *RNA editing,* in which the base sequence of the RNA transcript is actually changed by the addition of bases to the RNA molecule or by the chemical transformation of one base to another. The process was discovered in 1986 in the mitochondrial transcripts of the *trypanosome,* a parasite that causes sleeping-sickness; but it has since been found in organisms as diverse as mammals, amphibians, plants, protozoa, and viruses, involving not only mitochondrial and chloroplast genes[7] but also nuclear genes.[8] It is likely to be a very common process in gene expression.

RNA editing does not occur at random, but whenever it occurs it is probably essential for the proper functioning of the organism. For example, in wheat mitochondria the transcript of a gene, *atp9,* is edited by removing an amino group, $-NH_2$, from cytosine, turning it into uracil. The edited mRNA gives rise to a functioning protein with an amino acid sequence that differs from that encoded in the gene. When unedited proteins were introduced in transgenic plants it resulted in male sterility.[9] RNA editing depends on RNA *editases,* enzymes that exist in different forms specific to different editing jobs.[10] Moreover, multi-protein complexes are involved in editing,[11] as in transcription.

> The causal loop for gene expression is circular and multi-dimensional. There is no simple, linear, one-directional instruction proceeding from the gene to RNA to protein. The mechanical concept of an isolatable gene does not accord with the organic reality of the dynamic, delocalised entanglement of gene function.

The gene may therefore not even determine the amino acid sequence of the protein it is supposed to encode. Instead, the precise sequence of amino acids depends on influences from the context—the cellular and physiological state—propagating backwards to the post-transcriptional levels, just as similar backward influences are propagated to the level of transcription through transcription factors and DNA methylation to determine which genes are transcribed and which genes are silenced. The causal loop for gene expression is circular and multidimensional. There is no simple, linear, one-directional instruction proceeding from the gene to RNA to protein. (We shall have the opportunity later to examine many 'reverse information flows' that proceed from the environment backwards to alter genes and genomes.)

What is becoming clear is that the mechanical concept of an isolatable sequence of DNA corresponding to a gene does not accord with the organic reality of the dynamic, delocalised entanglement of gene function. The transition between the molecular genetic determinism of the central dogma and the new genetics is reminiscent of the transition between the separate, mechanical objects of the Newtonian universe and the delocalised, mutually entangled entities of quantum reality.[12] The new-found dynamism in gene function is fully matched by the fluidity of genes and genomes.

The fluid genome[13]

'The application of new molecular techniques reveals that, beneath the level of the chromosome, the genome is a continuously changing population of sequences. Mobility, amplification, deletion, inversion, exchange and conversion of sequences create this unexpected fluidity on both an evolutionary and developmental time-scale.'[14] This quotation is from a historic publication, *Genome Evolution*. By using this title the joint editors, Gabriel Dover and Richard Flavell, have in effect defined a completely new subject area.

Genome organisation is infinitely variable

The genomes of eukaryotes are very big and messy. (*Eukaryotes* are 'higher' organisms whose genomes are enclosed in a membrane-bound nucleus in the cell, as opposed to *prokaryotes,* such as bacteria, which do not have a nucleus and whose genomes exist free in the cytoplasm of the cell.) They are also infinitely variable, as geneticists came to realise when they had a chance to dissect eukaryotic genomes with recombinant DNA techniques.

First of all, there is far more DNA than is required to code for all the proteins and to supply all the signals necessary for gene transcription. The overwhelming proportion of the DNA—perhaps up to 99 per cent in some genomes—has no known function. It has been described as 'junk DNA' or 'selfish DNA'—selfish because it serves no purpose except to get itself replicated along with the rest of the genome. Secondly, most of the DNA consists of repeated sequences. Repeats vary in number, from less than ten to hundreds of thousands or several millions. The length of the sequence repeated varies from two or three base pairs to thousands or hundreds of thousands of base pairs. These repetitive sequences may be clustered near the ends of chromosomes, towards the middle, in other parts, or dispersed through all parts of all the chromosomes. The number of repeats, and sometimes also their location, differ between individual genomes belonging to the same species or populations.

Repetitive sequences are making life difficult for DNA-sequencers of the human genome, apart from the obvious question of whose genome it is that is being sequenced, as individual genomes are unique in their DNA sequences and in their organ-isation. (We shall see in chapter 11 just how variable individual genes coding for proteins may be, and how the enormous variation in repeated DNA sequences in the human genome can be used to find genes and to provide identification of individuals for forensic purposes.) Though some of the repeated sequences are members of multigene families that code for functional proteins, the vast majority of them have no known function.

Some repeats are *mobile genetic elements,* also called *transposons* or 'jumping genes'—sequence elements that encode genes for enzymes that can cut out and re-insert the elements in different places in the genome, during which process they may make further copies of themselves. Transposons were discovered by the geneticist Barbara McClintock more than fifty years ago. For this she was awarded the Nobel Prize belatedly in 1983, and has since been elevated to the status of scientific folk-hero. She was study-ing a number of very unstable genes in maize that mutated spon-taneously at high frequencies. This was because of transposons that jump in and out of the genes, disrupting their function. Even when the transposon jumps out again, function may not be restored, as transposons usually leave behind their 'footprint', which is a duplication of short sequences flanking the site of insertion.[15] (Transgenic maize is probably especially hazardous in this regard, as there are already plenty of transposons providing helper functions to mobilise transgenes and marker genes.)

One class of transposons is *retrotransposons,* which depend on reverse transcription to move and to duplicate. These are very similar to retroviruses, from which they may have originated (see chapter 12).[16] A host of other retrovirus-like *relict sequences,* which have lost their ability to mobilise independently, are also present in the genome. However, these relict sequences do not necessarily cease to mobilise and duplicate themselves, for they can be helped by other elements. *That is why the so-called 'crippled' vectors of genetic-engineering biotechnology are so dangerous* (see chapters 9 and 12). In all cases, reverse transcription has made a cDNA copy from the corresponding RNA, which is then inserted into the genome.

Reverse transcripts turn out to be very common in eukaryotic genomes, accounting for up to 20 per cent of some genomes. One class of such reverse transcripts, called Alu sequences (so named because they are cut by one of the many DNA cutting enzymes, or *restriction enzymes,* called Alu), is the most abundant of the middle-repetitive DNA sequences in human and rodent genomes. In the human genome it is a 300bp (base-pair) sequence repeated some half a million times, the repeats being widely dispersed in the genome. It is homologous (that is, has a similar base sequence) to parts of an RNA molecule in the cytoplasm, referred to as the 7SL RNA, which makes up the signal recognition particle (SRP)—part of the molecular machinery required for moving proteins across intracellular membranes after they have been translated. The 7SL RNA consists, intriguingly, of an Alu sequence into which a sequence specific to 7SL RNA has been inserted.[17]

Finally, the genome also contains many *pseudogenes*—non-functional coding sequences that have been reverse-transcribed from their mRNAs and re-inserted into the genome. Reverse transcription constitutes a potential route of reverse information flow.

> Genomes are continuously changing as a result of many processes, operating constantly on developmental and evolutionary time-scales. These processes destabilise genes and genomes, move genes around, mutate, rearrange, recombine, replicate sequences, delete or insert sequences, and even exchange and convert sequences.

Genome dynamics: DNA turnover[18]

The reason genomes are so big and messy is that they are continuously changing as a result of many processes, operating constantly on developmental and evolutionary time-scales. These processes destabilise genes and genomes, move genes around, mutate, rearrange, recombine, replicate sequences, delete or insert sequences, and even exchange and convert sequences. Sequences in the genome can be amplified and contracted thousands or hundreds of thousands of times as part of normal development, or as the result of environmental challenges. They can undergo large reorganisations or rearrangements to form new chromosomes. Genomes can duplicate wholesale, subsequent to the formation of hybrids between species whose chromosomes are not sufficiently similar for them to pair properly in the special cell divisions (*meiosis*) that form germ cells. In such a case, doubling the hybrid genome wholesale allows every chromosome to pair with a partner identical to itself. This process—*polyploidisation*—is very common in the evolution of natural species. That is why closely related species may have genomes of vastly different sizes. The biggest genomes in the world belong to single-celled ciliate protozoa, which tend to selectively amplify, delete sequences and drastically rearrange their genomes as part of normal development.[19]

The fluidity and dynamic nature of the genome so impressed the molecular geneticist Richard Flavell that he envisaged cycles of 'DNA turnover' in the genomes of all species, involving mutations, rearrangements, translocations, amplifications, and deletions, providing major sources of variation for the evolution of new species.

Jumping genes

Transposable elements are responsible for much of the fluidity of genomes. Transposition not only leads to changes in the position of the transposable elements themselves but, in the case of replicative transposons, can spread copies of the transposons around the same genome or to other genomes by infection. One transposon, the P element, has spread to all *Drosophila* species within a period of fifty years.[20] *Drosophila* strains in the laboratory that were established before the spread of P elements were free from the element. A tiny mite, parasitic on many *Drosophila* species, is thought to have been responsible for spreading the P element across species barriers.[21] (We shall come across other examples of transposable elements in chapters 9 and 12.) Transposable elements are responsible for many 'spontaneous' mutations in maize, as mentioned above, in *Drosophila,* and also in human beings. Transpositions lead to sequence duplications, deletions, and chromosomal rearrangements. The genetic upheavals caused by transpositions can be considerable.

Transposable elements in the genome do not always move. Transposition appears to be regulated by cellular functions, so transposons may change from an active to an inactive state. Inactive transposons are correlated with an increased level of methylation,[22] which is strongly implicated in 'gene-silencing' (the failure of gene expression). The frequency of transposition, however, is greatly increased as a result of environmental stress, in both maize[23] and *Drosophila.*[24] While some geneticists see this as a potentially adaptive function, generating variants that may enable the organism to overcome the environmental challenge, the overall result of stress-induced transposition is to increase the rates at which genes become inactivated as the transposons insert randomly into them. This has implications for human health (see chapter 13).

Amplifying and contracting genes

Gene amplifications and contractions can occur as part of normal development. For example, it has been known since the nineteen-sixties that the genes encoding ribosomal RNA, which are necessary for translating mRNA into proteins, undergo waves of amplifications during maturation of the germ cell. This happens again in the fertilised egg of *Xenopus,* the African clawed toad (really a frog), so that eventually more than 70 per cent of the nuclear DNA in the egg codes for rRNA. Ribosomal RNAs already exist in the genome as multigene families. Amplification does not involve the entire cluster of repeats: instead there is often a predominant class, which is amplified in the cluster.

Gene amplifications and contractions occur in many plants that switch from juvenile to adult phases. This involves changes in the repetitive sequences of all the cells, presumably in the growing tip of the shoot.

The potential for gene amplification and contraction is actually very widespread. It happens readily in mammalian cells during drug treatment, as in chemotherapy against cancer, in which the cells develop resistance to the drugs. One of the best-studied examples is methotrexate-resistance.[25] Methotrexate inhibits the activity of the enzyme dihydrofolate reductase, which is necessary for making DNA, so that cells unable to make DNA will no longer multiply. Resistance to methotrexate can be caused by increased activities of membrane proteins that pump drugs out of the cell, or it can involve mutational changes in the dihydrofolate reductase enzyme, so that the new enzyme is no longer inhibited by the drug. A third mechanism is the overproduction of the normal enzyme, so that there is an excess of the enzyme in the cell, which overcomes the inhibition by the drug. Overproduction of the enzyme is accomplished by gene amplification. Whole segments of the chromosome containing the gene are amplified, the amplified unit being at least ten times as long as the gene itself. Amplifications are accompanied by gross changes in chromosome structure, chromosomal rearrangements, and the acquisition of extra chromosomes exhibiting a wide range of abnormal structures.

> Changes in the genome are repeatably generated by particular
> drugs in particular cell lines. *They do not involve the selection of
> random mutations* but are physiological responses shared by all
> the cells.

These changes in the genome are repeatably generated by
particular drugs in particular cell lines. *They have nothing to do
with the selection of random mutations* but are physiological
responses shared by all the cells in the population. Similar genetic
and genomic changes are induced in insects exposed to insect-
icides and in plants exposed to herbicides (see chapter 8). They
are part and parcel of the spectrum of physiological responses
common to all individuals in a population. (In chapter 10 we shall
find further examples in the origin of antibiotic-resistance in
bacteria.) The extent to which the genomes of both somatic and
germ cells can change in response to the environment should
make geneticists extremely cautious about 'cloning' from the cells
of adult animals (see chapter 9) or about making inferences about
the primary causes of diseases such as cancer (see chapter 13).

Gene amplifications are known to be involved in cancer itself
(see chapter 12). All gene amplifications share certain common
features. The amplified sequence is specific to each developmental or environmental stimulus; and the amplified DNA contains
a large proportion of extraneous sequences, which presumably
contain the regulatory signals for gene expression.

The environment changing genes directly[26]

One interesting class of environmentally induced changes in DNA
is associated with a spectrum of heritable modifications after
treatment with various mixtures of fertilisers in flax and other
plants. As is well known, plants do not have separate somatic and
germ cells, for every somatic cell is capable of developing into
germ cells, and so somatic modifications will be inherited by later
generations.

This phenomenon was discovered in the nineteen-fifties but
was not analysed by molecular genetics techniques until the

eighties, by Chris Cullis at the John Innes Institute in Britain. Cullis found that a $1\frac{1}{2}$ per cent solution of the fertiliser ammonium sulphate added to compost at the time of sowing gave a large type, L, whereas a $1\frac{1}{2}$ per cent solution of a triple-superphosphate with low-pH compost gave a small type, S. The L and S *geno-trophs,* as they are called, differ in many characteristics from each other and from the parental type from which they were derived. Differences found include size, hairiness, and distinct types of enzymes expressed, as well as genome size and the copy number of repeated ribosomal RNA genes. The changes are stably inherited in later generations in the absence of the inducing environment, under the usual conditions of growth. However, the stability is not absolute, and further changes can be induced by other circumstances.

Environmentally induced changes in DNA are specific to different environments, and can be repeatably generated.

Careful analysis of seedlings treated with fertilisers at different stages of growth showed that the changes in DNA occur simultaneously in all the cells of a *meristem* (the growing zone of a plant). Thereafter, the growth characteristics of the shoot tend to improve, suggesting that at least some of the changes are adaptive. These environmentally induced changes in DNA are specific to different environments, and can be repeatably generated. They are therefore not random changes. Similar environmentally induced changes in DNA have since been documented in other plants, including maize, pea, and broad bean.

Gene conversion and concerted evolution[27]

A puzzling phenomenon emerged as multigene families from different species were analysed. Members of multigene families were created by gene duplication events that happened a long time ago in the phylogeny of the species; so they are expected to accumulate mutations independently and become substantially different one from another. However, they turn out usually to be homogeneous *within* a species. Furthermore, individuals within each species are homogeneous for variants that are characteristic of the species. In other words, variation is accumulating between different species, but within a species all members of each multi-gene family tend towards uniformity. Actually there are degrees of uniformity, as each multigene family can consist of sub-families, the members of which are more similar to one another than they are to members of a different sub-family. But the puzzle remains the same. It is as though some invisible hand is keeping all the gene sequences the same throughout the course of evolution. What is responsible for this 'concerted evolution' of sequences, many of them dispersed throughout the genome? Gabriel Dover achieved a degree of notoriety among the more orthodox community by drawing attention to this phenomenon very early on, calling it by the colourful term 'molecular drive', on the grounds that it drives evolution much more substantially and rapidly than natural selection.

There are several mechanisms that can generate uniform sequences. The first is gene amplification, in which an enormous number of tandem repeats are generated all at once. Another is unequal exchange between homologous chromosomes, which occurs during chromosome pairing in the formation of germ cells, so that one chromosome acquires more copies and the other fewer. However, these mechanisms cannot explain the homo-geneity of dispersed copies; and even tandemly repeated copies will be expected to accumulate mutations independently. A third mechanism is replicative transposition; but again the replicated copies will still tend to diverge after the event. So the evidence points to some process (or processes) of *gene conversion*—changing DNA sequences from one to another. In the case of multigene families it appears that all the family members tend to be converted to a uniform sequence, so that those sequences that have diverged are simply eliminated.

When sequences belonging to the hundred or so ribosomal RNA genes from *Neurospora* (the bread mould) were analysed they were found to belong to four sub-families. Within each sub-family the coding regions differed in sequence by less than 0.2 per cent, whereas the flanking 'spacer' regions differed by $3\frac{1}{2}$ to 7 per cent. Differences between the sequences of each sub-family were such that they preserved the same secondary structure of the ribosomal RNA necessary for its function, suggesting that gene conversion may depend on gene function. One way in which this may work is by means of reverse transcription, which appears to be a very active process in eukaryotic genomes, for which no other obvious function exists (though we shall have more to say on this later). Gene product ribosomal RNAs that are efficiently transcribed and stable escape destruction by ribonucleases, the enzymes that break down RNAs. This means that only genes that function well may be reverse-transcribed into complementary DNA (cDNA), which is inserted into the genome in place of those sequences that do not work well. A similar mechanism has been postulated for transfer RNA (tRNA) genes in yeast. The tRNAs are yet other genes required in the complicated process of translating mRNA into protein.

> The fluidity of the genome is involved in actively maintaining the stability of genes and genome. This is what organic stability—as opposed to mechanical stability—is all about.

Gene conversion is an example of a mechanism that operates not only at the level of the organism but at the level of the entire species. It is also a clear instance where the fluidity of the genome is involved in actively maintaining the stability of genes and genome, not just in changing genes and genomes. This is what organic stability—as opposed to mechanical stability—is all about. Genes and genomes need to be fluid in order to maintain stability under normal, everyday conditions, and also to be able to change promptly in response to environmental challenges (see chapters 9 and 12).

Wandering genes

As we have seen, transposons can travel between species that do not interbreed. The extent to which horizontal gene transfer has contributed to genome evolution has been a subject of dispute among geneticists. Not any more. The full scope of actual and potential horizontal gene transfer has come to light within the past five years. At least two hundred papers have been published in mainstream scientific journals since 1993 giving direct or indirect evidence of horizontal gene transfer. Transfers occurred between very different bacteria, between fungi, between bacteria and protozoa, between bacteria and higher plants and animals, between fungi and plants, and between insects. A transposon called 'mariner', first discovered in *Drosophila*, has recently been found to have jumped into the genomes of primates, including humans, where it causes a neurological wasting disease (see chapter 12).

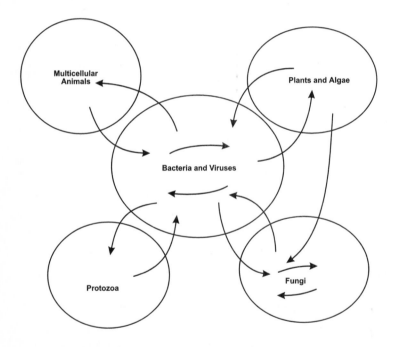

Fig. 7.1: Horizontal gene transfer links the whole biosphere

The present state of our understanding is presented in fig. 7.1, where the arrows indicate transfers for which direct or circumstantial evidence already exists. Genetic-engineering biotechnology poses unique dangers. It greatly facilitates horizontal gene transfer through vectors that are designed to break down species barriers and to overcome cellular mechanisms that break down or inactivate foreign DNA. (Horizontal gene transfer will be dealt with in greater detail in chapters 8 and 9.)

The inheritance of acquired characteristics

The issue of the 'inheritance of acquired characteristics' has been hotly debated for almost a century. The reality, which would take whole books to describe properly, is that there is no longer any doubt that acquired characteristics are inherited, and in many different forms. A number of them have already been identified in this chapter; I shall briefly review these below.

Epigenetic inheritance

Epigenetic inheritance is the inheritance of cellular states or gene expression states.[28] Cellular gene expression states, such as the pattern of DNA methylation, are inherited in somatic cells. In species where germ cells and somatic cells are not permanently differentiated, which include plants, fungi, bacteria, single-cell animals, and the majority of multicellular animals, patterns of DNA methylation will be inherited in subsequent generations. In vertebrates a demethylation of genes that are tissue-specific in expression occurs as part of the 'reprogramming' of the genome in the germ cells; but sometimes genes escape this reprogramming, leading to germ-line inheritance of acquired gene expression states.

There are many other forms of such epigenetic inheritance that do not involve changes in DNA base sequences, among them the ill-defined cytoplasmic states that give rise to cytoplasmic inheritance, which is not directly associated with DNA or RNA. They are known as *dauer modifications* (lasting modifications) or *paramutations,* and they tend to diminish in successive generations. In my laboratory we documented a case of such cytoplasmic inheritance in the fruit fly some years ago.[29] It may be similar to the changes that occur in cells exposed to carcinogens, X-rays, and metabolic stress. These epigenetic changes, rather than mutations in putative cancer genes, have been proposed as the primary cause of cancer (see chapter 13).

The inheritance of induced changes in genomic DNA

As described above, the inheritance of induced changes in genomic DNA occurs in cells and organisms exposed to a whole range of substances, including cytotoxic drugs (drugs toxic to cells), insecticides, and herbicides (see also chapter 8). They also occur in plants exposed to various fertiliser treatments. As plants and the majority of animal phyla do not have distinct germ cells and somatic cells, these modifications will be inherited in subsequent generations. Even in animals with apparently distinct germ cells, the germ cells may also respond directly to the same stimuli, or have communication channels with somatic cells, such as by way of reverse transcription.

Feedback from somatic cells to germ cells

Again we have seen this illustrated already in the intriguing phenomenon of gene conversion. There seems to be a cellular mechanism that in effect reports back to the germ-line, to change the genes for the next generation or to stabilise them according to the experiences of somatic cells of the parent. Reverse transcription, as we have seen, is extremely common in the genome. This has led to many speculations that it may be a normal physiological regulatory mechanism[30] for maintaining the stability of organisms while preparing them to deal with environmental changes (see chapter 8).

Reversed transcripts are abundant in the genome. Many are cDNA copies of the mRNA of cellular genes and are largely non-functional; but functional 'pseudogenes' have been identified in the genome. For example, one of the rat insulin genes was shown to be part of a functional retrotransposon.[31] Moreover, there is evidence suggesting that a certain family of repeated DNA sequences in primates, the L1, may be a reverse transcriptase.[32]

The immunologist Ted Steele proposed in 1979 that acquired immunological tolerance to foreign antigens is inherited via the male line, the implication being that it involves specific changes in germ-line DNA. That was a bombshell in those days. With characteristic proselytising zeal, Steele not only published the result of his experiments in *Nature* (after a wrangle with the then editor, John Maddox) but went on a world lecture tour to publicise the results as widely as possible. Some of us cheered him from the sidelines, while the orthodox community felt so threatened that they did their best to discredit him. But he was right all along; only the details needed filling in.

Now, twenty years later, Steele's group has obtained molecular genetic evidence of feedback between somatic cells and germ cells that has functional significance. Immunoglobulins are antibodies produced by leukocytes (white blood cells) during an immune response to antigens or foreign substances. They are unusual in that major chromosomal rearrangements have to take place to bring together different genes—each belonging to a multigene family—in the maturing leukocytes in order to produce an immunoglobulin protein. Each leukocyte (and its progeny) will have a different combination of genes and hence a distinct immunoglobulin protein with different binding affinity for the foreign antigen. The cell producing a high enough binding affinity at first will be selectively stimulated to multiply to generate a clone of cells. In the later stages of the immune response there is a process of 'directed hypermutation', a million times the rate of ordinary mutation, only in the antigen-binding region of the protein (encoded by the V gene), until an immunoglobulin protein with very high binding affinity is produced. Evidence suggests that the hypermutations are produced by successive rounds of transcription and reverse transcription, which are known to be prone to errors.

> This direct feedback to the germ-line is so controversial because it goes against the neo-Darwinian orthodoxy.

The leukocyte making this high-affinity immunoglobulin is then stimulated to multiply until its clone dominates the leukocyte population. The mRNA molecules resulting from the transcription then enter the germ cells and convert the immunoglobulin

V genes in the germ-line.[33] The mRNA may gain entry to the germ cells by being packaged inside retroviruses, as suggested by the authors. This is then followed by reverse transcription of the mRNA into cDNA and insertion of the cDNA into the germ cell genome in place of an existing gene.

This direct feedback to the germ-line is so controversial because it goes against the neo-Darwinian orthodoxy. The orthodoxy decrees that all genetic variations or mutations arise at random, and are then subject to subsequent selection. Moreover, there can be no feedback between soma and germ-line. However, the weight of evidence is overwhelmingly against the idea that mutations are random, in the sense that they are not correlated with the environment. Similarly, feedback between soma and germ-line is simply not an issue with the majority of organisms that do not have distinct germ cells, so somatically acquired DNA modifications are directly inherited. For organisms with some degree of separation between soma and germ-line it may be that reverse transcription provides a feedback channel from somatic to germ cells.

Adaptive mutations to order

The first indications that mutations are neither random nor rare were obtained when populations of *Escherichia coli* were plated on media containing high concentrations of a metabolite that they cannot use, together with very low concentrations of nutrient that can keep them alive but non-growing. Under such conditions the starving bacteria mutate at high rates, apparently only in genes that subsequently enable them to use the metabolite and hence to grow. These mutants do not exist already but arise only *after* the cells are plated; and they do not arise unless the metabolite is present. At least some of them bear a certain resemblance to the hypermutations in mammalian immunoglobulin V genes described above.

One of the first experiments involved mutant strains of *E. coli* in which a gene that breaks down lactose, β-galactosidase, had been deleted, so it could not metabolise the sugar. It was plated on a medium with high concentrations of lactose and some minimal nutrient. When the other nutrient was exhausted, mutant colonies began to appear that possessed lactose-splitting activity. The enzyme responsible was not the β-galactosidase that had been deleted but another enzyme altogether, called *ebg* (evolved galactosidase), mapping to the opposite side of the bacterial genome.[34] This had undergone mutations that gave it lactose-metabolising activity. By itself this result was unremarkable, as it could be explained away as the artificial selection of a fortuitous variation. However, the experiment was repeated by other geneticists,[35] who isolated thirty-four independent lactose-using strains by the same method. All of these contained enzyme activity identical to *ebg*. Moreover, in thirty-one of the strains the synthesis of the newly evolved enzyme was regulated by lactose, that is to say, there must have been a mutation in another gene that interacted with lactose to regulate *ebg*. The chance of two random mutations arising in the manner suggested by orthodox neo-Darwinian theory was 1 in 10^{18}. That means one would have to grow about 100,000 litres of bacterial culture—enough to fill a football stadium—to get one of those mutants arising by chance.

> It is becoming clear that the 'fluid genome' processes are a complex regulatory system for carrying out the 'natural genetic engineering' on which life depends. Natural genetic engineering is nothing if not precise. The artificial genetic engineering done by human beings, by contrast, ends up being random, because it is controlled neither by the organism nor by the human being. It is also dangerous, because it attacks the very mechanisms that maintain the integrity and autonomy of living organisms, even as they are inextricably entangled within their ecological environment.

Many later experiments have confirmed that these hyper-mutations arise at frequencies many orders of magnitude above the 'spontaneous', 'random' mutation rate, which is about 10^{-9} or less. These findings led John Cairns and his colleagues to suggest that 'bacteria in stationary phase, have some way of producing (or selectively retaining) only the most appropriate mutations.'[36] The phenomenon has since been referred to as 'directed mutations' or 'adaptive mutations'.

The phenomenon clearly exists not only in bacteria but in yeast cells and possibly also in fruit flies.[37] But there does not seem to be one single mechanism responsible. DNA replication appears to be necessary at least in some cases, but beyond that, a variety of mechanisms may be involved, including hyper-mutations caused by ineffective DNA repair or reverse transcription, genetic recombination, and single base-pair deletions. Adaptive mutations in starving bacteria are caused by a spectrum of genetic changes distinct from the 'spontaneous', random ones.[38] Despite this, neo-Darwinists are still trying hard to salvage the 'random-ness' hypothesis by saying that random errors are generated that are subsequently selected. But as *all* the cells in the population are genetically uniform, and all the cells are capable of generating those variations, there can be no question of selection in the usual neo-Darwinian sense. Instead it is a physiological response of starving cells involving genetic changes that enable them to overcome the starvation.

The molecular geneticist James Shapiro offers an appropriate perspective of genomic fluidity in bacteria that sums up the discoveries of molecular genetics over the past twenty-five years. He states that bacteria may have 'little tolerance for purely random variability.'[39] Bacterial cells possess a wide range of repair and proof-reading functions to remove accidental change to DNA sequences and to correct errors resulting from physiological insults. But the same cells also possess numerous biochemical mechan-isms for changing and reorganising DNA, suggesting that such changes are the consequence of 'natural genetic engineering', which enables bacteria to respond to environmental challenges. The ability to activate these mechanisms under stress can significantly accelerate evolutionary change in crisis without threatening genetic stability in ordinary circumstances. Shapiro feels it is not too unreasonable to predict that further studies of mobile genetic elements and DNA rearrangements will ultimately uncover truly directed mutations. Just as signal-transduction systems of the cell can direct the transcriptional apparatus to specific places in the genome to express particular genes, so mutational apparatus can be similarly directed to mutate specific genes. Such a mutational apparatus appears to be associated with the immunoglobulin V genes.[40]

Another observation relevant to adaptive mutations is that defective genes in organisms can become corrected to regain normal function. This was known for bacteria and yeast but has recently been discovered in human beings. Some patients suffering from a range of genetic defects, such as tyrosinaemia, adenosine deaminase deficiency, X-linked combined immuno-deficiency, and Fanconi anaemia, have regained functional genes by many different mechanisms. These include reverse mutation, recombination, and gene conversion, as well as compensatory deletions, insertions and mutations that result in a functional gene different from the wild type.[41] In view of the remarkable fluidity and adaptability of genes and genomes, the present exclusive preoccupation with genetic engineering is misplaced as well as dangerous. Molecular geneticists ought to direct their attention to the physiological and environmental factors that favour the regulation of gene function and structure in the organism as a whole, which can even repair defective genes.

It is becoming clear that the 'fluid genome' processes are a complex regulatory system for carrying out the 'natural genetic engineering' on which life depends. Natural genetic engineering is genetic engineering in the true sense of the term, as it is nothing if not precise. The artificial genetic engineering done by human beings, by contrast, ends up being random, because it is controlled neither by the organism nor by the human being. It is also dangerous, because it attacks the very mechanisms that maintain the integrity and autonomy of living organisms, even as they are inextricably entangled within their ecological environment.

Eight

PERILS AMID THE PROMISES OF GENETICALLY MODIFIED FOOD

Agricultural biotechnology cannot 'feed the world.' On the contrary, it is inherently unsustainable, and hazardous to biodiversity and to human and animal health. A drastic change of direction will be required to support conservation and the sustainable development of indigenous agricultural biodiversity that both satisfies the stated aims of the Convention on Biological Diversity and guarantees long-term food security for all.

The 'food crisis'

By the year 2000, we were told, the world would need to consume over 2 billion tonnes a year of wheat, rice, maize, barley, and other crops—an increase of 25 per cent over the figures for 1995.[1] This view was echoed by the report of the World Bank for the World Food Summit in Rome in 1996,[2] which warned that the world would have to double food production over the next thirty years. One solution on offer for 'feeding the world' is agricultural biotechnology. Crops will have to be genetically modified for herbicide, pest and disease-resistance, to improve nutritional value and shelf life and also, for the future, to bring about drought-resistance and frost-resistance, nitrogen-fixation,[3] and increased yield.[4]

Agricultural biotechnology is big business, and the mission to 'feed the world' has the irresistible ring of a noble obligation. The same goes for improving the nutritional value of foods. Despite prices having dropped to the lowest on record, a billion people still go hungry,[5] and eighty-two countries (half of them in Africa) neither grow enough food nor can afford to import it. Infant mortality rates—a sensitive indicator of nutritional stress—have been experiencing an increase in recent years, reversing a long-term historical trend. Large numbers of children in developing countries suffer from malnutrition. In India alone, 85 per cent of children under five are below the normal, acceptable state of nutrition.[6]

In the light of the putative crisis in food production, and the support for agricultural biotechnology as a solution to the crisis (as expressed by the World Bank report and by chapter 16 of Agenda 21 of the UN Convention on Biological Diversity), it is all the more important that we examine the claims and promises of the technology, as well as the uncertainties and hazards that are not adequately taken into account in existing practices and regulations.

Can genetically modified food feed the world?
The poverty trap of unequal power relationships

Undernutrition and malnutrition, found everywhere in the developing world as well as the industrialised world, stem from poverty, as was admitted in the World Bank report. In fact there is enough food to feed everyone one-and-a-half times over; world cereal yields have consistently outstripped world population growth since 1980 (2.2 per cent a year, compared with 1.7 per cent).[7]

In the Third World, poverty was created in large measure by centuries of colonial and post-colonial economic exploitation under the free-trade imperative and has been exacerbated since the nineteen-seventies by the introduction of the intensive, high-input industrial agriculture of the 'Green Revolution'.[8] The concentration on growing crops for export has benefited the corporations and the elite of the Third World, at the expense of ordinary people. In 1973 thirty-six of the countries most seriously affected by hunger and malnutrition exported food to the United States—a pattern that continues to the present day.[9]

World hunger is usually blamed exclusively on population increases in the Third World, even by those who should know better.[10] They have failed to mention, for example, the effect of the large dam projects in the Third World, supported by Northern interests through the World Bank. A total of 40,000 large dams took 400,000 square kilometres of the best agricultural land out of production, displacing sixty million farmers. Still greater areas of arable land were subsequently ruined by unsustainable irrigation practices that result in salination, waterlogging, drought, and erosion.[11] At the same time the policy of liberalising trade pursued by governments of the industrialised North in the World Trade Organisation made it easy and profitable for companies to divert food-growing lands to non-food crops, such as flowers and other luxury commodities for export, and to leisure facilities such as golf courses, turning traditionally food-exporting countries into importers.[12]

The present WTO agreement will make things worse.[13] While Southern countries are obliged to remove subsidies for their farmers, subsidies for Northern producers have remained untouched. In addition, as part of the same WTO agreement the intellectual property rights of corporate gene-manipulators in the North will be protected (see chapter 2), and this will restrict the use of indigenous varieties previously freely cultivated and sold, and introduce seed monopoly. Seeds protected by patents can no longer be saved by farmers for replanting without royalties being paid to the company that owns them. Worse still, the corporations are planning to introduce a 'terminator technology' that genetically engineers harvested seeds so that they will not germinate, to make sure that their patents will not be infringed.

In Europe the Seed Trade Act is already adversely affecting agricultural biodiversity. This makes it illegal to grow or sell non-certified seeds produced by organic farmers from indigenous varieties, certification being biased towards the commercial varieties at present used in agricultural biotechnology.[14] Far from providing cheaper food for all, agricultural biotechnology will further undermine the livelihood of family farmers all over the world and at the same time accelerate the loss of indigenous agricultural biodiversity.

It is because of the increasing corporate monopoly on food production and distribution under a liberalised global economy that the poor are getting poorer, and hungrier. Family farmers have been driven into debt and suicide, not just in the Third World but also in the United States and Britain.[15] American farmers are now receiving prices below the average cost of production for their produce.[16]

Corporate giants already control more than three-quarters of the world trade in cereals.[17] They buy where and when it is cheapest and sell dear, and undercut farmers by the subsidised dumping of surpluses. The international trade of cereals was worth $20 billion in 1995, which was subsidised by American and European taxpayers to the extent of $15.7 billion. The average subsidy to a farmer in the North is already twenty-five times the average income per capita in forty-two low-income countries.

'Food scarcity', like 'overpopulation', is generated by the unequal power relationships between the industrialised North and the Third World. While populations in the North are suffering from obesity, cardiovascular diseases and diabetes because of over-consumption, populations in the South are dying of starvation. Simplistic 'solutions' that leave out the unequal power relations are oppressive and ultimately 'reinforce the very structures creating ecological damage and hunger.'[18]

Biological diversity, food security, and nutrition

Biological diversity and food security are intimately linked. Communities everywhere have derived a livelihood from natural diversity in wild and domesticated forms. Up to half of the food consumed by farming communities in the Third World may consist of wild resources.[19] Diversity is the basis of ecological stability.[20] Recent studies show that diverse ecological communities are more resilient to drought and other environmental disturbances that cause the population of individual species to fluctuate widely from year to year.[21] Species within an ecological community are connected in an intricate web of mutual as well as competitive interactions, of checks and balances, that contribute to the survival of the whole (see chapter 13). This has important implications for conservation *in situ,* particularly at a time when it is estimated that fifty thousand species will become extinct *each year* over the next decade.[22]

The same principles of diversity and stability operate in traditional agriculture.[23] Throughout the tropics, traditional agro-forestry systems commonly contain well over a hundred annual and perennial plant species per field. A profusion of varieties and land-races (local varieties) are cultivated, which are adapted to different local environmental conditions and possess a range of natural resistances to diseases and pests. Spatial diversity through mixed cropping is augmented by temporal diversity in crop rotation, ensuring the recycling of nutrients that maintain soil fertility. These practices have prevented serious outbreaks of diseases and pests and have buffered food production from environmental exigencies.

> A major cause of malnutrition throughout the world is the replacement of the traditionally varied diet provided by sustainable agriculture with one based on monoculture crops.

The diversity of agricultural produce is also the basis of a balanced nutrition. Nutrition depends not only on the right balance of protein, carbohydrates and fats but also on a combination of vitamins, essential metabolites, co-factors, inorganic ions, and trace metals, which only a varied diet can provide. A major cause of malnutrition throughout the world is the replacement of the traditionally varied diet provided by sustainable agriculture with one based on monoculture crops. The transfer of an exotic gene into a monoculture crop can do little to make up for the dietary deficiencies of those suffering from monoculture malnutrition. The nutritional value of beans, or a combination of rice and beans, will always be greater than that of the transgenic rice with a bean gene.

Monoculture and transgenic threats

It is now indisputable that the monoculture crops introduced since the 'Green Revolution' have adversely affected biodiversity and food security all over the world. According to a report by the Food and Agriculture Organisation of the United Nations (FAO), by the year 2000 the world will have lost 95 per cent of the genetic diversity employed in agriculture at the beginning of the century.[24] Monoculture crops are genetically uniform and therefore notoriously prone to outbreaks of disease and pests, particularly when they are grown in large monoculture stands. The corn belt of the United States was devastated by corn blight in 1970–1, while in 1975 Indonesian farmers lost half a million acres of rice to leafhoppers. Genetic modification for disease-resistance or pest-resistance will not solve the problem, as intensive agriculture itself creates the conditions for new pathogens to arise.[25] In 1977 a variety of rice, IR36, created to be resistant to eight major diseases and pests, including bacterial blight and tungro, was attacked by two new viruses, called 'ragged stunt' and 'wilted stunt'. As a result, not only have new varieties to be substituted every three years but they require a heavy input of pesticides to keep pests at bay. But the high input of pesticides tends to exacerbate the problem. Pesticides also kill beneficial prey species, while resistance rapidly develops among the pests, resulting in explosive growths of resistant pest populations.

The high input of fertilisers, water, pesticides and mechanisation required by monoculture crops has had devastating environmental effects.[26] Teddy Goldsmith, who started the ecology movement in Britain in 1970, has been a long-time critic of global financial institutions, such as the World Bank and the International Monetary Fund, for the anti-ecological projects they finance in the Third World, among which are big dams for irrigation and roads that hasten the clearing of forests for intensive agriculture.

Between 1981 and 1991 the world's agricultural base fell by some 7 per cent, primarily because of environmental degradation and water shortages. A third of the world's croplands suffers from soil erosion, which could reduce agricultural production by a quarter between 1975 and 2000. In India 800,000 square kilometres are affected, with many areas turning into scrub or desert. Deforestation in Indonesia has resulted in 8.6 million hectares of degraded land, which is unable to sustain even subsistence agriculture. Throughout the tropics, vast areas are vulnerable to flooding. Of the world's irrigated land, a fifth—40 million hectares—suffers from waterlogging or salination. The resulting pressures on agricultural land led to the further marginalisation of small farmers, swelling the ranks of the dispossessed and hungry, while indigenous natural and agri-cultural biodiversity are eliminated at an accelerated rate.

> Herbicide-resistant transgenic crops make it possible to apply broad-spectrum herbicides, killing many species indis-criminately.

Transgenic crops are created from the same high-input mono-culture varieties as the 'Green Revolution', and are even more genetically uniform, because each transgenic line originates ultimately from a single cell. Two main traits account for almost 100 per cent of the transgenic crops planted in the world today; 70 per cent are herbicide-tolerant, with companies engineering tolerance to their own particular herbicide in order to increase the sales of herbicides, while the rest are insect-resistant.[27] Each of these traits is associated with its own problems.

Herbicide-tolerant transgenic crops make it possible to apply powerful broad-spectrum herbicides, which kill many species indiscriminately. This is so for Monsanto's 'Roundup', and for other herbicides produced by rival companies to be used on their own resistant transgenic crops. In the United States the Fish and Wildlife Service has identified seventy-four endangered plant species threatened by the use of herbicides such as glyphosate.[28] This product reduces the nitrogen-fixing activity of soils and is toxic to earthworms and to many species of mycorrhizal fungi, which are vital for the recycling of nutrients. And glyphosate-type compounds are the third most commonly reported cause of pesticide illness among agricultural workers. The use of non-discriminating toxic herbicides will lead to the large-scale elimination of indigenous species and cultivated varieties, damaging soil fertility and human health besides.

Another hazard from herbicide-tolerant crops is the spread of transgenes to wild relatives by cross-hybridisation, creating 'super-weeds'. Herbicide-tolerant transgenic oil-seed rape released in Europe has now hybridised with several wild relatives.[29] Herbicide-tolerant transgenic crops also become weeds in the form of 'volunteer plants' germinated from seeds after the harvest, so that other herbicides have to be applied to eliminate them, with a further impact on indigenous biodiversity.

Food security depends on agricultural biodiversity and sustainable agriculture

To counteract the crisis of environmental destruction and the loss of agricultural land and indigenous biodiversity created by decades of intensive farming, there has been a global move towards holistic, organic farming methods that revive traditional practices. Previous advocates of the 'Green Revolution' are now calling for a move to sustainable agriculture. This is promoted in chapter 14 of Agenda 21 of the UN Convention on Biological Diversity, signed by more than 140 countries. Large-scale implementation of biodynamic farming and sustainable agriculture is succeeding in the Philippines.[30] In Latin America a number of non-government organisations have joined forces to form the Latin American Consortium on Agro-Ecology and Development, to promote agro-ecological techniques that are sensitive to the complexities of local farming methods.[31] Schemes that introduce soil conservation practices and organic fertilisation methods tripled or quadrupled yields within a year.

Successive studies have emphasised the productivity and sustainability of traditional peasant farming in the Third World as well as in the North,[32] according to a report published by the National Academy of Sciences in the United States.[33] Everywhere, yields tripled, doubled, or at least kept up with high-input agrochemical farming. In twenty countries more than 2 million families are farming sustainably on 4 to 5 million hectares.[34]

The recent experience of Cuba is instructive.[35] The American economic blockade since the nineteen-sixties has caused a shortage of agrochemicals, making it necessary for Cuba to go organic on a grand scale. It maintained a third of its 11 million hectares of agricultural land on agrochemicals, turned another third fully organic, and kept the rest transitional, as half agrochemical and half organic. The yields per hectare of the fully organic are equal to the fully agrochemical, while the yields of transitional fields are only half as much. This is the clearest evidence that organic agriculture can work even on a large scale, with energy-efficient minimal inputs and low impacts on the environment.

Many, if not all, Southern countries still possess the indigenous genetic resources—requiring no further genetic modification—that can guarantee a sustainable food supply.

> Over centuries of agricultural practice, traditional societies have developed an incredible variety of crops and livestock. Some 200–250 flowering plants species have been domesticated, and genetic diversity amongst each of these is astonishing: in India alone, for instance, farmers have grown over 50,000 varieties of rice *Oryza sativa*. In a single village in north east India, 70 varieties are being grown … Farmers (especially women) repeatedly used and enhanced some varieties which were resistant to disease and drought and flood, some which tasted nice, some which were coloured and useful for ritual purposes and some which were highly productive.[36]

Seed-savers for organic agriculture

In Brazil, hundreds of rural communities in the north-east have responded to the economic and ecological crisis in food production by organising communal seed banks to recover traditional indigenous varieties and to promote sustainable agricultural development, with little or no government support.[37]

In India, Vandana Shiva has been involved in the women farmers' Navdanya (Nine Seeds, or Seeds of Freedom) movement for some years, saving and recovering valuable indigenous pulses and grains that have been displaced and marginalised by the 'Green Revolution'.

Seed-saving movements are spreading among organic farmers in Europe and the United States. I recently visited Anita Hayes, originally from the United States, who has started the Irish Seed-Savers' Association near Galway. She is working wonders with tiny plots, crowded with perhaps sixty or more varieties of potatoes, strawberries, cabbages and other plants that have been cultivated by organic farmers in Ireland and elsewhere for hundreds if not thousands of years. These varieties are naturally resistant to diseases and produce high yields without artificial fertilisers. Varieties have also been bred for different purposes. For example, a wheat known as *spelt* is naturally rich in the wheat protein gluten, and a 'huskless' oat can be harvested and cooked directly. What impressed me most was a winter cabbage that had been cultivated for generations in the family of a farmer who is now eighty-four years old. Keen to preserve the line, the farmer's daughter gave some seeds to Hayes, who had grown only five plants in her garden, each of which is about a metre high and the same in diameter. This hardy and vigorous biennial withstood winds of up to a hundred miles an hour, yielding delicious green leaves, which can be harvested throughout the growing seasons. At the end of the second year it is giving the most profuse return of perhaps 10,000 seeds per plant—an eloquent affirmation of nature's fruitfulness and abundance.

> Genetic-engineering agriculture is an assault on life and on our entire life support system. The organic seed-savers movement is the most concrete way to resist this assault, and it needs all our support.

It is impossible not to contrast this with the latest that the biotech industry has to offer: a 'terminator technology' owned by a subsidiary of Monsanto that genetically engineers seeds *not* to germinate.[38] The purpose is to protect corporate patents on seeds, to prevent farmers from saving seeds for replanting. This brings it home to us that the issue is not simply whether we should accept genetically engineered foods: genetic-engineering agriculture is an assault on life and on our entire life support system. The organic seed-savers movement is the most concrete way to resist this assault, and it needs all our support. The Soil Association in Britain, which sets organic standards, has announced that an organic seed certification scheme will be in operation by 2005.

The World Bank is reported to be planning sharp changes in policy to concentrate its efforts on small farmers in developing countries. Unfortunately this consists of offering agricultural bio-technology to the Third World, with the World Bank as the main broker.[39] At the same time companies such as Monsanto are trying to insinuate themselves into the Third World by way of the micro-credit schemes that lend money to farmers at low interest while the International Biosafety Protocol is being negotiated (see chapter 2). Fortunately, the Third World countries have been alerted. Resistance campaigns are going hand in hand with seed-savers campaigns throughout south Asia and Latin America as this edition goes to press. Brazil has banned the planting of Monsanto's transgenic soya.

> There is no need for genetically modified crops. They will not feed the world; on the contrary, they will undermine food security and biodiversity.

It seems obvious that to guarantee long-term food security and to feed the world we can do no better than take to heart the aim of the Convention on Biological Diversity, that is, help to conserve and sustain existing indigenous agricultural diversity, and to develop this diversity in all forms of sustainable agriculture as the basis of a secure and nutritious food base for all.

There is no need for genetically modified crops. They will not feed the world; on the contrary, they will undermine food security and biodiversity. Under the combined effects of monopoly of transnational genetic manipulators' intellectual property rights and 'free trade' agreements of the World Trade Organisation, the livelihood of family farmers will be further compromised by seed royalties and the restrictive practices of seed certification and unfair competition from subsidised Northern produce. Family farmers will be placed completely at the mercy of the corporations, which not only set the price for selling them seeds but buy their produce and sell them back the food they need. At the same time the use of toxic, wide-spectrum herbicides with herbicide-resistant trans-genic crops will result in the irretrievable loss of the indigenous agricultural and natural biological diversity on which food security depends.

There are, in addition, problems and hazards inherent to the technology and its practice that make the regulation of the technology by a strong, legally binding international biosafety protocol under the Convention on Biological Diversity a matter of urgency.

Agricultural biotechnology and wilful ignorance of genetics

In a publication that aims to 'provide consumers with clear and comprehensible information about products of the new technology [i.e. biotechnology]' we are told: 'Research scientists can now precisely identify the individual gene that governs a desired trait, extract it, copy it and insert the copy into another organism. That organism (and its offspring) will then have the desired trait.'[40]

This neatly encapsulates the genetic-determinist idea that one gene controls one trait, and that transferring the gene results in transferring that trait to the genetically modified organism, which can then pass it on indefinitely to future generations. It also presents the process of genetic modification as a precise and simple operation. This account—so typical of that found in publications promoting 'public understanding'—is based on a simplistic assumption regarding genetics that both classical geneticists and plant-breeders have rejected for many years and that has been thoroughly invalidated by the research findings in the new genetics (see chapters 3 and 7). Unfortunately, most molecular geneticists, apart from being absorbed into industry, also lack training in classical genetics and suffer from a severe narrowness of vision that prevents them from appreciating the implications and the broader perspective of the scientific findings in their own discipline, and most of all of the dangers involved.

The dangers of ignoring the interconnected genetic network

Because no gene ever functions in isolation, there will almost always be unexpected and unintended side effects from the gene or genes transferred into an organism.

> Transgenic plants engineered for resistance to diseases and pests may have a higher allergenic potential than unmodified plants.

One serious concern over transgenic foods relates to their potential to be toxic or allergenic, which has become a concrete issue since a transgenic soybean containing a brazil nut gene was found to be allergenic to those sensitive to brazil nut.[41] Recent studies suggest that allergenicity in plants is connected to proteins involved in defence against pests and diseases. Transgenic plants engineered for resistance to diseases and pests may therefore have a higher allergenic potential than unmodified plants.[42]

New proteins from bacteria, such as the *Bt*-toxin engineered into many transgenic crops to make them resist insect pests, cannot be tested for allergenicity, because allergic reactions depend on previous exposure. So, monitoring and the clear segregation and labelling of transgenic products after they have been put on the market are essential for the proper protection of consumers. Most identified allergens are water-soluble and acid-resistant. Some, such as those derived from soya, peanut, and milk, are very heat-stable and are not degraded during cooking.[43]

A transgenic yeast was engineered for an increased rate of fermentation with multiple copies of one of its own genes, which resulted in the accumulation of the metabolite methylglyoxal at toxic, mutagenic levels.[44] This should serve as a warning against applying the 'familiarity principle' or 'substantial equivalence' in risk assessment. We simply do not have sufficient understanding of the principles of physiological regulation to enable us to categorise, *a priori,* those genetic modifications that pose a risk and those that do not.

The 'principle of substantial equivalence', on which all risk assessment is at present based, is elaborated in a joint report by the Food and Agriculture Organisation of the United Nations (FAO) and the World Health Organisation (WHO),[45] whose *Codex Alimentarius* sets world safety standards. The principle is validated by the same reductionist science that drives the biotech industry, which pronounces that there is 'no essential difference' between transgenic lines and conventional varieties produced by selective breeding. A product assessed as substantially equivalent is regarded as safe and fit for human consumption.

> Risk assessment based on the principle of substantial equivalence is the stuff of farce. It is a case of 'don't need—don't look—don't see.' Biotech companies are in effect given carte blanche to do as they please, while regulators are serving to defuse and allay legitimate public fears and opposition.

However, substantial equivalence can be claimed in advance, in which case subsequent risk assessment is perfunctory. Furthermore, 'substantial equivalence' does not mean equivalence to the unengineered plant or animal variety. The genetically engineered food could be compared with any and all varieties within the species. It could have the worst characteristics of all the varieties and still be considered 'substantially equivalent'; it could even be compared with a product from a completely unrelated species or collection of species. Worse still, there are no defined tests that products have to go through to establish substantial equivalence. The tests are so undiscriminating that unintended changes, such as new toxins and allergens, could easily escape detection. A genetically engineered potato, grossly altered, with deformed tubers, was nevertheless tested and passed as substantially equivalent.

Risk assessment based on the principle of substantial equivalence is the stuff of farce. It is a case of 'don't need—don't look—don't see.' Biotech companies are in effect given carte blanche to do as they please, while regulators are serving to defuse and allay legitimate public fears and opposition.[46] A legal case challenging the policy of the Food and Drug Administration in the United States on genetically engineered foods was begun in May 1998 by a coalition of scientists, health professionals, religious leaders, and chefs, demanding adequate safety testing and mandatory labelling. It also alleges that the policy of the FDA is scientifically unsound and ignores significant health risks.[47]

Serious doubts over the safety of transgenic foods were raised by the recent experiments of Arpad Pusztai at the Rowett Institute. Potatoes engineered with snowdrop lectin were found to be toxic to rats, with effects on many organs, including the brain, impairment of the immune system, and signs suggesting viral infection. The experiments further suggested that the main toxicities were associated with the transgenic process itself, as rats fed non-transgenic potatoes spiked with snowdrop lectin did not show the same effects.[48] This draws attention once again to the reductionist science that is used to justify concentrating on the particular genes and gene products transferred into the transgenic line, ignoring all unintended effects arising from the interaction between genes and from the random gene insertion process itself.

The danger of ignoring the ecology of genes and organisms
The impact of single genes on the ecosystem

The most immediate and easily observable impacts of transgenic plants on the ecological environment are due to the cross-pollination of transgenic plants and their wild relatives to generate superweeds. Field trials have shown that cross-hybridisation has occurred between herbicide-resistant transgenic *Brassica napa* and its wild relatives, *B. campestris*,[49] *Hirschfeldia incana*,[50] and *Raphanus raphanistrum*.[51] These impacts have been predicted by ecologists such as Rissler and Mellon[52] and arise from the introduction of any exotic species, whether genetically engineered or not. However, in the case of transgenic plants the spread of novel combinations of genes may increase the ecological impact. Typically, the novel genes are placed next to strong viral promoters, which make them express continuously at high levels, in effect placing them outside the regulation of the cell (see chapters 3 and 7).

Impacts that are generally underestimated are those caused by transgenic soil bacteria. As very few molecular geneticists have any training in soil ecology, they may be ignorant of the important role played by soil microbes in recycling nutrients for the growth of crop plants. The soil microbiologist Elaine Ingham and her student tested a common soil bacterium, *Klebsiella planticola,* engineered to produce ethanol from crop waste. The bacteria were introduced into jars containing different kinds of soil in which a wheat seedling had been planted.[53] In all soil types the growth of the wheat seedling was drastically inhibited. This was due to the ethanol produced, which had adverse effects on microbes involved in recycling nutrients for the wheat seedling. Ingham has talked about this in several seminars sponsored by the Third World Network, to great effect. She and her colleagues now run a consultancy and research firm for organic farming in the United States, which is a marvellous way to resist the agrochemical biotechnological encroachment.

About 30 per cent of all transgenic crops are now engineered with one of several δ-endotoxin genes from the soil bacterium *Bacillus thuringiensis* to protect them from insect pests. Suspensions of the bacteria have been used traditionally by organic farmers as a spray for controlling pests, and so the toxin is considered to be an environmentally friendly biopesticide. However, the transgenic plants were found to harm beneficial species, both directly and indirectly, down the food chain. In a field trial of *Bt*-cotton in Thailand, 30 per cent of the bees around the test fields died; while lacewings fed on prey that have eaten *Bt*-maize plants also suffered ill-effects. Recently it has transpired that pollen from *Bt*-maize is highly lethal to monarch butterflies.[55]

It turns out that because the toxin gene is incorporated into the transgenic plants with a viral promoter that makes it over-express, the toxin is produced at ten to twenty times the lethal dose.[56] Also, the toxin gene is often incorporated in a pre-activated form, which is non-selective. While sprays of bacterial suspensions remain exposed to the sunlight, which rapidly breaks down the toxin, high concentrations of the toxin from transgenic plant debris can build up in the soil, with further impacts on pollinators and other beneficial insects.[57]

> The long-term agronomic viability of transgenic crops has yet to be proved.

The instability of transgenic lines

Traditional breeding methods involve crossing closely related varieties or species containing different forms of the same genes. Selection is then practised over many generations under field conditions, so that the desired characteristics and the genes influencing those characteristics, in the appropriate environment, are tested and harmonised for stable expression over a range of genetic backgrounds. Different genetic combinations, moreover, will perform differently in different environments. This genotype-environment interaction is well known in traditional breeding, so it is not possible to predict how a new variety will perform in untested environments. In many cases new varieties will lose their characteristics in later generations as genes become shuffled and recombined or as they respond to environmental changes.

The problem of instability is greatly exacerbated in genetic engineering. First of all, completely exotic genes are often introduced into organisms. Secondly, the procedures for creating transgenic organisms inherently generate increased genetic instability. In plants, the genes are often introduced into cells in tissue culture, and transgenic plants are then regenerated from the cells after selection in culture.

Transgene instability occurs both in farm animals and in plants.[58] The transgenic sheep Tracy, engineered to produce human α-antitrypsin at high levels in her milk, failed to reproduce a single female offspring that matches her performance. Much more is known about instability in plants. In tobacco, between 64 and 92 per cent of the first generation of transgenic plants become unstable. The frequency of transgene loss in *Arabidopsis* ranges from 50 to 90 per cent. Instability arises both during the production of germ cells and in cell division during plant growth. It can be triggered by transplanting or by mild trauma. Transgenic lines, therefore, often do not breed true, and do not perform consistently in the field. Small and large failures are common even among the crops that have been approved for commercial planting (see chapter 3).

The long-term agronomic viability of transgenic crops has yet to be proved. A recent survey of 8,200 field trials of glyphosate-tolerant transgenic soya varieties in American universities reveals that transgenic crops yield on average 6.7 per cent less and require two to five times more herbicide than non-transgenic soya.[59] Farmers should beware.

By contrast, the long-established indigenous local varieties and land-races are the most stable, as genes and environment have mutually adapted to reinforce the stable expression of desirable characteristics for hundreds, if not thousands, of years. There is no 'quick fix' in establishing ecological balance; yet it must be restored in order to guarantee our long-term food security.

The empty promise of 'high-yielding' and 'nitrogen-fixing' crops

It is irresponsible to claim that genetic modification can make high-yielding or nitrogen-fixing transgenic plants. Yield is a complex characteristic—a polygenic trait (see chapter 5)—dependent on many still largely unknown genes as well as on environmental conditions.[60] Furthermore, it cannot be identified and therefore cannot be selected for in tissue culture. Hopes of discovering individual 'genetic markers' for yield may be unrealistic. A complex characteristic such as yield cannot be 'transferred' by transferring one or two genes; even if all the genes required could be transferred, the problems of genetic instability would only be correspondingly multiplied.

Transgenic lines are inherently unstable

- The tissue culture technique itself introduces new genetic variations at high frequencies (known as *somaclonal variations*).[61] This is most probably because the cells are removed from the internal, physiological environment of the plant, which, together with the ecological environment, keeps gene expression, genes and genome structure stable in the cells and in the organism as a whole. Unilever used tissue culture techniques to regenerate oil palms for planting in Malaysia several years ago; this has now been abandoned, as many plants aborted in the field or failed to flower.[62]

- The process of gene insertion is random, and many secondary genetic effects can result, as mentioned in chapter 3.

- The extra DNA integrated into the transgenic organism's genome disrupts the structure of its chromosome and can itself cause chromosomal rearrangement,[63] further affecting gene function.

- The integrated vector containing the transgene and marker gene has the potential to move out again or to reinsert into another site, causing further genetic disturbances.

- The highly mosaic character of most vector constructs makes them structurally unstable and prone to re-combination. This may be why viral-resistant transgenic plants generate recombinant viruses more readily than non-transgenic plants.

- The use of aggressive promoters, often from viruses, to boost the expression of transgenes stresses and unbalances the physiological system and may thereby increase instability.

- All cells have mechanisms that inactivate or silence foreign genes.[64] One common mechanism is methylation (a chemical reaction that adds a methyl group to the base adenine or cytosine in the DNA), as a result of which the gene is no longer expressed.

The same goes for nitrogen-fixation, the ability of a relatively small number of bacterial species to reduce atmospheric nitrogen to ammonia, a product that can be used by plants and other microbes to make amino acids and, hence, proteins and other nitrogenous compounds essential for life.[65] Throughout the world, 200 million tonnes of nitrogen is fixed by these bacteria each year, while the Haber-Bosch chemical-industrial process produces only 40 million tonnes of nitrogen fertiliser. Of special importance are nitrogen-fixing *Rhizobium* bacteria, which live in symbiotic relationship in the root nodules of legumes.

Shifting from chemical to biologically fixed nitrogen is desirable, as much of the chemical fertiliser applied to soil is leached from it, polluting drinking-water and leading to algal blooms in the water system, anoxia, and hence a decline in fish and shellfish populations. The most important nitrogen-fixing bacteria, on the other hand, work in symbiotic relationship with higher plants. The reason is that the process is thermodynamically uphill and extremely costly in energy. It depends on at least seventeen genes in the bacterium and fifty genes in the plant.[66] Moreover, it has to take place in the absence of oxygen (which is toxic to the principal nitrogen-fixing enzyme complex). Most serious molecular geneticists do not rate as realistic the prospect of creating transgenic nitrogen-fixing crop plants; however, they recognise the value of traditional methods in improving the existing symbiotic relationship between nitrogen-fixing bacteria and higher plants and thereby reducing the need for chemical fertilisers.

The dangers of ignoring 'fluid genome' processes
Herbicide-tolerance and pesticide-resistance

Transgenic crops with insecticidal genes or herbicide-tolerance genes actually favour the evolution of pesticide-resistance and herbicide-tolerance. In other words, they exacerbate the problems they are supposed to solve. Pesticide-resistance has been a serious and persistent problem in intensive agriculture. The rapid evolution of resistance among insect pests has become a textbook example of the supposed power of neo-Darwinian natural selection to increase the frequency of 'rare random mutations' that confer resistance. In reality, insecticide-resistance is a result of genetic changes that can occur in all individuals in insect populations, including mosquitoes, houseflies and aphids exposed to sub-lethal levels of insecticide, and this has been known for close to twenty years. Resistance often involves the hypermutation or amplification of genes encoding enzymes that detoxify the chemical and is part and parcel of the 'fluid genome' mechanisms common to all cells challenged with toxic substances (see chapters 7 and 10). Tolerance to glyphosate readily arises in plant cell lines exposed to the herbicide, and also involves amplifications of detoxifying genes.[67] In the light of this knowledge one could have predicted that transgenic plants with built-in insecticide would favour the acquisition of resistance by insect populations, which are in effect exposed continuously at sub-lethal levels. Similarly, herbicide-tolerant transgenic plants will also hasten the widespread evolution of herbicide-tolerance among weeds, *even in the absence of cross-pollination.*

As we have seen, transgenic crops with *Bt*-toxin genes are already known to be harmful to beneficial insects. The other serious problem that has arisen is *Bt*-resistance among insect pests in the United States, where these transgenic crops have been released over the past four years.[68] *Bt*-resistance contributed substantially to the problems experienced by the *Bt*-cotton crop in the United States and Australia in 1996–7. Strategies for crisis management had to be adopted, such as supplementary sprays, the creation of non-transgenic 'refugia' to continue breeding non-resistant insect pests, the promise of transgenic plants engineered with multiple toxins, and an intensified search for new toxins.[69] Unfortunately, the resistance trait is highly stable, and also exhibits broad-spectrum cross-resistance to other δ-endotoxins, which undermines many potential options for resistance management.[70]

> This continual warfare with nature has already been shown to
> fail, as losses due to insects are at present estimated at 20 to 30
> per cent when they are being fought with a deadly arsenal of
> chemical pesticides.

These measures betray the short-termism of reductionist, non-ecological thinking. From past experience it can be predicted that newer and more powerful resistances and multiple resistance will be acquired by insect pests. This continual warfare with nature has already been shown to fail, as losses due to insects are at present estimated at 20 to 30 per cent of total production when they are being fought with a deadly arsenal of chemical pesticides. The new generations of transgenic plants with biopesticide genes may be destroying the last stronghold of the ecosystem's ability to readjust and rebalance itself in the face of the assaults of intensive agriculture. The biopesticides have all been isolated from soil bacteria; it does not take much imagination to see that these may play an indispensable role in natural pest control. If, as the result of commercial releases of biopesticide-producing transgenic plants, insect pests develop resistance on a large scale, there will be nothing left for the ecosystem to fall back on. The future of agriculture in such a situation may be among the first of the genetically engineered nightmares.

The hazards from horizontal gene transfer and recombination

The most underestimated hazards of agricultural biotechnology are those from horizontal gene transfers (see chapters 7 and 9). This is the very process that is exploited for creating transgenic organisms. Secondary horizontal transfer from the transgenic plants may spread the novel genes and gene constructs to unrelated species. This can, in principle, occur in all species that interact with the transgenic plants, either directly or indirectly: microbes in the soil and in other parts of the plants, worms, insects, arthropods, birds, small mammals, and human beings. Horizontal gene transfer is the subject of a report commissioned by the Norwegian government from the virologist Terje Traavik.[71]

Existing transgenic plants often contain antibiotic-resistance marker genes. When released into the environment, these genes will spread and exacerbate the present public health crisis in antibiotic-resistant infectious diseases. This consideration was behind the British government's initial rejection of Ciba-Geigy's transgenic maize, which contains the marker gene for ampicillin-resistance,[72] as ampicillin is still in use. Nevertheless, Britain has authorised the marketing of Zeneca's transgenic tomato paste, as well as Calgene's transgenic tomato, both of which carry the marker gene for kanamycin-resistance. Though it is claimed that kanamycin is no longer in use, as it has already been supplanted by new generations of aminoglycoside antibiotics, at least one kanamycin-resistance gene used as a genetic marker has been found to confer cross-resistance to two new-generation aminoglycosides, amikacin and tobramycin.[73]

Several factors make it more likely that the foreign genes that were introduced into the transgenic organisms, rather than the organisms' own genes, will take part in secondary horizontal gene transfer.[74] First, the mechanisms that enable foreign genes to insert into the genome may enable them to jump out again, or to re-insert at another site or to another genome. For example, the enzyme integrase, which catalyses the insertion of viral DNA into host genomes, also functions as a 'disintegrase', catalysing the reverse reaction. These integrases belong to a superfamily of similar interchangeable enzymes present in all genomes, from viruses and bacteria to higher plants and animals.[75] Second, the unnatural gene constructs tend to be unstable and therefore prone to recombine with other genes. Third, the metabolic stress on the host organism caused by the continuous over-expression of the foreign genes may contribute to the instability of the insert. Fourth, the foreign gene constructs and the vectors into which they are spliced are typically mosaics of DNA sequences from many different species and their genetic parasites and therefore more prone to recombine with, and successfully transfer to, the genomes of many species.

There is evidence that a herbicide-tolerance gene introduced into *Arabidopsis* by means of a vector may be up to thirty times more likely to escape and spread than the same gene obtained by induced mutation.[76] One way in which this could happen is by the secondary horizontal transfer of the transgene itself by way of insects visiting the plants for pollen and nectar and carrying it on to infect the next plant.

Spreading genes via the natural microbial populations

The most obvious route for spreading transgenes and marker genes from transgenic higher plants and animals (transgenic fish and shellfish) as well as micro-organisms is by way of the teeming microbial populations. Microbial populations in all environments form large reservoirs supporting the multiplication of the transgenes and marker genes, enabling them to spread to all other species. They also provide an opportunity for the genetic elements to recombine with other viruses and bacteria to generate new genetic elements and pathogenic strains of bacteria and viruses, which will, at the same time, be antibiotic-resistant.

> In the light of the documented propensity for horizontal gene transfer and the potential health hazards involved, it is irresponsible to continue releasing transgenic organisms into the environment.

Secondary horizontal transfers of transgenes and marker genes from transgenic plants to soil bacteria and fungi have been experimentally demonstrated in the laboratory.[77] Transfer between transgenic plants and fungi was achieved simply by cultivating them together.[78] Successful transfers of a kanamycin-resistance marker gene to the soil bacterium *Acinetobacter* were obtained using DNA extracted from homogenised leaf from a range of transgenic plants: potato, tomato, oil-seed rape, sugar beet, and tobacco.[79] It is estimated that about 2,500 copies of the kanamycin-resistance gene (from the same number of plant cells) is enough to successfully transform one bacterium, despite the 6,000,000-fold excess of plant DNA present. A single plant with, say, 2.5 trillion cells would be enough to transform one billion bacteria. In an experiment with transgenic potato, a high 'optimal' gene transfer frequency of 6.2×10^{-2} was observed in the laboratory, from which, using dubious assumptions, an extremely low frequency of 2.0×10^{-17} was 'calculated' under 'natural idealised conditions'.[80] It is impossible to know the precise frequencies for such horizontal gene transfer under natural conditions, as very few actual studies have been carried out. Nor has horizontal gene transfer been monitored in previous field trials or releases until very recently.[81] Transgenic DNA was found to have persisted two years after field release. No horizontal gene transfer was detected in bacterial isolates; however, it must be stressed that present culture methods can isolate at most 1 per cent of the bacteria in the environment.

Many transgenic plants have been made with a vector constructed from the *Agrobacterium tumefaciens* (tumour-inducing) plasmid, which is already known to be able to integrate into plant cell genome (see chapter 9). It is possible for the integrated vector to undergo secondary mobilisation to end up in other plants, either via microbes in the environment or via insect vectors. The same vector system is now found to be effective for carrying genes into mammalian cells and is being developed for human gene therapy.[82] The researchers seem to be completely unaware of the health hazards posed by many transgenic crops that are made with vectors derived from the tumour-inducing plasmid.

The new 'terminator technology' engineers genes to splice in and out of genomes by 'site-specific' recombination.[83] (Splicing means cutting and rejoining the cuts, rather like what one might do with magnetic tape.) Part of the system is an enzyme, recombinase, which cuts and joins DNA at specific sites, which is regulated by an external chemical signal. The other part is a promoter flanked by the specific sites and inserted in front of a second gene, whose expression is to be controlled. When the recombinase is activated by the external chemical signal it cuts out the promoter, thus disabling the second gene. In another version a blocking sequence can be placed between the specific sites so that when removed by the recombinase the gene downstream is unblocked. However, the specificity of the sites recognised by the recombinase may not be precise. There is no guarantee that sites recognised by the recombinase do not exist elsewhere in the genome, or that during the engineering process the sites were not inserted as multiple copies in the genome. These gene constructs, once released, may rapidly spread out of control. Not only will they contribute to creating new pathogens but they may scramble up genes and genomes, including our own, by splicing at inappropriate places.

In the light of the documented propensity for horizontal gene transfer and the many potential health hazards involved, it is irresponsible to continue releasing transgenic organisms into the environment, even as field trials.

Viral-resistance transgenes generate live viruses

An important class of transgenic plants is engineered for resistance to viral diseases by incorporating the gene for the virus's coat protein. Some molecular geneticists have expressed concern that these transgenic crops might generate new diseases, by several known processes. The first, *transcapsidation,* has already been detected. It involves the DNA or RNA of one virus being wrapped up in the coat protein of another, so that viral genes can get into cells that otherwise exclude them. The second possibility is that the transgenic coat protein can help defective viruses multiply by *complementation.* The third possibility, *recombination,* has been demonstrated in an experiment in which *Nicotiana benthamiana* plants, expressing a segment of a cow-pea chlorotic mottle virus (CCMV) gene, were inoculated with a mutant CCMV, missing that gene. The infectious virus was indeed regenerated by recombination.[84] There is now also evidence that transgenic plants increase the frequency of viral recombination, because of the continual expression of the viral coat protein gene.[85] Similar recombination events have been demonstrated in transgenic plants engineered to be resistant to red clover necrotic mosaic virus[86] and cauliflower mosaic virus,[87] in which superinfectious viruses often arise. In one experiment the host range of the recombinant virus was expanded, so that it was able to cause disease in a plant species not susceptible to the original virus.[88]

Viral recombination is well documented in animals, and the resulting recombinant viruses are strongly implicated in causing diseases (see chapter 12). As in animals, plant genomes also contain many endogenous proviruses and related elements that can potentially recombine with the introduced transgene.

Another strategy for viral resistance made use of benign viral 'satellite RNAs' as transgenes, thereby attenuating the symptoms of viral infection. However, transgenes were found to readily mutate to pathogenic forms.[89] These documented pathogenic recombinants and mutants, regenerated from viral-resistant transgenic plants, are particularly significant, as viruses are readily transmitted from one plant to another by many species of aphids and other insects that interact with the plants. There is a distinct possibility of new broad-range recombinant viruses arising, which could cause epidemics.

A potentially serious source of new viruses arising from recombination has been pointed out by the molecular geneticist Joe Cummins.[90] This is the powerful promoter from cauliflower mosaic virus (CaMV), which is routinely used to drive gene expression in transgenic plants. The CaMV is closely related to the human hepatitis B virus and also has sequence homologies to human retroviruses such as the AIDS virus.[91] The CaMV promoter can drive the synthesis of related viruses.[92] It is functional in most plants, in yeast, in insects, and in *Escherichia coli*.[93] Two kinds of potential hazards can be envisaged: the reactivation of dormant viruses, and recombination between the CaMV promoter and other viruses, dormant or otherwise, to generate new super-infectious viruses or viruses with a broadened host range.[94]

Vectors infect mammalian cells and resist breakdown in the gut

Among the important factors to consider in the safety of transgenic organisms used as food are the extent to which DNA, particularly vector DNA, can resist breakdown in the gut and the extent to which it can infect the cells of higher organisms.

Studies made since the nineteen-seventies have documented the ability of bacterial plasmids carrying a mammalian virus to infect cultured mammalian cells, which then proceed to synthesise the virus. Similarly, bacterial viruses or baculovirus can also be taken up by mammalian cells.[95] Baculovirus is so effectively taken up by mammalian cells that it is now being developed as a gene transfer vector in human gene replacement therapy.[96] At the same time, baculovirus is genetically engineered to kill insects more effectively, with genes encoding diuretic hormone, juvenile hormone, *Bt* endotoxin, mite toxins, and scorpion toxin. The recombinant virus is sprayed directly onto crops.[97] A recombinant baculovirus has even been made containing an anti-sense sequence of a human cancer gene, *c-myc*. What happens when humans eat foods containing vectors and viral sequences?

> In experiments with mice, large fragments of viral DNA were found to survive passage through the gut and to enter the bloodstream.

It has long been assumed that our gut is full of enzymes that can rapidly digest DNA. In a study designed to test the survival of viral DNA in the gut, mice were fed DNA from a bacterial virus. Large fragments were found to survive passage through the gut and to enter the bloodstream. The ingested DNA ended up not only in the gut cells but also in leukocytes (white blood cells) and in spleen and liver cells. In some cases as much as one cell in a thousand had viral DNA. There is also evidence that the viral DNA is incorporated in the mouse genome. Similar results were obtained with plasmid DNA.[98] When the viral DNA was fed to pregnant mice it ended up in the cells of the fetus and the newborn.[99]

A group of French geneticists found that certain pathogenic bacteria have acquired the ability to enter mammalian cells directly by inducing their own entry. They found invasive strains of *Shigella flexneri* and *E. coli* that break up on entering the mammalian cells because of an impairment in cell wall synthesis. They developed these strains as gene transfer systems into mammalian cells. This transfer was described as 'efficient, of broad host cell range and the replicative or integrative vectors so delivered are stably inherited and expressed by the cell progeny.'[100] Once again the researchers are completely unable to recognise the tremendous health risks involved in developing such a vector. These cross-kingdom transfer vectors are extremely hazardous, as are transgenic vaccines constructed in plants and plant viruses, which are chimeras of animal viral genes inserted into plant viruses. These will have an increased propensity to invade cells, recombine with endogenous viruses and proviruses, or insert themselves into the cell's genome (see chapter 12).

Within the gut, vectors carrying antibiotic-resistance markers may also be taken up by the gut bacteria, which would then serve as a mobile reservoir of antibiotic-resistance genes for pathogenic bacteria. Horizontal gene transfer between gut bacteria has already been demonstrated in mice and domestic fowl and in human beings (see chapter 9).

In the light of all this evidence one would be foolish to eat transgenic foods, as the manipulated DNA may resist digestion. It may be taken up by gut bacteria as well as by gut cells and, through the gut, into the bloodstream and other cells. The uptake of the manipulated DNA into cells can lead to the regeneration of viruses. If the DNA integrates into the cell's genome, a range of harmful effects can result, including cancer. Moreover, one cannot assume, without adequate data, that DNA is automatically degraded in processed transgenic foods, such as Zeneca's tomato paste, and the many foods containing processed transgenic soybean or maize. A scientific report commissioned by UK MAFF indicates that plant DNA is not readily degraded during most commercial processing.[101] The public are already being experimented on, without informed consent. This is surely against the European Bioethics Convention, as well as the Universal Convention on Human Rights. There is a strong case for a moratorium, at the very least, and for all transgenic foods containing DNA to be withdrawn from the market.

Check-list of hazards from agricultural biotechnology

As a summary of this somewhat complex chapter, I shall reiterate the arguments about why agricultural biotechnology does not feed the world, is unsustainable, and poses unique hazards to health and biodiversity.

Socio-economic impacts

(1) The increased drain of genetic resources from South to North.
(2) The increased marginalisation of family farmers caused by intellectual property rights and other restrictive practices associated with seed certification and by the intensified corporate control of food production and distribution.
(3) The replacement of traditional technologies and produce.
(4) The inherent genetic instability of transgenic lines, resulting in crop failures.
(5) The diverting of resources and efforts from organic sustainable agriculture, which can improve yields and regenerate degraded land.

Hazards to human and animal health

(1) Toxic or allergenic effects caused by transgene products arising from interactions with host genes and genomes.
(2) The increased use of toxic pesticides with pesticide-resistant transgenic crops, leading to pesticide-related illnesses in farm workers and the contamination of food and drinking-water.
(3) The spread of antibiotic-resistance marker genes to gut bacteria and to pathogens by horizontal gene transfer.
(4) The spread of virulence among pathogens between species by horizontal gene transfer and recombination.
(5) The potential for horizontal gene transfer and recombination to create new pathogenic bacteria and viruses.
(6) The potential for transgenic DNA to infect cells after the ingestion of transgenic foods, to regenerate disease viruses, and to insert itself into the cell's genome, causing harmful or lethal effects, including cancer.

Hazards to agricultural and natural biodiversity

(1) The spread of transgenes and gene constructs to related weed species by cross-pollination, creating superweeds (for example herbicide-resistance).

(2)   An increase in the indiscriminate use of broad-spectrum herbicides with herbicide-resistant transgenic plants, leading to the large-scale elimination of indigenous agricultural and natural species.

(3)   An increase in the use of other herbicides to control herbicide-resistant 'volunteers', further affecting indigenous biodiversity.

(4)   An increase in the use of toxic herbicides, destroying soil fertility and decreasing yield.

(5)   Acceleration of the evolution of biopesticide-resistance in major insect pests, resulting in the loss of a biopesticide used by organic farmers for years.

(6)   The harm to beneficial insect species.

(7)   The increased exploitation of natural biopesticides in transgenic plants, leading to a corresponding range of resistant insects, depriving the ecosystem of its natural pest controls and the ability to rebalance itself to recover from perturbation.

(8)   The horizontal transfer of transgenes and marker genes to unrelated species via bacteria and viruses, with the potential to create many other weed species.

(9)   The increased potential to generate new virulent strains of viruses, especially in transgenic plants engineered for viral-resistance with viral genes.

(10) The fact that transgenic DNA, unlike chemical pollution, can be perpetuated and amplified, given the right environmental conditions, and as a result the potential to unleash cross-species epidemics of infectious plant and animal diseases that will be impossible to control or recall.

Conclusion

The report of the World Bank for the 1996 Food Summit advocated sustained support for research to develop new plants and technologies, but it also called for 'whole new ways' of dealing with the problem of the present food crisis, one of which was concentrating on helping small farmers. A later report, however, recommends transgenic crops for the Third World.[102]

In this chapter I have presented the reasons why transgenic crops cannot alleviate the food crisis. *On the contrary, they are inherently unsustainable, and extremely hazardous to biodiversity and to human and animal health.* A sharp change of direction is required, aimed at supporting conservation and sustainable agriculture and restoring indigenous agricultural biodiversity. That would both satisfy the stated aims of the Convention on Biological Diversity and guarantee long-term food security for all.

Nine

THE IMMORTAL MICROBE AND PROMISCUOUS GENES

Drug-resistant and antibiotic-resistant infectious diseases account for a third of the 52 million deaths from all causes in the world. They have been increasing dramatically over the past twenty years, coinciding with the development of commercial genetic-engineering biotechnology. The evidence is overwhelming that horizontal gene transfer across species barriers is responsible for creating new viral and bacterial pathogens and for spreading drug-resistance and antibiotic-resistance. Genetic engineering is inherently hazardous, because it depends precisely on designing artificial vectors to cross all species barriers, greatly increasing the potential for generating new viral and bacterial pathogens by horizontal gene transfer and recombination. This very danger persuaded the first genetic engineers to declare a moratorium on their own work in 1975; but pressures to go ahead with commercial exploitation led to regulatory guidelines that were drawn up largely on the basis of assumptions. Every one of those assumptions has since been invalidated by scientific findings. We may already be experiencing the prelude to a nightmare of uncontrollable, untreatable epidemics of infectious diseases. We must call a halt now; there is no time to lose.

The world health crisis

The world is facing a public health crisis. At least thirty new diseases, such as AIDS, several kinds of hepatitis and various other deadly viruses, have emerged over the past twenty years, while new variants of old infectious diseases, such as TB, cholera, malaria and diphtheria, are coming back. Practically all the diseases are resistant to treatment, many to multiple drugs and antibiotics. A third of the 52 million deaths from all causes in the world in 1995 were due to drug-resistant and antibiotic-resistant infectious diseases. The biggest killers were TB (3.1 million), malaria (2.1 million), hepatitis B (1.1 million), and AIDS (more than 1 million).[1]

'The optimism of a relatively few years ago that many of these diseases could easily be brought under control has led to a fatal complacency among the international community,' according to the director-general of the World Health Organisation, Dr Hiroshi Nakajima. Since the WHO report of 1996, the situation has become considerably worse. Strains of four dangerous bacteria, including that associated with TB, are now resistant to treatment by all antibiotics.[2] No-one knows for certain why infectious diseases have staged such a dramatic return since the late nineteen-seventies. Many causes have been suggested, including population growth and increasing urbanisation, destruction of the environment, deterioration of living conditions, increase in international travel, wars and natural disasters, and most of all the overuse and abuse of antibiotics in intensive farming and medicine. One factor that has not been considered is genetic-engineering bio-technology; and that is what I propose to do in this chapter.

Microbes as friend and foe

To understand why genetic-engineering biotechnology is so inherently hazardous we have to appreciate the prodigious power of microbes to proliferate, and the protean promiscuity of the genes they carry, which have the ability to jump, to spread, to mutate and recombine.

Microbes are ubiquitous. They live in abundance in the soil, in the terrestrial and aquatic environments, in the air we breathe, on our skin and in our bodies. Most of the time they have a benign, balanced relationship with us, so that they do us no harm and, in many cases, a lot of good. Jim Lovelock and Lynn Margulis, proponents of the Gaia hypothesis—the idea that the entire earth is a self-regulating system—show how different microbes are essential participants in the regulatory mechanisms that maintain conditions on earth congenial for all life forms.[3] It is well known that microorganisms in the soil are indispensable for recycling nutrients for the growth of crop plants, and that bacteria in the gut of a healthy person can provide vitamins and co-factors and aid digestion. Humans indeed have used microbes for centuries, to make beer and wine, bread, yoghurt, cheese, sausages, miso, soy sauce and many other products, without experiencing harm. However, when that balanced ecology is disturbed, bacteria can turn virulent and cause debilitating or lethal diseases. And when we wage war on them with a succession of increasingly potent drugs and antibiotics, they counter with ever more complex drug-resistance and antibiotic-resistance.

While mammalian cells, like our own, typically take a day or more to double in number, most bacteria take only minutes. A millilitre of tightly packed *Escherichia coli* contains a trillion cells, enough to infect the entire population of the world. A single bacterium will require only forty doublings, or less than a day, to multiply to that number when conditions are right. On the other hand, it can persist indefinitely either as a metabolically inactive form or in a metabolically active but non-proliferating state, during which it will continue to mutate its genes and to acquire new genes, so that, given the right opportunity, it will once again proliferate. Microbes, to all intents and purposes, are immortal.

> The problem we face is that commercial-scale genetic engineering, together with the profligate use of antibiotics in intensive farming and medical practice, is creating just the sort of conditions for microbes to do the greatest harm.

The genes these microbes carry have an even more tenacious hold on life. They have a greater propensity to multiply and to spread promiscuously to different microbes as well as to 'higher organisms', giving them the opportunity to mutate and recombine into new variants, to fully realise their protean potential, to do great harm or not, in response to different ecological conditions.

The problem we face is that commercial-scale genetic engineering, together with the profligate use of antibiotics in intensive farming and medical practice, is creating just the sort of conditions for microbes to do the greatest harm.

Antibiotic-resistance: from boom to bust

Antibiotics were introduced in the nineteen-forties for treating microbial infections. Microbial geneticists in those days did not foresee the rapidity with which antibiotic-resistance would evolve, based on the very low spontaneous mutation rates observed.[4] Antibiotics came to be widely used to control infectious diseases, with stunning success. But the euphoria was short-lived, as microbes soon developed resistance to antibiotics. By the early eighties fewer than 10 per cent of all cases of *Staphylococcus* infection responded to treatment with penicillin, compared with almost 100 per cent in 1952. Resistance to antibiotics has become widespread, with new resistances arising as soon as novel antibiotics come into use; and outbreaks of resistant bacteria are now commonplace in hospitals. By 1990 nearly all common pathogenic bacterial species had developed varying degrees of antibiotic-resistance.

Multi-antibiotic-resistance has also emerged. An Australian research team treated a patient infected with a strain of *Staphylococcus* that was resistant to thirty-one drugs, including cadmium, penicillin, kanamycin, neomycin, streptomycin, tetracycline, and trimethyloprim.[5] In a series of investigations they showed that the various resistance capabilities were due to genes carried on different plasmids that could be separately passed on from one bacterium to another.

Soon after antibiotics were introduced in medicine it was discovered that livestock lived longer and grew faster when they were fed antibiotics to overcome infections. Antibiotics were therefore routinely fed to domestic fowl, cattle, pigs, and dairy cows, which also extended the shelf life of meat, poultry, eggs, and dairy products. In the nineteen-seventies it was discovered that giving domestic fowl high doses of antibiotics resulted in the appearance of resistant *Salmonella* strains in both the meat and the eggs. In 1983 mutant strains of antibiotic-resistant *Salmonella* that attacked human beings emerged.[6]

One of the clearest and most disturbing examples of mutant bacteria crossing from domestic animals to human beings, and of the transformation of a previously benign strain into a pathogen, is *Escherichia coli,* a common bacterium inhabiting the intestine of all human beings and other mammalian species. Most of the time *E. coli* is harmless, which is why it is the darling of genetic engineers, who have routinely used it and its plasmids since the seventies to clone genes. *E. coli* is the most manipulated organism, and genes from species in practically every kingdom have been transferred to and cloned in it. Perhaps it is not surprising that *E. coli* has emerged as a major pathogen.

In 1982 a new strain, *E. coli* O157:H7, appeared, which, far from being benign, caused dangerous haemorrhages of the colon, bowel and kidneys in human beings. It broke out suddenly in several regions in the Unites States.[7] Like most *E. coli* strains in the eighties, it was moderately resistant to the antibiotics ampicillin and tetracycline. Since then there have been many outbreaks all over the world, and with increasing frequency. A mass outbreak in Japan in 1996 affected nine thousand people, with twelve deaths in children, and a further outbreak occurred in 1997. In Scotland a series of outbreaks in 1997 killed twenty people and made hundreds ill.[8]

'DNA fingerprinting' (see chapter 11) supports the epidemiological evidence that *E. coli* O157:H7 arose recently and, up to 1993, was restricted to cattle in the United States, Canada and Britain but absent in cattle in eastern Asia.[9] *E. coli* mutates fairly rapidly; therefore, the low degree of genetic variation observed among the O157:H7 isolates up to 1993 suggests that they originated from a single clone, which may since have spread to Japan. Most cases came from contaminated meat, but outbreaks have also been associated with cheese, salami, raw vegetables, unpasteurised apple juice, and water.[10] *E. coli* O157, like other water-borne pathogens, such as *Crytosporidium, Giardia,* and *Shigella,* had developed resistance to chlorine.[11] The mass outbreaks in Japan were linked to white radishes, which most probably came from contaminated soil. The specific toxicity of the strain is attributed to the Shiga-like toxin genes acquired by horizontal gene transfer from *Shigella*.[12] One of these genes, *VT1,* is almost identical in base sequence to that of *Shigella,* indicating that the gene transfer was a very recent event.

> Strains of four dangerous bacteria, including the one causing TB, are already invulnerable to all known antibiotics.

Studies of dozens of emergent species showed that genes for antibiotic-resistance and virulence often reside in the same regions of the bacterial DNA. *E. coli* strains were rapidly acquiring broad ranges of antibiotic-resistance during the nineteen-seventies and eighties. By the nineties, 'superstrains' resistant to multiple anti-biotics were isolated. Two strains of *E. coli* appeared in a hospital transplant ward outside Cambridge that were resistant to an astonishing range of antibiotics.[13] Only one commonly used anti-biotic, amikacin, remained effective; if the strains ever become resistant to that drug, they will be completely invulnerable to treatment by antibiotics.

Up to May 1998, strains of four dangerous bacteria, including *Staphylococcus aureus* (toxic shock syndrome), *Enterococcus faecalis* (blood poisoning and infection of wounds), *Pseudomonas aeruginosa* (blood poisoning and pneumonia) and *Mycobacterium tuberculosis* (TB), have become invulnerable to all known antibiotics.[14]

> A profusion of biochemical mechanisms and genes is involved in antibiotic-resistance, fully matching, if not surpassing, the variety of targets at which antibiotics are aimed.

A profusion of mechanisms and genes

A profusion of biochemical mechanisms and genes is involved in antibiotic-resistance, fully matching, if not surpassing, the variety of targets at which antibiotics are aimed.[15] Most antibiotics have a single primary target—usually a single step in the synthesis of constituents essential to the bacterial cell—and preferably do not affect the infected host cells. Several classes of antibiotics are therefore aimed at the synthesis of the bacterial cell wall. Other classes of antibiotics are aimed at the synthesis of DNA, RNA, and proteins, which differ from their eukaryotic counterparts—though their effects may not always be so selective—and are therefore toxic to varying degrees. Translation is targeted by a wide variety of antibiotics. In addition, anti-metabolites inhibit the synthesis of essential metabolites in the bacterium.

Resistance to every class of antibiotics has been found. One of the commonest mechanisms is the degradation or modification of the antibiotic by specific enzymes. The β-lactams, for example, which inhibit cell-wall synthesis, are degraded by lactamases, all of which have arisen from one ancestral gene. On the other hand, aminoglycosides, which inhibit translation, are inactivated by specific modifying enzymes encoded by at least thirty different genes; while chloramphenicol, also inhibiting translation, is in-activated by many acetyltransferases encoded by at least a dozen genes.

Mutation of an antibiotic's specific target is also frequently involved in resistance. Streptomycin is overcome in *Mycobacterium* by mutations in the ribosomal RNA (rRNA) molecules required for protein synthesis, so that they have reduced affinity for strepto-mycin. Antibiotics may be inactivated by binding permanently to specific proteins. A metabolic bypass may appear to be a reaction inhibited by the antibiotic, or the inhibited protein may simply be overproduced by the bacteria in order to overcome the inhibition.

Apart from those mechanisms that are specific to each antibiotic or chemical class of antibiotics, broad-range resistances are achieved by setting up permeability barriers to antibiotics entering the cell or, more importantly, by increased rates of pumping them out of the cell. More than twenty different genes in four gene families have been identified in the latter category. They code for proteins that penetrate the cell membranes as molecular pumps, which transport substances out of the cell, using ATP or protons as sources of energy. Many efflux pumps confer multi-drug-resistance, as they recognise a broad range of unrelated chemical substances. Quite often several mechanisms are involved in giving protection against a single antibiotic, resulting in a very high level of resistance. Cross-resistances are also common within a class of antibiotics such as the aminoglycosides (see chapter 8).

Where do the genes conferring antibiotic-resistance come from? And how do they manage to spread so quickly? Let us first consider the question of the origin of the genes.

The origins of antibiotic-resistance genes

There are several sources of antibiotic-resistance genes. The first is organisms producing the natural antibiotics, such as penicillin, which also produce the inactivating enzyme. As new β-lactams are introduced, the gene coding for the β-lactamase undergoes mutational changes, often involving only one base substitution, leading to a single amino acid difference in the enzyme, which would be enough to enable the enzyme to recognise the new drug and to break it down. In this way the enzyme readily extends its ability to inactivate new drugs.

Numerous mutational variants of β-lactamase have been identified, showing the ease with which appropriate mutational changes can arise in this gene. The variants derive from different genes, all of which can be traced to a single ancestral gene. The β-lactamase gene is so versatile that when a series of inhibitors is made against the enzyme and used in combination with the β-lactam antibiotic—a 'belt and braces' approach—mutant enzymes arise that not only break down the new antibiotic but are also insensitive to the inhibitor.

More often, however, it is not at all clear where the antibiotic-resistance genes come from. New genes seem to appear from nowhere. The many genes involved in resistance to different aminoglycosides are not related to one another. Some are thought to have arisen from mutations of existing genes coding for enzymes that catalyse normal metabolic reactions in the cell. Others may involve the activation of previously 'cryptic' or hidden genes in the bacterial genome; or they may have been acquired by gene transfer from another bacterium. The molecular efflux pumps associated with multi-drug-resistance in *E. coli* are believed to have originated from *operons* (multigene units under the control of a regulator gene) in free-living bacteria that enable the latter to respond to noxious substances in the environment by synthesising enzymes to break those substances down.

Before we go on to consider gene transfer in the spread of antibiotic-resistance, I shall deal with the supposed natural selection of random mutations in the origin of antibiotic-resistance genes.

The irrelevance of 'random' mutations

To measure the rate of 'spontaneous' mutations to antibiotic-resistance in a strain of bacteria, a small amount of a dilute suspension of the bacteria is spread on a nutrient agar-plate. The agar-plate has been impregnated with antibiotic at a concentration high enough to kill non-resistant bacteria, so that only those with an existing mutation that happens to confer resistance will survive and form colonies. A colony appears as a round greyish-white spot on the agar plate, formed by the growth and multiplication of one original resistant bacterium.

> The evolution of antibiotic-resistance is paradigmatic of the fluid genome that bacteria share with all organisms. Bacteria may specifically increase the mutation rates in those genes that will eventually give them resistance against the antibiotic (or antibiotics). In addition, because bacteria are potentially so good at exchanging genes, their fluid genomes are becoming rapidly delocalised. Parts of them have semi-autonomous or auto-nomous existence and can travel between species that do not interbreed; in the process, they recombine and further mutate.

The spontaneous mutation rate for antibiotic-resistance estimated in this way is typically 10^{-9} or less, and is about the same for all other genes in the genome. This is the rate of random mutations—in other words, mutations that have no direct correlation with the environment, or the selective regime. Based on these estimates, the early microbiologists did not believe that resistance to antibiotics would pose a problem when antibiotics first came into use. So why did antibiotic-resistance evolve and spread so rapidly?

The neo-Darwinian explanation is that it is because of the intense 'selective pressures' exerted by the antibiotics, so that even extremely low rates of 'spontaneous' random mutations that happen to confer resistance on the antibiotic will be rapidly selected for, while those that do not happen to have the mutation will die out. This account is so far from the truth that I am appalled to read how many staunch neo-Darwinists are still at pains to defend it.

The evolution of antibiotic-resistance is paradigmatic of the fluid genome that bacteria share with all organisms. Bacteria may specifically increase the mutation rates in those genes that will eventually give them resistance against the antibiotic (or antibiotics). In addition, because bacteria are potentially so good at exchanging genes, their fluid genomes are also rapidly becoming delocalised. Bacterial genomes mutate, expand, contract, and rearrange. Parts of them have semi-autonomous or autonomous existence and can travel between species that do not interbreed; in the process, they recombine and further mutate.

Though bacteria will be killed by high enough concentrations of antiseptics or antibiotics to which they are susceptible, at lower concentrations of the noxious agent a bacterium may fail to grow at first but after some time will develop the required resistance to the drug and so can grow, multiply, and form colonies. This ability to develop drug-resistance (described in chapter 7) is common to cells of all species—bacteria, fungi, plants, and animals—without exception. It is a physiological response shared by all the cells or organisms of the population and is not a result of the selection of existing random mutations. To insist on interpreting them in this way is simply a desperate attempt to salvage the neo-Darwinian dogma that continues to serve the existing orthodoxy, as well as biotech interests.

During a discussion on one of the papers presented at a conference on antibiotic-resistance, precisely this question was raised: whether antibiotic-resistance in bacteria is related to multi-drug-resistance, which regularly arises in cancer cells during chemotherapy. The answer, provided by S. B. Levy of Tufts University School of Medicine, Massachusetts, was as follows:

> We have described an analogous multi-drug-resistance system in *E. coli*. Chromosome-mediated multi-resistance emerges upon the use of a single drug, tetracycline or chloramphenicol. The mechanisms of resistance to the different antibiotics are very different. A similar phenomenon has been described among parasites. One must distinguish between extrachromosomal-resistance elements, e.g. plasmids and transposons, and chromosomal adaptations to environmental stress. Mammalian cancer cells, bacteria and parasites all seem to be able to respond to toxic external agents by turning on cryptic chromosomal genes that aid their survival.[16]

Levy was distinguishing between mechanisms that turn on cryptic chromosomal genes and genes acquired by horizontal gene transfer through extrachromosomal elements or plasmids. We shall see later that this distinction is no longer useful, as genes can move easily between chromosomes and plasmids.

> Horizontal gene transfer has emerged as a major mechanism for the spread of antibiotic-resistance.

Horizontal gene transfer: the genetic melt-down

The other main reason why neo-Darwinism got it wrong is that competition is irrelevant among bacteria; they share their most valuable assets for survival: genes coding for resistance mechanisms against antibiotics. Horizontal gene transfer has emerged as a major mechanism for the spread of antibiotic-resistance only since the late nineteen-eighties, when a Conference on Antibiotic Resistance was jointly sponsored by the US Environmental Protection Agency and the National Science Foundation to look into the possible mechanisms and factors affecting such gene transfer.[17] The first definitive evidence for horizontal gene transfer came from DNA sequence analysis of the genes for neomycin-kanamycin-resistance from *Staphylococcus aureus, Streptococci,* and *Campylobacter* sp., which were found to be essentially identical.[18] Identity of gene sequence not only gives evidence for horizontal gene transfer but also indicates that the transfer is a very recent event. Further evidence of horizontal gene transfer, by DNA sequencing or other methods of characterising DNA, were later obtained for many other antibiotic-resistances.[19]

The scope of horizontal gene transfer

The scope of horizontal gene transfer is essentially the entire biosphere.[20] Genes are found to have been transferred not only among micro-organisms and viruses but among eukaryote species and between traditional kingdoms of organisms. Among eukaryotes the main transfers have involved transposable elements such as the P element among Drosophilids (the group of insects to which fruit flies belong) and transposable introns (non-coding segments of genes) among lower eukaryotes and bacteria. Some especially promiscuous elements, such as *mariner*, have been found in arthropods and vertebrates, including primates and humans, where it is associated with a neurological wasting disease. Gene transfer mediated by transposable elements does not require DNA base sequence homologies or similarities.

Transfers have occurred from bacteria to higher plants, and vice versa. The best-known example is the direct demonstration of transfer between the soil bacterium *Agrobacterium* and plants. In a process bearing a strong resemblance to conjugation between bacteria, the tumour (*T*) segment of the tumour-inducing (*Ti*) bacterial plasmid is transferred and incorporated in the plant genome. However, it must be noted that nearly all cases of directly demonstrated horizontal gene transfer, especially those involving phylogenetically distant species, made use of artificially constructed hybrid shuttle vectors, which can transfer between distant species and replicate in both. These shuttle vectors possess signals for replication (*origins of replication*) in more than one species as well as the signal for DNA transfer (*origin of transfer*) and are therefore much more likely to be successful in horizontal transfer than unmodified plasmids found naturally. The *Ti* plasmid is indeed the basis of a gene transfer vector system widely used for genetically engineering crop plants (see chapter 8).

> Bacteria can transfer DNA to animal cells by conjugation, or direct injection.

Cross-kingdom horizontal gene transfer by conjugation has also been demonstrated between bacteria and yeast, using shuttle vectors derived from promiscuous plasmids with a broad host range, which are already transferable between many bacterial species. Such vectors can even substitute for the *Ti* plasmid in transferring genes from *Agrobacterium* to plants. The direct transfer of transgenes and marker genes from transgenic plants to soil fungi and soil bacteria has been documented in the laboratory (see chapter 8), indicating that secondary, unintended gene transfers can occur from genetically engineered crop plants that are now released commercially into the environment. Debris and exudates from transgenic plants will therefore be expected to transform bacteria and other micro-organisms in the soil. *E. coli* cells have been successfully transformed in the laboratory by T-DNA transferred to a transgenic plant; and the *T*-DNA vector was recovered as a circular plasmid in the transformed cells.[21] In addition, other vectors, such as viruses, insects and nematodes, can also mediate unintended, secondary horizontal gene transfer.

Mammalian cells are known to take up foreign genes by a number of mechanisms (see chapter 8). Gene transfer from bacteria to animal cells can even occur by *conjugation,* a mating process previously thought to be confined to bacteria, in which a bacterium directly injects DNA into the animal cell. This has been demonstrated with artificially constructed shuttle vectors.[22] The ability of retroviruses to capture and transfer genes among mammalian cells is well known and is associated with many animal cancers.[23] Numerous 'illegitimate' genetic recombinations, that is, those requiring no sequence homologies, are a result of retroviral insertion into the genome, thereby transferring genes horizontally between individuals of the same or different species. In short, a given gene from any organism has the potential to spread to all other organisms in the biosphere.

However, DNA uptake by itself is *not* sufficient for successful gene transfer. *After* the uptake of foreign DNA, important barriers operate that break down or otherwise block the integration, use and maintenance of the foreign genes. Plasmid DNA requires an origin of replication that is recognised and used by the host cell before it can be replicated and maintained. Similarly, promoter sequences that can be recognised by the host are necessary for expressing the viral genes that make the virus, as well as expressing any other foreign genes carried by the virus. (Though of course origin of replication and promoter sequences can be acquired by recombination.) However, small pieces of DNA coding for domains or parts of proteins, or short regulatory sequences that bind transcription factors or otherwise increase or repress gene expression, may also be integrated. And these may have significant genetic effects, including cancer.

> Genetic engineering may have created new avenues and possibilities for increasing the scope and frequency of horizontal gene transfer.

Though the host cell DNA has its own origins of replication, methylation patterns (chemical markers) and promoter sequences that are specific to its species, artificial gene transfer vectors and other manipulated DNA have recombined origins of replication and promoter sequences from different species, which can be recognised by a variety of host species. The cauliflower mosaic viral promoter that is used in practically all transgenic plants is active in many species, and raises special safety concerns (see chapter 8). In addition, vectors are designed to overcome the restriction systems that break down and 'silence' foreign DNA. *Genetic engineering may therefore have created new avenues for increasing the scope and frequency of horizontal gene transfer.*

Mechanisms for horizontal gene transfer

There are three mechanisms for gene transfer in bacteria: by direct uptake of DNA (*transformation*), through genes being carried by viruses that infect bacterial cells (*transduction*), and through a mating process requiring cell-to-cell contact (*conjugation*). These processes have been studied most extensively in *E. coli*, though it is becoming clear that what is true for *E. coli* does not necessarily apply to other species. The extent of our ignorance is enormous, but enough is already known to give serious cause for concern.

Transformation frequencies are high

Transformation among microbial populations in the environment has been extensively reviewed recently,[24] showing that it is extremely widespread. DNA is released into the environment; it then binds to the surface of bacteria, enters the cell, and recombines with the bacterial chromosome, or, in the case of plasmids, it becomes reconstituted. All these processes are facilitated by bacterial proteins. Both chromosomal and plasmid DNA are able to transform bacteria, the frequency of transformation varying with the physiological state of the cell, the presence of salts, and the participation of diffusible factors excreted from the bacteria. The nature of the DNA, its source, size and state, may also be important. Generally, transformation is most frequent within the same species, as its successful integration into the recipient genome depends on the degree of homology (similarity in base sequence) between the transforming DNA and the host DNA. It also depends on the DNA being resistant to the restriction enzymes in the host cell that break down foreign DNA. However, homology is not necessary for successful transformation to occur.

Cross-species, cross-genus and even cross-order transfers have been observed with chromosomal DNA; and plasmid DNA in particular has effected cross-kingdom transformations among Eubacteria, Proteobacteria, and Cyanobacteria.

> DNA released into the environment can survive indefinitely and maintain its potential to transform other species.

DNA is not released into the environment only from dead cells: it is actively excreted by living cells during growth. Some species export DNA wrapped in membrane-derived vesicles. The DNA in a culture slime can be more than 40 per cent of the dry weight. The environment is therefore extremely rich in DNA. Sea water contains between 0.2 and 44 μg per litre; fresh water contains between 0.5 and 7.8 μg per litre; fresh-water sediment has a high concentration of 1 μg per gram. Though enzymes breaking down DNA (*deoxyribonucleases* or *DNases*) are found in the environment, DNA is protected from degradation by sticking to detritus, humic acid, and, in particular, clay and sand particles; and such DNA is equally efficient in transforming cells. The half-life of DNA in soil is 9.1 hours for loamy sand soil, 15.1 hours for silty clay soil, and 28.2 hours for clay soil. While half-life in waste water is typically less than an hour, that in fresh water and sea water is 3 to 5 hours, with a maximum of 45 to 83 hours on the surface of the sea and extremely high values of 140 and 235 hours for the marine sediment. (The half-life is the time it takes for half the DNA to degrade; it does *not* mean half the time for all the DNA to disappear, which is far longer, as the rate of decay slows down exponentially.)

The adsorption of DNA to solid particles is a very rapid process, which means that DNA released into the environment can survive indefinitely and can maintain its potential to transform other species. Transformation may be a major route of horizontal gene transfer: frequencies obtained under different environmental conditions, using artificial vectors, are found to be generally quite high, ranging between 10^{-2} and 10^{-5} per recipient cell. A special form of bidirectional transformation by cell contact and fusion is now known to be widespread.

Transduction is substantial in aquatic environments

Transduction takes place by means of bacteriophages (viruses that infect bacteria). They consist of viral DNA wrapped in a protein coat that binds to specific receptor sites on the bacteria. Once bound to the receptor sites, the bacteriophage injects its DNA into the bacterium, where either it directs the synthesis of yet more bacteriophages that lyse (break open) the cell, or the phage DNA may insert itself into the bacterial chromosome. The bacteriophage can transfer genes by mispackaging a piece of bacterial DNA in the viral protein coat, or by packaging viral DNA that had a piece of bacterial DNA spliced into it. When the virus infects a second cell, the bacterial DNA is transferred and may then become integrated into the new bacterial chromosome.

Though transduction is normally limited by the host range, it may be a vehicle for transposable elements to establish themselves in an otherwise unrelated host and so contribute to cross-species or cross-genus gene transfer. Also, bacteriophages themselves evolve by horizontal gene transfer and recombination, leading to broadening of their host ranges.[25] As many as 10^8 to 10^{11} bacteriophages per millilitre have been found in aquatic environments,[26] so that a third of the total bacterial populations is attacked up to two thousand times every twenty-four hours, each attack being capable of transducing genes from another species.

Conjugation is promiscuous

Conjugation—mating between bacteria—was previously thought to be a species-specific process requiring complex complementary interactions between the genetic 'donor' and the genetic 'recipient'. Conjugation depends on certain conjugative plasmids, extrachromosomal pieces of DNA replicated independently of the chromosome, which carry genes required for the process of conjugation. These plasmids fall into different incompatibility groups, which define mating relationships. A review in 1993 lists seven or more *incompatibility groups* of over a hundred known plasmids, *most of them carrying one or more antibiotic-resistance genes.*[27] Several incompatibility groups of plasmids are 'promiscuous', in that they have a very broad host range.

Conjugative plasmids can integrate themselves into the bacterial chromosome. In such cases conjugation will take place, and the integrated plasmid will also drag the bacterial chromosome with it across the 'conjugation tube' from donor to recipient, leading to the transfer of bacterial DNA as well as plasmid DNA. Donor DNA will then recombine with recipient DNA to generate new genetic recombinations. The DNA is thought to be passed in a single-stranded form, which is resistant to breakdown by enzymes attacking double-stranded DNA (such as nucleases and restriction enzymes), thus ensuring a high success rate of gene transfer. The single-stranded DNA then directs the synthesis of the complementary strand to restore double-stranded DNA in both donor and recipient.

Recent studies suggest that conjugation has an extraordinarily wide host range, involving diverse, complex mechanisms that are not yet well understood.[28] The 'promiscuous' plasmids overcome species barriers, effecting horizontal gene transfer between unrelated species. In addition, conjugative transposons (mobile genetic elements) mediate their own transfer to recipient cells during conjugation and insert into the recipient chromosome. They can also jump from one site to another on the same chromosome, or from chromosome into plasmids, and vice versa.[29]

There could be very few barriers remaining to horizontal gene transfer. Antibiotic-resistance genes, especially those carried on plasmids and transposons, can, in principle, cross species as well as genera and even kingdoms.

A special class of such conjugative transposons are the 'integrons',[30] which support the site-specific integration of antibiotic-resistant gene 'cassettes' within the integron, so that each cassette is then provided with ready-made promoters for expression. Each integron can carry several cassettes, with different antibiotic-resistances. It can facilitate recombination between different cassettes to form exotic gene fusions that code for multi-functional proteins. Integrons can also jump from the bacterial chromosome into a plasmid and become transferred to another bacterium during conjugation. Genetic material during conjugation goes not only from donor to recipient but also in the other direction. Such *retrotransfers* of genetic material have only been discovered recently.

The result is that there could be very few barriers remaining to horizontal gene transfer. Antibiotic-resistance genes, especially those carried on plasmids and transposons, can, in principle, cross species as well as genera and even kingdoms, as we shall see.

Tetracycline-resistant genes are now found to be shared between many genera. One of them, the *TetL* gene, is found in *Actinomyces, Clostridium, Enterococcus, Listeria, Peptostrepto-coccus, Streptococcus, Staphylococcus,* and *Bacillus*. Another gene, the *TetK,* is found in *Bacillus, Clostridium, Enterococcus, Eubacterium, Listeria, Peptostreptococcus, Staphylococcus,* and *Streptococcus.*[31] More recently, both these genes have been found for the first time in soil species belonging to the genera *Mycobacterium* and *Streptomyces,* which can cause soft-tissue and skin infections.[32] Antibiotic-producing *Streptomyces* are believed to be the ancestral source of many aminoglycoside antibiotic-resistance genes, and the bacteria are now regaining more of these genes from other species. These findings are of particular significance, as they 'suggest the potential for the spread of an antibiotic-resistance gene into all environmental mycobacteria, including *Mycobacterium leprae.*[33] This will make leprosy very difficult to treat.

Even genes in the chromosome, such as those coding for penicillin-resistance (penicillin-binding proteins, *pbps,* required for the uptake of penicillin), are readily transferred. Transfers of pbp genes were found between *Streptococcus pneumoniae* and *Neisseria gonorrhoeae*. These later recombined to generate new hybrid genes.[34]

The acquisition of virulence

The very same genetic mechanisms for horizontal gene transfer have been shown to be involved in the emergence of virulence among old and new pathogens since the mid-eighties. For example, there has been an increase in sporadic cases of very severe invasive *Streptococcus pyogenes* infections in Europe, North America, and elsewhere. In an analysis of 108 isolates from patients in the United States with streptococcal toxic shock syndrome,[35] a toxin is frequently found encoded by a gene, *SpeA,* belonging to a bacteriophage that has become inserted into the bacterial genome. This gene was spread horizontally among divergent strains of *S. pyogenes.* Similar findings were produced by the analysis of group A *Streptococci* isolated from a cluster of cases of serious infections over a three-month period in Tayside, Scotland, in 1993.[36] DNA sequence analysis of virulence factors suggests that they may have been recently acquired by horizontal gene transfer.

In the past, only *Vibrio cholerae* strains of the type O1 were known to cause epidemics, while non-O1 strains were associated with sporadic cases. But a recent epidemic in Asia was caused by a non-O1 strain, *Vibrio cholerae* O139. It turns out that the new strain is identical to an earlier pandemic strain, O1 EL Tor, except for proteins involved in the capsule and the O antigen. This was due to the acquisition of DNA inserted into and replacing part of the O antigen gene cluster. This suggests that O139 arose by horizontal gene transfer from a non-O1 strain into a type O1 strain.[37]

At least ten unrelated bacterial pathogens, causing diseases from tree blight to bubonic plague, share an entire set of genes for invading host cells, which have spread by horizontal gene transfer.

Pathogenic mycoplasmas possess proteins called *adhesins* and related accessory proteins that are required for adhering to cells and subsequent disease development. *Mycoplasma genitalium,* implicated in urethritis, pneumonia, arthritis and AIDS progression, was found to encode one adhesin and two adhesin-related proteins that shared substantial sequence similarities, as well as genome organisation, with those of another species, *M. pneumoniae.*[38] These were attributed to horizontal gene transfer events between the two species.

Most disturbing of all is the recent discovery that at least ten unrelated bacterial pathogens, causing diseases from tree blight to bubonic plague, share an entire set of genes for invading host cells, which have almost certainly spread by horizontal gene transfer.[39] More than twenty genes are involved in a system that secretes damaging proteins directly into host cells. They were first discovered in *Yersinia,* a genus of several species that cause human disease, including bubonic plague and intestinal infections. These proteins prevent bacteria from being taken up and destroyed by leukocytes (white blood cells). The system differs in different bacterial species. In general, it disables the host cell and makes it more hospitable to the bacterium. In some species, such as *Shigella,* the secreted proteins induce non-immune cells to take in the bacteria. In *E. coli* these proteins allow the bacteria to stick to the intestinal epithelium. At least some of the proteins are typical of eukaryotic cells and are directed at eukaryotic bio-chemistry, leading to the speculation that the genes were originally acquired from eukaryotic cells. One way in which this might have happened is through genetic-engineering biotechnology, in which arbitrary recombinations of gene sequences of infectious genetic elements are routinely made.

Like antibiotic-resistance genes, many virulence genes reside on transposons or plasmids. For example, the ST-enterotoxin genes of *E. coli* are part of a transposon, while important virulence factors of both Gram-negative pathogens (*Shigella flexneri, Salmonella* spp., *Yersinia* spp.) and Gram-positive pathogens (*Clostridium tetani*) are encoded in plasmids. Other factors, including the Shiga-like toxins of *E. coli*, the cholera toxin of *Vibrio cholerae,* the diphtheria toxin of *Corynebacterium diphtheriae,* neurotoxins of *Clostridium botulinum* and the cytotoxin of *Pseudomonas aeruginosa,* are encoded by bacteriophages. All these toxins and virulence factors obviously have the capacity to spread horizontally and to create new pathogens by recombination.

Virulence genes are often also located in the chromosome, where they form large unit-blocks, which came to be called *pathogenicity islands*.[40] These are acquired from unrelated species by horizontal gene transfer. The ubiquitous twenty-gene system mentioned above belongs in a pathogenicity island. These islands have very mixed characteristics, reminiscent of both plasmids and phages, and have come about through numerous recombination events. Have some of these recombinations been inadvertently created by genetic engineering? Now that the entire genome sequences of pathogenic bacteria are coming in thick and fast, it will be possible to answer this question by comparing gene sequences of artificial gene transfer vectors with those of pathogenicity islands. A scientist from the Center for Complex Infectious Diseases in Rosemead, California, isolated an unusual virus from patients with various chronic fatigue syndromes that has more than fifty bacterial genes.[41] He regards the hybrid virus-bacterium as a new organism and has coined the name 'viteria' for it. Viteria most closely resemble a cytomegalovirus, one of the first viruses to be exploited as a vector for the genetic manipulation of animals. And top of the list of bacteria from which it has captured genes are *Escherichia coli* and *Bacillus subtilis,* the two most commonly used bacteria in genetic engineering. Could viteria be a pathogenicity island in viral clothing?

> The evidence is now overwhelming that horizontal gene transfer has been responsible for both the rapid spread of antibiotic-resistance and the emergence of virulent strains of pathogens.

As the many virulence genes required for causing disease are all clustered together on mobile, infectious units, non-pathogens could be converted into pathogens in a single horizontal transfer event. This emphasises the danger of releasing transgenic micro-organisms into the environment, even those that are not known to be pathogenic. And yet this has been routinely done since genetic engineering began.

The evidence is now overwhelming that horizontal gene transfer has been responsible for both the rapid spread of antibiotic-resistance and the emergence of virulent strains of pathogens. This raises the question whether the full range of mechanisms for horizontal gene transfer has always existed. A study in 1983 on strains of bacteria isolated between 1917 and 1954—well into the antibiotics era—showed that none of the strains carried any antibiotic-resistance.[42] However, 24 per cent of them encoded genetic information for the transfer of DNA from one bacterium to another; and from at least 19 per cent of the strains conjugative plasmids carrying no antibiotic-resistance were transferred to the laboratory strain *E. coli* K12. While conjugative plasmids do predate the antibiotics era, therefore, their prevalence and the range of drugs to which they confer resistance have greatly increased since.

Horizontal gene transfer may have increased recently

I do not think it is an exaggeration to say that horizontal gene transfer (and consequent recombination) is the greatest threat to public health facing us today, especially if commercial-scale genetic-engineering biotechnology is allowed to continue unchecked and unregulated.

Precise epidemiological data is not yet available, but the signs are that both the incidence and the severity of outbreaks of multi-drug-resistant pathogens have sharply increased within the past ten to fifteen years. For example, there has been a twenty-fold increase in the number of *Salmonella* infections in some European countries since 1980.[43] Similar increases have been reported for haemorrhagic *E. coli* O157 food poisoning: between 1986 and 1996 there was a ten-fold increase in the frequency of infection in England and Wales and a hundred-fold increase in Scotland.[44]

The first widely used anti-malarial drug, chloroquine, came into use during the Second World War; resistance did not appear until the early nineteen-sixties. By contrast, the new drug mefloquine, released in 1985, became useless in 60 per cent of malaria cases within five years.[45] Comparable accelerations in the development of antibiotic-resistance have taken place in the same period. Antibiotics were introduced in the early nineteen-forties, and resistance did not appear until the early fifties. Resistance to penicillin, ampicillin and anti-pseudomonas penicillins in *Staphylococcus aureus* went from approximately nil in 1952 to more than 95 per cent in 1992.[46] By the eighties, *S. aureus* had also developed high levels of resistance to the synthetic penicillin methicillin and all other β-lactams. The new fluoroquinolone anti-microbial, ciprofloxacin, was introduced in the mid-eighties; resistance to it had reached more than 80 per cent by 1992. A study carried out by the Centres for Disease Control showed that ciprofloxacin-resistance in *S. aureus* went from less than 5 per cent to more than 80 per cent within one year. Recent data shows that vancomycin-resistance in *Enterococci* in hospitals in San Francisco grew from 3 per cent in 1993 to 95 per cent in 1997.[47] In Italy there was a twenty-fold increase in erythromycin-resistance in *Streptococcus* between 1993 and 1995.[48]

> Antibiotics are hazardous, not only because they provoke antibiotic-resistance to evolve but because the presence of antibiotics can actually increase the frequency of horizontal gene transfer ten-fold to 10,000-fold.

The dramatic increase in virulent infections and antibiotic-resistance within the past ten to fifteen years is usually attributed to the profligate use of antibiotics in intensive farming and in medicine. Antibiotics are hazardous, not only because they provoke antibiotic-resistance to evolve but because the presence of antibiotics can actually increase the frequency of horizontal gene transfer ten to 10,000-fold.[49] In one experiment the antibiotic oxytetracycline increased the frequency of transfer of a plasmid encoding multi-antibiotic-resistance by three to four orders of magnitude.[50]

It is known that ancestral antibiotic-resistance genes have originated from antibiotic-producing micro-organisms themselves.

It has been suggested, therefore, that what we call antibiotics may really be sex hormones for the bacteria, enhancing conjugation between cells—and, furthermore, that the process is naturally regulated by the product of the 'antibiotic-resistance' gene that shuts off the signal. The use of antibiotics therefore not only leads to mutational transformations of antibiotic-resistance genes but increases the spread of those very genes among pathogens.

The other factor to take into account is commercial-scale genetic-engineering biotechnology. The spread of virulence genes and the generation of new pathogenic strains of bacteria and viruses cannot be attributed to the overuse and abuse of antibiotics *per se*. Forty new viruses making human beings ill have been identified between 1988 and 1996 alone.[51] This does not include the numerous other viruses that attack wild and domestic species of animals and plants. New virulent strains of viruses and bacteria may well be the consequence of other practices, such as the extensive genetic manipulations of microbial and other genomes, which are throwing the ecology of microbes seriously out of balance. Though there is no direct evidence linking genetic-engineering biotechnology to the spread of virulence and antibiotic-resistance, there is clear evidence that horizontal gene transfer is responsible for both. And there is no escaping the fact that the *raison d'être* and aspiration of genetic engineering is to facilitate horizontal gene transfer, so as to create ever more exotic transgenic organisms.

Artificial gene transfer vectors make it much more likely to occur

It is not easy to transfer genes naturally between species. That is why such events were relatively rare in our evolutionary past. For example, analyses of 145 non-vertebrate globin gene sequences showed that there were probably two cases of horizontal gene transfer, one from the common ancestor of ciliates and the green algae to the ancestor of cyanobacteria and the other from the ancestor of the yeasts to the ancestor of bacteria.[52] Natural gene transfer vectors—viruses, plasmids, and transposons—have probably always existed, especially in the microbial species; but they are, to varying degrees, host-specific, so that the frequency of conjugal transfers is higher between the same species than with other species.[53] Furthermore, there are cellular mechanisms that break down foreign DNA, fail to replicate it, and excise or inactivate foreign genes that do get inserted into the genome (see chapter 7).[54] These mechanisms are also responsible for the instability and silencing of transgenes, which is posing a problem for the technology (see chapter 8).

Genetic-engineering biotechnology depends on constructing a wide range of artificial vectors designed both to break down species barriers and, increasingly, to overcome cellular mechanisms that break down or inactivate foreign DNA. The artificial vectors constructed by genetic engineers have the following important characteristics that increase horizontal gene transfer:

- They are already derived from infectious agents that mediate horizontal gene transfer most effectively.
- Their chimeric nature means that they possess sequence homologies (similarities) to DNA from widely different species and their viral pathogens, plasmids and transposons, thus facilitating successful horizontal transfer and recombination.
- They routinely contain antibiotic-resistance marker genes, increasing their successful transfer in the presence of anti- biotics, either intentionally applied or as pollutants in the environment.
- They often contain origins of replication and transfer sequences, all of which facilitate horizontal gene transfer and recombination. In this context, the fact that they are 'crippled', so that genes for mobility or virulence are removed, is irrelevant, as 'helper' functions can be supplied by other viruses, plasmids and mobile genetic elements present in the donor, the recipient, or a third strain of bacteria present in the environment. And virulence genes can be regained by recombination.
- It is well known that chimeric plasmids and viral vectors are subject to structural instabilities that make them more prone to recombination.[55] Vector instability is a continuing problem for

genetic engineers and the biotech industry as far as the stability of the transferred genes is concerned. It also increases the probability and scope for unintended, secondary horizontal gene transfer, which has already been directly demonstrated, even from transgenic plants to soil micro-organisms (see chapter 8).

- The now routine incorporation of strong promoters and enhancers in vectors to boost the expression of transgenes is one main cause of structural instability, additional to the instability arising from the attendant metabolic stress to the organism and which again may increase unintended horizontal gene transfer.[56]

- Finally, artificial vectors are designed to escape being broken down by restriction enzymes, thereby also increasing the probability of successful horizontal gene transfer.

> Genetic-engineering biotechnology has in effect opened up highways for horizontal gene transfer and recombination where previously there was only restricted access through narrow, tortuous paths.

All the classes of genetic elements that mediate horizontal gene transfer have been used: plasmids, phages, transposons, and a range of pathogenic plant and animal viruses. Though different classes of vectors are distinguishable according to the main framework sequence, practically every one of them is chimeric. Important chimeric vectors are the shuttle vectors that enable genes to be cloned (multiplied) in *E. coli* and transfected (transferred) into unrelated species in every kingdom. Similarly, vectors used in manipulating plants and animals typically contain sequences from a range of plant and animal viral pathogens, as well as antibiotic-resistance genes, often originating from promiscuous-resistance plasmids and transposons. Phage vectors and phasmid vectors (hybrids of phage and plasmid) are also extensively used and may have special relevance for the evolution of pathogenicity islands in bacterial pathogens.

Genetic-engineering biotechnology has in effect opened up highways for horizontal gene transfer and recombination where previously there was only restricted access through narrow, tortuous paths. These gene transfer highways connect species in every domain and kingdom with the microbial populations via the universal mixing-vessel, *E. coli.*

As mentioned in chapter 7, the microbial populations in the environment serve as a gene transfer highway and reservoir, enabling genes to be replicated and recombined, to spread from non-pathogens to pathogens, and to infect all other organisms. The release of genetically engineered micro-organisms is especially hazardous.

Horizontal gene transfers have been directly demonstrated between bacteria in the marine environment,[57] in the fresh-water environment,[58] and in the soil;[59] and in all the experiments, horizontal gene transfers are mediated by specially constructed hybrid plasmid vectors, of the sort used in genetic engineering.

Horizontal gene transfer occurs preferentially in interfaces between air and water and in the sediment, and especially under conditions of nutrient depletion,[60] which disproves the claim that nutrient-rich media are necessary to support horizontal gene transfer. Horizontal gene transfer has even been demonstrated in waste-water treatment ponds, the effluent from which is increasingly being used for irrigation in developing countries.[61]

Horizontal gene transfer is not limited to the external environment: it has been demonstrated between gut bacteria in mice and domestic fowl,[62] and in the mouth and gut[63] as well as the urogenital and respiratory tracts of human beings.[64]

While some geneticists recommend caution in the face of the existing evidence for horizontal gene transfer, those still dominated by the genetic engineering mentality see the potential for horizontal gene transfer as a new opportunity to be further exploited, dismissing those who present the evidence as expressing 'scenario-based concerns of lesser validity.'[65]

> We may be experiencing the prelude to a nightmare of uncontrollable epidemics of infectious diseases arising from horizontal gene transfer and recombination.

What the public are up against is a selective blindness to evidence among the genetic engineers and a single-minded commitment to look solely for the exploitable, which is the hallmark of bad science. To make things worse, the public are getting little or no protection from existing regulations. I am certainly not the first nor the only person to draw attention to the hazards of genetic-engineering biotechnology. The pioneers of genetic engineering imposed a moratorium on their own work in the Asilomar Declaration of 1975 (see chapter 2), because they were concerned about the possibility of generating new viral and bacterial pathogens through horizontal gene transfer and recombination. However, commercial pressures led to regulatory guidelines based largely on assumptions, every one of which has since been invalidated by scientific findings.

Evidence presented in this and earlier chapters (chapters 1 and 8 in particular) suggests that the original concerns of the Asilomar Declaration may have been borne out. We may be experiencing the prelude to a nightmare of uncontrollable epidemics of infectious diseases arising from horizontal gene transfer and recombination.

Let us examine some additional recent evidence suggesting that existing regulatory guidelines are seriously out of date and have failed to keep pace with scientific findings.

The health hazards of 'naked DNA'

'Naked DNA'—DNA by itself, outside of viruses or organisms—is a major new source of hazards, both to laboratory workers and to those exposed to products of genetic engineering, such as farm workers, those who process food and those who handle produce, as well as the general public. It has long been assumed that DNA cannot be taken up through intact skin, surface wounds, or the intestinal tract, or that it would be rapidly destroyed if taken up. But these assumptions have been overtaken by events. Geneticists are already contemplating the uptake of DNA through the skin and through the intestinal tract as a means of delivering genes for human gene therapy,[66] as naked DNA can indeed penetrate intact skin and survive passage through the gut to enter the bloodstream and cells (see also chapter 8). Naked DNA can even be taken up by sperm cells of marine organisms and mammals, and transgenic animals created.[67] So-called 'somatic' gene therapy may therefore be a misnomer, as the patient's germ cells may also be transformed and the effects passed on to the next generation.

The ability of naked DNA to penetrate intact skin has been known since at least 1990. Cancer researchers found that within weeks of applying the cloned DNA of a human oncogene to the skin on the back of mice, tumours developed in endothelial cells lining the blood vessel and lymph nodes.[68]

The Norwegian virologist and genetic engineer Terje Traavik has described how he was alerted to the dangers of naked DNA. He found that injecting DNA from the human polyomavirus into rabbits gave a full-blown infection, whereas the intact virus failed to have any effect.[69] The DNA of the virus is therefore much more infectious and has a wider host range than the virus itself. This has been found to be the case for other viruses.

The synthetic nucleic acids and gene constructs created by the biotech industry are therefore potentially the most dangerous class of xenobiotics (substances foreign to living organisms) to pollute our environment in increasing volumes, for which risk assessment has hardly even been considered. These include transgenic DNA from transgenic crops and genetically engineered micro-organisms; the artificial vectors for gene transfer, including human gene therapy vectors and other naked DNA constructs for somatic gene therapy; naked DNA vaccines (see chapter 12); DNA sequences amplified by laboratory procedures; and synthetic anti-sense RNA and ribozymes (RNAs that act as enzymes).

Novel genes and gene constructs can persist indefinitely in the environment

The survival of crippled laboratory strains of bacteria and the persistence of DNA in the environment were first brought to our attention by Dr Beatrix Tappeser of the Ecological Institute of Freiburg, who has been campaigning for many years in Germany and elsewhere against the inadequacy of regulation on genetic-engineering biotechnology.[70] She was a regular member of the group working with the Third World Network and presented what must have been the most significant paper in the first of the TWN seminars, in New York in 1995.

In one study in eastern Germany beginning in 1982, streptothricin was administered to pigs. By 1983, plasmids encoding streptothricin-resistance were found in the pig gut bacteria. These had spread to the gut bacteria of farm workers and members of their families by 1984, and to the general public and pathological strains of bacteria by 1985. The antibiotic was withdrawn in 1990. Yet the prevalence of the resistance plasmid had remained high when monitored in 1993, confirming the ability of microbial populations to serve as stable reservoirs for replication, recombination and horizontal gene transfer in the absence of 'selective pressure'.[71]

> Bacteria and viruses can indeed apparently disappear as they go dormant, and then reappear in a more competitive form.

In a direct test of the persistence of streptomycin-resistance in the absence of selection, researchers cultured many independent lines of a streptomycin-resistant mutant of *E. coli* without the antibiotic.[72] They found that all retained the resistance after 180 generations. Furthermore, the lines had also in the meantime accumulated compensatory mutations in other parts of the genome, which increased their competitive ability relative to the wild type. This demonstrates the irrelevance of the neo-Darwinian explanation that antibiotic-resistance evolves because of the intense 'selection pressure'; for that would predict the gradual disappearance of the antibiotic-resistance once the antibiotic is no longer in use.

Bacteria and viruses can indeed apparently disappear as they go dormant, and then reappear in a more competitive form. This has been documented for a laboratory strain of *E. coli* K12, which, when introduced into sewage, went dormant and undetectable for twelve days before reappearing, having acquired a new plasmid for multi-drug-resistance that enabled it to compete with the naturally occurring bacteria.[73] Dormant forms of bacteria and viruses can survive indefinitely as *biofilms* made up of extra-cellular matrices containing multiple-species communities. These are organised assemblages that can be found in the digestive and circulatory systems of our bodies as well as in the environment.[74] In this state the bacteria continue to accumulate new mutations, to exchange genes, and to come back with a vengeance when the ecological conditions are ripe.

These findings take on additional significance in the light of a report that the chemical treatments in waste tanks of commercial aircraft are insufficient to inactivate pathogens.[75] Commercial-scale contained users of genetically modified micro-organisms (GMMs) routinely release large amounts of wastes after chemical or phys-ical 'inactivation'. How adequate are those inactivation measures? Even if inactivation is effective, we now know that the large amount of recombinant DNA released can still be readily trans-ferred to other bacteria by direct uptake. There is an urgent need to reassess the regulation of contained use, as inadequately inactivated pathogenic and other dangerous GMMs and transgenic DNA may already be routinely discharged into the environment.

One 'environmentally conscientious' biotech company has even turned its inactivated transgenic sludge into a fertiliser for crops.[76] Far from contemplating such reassessment, the Health and Safety Executive in Britain drafted a document that would allow commercial and other contained users to release certain classes of live GMMs into the environment as liquid wastes, simply on notification and without the need to monitor for the survival and subsequent evolution of the GMMs.[77] I was advised by Professor Günther Stotzky, an expert on horizontal gene transfer, to fight this at the 'highest level of government', which I did. I am still awaiting the outcome. As this edition goes to press, the Health and Safety Executive is still allowing the release of dangerous transgenic DNA into the environment without any requirement to degrade it beforehand. At the same time some of the British government's own commissioned scientific reports are warning of the dangers of horizontal gene transfer from transgenic crops and products, and DNA is found not to be readily degraded by most commercial processing procedures.[78]

Conclusion

Little doubt can remain that horizontal gene transfer is responsible for the emergence of both new and old pathogens and of multi-antibiotic-resistance. The huge increase in the emergence of pathogens and antibiotic-resistance over the past fifteen years coincides with the commercialisation of genetic-engineering biotechnology. Many pathogens have crossed species barriers in acquiring genes that are involved in their ability to cause diseases. Genetic engineering is inherently hazardous, because it depends precisely on designing gene transfer vectors to cross wide species barriers and because many arbitrary combinations of genes are created and transferred between species that would never interbreed in nature. Genetic engineers are motivated solely by the ambition to design more and more aggressive gene transfer vectors with ever wider host ranges and are apparently unable to see the hazards involved. It is time to call a halt—for the future of humanity and all other living species.

Ten

DOWN AT THE ANIMAL PHARM

Who would want to clone a sheep, or a cow, let alone a human being? No-one except the genetic-determinist who believes an organism is nothing more than the sum of its genetic make-up. Dolly was not even a clone. Somatic cells accumulate systematic and non-systematic changes in genomic DNA during development, which accounts for the low success rate of this so-called 'cloning' technique. The experiment is misguided. It is not the best way to generate identical clones but to generate monstrous failures. It is irresponsible and unethical to claim otherwise. The cloning and 'pharming' of livestock, the creation of transgenic animals for xenotransplantation and to serve as animal models of human diseases, are all scientifically flawed and morally unjustifiable. They also carry inherent hazards in facilitating cross-species exchange and the recombination of viral pathogens. These projects ought not to be allowed to continue without a full public review.

A Frankenstein beyond reproach

On Sunday 23 February 1997, Ian Wilmut, an embryologist at the Roslin Institute outside Edinburgh, announced that they had succeeded in 'cloning' a sheep from a cell taken from the mammary gland of an adult. The clone, then seven months old, was said to be genetically identical to the adult from which the cell had been taken.

Public reaction was swift. Did it mean, people asked, that this could be done in humans? Were we nearer to cloning human beings? Why was this research allowed to go on at all? And why was it only coming to public attention now, some ten years after the work had begun?

The newspaper stories for the next few days were sensational. 'Galileo, Copernicus—and now Dolly!'[1] ... 'The spectre of a human clone' ... 'In the past few days, we have lived through a change in our condition as momentous as the Copernican revolution or the splitting of the atom' ... 'Scientists "able to create human clone".'[2]

President Clinton of the United States declared that the 'cloning' of the sheep raised 'serious ethical questions, particularly with respect to the possible use of this technology to clone human embryos.' He told a panel of bio-ethics experts to report back to him in ninety days on the ethical and legal implications. (In June, a ban was imposed on human cloning for five years.) The same week Sir Ian Campbell, chairman of the Human Genetics Advisory Commission in Britain, announced that the commission was meeting to deliberate the implications of the new 'cloning' science.

The story dominated front pages and television news and gave rise to endless streams of articles and talk shows. By Wednesday the share price for PPL Therapeutics, which carried out the work in collaboration with scientists at the Roslin Institute, had risen by more than a third, to increase its market value by £25 million. We should make no mistake about what is driving this science. The Roslin scientists own no shares in the company, and will not benefit directly; however, the 'cloning' technology has been patented jointly by PPL Therapeutics and the Roslin Institute, so the institute will certainly expect to benefit from royalties, if not from continued research contracts and grants.

At first the scientists involved, including Wilmut, dismissed the whole subject of cloning humans as science fiction. The technique was very difficult, they said. They had manipulated nearly three hundred embryos to get one success. The fact that it could be done in sheep did not mean it could be done in humans; besides, there was no need, and it was illegal in Britain in any case.[3] A few days later Wilmut admitted that it could be done in humans, though the director of the Roslin Institute, Professor Grahame Bulfield, insisted that they would not allow cloning to be used in harmful ways, and especially not for work on humans. Instead he emphasised that the breakthrough could, in the long term, lead to 'a myriad new ways' to help humans. Herds of transgenic animals could be farmed for proteins, blood, and organs. Gene therapy could provide cures for fatal diseases.[4]

> Human embryos created like Dolly would then be grown until important cells could be extracted from the embryo and used to treat human diseases.

Wilmut himself offered the prospect of human embryos, produced by the same methods, being used to treat cancer and other life-threatening diseases. Human embryos created in the same way as Dolly would then be grown until important cells could be extracted from the embryo and used to treat human diseases. During the work, the embryo would die. In other words, human embryos would be farmed, like the transgenic animals mentioned by the director of the institute. The horror of this thought is tempered only by Wilmut's reaffirmation that cloning a human would be 'technically difficult and ethically unacceptable.'[5] However, it transpired that patents on the technology applied for by the Roslin Institute would cover all 'animals', including human beings.[6]

A newspaper article later in the year reported on headless frogs having been created by a scientist, who raises the prospect of engineering headless human clones to grow organs and tissues for transplant surgery. He thought these headless human embryos could not possibly suffer, and would reduce public objection on ethical grounds.[7]

There are laws against human cloning in some countries, but not all: in Britain, Spain, Germany, Canada, and Denmark, for example. In the United States, though government funds cannot be used for research on human embryos, the position regarding privately financed research is unclear. Joseph Rotblat, a British physicist and Nobel laureate, called for the establishment of an international ethical committee.[8]

The 'pharming' of human embryos has not gone away. It is now presented to us as a real health bonus. Everyone can have a genetic twin, we are told, a human embryo clone kept in the freezer until the time comes when we need extra organs. What we are not told is that it's all done to make lots of money for the companies that hold patents on these services, were they to succeed (and there is no guarantee they would). But scientists have been given the go-ahead to experiment, which is irresponsible. According to the news report, each newborn baby would have some of its germ cells removed for culture in order to create embryonic stem cells that could be propagated indefinitely, or stored frozen. When required, these cells could be stimulated to grow and differentiate into an embryo or any of a number of cells, tissues, or organs.[9] Would the procedure be harmful for the baby? Why would we want to do such a thing when there is now a perfectly acceptable way of generating replacement tissues and organs using the patient's own cells? That approach was pioneered by two researchers in Boston, who shocked the public a couple of years before by growing a human ear on the back of a laboratory mouse. (It is actually possible to accomplish the same thing by seeding the cells on an artificially sculpted scaffold in tissue culture.)

While Wilmut welcomed Clinton's reaction and accepted the need for the issues raised to be considered by biologists and professors of ethics, he was unapologetic about the technique and expressed irritation at the continuing 'atmosphere of criticism' surrounding his success.

> Here we have a remarkable achievement, a world first, and there are people who seem to make a living out of spreading angst. You cannot blame the scientists for making those kind of discoveries. We are not Frankenstein-type people. If we hadn't made the breakthrough somebody else would; the technology is out there. It is now up to society to decide how it should be used and we welcome any discussion of these matters.[10]

These are significant words, not least because they reveal the scientist's unspoken assumption that he can do no wrong. He is, by implication, simply following a natural obligation to the 'advancement of science', an aim above reproach. In fulfilling this noble obligation there can be no question of any personal responsibility to decide whether or not he should.

Many forces are at work that converge towards this eventuality. The pure motive of the advancement of science may be only one among them, personal advancement and prestige a strong other. And one must not underestimate the importance of financial support from the pharmaceutical industry, eager to reap the rewards of a growing market in reproductive biotechnologies. And a substantial amount of the financial support for the research actually came from the taxpayer, via the Ministry of Agriculture, Fisheries and Food, as was revealed when the ministry announced it was withdrawing the group's funding barely a week afterwards.[11] The ostensible reason was that the group had already succeeded in what it had proposed to do with the grant: cloning sheep.

> This 'cloning' technique is the latest development in an accelerating trend in industrialised societies to wrest control of reproduction from women and place it in the hands of expert scientists and, ultimately, of faceless corporations.

It is significant that not one among the luminaries invited to comment on the cloned sheep in Britain within the first week of the discovery was a woman. Women have been conspicuously absent from the scene. (The only allusion to women was Wilmut's revelation that the world's first cloned animal was named after the singer Dolly Parton, because the cell used to create it came from the 'impressive mammaries' of the adult sheep.)[12]

This 'cloning' technique is the latest development in an accelerating trend in industrialised societies to wrest control of reproduction from women and place it in the hands of expert scientists and, ultimately, of faceless corporations that turn reproduction into services and commodities.[13] (I have put 'cloning' in quotation marks deliberately because, as I shall reveal later, the technique does not actually result in a genetically identical clone.)

It all began with the contraceptive pill and other methods of contraception that are predominantly aimed at women. Though the contraceptive pill is generally seen to give women more choice and control, it also puts the entire burden of responsibility for parenthood and otherwise on them, leaving men completely free and 'blameless'. That is why we live in a society that still stigmatises single mothers. Women are not in control when they take the pill (and suffer all the side effects besides), because their partners are automatically absolved from any responsibility.

After the contraceptive pill came in-vitro fertilisation and infertility treatments, determination of the sex of embryos, surrogate motherhood, germ-line gene replacement therapy—and now 'cloning', a method that bypasses fertilisation altogether. It is the logical culmination of the instrumental, exploitative science that treats nature as a collection of so many objects to be manipulated for the benefit of 'mankind'. So embryos, even human embryos, can be turned directly into commodities, or else into 'pharm' animals to produce proteins, cells or organs to order (for those who can afford to pay).

But who would want to clone a sheep, or a cow, let alone a human being? No-one except the genetic-determinist who believes an organism is nothing more than the sum of its genetic make-up, and perhaps those who believe it is their right to exploit cloned animals or human beings for spare body parts. It is indeed genetic determinism that inspires the act, that simultaneously validates and legitimises it and makes it so compelling, not only for the scientists concerned but for a substantial sector of the public who have become hooked on the genetic-determinist propaganda.

'A human triumph that humbles mankind'

A journalist writing in one of the leading British newspapers surpassed himself in the euphoria he experienced over the 'cloning' of the sheep. 'In the sheepish gaze of Dolly from Edinburgh, awesome possibilities glitter. We can imagine, just a little, how it must have felt to be a Tuscan Jesuit reading Galileo's Dialogue on astronomy, or a pious Londoner settling down 250 years later with a first edition of *Origin of Species*.[14] The reason for his euphoria was that he really believed geneticists had begun to reveal how much is determined in our genes, and that in gaining control of our genes we are gaining control of our destiny. E. O. Wilson, the founder of the discipline of sociobiology, which purports to explain all human behaviour according to the natural selection of genetically determined behavioural traits, was quoted in the same article as describing the human brain (presumably human consciousness) as 'an exposed negative waiting to be slipped into developer fluid ... The print is the individual's genetic history, over thousands of years of evolution, and there is not much anybody can do about it.'

> 'Instead of watching a mixture of yourself and your partner's genes playing on the swings, you could watch the unadulterated you.'

In the same vein Jonathan van Bierkom, professor of genetics at the University of Colorado, commented: 'After all, if you believe in the selfish DNA theory—the evolutionary imperative to propagate one's gene—then this is the ultimate.'[15] Richard Dawkins—arch-neo-Darwinian and genetic-determinist, famous for the utterly banal idea that human beings are nothing but automatons acting under the influence of their 'selfish genes', whose only imperative is to replicate—also declared himself delighted. He confessed he would like to be cloned himself; he would love to watch a tiny copy of himself grow up. And fundamentally, he asked, was that not what we were all after when we had children? 'So instead of watching a mixture of yourself and your partner's genes playing on the swings, you could watch the unadulterated you.'[16] It was all too predictable that a letter in support of cloning circulated on the internet was signed mostly by philosophers, together with the three arch-genetic-determinists Richard Dawkins, E. O. Wilson, and Francis Crick.

'Now we can reproduce ourselves without sex,' Andrew Marr wrote triumphantly in the *Independent,* chiding both 'religious fundamentalists' and 'open-eyed liberals' for calling attention to eugenics (while admitting that they had a point) but citing with approval the tongue-in-cheek comment by the novelist Fay Weldon that nature hasn't done such a good job that we can't improve on it, and that it is rather primitive of us to be so fearful of ourselves.[17] It would definitely be a sin, Marr said, to use political authority to ban new thinking or new research. Tom Wilkie, a science journalist (now senior policy analyst with the Wellcome Trust), was quoted as saying that moral attitudes evolve and that, up until 1950, it was illegal and considered immoral to use the corneas of dead people for transplants.

If people like Wilkie and Marr cannot tell the difference between transplanting corneas and cloning human beings, we have not only descended into complete moral relativism but have also substituted science for God. There is an underlying attitude that science is, indeed, beyond reproach, that it can never be wrong, while 'moral attitudes' or ethics are infinitely negotiable and evolvable. So let us examine the science to see if it bears out the claims that have been made for it. To begin, let us look at how the 'cloning' was done, and the claims that were made by scientists in a scientific journal, as opposed to those that appeared in the popular media.

What do the experiments actually say?

In the 'cloning' procedure, cells from an adult sheep's udder are cultured until they reach a 'stationary state' and cease to grow or divide. A cell is taken from the culture and fused with an egg from another sheep from which the nucleus has been removed. This allows the nucleus of the cell containing the genome of the first adult sheep to replace the egg's genome. The egg then starts to develop *in vitro,* and after it has been confirmed that it is developing normally it is transferred to the womb of a surrogate mother sheep, who carries it to term.

Out of a total of 277 embryos created in this way, only twenty-nine developed sufficiently 'normally' to be transplanted into

foster-mothers. And of those twenty-nine, only one lamb resulted.[18]
In the same series of experiments, cells were also taken from an
early embryo and a fetus with which cloning was attempted. Of
the 172 embryos created from fetal cells, three live lambs were
born, one of which was very weak at birth and died soon afterwards. A total of 385 embryos were created from the cells taken
from the embryo, and these gave rise to four live lambs, two of
which were delivered by caesarean section. The success rate
therefore was no greater than 1 per cent.

In fact neither this idea nor the technique is new. Extensive
experiments of this kind were carried out on the frog in the
nineteen-sixties by John Gurdon's group in Oxford, and on the
axolotl by other developmental biologists. *In no case, however,
did the scientists involved claim they were creating clones. Far
from it, for they knew they were doing no such thing.*

The intellectual motivation for the experiments came from a
deep problem in developmental biology. Organisms, no matter how
complex, typically start development from a single fertilised egg cell,
which goes through successive cell divisions to produce many
cells. These cells then undergo a hierarchical process of *determination* to form different organs and, later on, to become progressively
differentiated into distinctive nerve cells, skin cells, liver cells, and
so on. The process of determination commits distinctive parts of
the embryo to developing into different organs long before these
organs are actually formed; the process of differentiation into
specific cells occurs much later. The fertilised egg and its genetic
material are, as it were, 'totipotent' at the start of development,
that is, they have the ability to become all organs and all cells.

There are two related questions that nuclear transplantation
experiments address. First, when cells become determined to
form different organs, do they lose the potential to become part
of other organs or other kinds of cells? Second, does cell
differentiation involve irreversible changes in the genetic material
carried in the nucleus of the cell?

It is significant that the scientific paper on Dolly published in
Nature did not claim that the sheep had been cloned. The article

was entitled 'Viable offspring derived from foetal and adult mammalian cells.' Cloning was claimed, however, in the press statements and official comments to the public. The implication of their claim was that the viable offspring contained the original 'genetic blueprint' intact, and therefore the genetic material contained in the nucleus of the adult cell has remained totipotent and unchanged in development, and could be used to produce another organism like the original.

In the earlier amphibian experiments, many developmental abnormalities resulted, and the furthest any embryo resulting from the nuclear transplant developed was to the juvenile, tadpole stage. However, by repeating the nuclear transplant serially—that is, taking cells from the first nuclear transplant embryo and transplanting the nucleus into a second egg cell—it was found that adult frogs could be created, most of which were infertile and abnormal in some way.[19] In one set of results a total of 3,546 nuclear transplants were done using cells grown from adult frog skin.[20] The success rate of the first transplants to produce tadpoles was 0.1 per cent—in other words, the failure rate was 99.9 per cent. Serial transfers improved the success rate to 12 per cent, but these tadpoles came from that 0.1 per cent that had developed to tadpoles on the first transplant and were therefore pre-selected. And even the 'successes' showed varying degrees of abnormality. Why should this be?

> There is no evidence that the original 'genetic blueprint' remained intact in any cell, except those obtained in the very earliest stages of development, when the number of cells in the embryo could be visibly counted.

The technique of nuclear transplantation was actually invented by Thomas King and Robert Briggs in the nineteen-fifties.[21] They, and later others, carried out extensive series of experiments. Some of the main conclusions arising from these experiments are as follows:

- The developmental capacity of transplanted nuclei to support development decreases with the increasing age of the donor cells.
- The reduced developmental capacity of the nuclei is irreversible, so that it is propagated over serial transplants and may involve DNA changes, such as chromosomal damage, as well as other alterations.
- The developmental abnormalities resulting from the nuclear transplant experiments show no correlation with the kind of cells used.

There is therefore no evidence that the original 'genetic blueprint' remained intact in any cell, except those obtained in the very earliest stages of development, when the number of cells in the embryo could be visibly counted. That is why such a large number of abnormal embryos resulted from the transplanted nuclei. Small and large changes in DNA are now known to occur during development, either as part of normal development or in response to different environments (see chapter 7). Nevertheless Gurdon stated: 'The main conclusion to be drawn from the experiments summarised in this chapter is that the nuclei of different kinds of cells in an individual appear to be *genetically identical* [emphasis added].' Gurdon's claim was not supported by the data and contradicted the subsidiary conclusions made just before. This was surely someone who was trying to salvage the accepted dogma that genes (DNA) do not change in development, only the expression of genes, *in the face of evidence to the contrary.* This misreading or misinterpretation of evidence is now familiar in the long history of genetic determinism. (We shall come across yet more instances in the next chapter.)

The only real novelty involved in the Roslin Institute experiment was that it was done with sheep, and the experimenters apparently succeeded in obtaining an apparently healthy live birth without serial nuclear transplants. The interpretation of the results in the *Nature* paper was more cautious. Though it did not comment on the large proportion of failures, it stated: 'The fact that a lamb was derived from an adult cell confirms that differentiation of *that* cell did not involve the irreversible modification of genetic material required for development to term [emphasis added].'[22] I have italicised 'that' to emphasise that the conclusion that differentiation did not involve the irreversible modification of the genetic material applies only to one out of the 277 nuclei that were transplanted.

But why were these experiments attempted? They were attempted in the hope of replicating animals with proven performance within 'elite selection herds'. In addition, the technique might make possible the rapid creation of transgenic animals simply by making transgenic cells in culture for nuclear transplantation. As an afterthought, the authors mentioned that the technique could also be used to study possible persistence and impact of developmental changes on DNA during cell differentiation.

The science is seriously flawed

The science is fundamentally flawed in assuming that an individual is determined entirely by its genetic make-up, and that the genetic make-up of adult cells remains unchanged. This is not supported by the results of the nuclear transplantation experiments. Many commentators have pointed out that the clone is not identical to the original individual, because of the different life experiences the clone will have. Even identical twins, which are more 'clones' in the strict sense of the word, are different individuals. The development of their brains, for example, differs according to their individual experiences, as recent studies clearly show.[23]

There are more specific errors involved. First of all, as described above, one cannot clone any organism simply from a cell taken from the adult organism: it cannot be done without the egg from the second sheep, which plays the main role in 'rejuvenating' and 'reprogramming' the nucleus introduced with the cell, erasing all the 'imprinting marks' and other modifications in its DNA that make it a mammary gland cell and, most probably, changing the introduced DNA in other ways so that it is appropriate to be the genome of a fertilised egg at the start of development. In addition, the egg cytoplasm provides important cues for making the proper body plan characteristic of the species—something that is still very imperfectly understood, despite the isolation of large numbers of genes affecting the determination of body plan in the fruit fly in recent years. The egg also provides the food store, as well as the *mitochondria* or sub-cellular 'power-houses' that generate the energy intermediate, ATP, which is used in all the energy transformations necessary for growth and development. The mitochondria, as it happens, have their own complement of DNA, and each mitochondrion with its DNA is replicated independently in the cytoplasm, so that when the cell divides, each daughter cell will have the right number of mitochondria. Lineages of organisms can be traced through the mitochondrial DNA, and mutations in mitochondrial genes are involved in a number of diseases. No cell can live without mitochondria.

The really interesting aspect of this experiment is the role played by the egg cytoplasm, which is almost uniformly ignored by commentators, reflecting the patriarchal bias in mainstream science. Nuclear-cytoplasmic interactions are well known; development cannot proceed if the nucleus and the cytoplasm are incompatible.[24] Many characteristics are so strongly influenced by the cytoplasm that 'cytoplasmic inheritance' used to be a subject of its own, before it was eclipsed by the general obsession with DNA since the nineteen-fifties.

> The experiment is misguided. This is not the best way to generate identical clones but to generate monstrous failures of development. It is irresponsible and unethical to claim otherwise.

Another scientific error is the assumption that the genetic make-up of all the cells in the adult organism is the same, and identical to the fertilised egg from which the adult has developed. This myth has really been exploded since the early nineteen-eighties by the discovery of the fluid genome (see chapter 7). As pointed out above, it was already refuted by the nuclear transplantation experiments in amphibians. It is therefore a case of bad science to ignore, if not wilfully misread, the evidence. In fact somatic cells (cells of the body apart from germ cells) accumulate point mutations and other changes—insertions, deletions, rearrangements, duplications, amplifications, and so on—during the lifetime of the organism. Some of these mutations are implicated in cancer (see chapter 12). These DNA changes may account for the low success rate of the 'cloning' technique.

All in all, the experiment is misguided. This is not the best way to generate identical clones but to generate monstrous failures of development. It is irresponsible and unethical to claim otherwise.

Animal Pharm

Dolly draws our attention to a disturbing trend in genetic engineering as applied to domestic livestock and laboratory animals. The transgenic technology as a whole is very inefficient and the rate of success very low. Many embryos have to be manipulated and discarded because of abnormal, arrested developments before a few animals are obtained carrying the transgene, as was the case in making Dolly. Even the few that carry the transgene may turn out very sick, though they were not meant to be. This is simply because gene insertion is random. The insert can inappropriately turn host genes on or off, can scramble host genomes, or cause cancer (see chapter 8). Furthermore, the disturbance can propagate far away from the site of insertion, as recent findings have revealed.[25]

The introduced gene is bound to interact with other genes in the host gene, as we saw earlier. The most publicised failure of this kind concerned pigs engineered with a human growth hormone gene to make them grow faster. Unfortunately they were arthritic, ulcerous, partially blind, and impotent.[26]

After Dolly came Polly, who should be able to produce milk, when old enough, containing factor IX—the blood-clotting protein deficient in people with haemophilia B. Cells from Polly were cloned in the hope of creating an 'elite herd' that, like her, would produce the same factor IX in their milk. However, the cloned lambs were abnormal and eight times as likely to die at birth as ordinary lambs.[27]

Another group of researchers reported high rates of success in mice by transplanting nuclei from certain adult cells.[28] But this was still only 2–3 per cent of the embryos implanted and 1–2 per cent of the total number of eggs receiving nuclear transplant.

The widespread use of mice made transgenic with mutant human genes to serve as models of human diseases is both ethically and scientifically questionable. Is it justifiable to create animals that are meant to be sick? The most notorious is the 'onco-mouse', engineered to develop cancer, which has been patented and licensed to be marketed by Du Pont—without success.[29]

The principal scientific flaw in the whole endeavour is that single human genes are put into a completely different genetic background, and so it is doubtful that they can act as genuine models of human conditions. For example, mice engineered to carry a mutation in a gene that predisposes humans to retino-blastomas (tumours in the retina of the eye) did not show any such symptoms. Similarly, mice engineered to have Lesch-Nyhan disease turned out to be completely without symptoms, while those manipulated to have Gaucher's disease died within a day of birth.[30] (We shall see in the next chapter that human genes can even give completely different effects in different human populations.)

It is in the world of commerce that genetic engineers have dreamt up ever more exotic ways to exploit animals to dubious ends.

Much harm for so little benefit

One project that has gained considerable momentum is xenotrans-plantation, the transplanting of organs of other species into human beings. There is already a thriving market in the sale of human body parts, as graphically documented in Andrew Kimbrell's book *The Human Body Shop*.[31] Where once organ donors offered the gift of life to those in need, without any recompense, body parts are now commercial commodities. In the United States alone it is estimated that the market for human organs may be worth

$6 billion a year.[32] The biotech company Imutran in Cambridge is one of the leaders in producing pigs with human genes to overcome the immune reactions that lead to the rejection of transplanted organs.

Another development is the engineering of domestic livestock, such as sheep and cows, to secrete useful drugs in their milk. In 1990 the same partnership of laboratory and biotech company that produced Dolly had already produced Tracy, a transgenic sheep that secreted huge quantities of the human protein α-antitrypsin in its milk.[33] This protein is secreted mainly from the liver in human beings and is an inhibitor of elastase, which breaks down a connective-tissue protein. The deficiency of α-antitrypsin is associated with emphysema (obstruction of the airways of the lungs). Tracy was made with a large segment of human genomic DNA surrounding the human gene, as previous experiments showed that the gene by itself was not expressed at a high enough level to be commercially viable. The researchers did not know what was in the rest of the DNA but inferred that it must contain a regulatory sequence for high expression. However, Tracy's transgene was not stable and failed to be passed on to her offspring. This was presumably the main reason why 'cloning' was attempted: to preserve the characteristic of Tracy without going through the process of germ cell formation, which is where the transgene (or transgenes) can most easily get lost. Transgenic instability is a major problem in livestock, as it is in crop-plants (see chapter 8).

There are at least two aspects to consider in the 'pharming' of animals. The first is the ethical concern regarding animal welfare. Is the suffering of the animal justified by the amount of 'good' involved? The second is the question whether it is safe. According to Richard Nicholson, editor of the *Bulletin of Medical Ethics*, the whole transplant scheme in rich countries adds 0.003 per cent to life expectancy, which amounts to about a day. The use of xenotransplantation, assuming it works perfectly, will only increase life expectancy by 0.02 per cent.[34] Clearly the good this policy can bring is extremely limited. The same may be said for 'pharming' drugs in milk. The animal is made to lactate early with hormone treatment and thereafter is kept lactating permanently in order to keep up production. The protein the animal has to produce is *in addition to* all the normal proteins in her milk, which in transgenic sheep like Tracy is more than twice as much protein as in ordinary sheep milk. So she is under permanent metabolic stress.

A biotechnology company in Montréal has now cloned three goats to produce spider silk in the goat's milk.[35] Why not at least harvest spider's silk from spiders instead of making the poor goat produce what it was never intended to produce? Apart from the unacceptable suffering caused to these female animals being exploited as 'bioreactors', the hazards involved also far outweigh any potential benefits.

A moratorium was imposed by the regulatory body in Britain on clinical trials of xenotransplants, because of the recognised possibility that pig viruses can cross into human beings (see chapter 12). But it has now been lifted, and clinical trials seem set to go ahead. As we have already seen, the mere act of transferring genes between unrelated species with chimeric vectors is enough to facilitate the generation of new pathogenic viruses by recombination. Eukaryotic genomes are full of proviruses and related elements (see chapters 7 and 12), which can help 'crippled' vectors mobilise and recombine with them. Recombination between external and resident viruses is strongly implicated in cancer in many mammalian species (chapter 12). The large segment of human DNA transferred into transgenic sheep like Tracy and other species is particularly worrying, as researchers have no idea what other sequences are in the extra DNA. It is very likely to contain human proviral sequences that could recombine with sheep sequences to generate new viral pathogens. Yet the trend towards constructing transgenic animals will transfer large segments of the human genome to the other species. Scarcely a month after the announcement of the creation of the first artificial human chromosome in cultured human cells,[36] Japanese scientists made the first transgenic mouse line containing an entire human chromosome.

After all that, is the product safe to use? In the case of α-antitrypsin, which is marketed as a purified product, it may be possible to make sure that other protein contaminants, especially the prion proteins responsible for scrapie in sheep, BSE in cattle and Creutzfeldt-Jakob disease (CJD) in humans, can be excluded, as well as viral particles. The animal, it is claimed, will be kept in a special disease-free environment. It is admitted, however, that 'practically speaking, it is impossible to ensure that production animals retain the same disease status from day to day. Certain viruses are endemic to particular livestock species in all parts of the world, and sub-clinical infections could go unnoticed.'[37] The same company, PPL Therapeutics, is hoping to produce novel cow's milk for human consumption, claiming to use 'BSE-free' cows from the United States, and hopes to get approval for doing so. After all, it says, human blood is not at present checked for prion contamination associated with BSE. It expects 'less stringent guidelines in instances in which the products are for oral use.'[38] As described in detail in chapters 8 and 9, viruses and even naked DNA may survive passage through the gut and, from there, get into bacteria in the gut, and also into the cells in our body.

Conclusion

The cloning and 'pharming' of livestock, the creation of transgenic animals for xenotransplantation and to serve as animal models of human diseases, are all scientifically flawed and morally un-justifiable. They also carry inherent hazards in facilitating cross-species exchange and the recombination of viral pathogens. These projects ought not to be allowed to continue without a full public review.

Eleven

THE BRAVE NEW WORLD OF GENETIC DETERMINISM

Ethical committees, by not questioning the scientific basis of the practices being considered, end up serving vested interests rather than humanity at large. The science of genetic determinism is both master and handmaiden to the industrialisation of eugenics. If screening is eventually going to be applied to 'predisposing' genes and to genes whose connection with dubious conditions is increasingly tenuous, we shall slip insensibly into an era of human genetic engineering dictated purely by corporate interests. This will lead to the exploitation of the sick and the gullible for profit, at the same time giving rein to the worst excesses of human prejudices. Inherent in genetic-determinist thinking is the tendency to be blind to the enormous variation that exists in all natural populations. Genetic tests are poor predictors for the condition of any individual, because the genetic backgrounds of all the other genes are different. Genes associated with certain conditions in one population turn out to have no associations at all in another. Genes cannot be considered except in the context of the whole organism in its socio-ecological environment.

Genetic and Ethics

In November 1996 a meeting was held in Nürnberg to mark the fiftieth anniversary of the trials of doctors who experimented on concentration camp prisoners in the Nazi era. During the meeting the German section of International Physicians for the Prevention of Nuclear War (IPPNW) called for a full debate in the German parliament on the Council of Europe's proposed Bioethics Convention, claiming that it was not sufficiently restrictive to provide adequate protection for the mentally handicapped.[1] The meeting endorsed a declaration that if the draft Bioethics Convention were to be approved, there was a serious risk that Germany's dark history of human experimentation would repeat itself. This declaration has already been signed by more than fourteen thousand people, including representatives of the medical, academic and political communities, as well as groups such as charities for the mentally handicapped.

The declaration was originally drawn up for a meeting of the IPPNW's working group on the history of euthanasia, held in June 1995 in Grafenecker, a small town in south-west Germany where ten thousand mentally handicapped and psychologically ill people were gassed by the Nazis in 1940.

Michael Wunder, a psychologist, who drew up the declaration, argued that the draft convention compromised the first article of the Nürnberg Code of 1947, which says that voluntary consent of the human subject in medical experiments is essential and also specifies that anyone taking part in an experiment must be capable of giving consent. In contrast, the proposed Bioethics Convention would allow research to be carried out to determine the general mechanisms of a disease suffered by a person incapable of giving consent. This would be of no direct benefit to the patient, though it might benefit others afflicted with the same disease. The declaration also argued that the convention was too liberal towards human embryo experimentation and genetic screening. It took no stand on the issue of embryo research (this omission is especially glaring in view of the possibility of human cloning raised by subsequent events) but confirmed that genetic testing would be permitted for health purposes or for scientific research linked to health purposes, accompanied by appropriate genetic counselling. At the same meeting the IPPNW also called for a moratorium on the development and use of new genetic screening tests until laws had been introduced protecting people against their possible misuse.

But Ludger Honnefelder, director of the Bonn Institute for Science and Ethics and a member of the Council of Europe's expert committee responsible for drawing up the convention, rejected these criticisms, claiming that the convention had been wilfully mis-interpreted with a political intention to 'hinder genetics research.' The convention was approved by the Council of Europe's parliamentary assembly in September 1997, when the German representatives were the only source of significant objection.

Once again the underlying assumption is that science must go on, with ethics being negotiated around it. The laws of nature, the reasoning goes, are ineluctable, for they are God-given; while the laws of 'man' must accommodate themselves to the progress of science and not hinder it.

China has already legislated for eugenics in a new law that came into effect in June 1995.[2] It requires couples planning to marry to undergo screening for 'serious' hereditary diseases, as well as contagious diseases such as AIDS, sexually transmitted diseases, leprosy, and mental illnesses, including schizophrenia, manic depression, and other major psychoses. If either partner suffers from infectious or mental illnesses, the marriage must be postponed. In the case of genetic diseases, marriage is allowed only if the couple agree to long-term contraception or sterilisation.

> Genetic discrimination and eugenics are being privatised and depersonalised and are therefore much more insidious than the state-sanctioned forms, because they cannot be effectively opposed. They are being promoted under the banner of scientific progress and free choice.

Genetic screening, including prenatal genetic screening and gene replacement therapy, are already widely available in the West. The British government's Advisory Committee on Genetic Testing has produced a code of practice for companies selling genetic tests by post, but the code is not legally binding.[3] It restricts testing to heterozygotes (carriers) of recessive diseases, such as cystic fibrosis, and requests companies to notify it in case they want to sell tests for other types of genetic disorders. Genetic data should be kept confidential, though samples may be transferred to third parties with the consent of the person whose sample it is. This permissive attitude is at odds with the recommendation of the government's own Science and Technology Committee that commercial screening should be strictly regulated, on the grounds that 'there is a very real danger that unscrupulous companies may prey on the public's fear of disease and genetic disorders and offer inappropriate tests, without adequate counselling and even without laboratory facilities necessary to ensure the tests are conducted accurately.'[4]

Genetic discrimination and eugenics are being privatised and depersonalised and are therefore much more insidious than the state-sanctioned forms, because they cannot be effectively opposed. They are being promoted under the banner of scientific progress and free choice. It is significant that 'genetic science and industry' ranks before 'human rights' in the report of the Science and Technology Committee, demonstrating the importance of gaining access to the health care market in the United States and elsewhere.[5] Has no-one questioned the ethics of profiting from ill-health? In the same way, by not questioning the scientific basis of the practices being considered, ethical committees end up serving vested interests rather than humanity at large.

The science of genetic determinism is both master and handmaiden to the industrialisation of eugenics. It proliferates, like a virus, into every aspect of our lives. There is, admittedly, a better scientific rationale for hunting for traditional 'single-gene' diseases—such as cystic fibrosis and sickle-cell anaemia—than for those that are clearly shown to be associated with mutations in a corresponding gene, which constitute less than 2 per cent of all human diseases. But screening for these diseases is not without problems, as we shall see later. The hunt goes on, however, for genes said to predispose people to diseases such as cancer, diabetes, asthma and allergies and to conditions such as obesity, manic depression, schizophrenia, alcoholism, homosexuality, criminality and even attributes such as longevity, novelty-seeking, and so on.[6] They have made sensational newspaper headlines; but behind the headlines many of the genes have come and gone like will-o'-the-wisps, because they never existed in the first place. Of the rest, all that remains to be said is that they give varying degrees of association with the given condition, which differ for different human populations.

> The effects of genes are complex [and] subtle and depend on interactions with the environment. In many cases, possession of the gene variants associated with a disease will only increase the risk and will not necessarily indicate that their possessor will suffer from the complaint. Even in the minority of cases where the possession of a defective gene inevitably leads to the development of a condition, it cannot predict its severity or, in late-onset diseases, show when it might appear.[7]

Nevertheless, tangible demand has been created for screening, not just for the single-gene diseases but for any other condition potentially on offer. A survey in the United States found that 43 per cent of those with genetic disorders were experiencing discrimination in employment, health, or life insurance.[8] If genes make people susceptible or allergic to environmental pollutants, or to pollutants in their work-place, then employers will demand those forms of genetic screening for employment.[9] And why stop there? Geneticists claim to have identified a mutation in a gene encoding monamine oxidase inhibitor that causes aggressive behaviour and may be implicated in attention-deficit hyperactivity disorder (ADHD) in young children, conduct disorder in adolescents, and anti-social personality disorder in adults.[10] One scientist even suggested that six-year-olds diagnosed with ADHD might be saved from a criminal career if they were given prophylactic drug treatment.

The fact that some people may be able to tolerate poisonous chemicals does not make it ethical to make them work in places where such pollution is the norm. And branding a child a potential criminal on account of its genes is simply to relinquish responsibility for its care and proper upbringing. By a seemingly harmless, subtle shift in emphasis from the environment to the genes, we are saying in effect that it is all right for the environment to deteriorate and to be polluted, and that it is all right for communities to undergo social disintegration, which drives adults to drink and crime, and children to misbehave; what's wrong lies in people's genes. Therefore, what we need to do is genetically engineer people not to be susceptible, commit crimes, become ill, and so on. Environmental factors are the main cause of ill-health, but they continue to be ignored by the establishment in favour of 'genetic predispositions'.

> Research on 'genetic predispositions' is not only a drain on public resources, diverting them away from the real causes of society's ills: it is pernicious, because of the ideology of genetic determinism that motivates it and that it in turn reinforces.

A group of biologists has completed a five-year experiment on the effect of low levels of mixtures of pesticides and agro-chemicals on male mice, levels that are similar to those found in the ground water of agricultural areas in the United States. They found detrimental effects on the nervous, immune and endocrine systems. They also observed increased aggressive behaviour in mice exposed to atrazine and nitrate and to atrazine, aldicarb and nitrate together.[11] A recent study compared the mental ability and aggressive behaviour of two groups of Yaqui children in the Yaqui Valley in Mexico. One group lives in the lowlands, dominated by pesticide-intensive agriculture, while the other group lives in the nearby foothills, where ranching is practised without pesticides. The children exposed to pesticides had far less physical endurance, inferior hand-eye co-ordination, and less ability to draw. They were also much more prone to aggressive behaviour.[12]

Research on 'genetic predispositions' is not only a drain on public resources, diverting them away from the real causes of society's ills: it is pernicious, because of the ideology of genetic determinism that motivates it and that it in turn reinforces. Let us examine the shaky foundations of the claims of genetic determinism and the difficulties it generates, beginning in the area of classic Mendelian genetic disorders, then going on to the more elusive human conditions.

Hunting for the snark

Gene hunts are based on the simplistic assumption that there is a gene, or a limited number of genes, that can be pinpointed for every known human condition, however complex and irrespective of whether it is known to be significantly influenced by environmental factors. Recombinant DNA techniques now provide the means to follow the association of any given condition with a large number of genetic markers for which there is variation, or polymorphism, in the population. These genetic markers are banding patterns produced on electrophoresis by pieces of DNA with unknown function, resulting from cutting the DNA in the human genome with specific restriction enzymes, or from amplifying specific sequences using the PCR chain reactions (see chapter 3).[13] The hope is that one of these markers will be closely linked on the same chromosome with the putative gene, also of unknown function, determining the condition, and so will be more likely to be inherited together with the gene. By screening members of those families in which the condition is known to occur, the marker most likely to be present together with the condition can then be identified. This technique has been successfully used to find the gene in cases of so-called single-gene diseases. In other cases most of the markers turn out to have little or no relevance to the condition when more data is analysed or other families are examined.[14]

The human genome is huge, containing some three billion base pairs, only a small fraction of which code for functional proteins and RNAs or are involved in providing signals for making functional proteins and RNAs. Some estimates put the proportion of useful DNA at between 1 and 5 per cent, others at up to 33 per cent. The rest, of unknown function, is referred to as 'junk DNA'.

This is typical of eukaryotic genomes, with 'junk DNA' vastly predominating. No-one knows why so much apparently useless DNA is carried around. The number of polymorphic genetic markers is enormous. By 1995, 10,468 of these had been mapped to locations scattered throughout the twenty-three human chromosomes.[15] The idea of picking up functional genes by looking at their association with these markers is like hunting for a needle in a haystack, even assuming that the needle exists.

Hunts for genes involved in single-gene diseases have a much better chance of success, because most of the effects can be attributed to a single gene, even if no-one has any idea what that gene does. This is the power of 'reverse genetics', which recombinant DNA techniques enable geneticists to do. One first isolates the gene, then finds out what the gene does. Classically, it had to be done the other way round: it was necessary first to identify the biochemical idiosyncrasy before establishing the gene involved. Finding a gene is simple if the biochemical basis is known, or if classic linkage analyses and other studies have already supplied important clues about where the gene might be.

Cystic fibrosis was the first disease for which a gene of largely unknown function was found by such methods. Its approximate position was already known from classic linkage studies, but it was still not an easy task. It involved extreme, at times bitter competition between rival laboratories, and a couple of false reports, before the gene was finally found in 1989.[16] There was an immediate proposal for screening and prenatal diagnosis. And the case for this is strong, for it is a single-gene disease affecting a large proportion of the population.

> Not only can many different mutations in the same gene lead to the same syndromes, but so can mutations in one of several genes. Conversely, mutations in a single gene have been attributed to four different syndromes.

The practical problem of screening is that the gene is very, very big, some 230,000 base pairs in length, with twenty-seven exons, coding for a large protein that has 1,480 amino acids. A deletion of three base pairs, removing a single amino acid (in position 508) from the protein, occurs in 68 per cent of patients. But more than four hundred different mutations have since been found[17]—and others will turn up on further screening—involving changes in different positions within the same gene. Only some mutations result in cystic fibrosis, or similar syndromes. The same mutations, moreover, may be associated with different symptoms in different people. It would not be feasible to screen for all the variants. Screening for only the commonest variant will not reveal whether the other mutations may or may not also result in cystic fibrosis in combination with the common variant. This sort of problem is shared by many other single-gene diseases.

Not only can many different mutations in the same gene lead to the same syndromes, but so can mutations in one of several genes, as is found in a conglomerate of cranio-facial syndromes that includes achondroplastic dwarfism. Conversely, mutations in a single (tyrosine kinase) gene have been attributed to four different syndromes.[18] There is really no such thing as a single-gene disease.

At present, the sort of diseases where screening can give a definite result are those found in people with a known family history of the disease and where, as with Huntington's chorea (which affects one in twenty thousand people in mid-life), the mutation simply involves variable repeats of a trinucleotide sequence (CAG) within a particular gene, and the condition appears to be associated with forty or more repeats—there being a rough correlation between the age of onset and the number of repeats greater than forty.[19]

What about the genes that 'predispose' people towards cancer and other conditions? 'Breast cancer genes' have been in the news since 1994, when mutations in two genes, *BRCA1* and *BRCA2,* were discovered that were said to 'trigger' breast cancer.[20] Both were thought to be 'tumour-suppressors', though their real functions have remained elusive. Other putative 'cancer genes' continue to be identified, as for example *BRCA3*[21] and *BCSG4,*[22] there being such a big potential for the screening market. In the case of

BRCA1, women who inherit one copy of the mutated gene inherit the predisposition to breast cancer, since, when the unmutated copy is damaged in the cell, that cell will turn cancerous. The frequency of this gene in the northern European population is 0.0033 per cent, or one in three hundred.[23]

> 'Predisposition' conceals the fact that important environmental factors are left out of consideration.

The estimate in 1996 was that one in five women in Western societies is likely to develop breast cancer by the age of eighty-five, and 25 per cent of those will die from it.[24] However, only between 2 and 5 per cent of all cases are known to be hereditary, and the first two genes discovered account between them for only 80 per cent of those cases known to be hereditary. *But 'predisposing' mutations in those particular genes do not predispose women to develop breast cancer if they do not already have a family history of breast cancer*—possibly because they have a different genetic background. So a positive test for informative mutations in either one of those genes, if you have a family history of breast cancer, will tell you one of two things: either you belong to the 20 per cent where it doesn't matter that you have the gene, in which case your chance of getting breast cancer is still one in five (as in the general population), or you have an 80 per cent chance of developing the disease. These tests will give no information whatever on the great majority (95 per cent) of breast cancer cases.

A genetic test for *BRCA1* has been marketed in the United States for the last five or six years. By 1996, 254 mutations had been identified, of which 132 are unique and only 36 are 'disease-associated'.[25] The most common mutations, 185delAG and 5328insC, account for 11.7 per cent and 10.1 per cent, respectively, of all mutations shown. During screening, other mutations are bound to turn up in the gene whose effects will be utterly unknown. (It is relevant to mention here that in a study to ascertain whether breast cancer may be induced by mammographic screening,[26] as has been widely claimed, 99 per cent of mammographically induced breast cancers were found to have occurred in women who were carriers of a breast cancer gene. This identifies at least one important environmental factor in the aetiology of the disease, even in its familial form.)

The medical benefit of knowing about a predisposition to breast cancer, as for other conditions for which there is no cure, is unclear. It is more likely simply to cause increased anxiety, with some women even resorting to drastic prophylactic surgical removal of the breasts.[27]

'Predisposition' conceals the fact that important environmental factors are left out of consideration, as for example chemical carcinogens, of which there are at least several hundred in our environment, as admitted by the US National Cancer Institute.[28] It is also well known that the incidence of cancer increases with industrialisation and with the use of pesticides. Women in non-industrialised Asian countries have a much lower incidence of breast cancer than women in the industrialised North; however, when Asian women emigrate to Europe or the United States their cancer rate jumps to that of the native European women within one generation. Similarly, when DDT and other pesticides were phased out in Israel, breast cancer mortality in pre-menopausal women fell by 30 per cent.[29]

Environmental factors are left out of consideration not only with regard to cancer but in such conditions as late-onset diabetes. This is characterised by resistance to insulin treatment, for which genes have yet to be identified, though it is claimed that between two and eight genes may be involved. But even if they are eventually identified 'there will still remain the daunting task of interpreting the way these genes predispose to a disease that is strongly influenced by external factors such as poor diet and obesity.'[30]

Progress in identifying genes that predispose a person towards cardiovascular disorders fares no better. In the United States a quarter of men and women under the age of sixty-five and about half of those over sixty-five die from cardiovascular diseases.

Some cases—identified as familial hypercholesterolaemia—have been traced to a mutation in a gene, but most others are a result of general susceptibility and life-style. Even in familial hyper-cholesterolaemia, where a mutation in the cholesterol-carrying protein leads to the disease, the onset and severity of the condition are affected by diet.

In most cases, therefore, it will be impossible to interpret the results of a genetic screening test for the patient, or for the insurance company or prospective employer; the only people who stand to benefit in all circumstances are those selling the screening tests. But then, that is what the health care 'market' is all about.

Complexities confound prognosis

The other main problem is that prognoses can vary a lot, even for so-called single-gene diseases. A positive result in a screening test will not give an accurate prognosis of how the individual will fare. And in the case of 'predispositions', the individual may not develop the condition at all.[31] Even if one were to ignore environ-mental effects, the expression of each gene is entangled with that of every other. In other words, a prognosis will depend on the genetic background, consisting of all the other genes. Enormous variation exists in every known gene. Hundreds of mutants have already been uncovered, though many of the variants are essentially neutral, having few or no deleterious effects. Therefore, no two people on earth will have the same combination of genes, except for monozygotic twins at the beginning of their lives. The uniqueness of the individual applies not just to his or her life experiences but especially also to the genetic make-up.

> If screening is going to be applied to 'predisposing' genes, and to genes whose connection with dubious conditions is increasingly tenuous, we shall slip unwittingly into an era of human genetic engineering dictated purely by corporate interests.

The variable prognosis is particularly relevant in conditions such as cystic fibrosis and sickle-cell anaemia, which can be alleviated by treatments and appropriate management of crises. And one should never forget the classic case of phenylketonuria (PKU). This is a condition that resulted in some cases in severe mental retardation and early death before it was effectively treated by excluding foods from the diet containing the amino acid phenylalanine, which PKU sufferers cannot metabolise. Nevertheless positive test results for PKU have already created social pressures on parents to abort the fetus,[32] whether they wish to do so or not. So-called 'therapeutic' abortions will soon be seen as the logical follow-up to positive prenatal diagnosis, and no-one will be seriously looking for cures or treatments any more, except in the form of gene therapy, which creates its own problems (see chapter 12). The impetus now in so-called 'preventive medicine' is to isolate the gene for the purpose of screening and then to eliminate the affected gene before birth. And if screening is eventually going to be applied to 'predisposing' genes, and to genes whose connection with dubious conditions is increasingly tenuous, we shall slip insensibly into an era of human genetic engineering dictated purely by corporate interests exploiting the sick and gullible for profit, while simultaneously giving rein to the worst excesses of human prejudices.

A geneticist has recently screened pre-implantation embryos *in vitro* for a mutant gene that predisposes *adults* to bowel cancer. One embryo diagnosed as free from the mutant gene was implanted into the womb,[33] but it failed to develop to term. The procedure is not new. Up to fifty children in Britain have already been born as the result of pre-implantation genetic diagnosis, but all were in families at risk of genetic disorders that strike at an early age. Pre-implantation diagnosis on 'predisposing' genes that affect adults is a further step down a slippery slope. The geneticist who carried out the work has no misgivings, as it was 'up to the family concerned' to decide. She is, however, applying for funding that would enable five further couples to undergo pre-implantation diagnosis for genetic predisposition to other cancers.

> A variant that appears to predispose people to a certain disease in one population may not have the same effect in another, simply because the genetic background is very different.

It may seem that pre-implantation genetic diagnosis has undergone proper risk assessment and that the ethical issues raised have been thoroughly debated. Not at all. The procedure involves removing two cells for testing from the embryo at a very early stage, when it has a total of eight cells and is bound to have a high failure rate. Furthermore, the effects on children developed from embryos manipulated in this manner are completely unknown. A special ethics committee of the Human Fertilisation and Embryology Authority is only now scrutinising the ethical implications. Have people been informed of the risks there might be to the child resulting from the manipulated embryo? One member of the ethical committee dismisses the possibility of 'designer babies' on the grounds that the procedure is about 'ways of preventing children being born with genetic disorders.' In other words, negative eugenics—weeding out undesirable genes—is, in her view, quite acceptable.

Inherent in genetic-determinist thinking is the tendency to be blind to the enormous variation that exists in all natural populations. It ignores the fact that a variant that appears to predispose people to a certain disease in one population may not have the same effect in another, simply because *the genetic background is very different.* Cystic fibrosis mutations in the people of Yemen are found to be associated with a different syndrome—the bilateral absence of vas deferens—which can also result from some other unknown cause or causes.[34] Significantly, in the same population *none of those patients diagnosed as bona fide cystic fibrosis sufferers actually possessed the cystic fibrosis mutations.*

Another case in point was captured in a headline in the *Boston Globe* that proclaimed, 'Genes tied to cancer in Jewish women.' This referred to the finding that about 1 per cent of American Jews have the 185delAG variant of the cancer gene *BCRA1.* The assumption that followed was that there was a 'Jewish genetic flaw' that might predispose Jewish women to breast cancer. There are no grounds for such a conclusion. As Hubbard and McGoodwin point out, the variant 'may merely be a common form in which this gene occurs in the Jewish population';[35] it does not suggest that Jewish women have an increased predisposition to breast cancer. This example serves once again to stigmatise Jews. And already a biotech company has begun offering screening tests to Jewish women, for a fee. When screening was carried out on 108 Jewish women suffering from breast cancer who also had a familial history of breast cancer, no more than twenty-four (23 per cent) were found to have the mutation.[36] This is considerably lower than the figure of at least 40 per cent found to be associated with mutations in *BRCA1* among northern Europeans, the other 40 per cent being associated with mutations in *BRCA2*.

> Population geneticists have long ago demonstrated that eugenics does not make scientific sense. It makes even less in the light of the new genetics, when we know that genes and genomes are fluid and dynamic and that mutations are much more frequent than previously thought and can occur *in response to* environmental conditions.

An even more dramatic difference in association has been found for cases of male breast cancer.[37] An analysis of fifty-four patients showed that none of them had any *BRCA1* mutations. Two patients were found to carry novel mutations in *BRCA2,* but only one of the two had a family history of cancer.

One can confidently predict that, as more 'predisposing' genes are studied in other human populations, they will be shown to have different degrees of association with the corresponding conditions, or none at all. It will be a case of 'Now you see it, now you don't.' This is the consequence of the non-linear complexity and interconnectedness of gene function, where diversity is a hallmark.

Classical geneticists have continuously wrestled with the question of why there should be so much diversity in natural populations, and the debate goes on. The most immediate explanation is that genes and genomes are inherently mutable and fluid. Mutations in both germ cells and somatic cells are much more frequent than previously thought (see chapter 12). Genes work together as an interconnected network, in which a lot of variations will have no net effect on the well-being of the individual concerned: that is, they are neutral. Potential metabolic blocks can also be bypassed because of redundancy of pathways within the system.[38] Another explanation is that while specific combinations of alleles may work particularly well with one another, some may give harmful effects in homozygous states. The sickle-cell anaemia allele is widely thought to give protection against malaria in the heterozygous state in the Afro-Caribbean genetic background, while the cystic fibrosis allele is thought to give protection against childhood diarrhoea[39] in the north European genetic background.

Classical genetics has long estimated that every individual in a population carries at least the equivalent of five lethal alleles in heterozygous forms. This means either heterozygous alleles in five genes, each of which will be lethal in homozygous form, or heterozygous deleterious alleles in many, many genes, equivalent to a total of five 'genetic deaths', if all of them were made homozygous.[40] This is referred to as 'the genetic load' of the population. Population geneticists have long ago demonstrated that eugenics does not make scientific sense. It makes even less sense in the light of the new genetics, when we know that genes and genomes are fluid and dynamic and that mutations are much more frequent than previously thought and can occur in response to environmental conditions (as extensively reviewed in chapter 7). Let us go on to deal with the even more tenuous connections between genes and patterns of human behaviour.

Neurogenetic determinism

Neurogenetic determinism purports to explain brain function and human behaviour according to their genes. It 'claims to be able to answer the question of where, in a world full of individual pain and social disorder, we should look to explain and to change our condition':[41] to our genes. According to this theory, people are homosexual because they have 'gay genes' and people are violent because they have 'criminal genes'. Of course the language is usually clothed in appropriate sophistry, but the message is unmistakable.

Neurogenetic determinism is a direct descendant of neo-Darwinism and operates in the same way. The first step in the process is to invent a characteristic (see chapter 5). 'Aggression' is a familiar characteristic, invented by Konrad Lorenz,[42] who did most to 'explain' all animal behaviour as the result of the natural selection of genes. Aggression is now firmly established in the literature of sociobiology—the discipline that 'explains' all social behaviour, including that of human beings, as the natural selection of genes determining behaviour. It comes as no surprise, therefore, that 'aggression' is used to lump together all kinds of behaviour, from temper tantrums in children to a man abusing his partner or child. The description offered in the study that claims to have identified the association of aggression with a mutation in the gene encoding monamine oxidase inhibitor is an example of the intellectual sleight-of-hand involved. The 'behavioural phenotypes' of the eight males in a family said to have the mutated gene include 'aggressive outbursts, arson, attempted rape and exhibition-ism'[43]—activities carried out by subjects living in different parts of the country at different times over three generations. 'Can such widely differing types of behaviour, described so baldly as to isolate them from social context, appropriately be subsumed under the single heading of aggression?'[44] Yet the 'evidence' provided by this paper is part of the argument employed by the Federal Violence Initiative in the United States to identify at least 100,000 inner-city children whose alleged biochemical and genetic defects will, it claims, make them prone to violent crimes in later life.

Similarly, claims and counter-claims for 'genes for schizo-phrenia' have been appearing since 1988, and the story is not over yet. This condition affects one in every two hundred people in the West at some time during their lives. They experience dis-turbances of thought and feeling, a belief that their actions, as well as thoughts and feelings, are under external control. They may experience visions, seeing, hearing or even smelling things that others cannot, and may be convinced of something for which there is no obvious justification.[45] But not only is the hereditary status of schizophrenia questionable, 'there is no general agreement about its cause, its diagnosis, its symptoms, its cure, or even whether it actually exists as such.'[46]

> Kallman's work on the putative genetic basis of schizophrenia is an example of how results can be distorted to fit an ideology, then uncritically accepted and used by a scientific community attuned to the same ideology.

There are at least four claimants at present to 'genes for schizophrenia'. One of them is located near a 'genetic marker for schizophrenia,' based on measuring anatomical features of the brain by magnetic-resonance computer tomography, an imaging technique, as well as diagnosis of 'schizophrenia-related' disorder, 'schizotypal personality disorder', and 'schizophrenia'—all lumped together in a single family.[47] Mutation in another gene, the human dopamine D-3 receptor, is said to display, in homozygous state, a 'two-fold higher risk of schizophrenia,'[48] while third and fourth candidates are those genes[49]—not yet identified—involved in the incorporation and removal of certain fatty acids in the phospholipids of the cell membrane. It is clear that in each case the connection is tenuous and weak, and not helped by lumping together different syndromes. And even if biochemical or anatomical differences do exist, they do not tell us whether these differences are the cause or the consequence of their conditions.

Nevertheless, a dominant hereditarian view of schizophrenia exists. It can be traced back to studies on identical twins carried out by Franz Kallman in the late nineteen-forties and early fifties. These studies claimed that a high level of concordance exists between identical twins—that is, where one twin suffers from schizophrenia, the corresponding twin is much more likely to suffer from it too; and conversely, where one twin does not suffer from schizophrenia, the other twin will also be free of the condition. Unfortunately, when re-examined by Richard Marshall in 1984, those studies were found to be riddled with distortion and fiction.[50] Kallman himself both made the diagnosis of schizophrenia and ascertained that the twins were identical. Kallman was a committed eugenicist who extolled the virtues of eugenics and biological psychiatry. He referred to people with schizophrenia who did not need to be admitted to hospital as 'disease trait-carriers'. When his methods and data were challenged he failed to produce clarification. Kallman's work is an example of how results can be distorted to fit an ideology, then uncritically accepted and used by a scientific community attuned to the same ideology. That was neither the first nor the last of such episodes in science, and genetic determinism has had more than its fair share (as we shall see with respect to the genetics of IQ).

It is significant that two years after the original claim that a gene for schizophrenia had been isolated, the British medical journal *Lancet* carried a report of a study suggesting that the improved health of mothers was a factor in the substantial fall in the number of people admitted to hospital for schizophrenia since the nineteen-fifties.[51] And genetics and nutrition by no means exhaust the factors that may be involved in schizophrenia. On the contrary, it is the totality of a person's experience of life, in which the genetic and nutritional, the 'social, cultural, spiritual and cosmological,'[52] are all inextricably entangled, that counts. There is no single, isolatable cause that applies universally to all cases, genetic or otherwise. To persist in thinking that this is the case, and to pursue a course of action based on it, is to perpetrate untold violence on the human spirit. And that is much of what the Brave New World is about.

The multigenic IQ fraud

When hereditarians fail to pinpoint the gene or genes determining a condition, they retreat to polygenic, or multigenic, inheritance. 'Intelligence quotient' (IQ) is claimed to be such a characteristic. Robert Plomin, who worked for many years in the United States on the genetics of IQ, has taken up a prestigious post in the Institute of Psychiatry at the Maudsley Hospital in London. His research group is proposing to identify the genes involved in intelligence by means of genetic marker associations. This has worked successfully for schizophrenia, criminality, and homosexuality, they claim; so why not for IQ? Plomin and his colleagues have applied to the Medical Research Council for a grant of £1.8 million to take DNA samples from ten thousand children.[53] This has aroused considerable public opposition.

The IQ test was invented by Alfred Binet, for the benign purpose of identifying children who were not profiting from instruction in the normal public schools of Paris so as better to help them. IQ, as he identified it, was strictly a quotient or ratio of performance between mental age and chronological age. Binet did not for a moment suggest that his test was a measure of some innate or fixed characteristic that could not be changed. To those who made this claim his answer was, 'We must protest and react against this brutal pessimism.'[54]

In the United States and Britain, IQ tests have shunted vast numbers of working-class and minority children onto inferior and dead-end educational tracks. In the United States the testing movement was also clearly linked to the adoption of compulsory sterilisation laws, aimed at genetically inferior 'degenerates' and 'imbeciles', which resulted in hundreds of thousands of people being sterilised between 1924 and 1974.

In the United States and Britain, IQ tests came to be used in a way diametrically opposed to that intended. Claims were made that these tests measured an innate quantity that reflected mental ability or intelligence, which was fixed by genetic inheritance at birth. Followers of Francis Galton—the Galtonian eugenicists—took control of the mental testing movement in all English-speaking countries. They claimed that IQ measures were indicative of genetic differences in intelligence not only between individuals but also between social classes and human races.

In England the principal translator of Binet's test was Cyril Burt, whose father was Galton's physician; and it was Galton's strong recommendation that secured Burt's appointment as the first school psychologist in the English-speaking world. From an early age Burt was motivated by eugenic ideas, which he later sought to confirm in voluminous publications. In both the United States and Britain, IQ tests have shunted vast numbers of working-class and minority children onto inferior and dead-end educational tracks. In the United States the testing movement was also clearly linked to the adoption of compulsory sterilisation laws, aimed at genetically inferior 'degenerates' and 'imbeciles', which resulted in hundreds of thousands of people being sterilised between 1924 and 1974.

Burt continued his eugenics research into the inheritance of IQ until his death in 1971, having been knighted in Britain and bemedalled by the American Psychological Association, his work an inspiration to further generations of hereditarians, such as Arthur Jensen and Hans Eysenck. But cracks soon began to appear in the eugenicist edifice that Burt constructed.

Burt's most impressive data on the heritability of IQ was a study on fifty pairs of separated twins—the largest on record. This showed strikingly high correlation between twins in their IQ and no correlation whatsoever in their environments. Furthermore, to fit a biometrical genetics model, Burt claimed to have measured the correlations for a considerable number of types of relatives—the only investigator in history to have administered the same IQ test to the whole gamut of relatives. And the correlations all added up to his satisfaction, allowing him to conclude that variation in IQ was completely determined by the genes, the environment having no effect whatever.

Let me digress to repeat what heritability estimates involve. As we saw in chapter 5, the heritability of a trait is the proportion of the total variation of the trait, in a randomly mating population, that can be attributed to the variation in the genes. Heritability therefore is strictly a population measure and says nothing about the proportion to which any person's IQ is determined, or fixed, by the genes. Heritability can be estimated by correlations between different pairs of relatives—from monozygotic twins, who have all their genes in common, to grandparent-grandchild pairs, who have a quarter of their genes in common, and so on. For estimates of heritability to be valid, the population has to be random-mating. That means mating purely as a result of chance, so there is no mating between close relatives, and those people with similar genes do not mate together more often than their frequency within the population would predict. This ensures that there is a sufficiently representative range of genetic variation in any sample taken. Another requirement is that there be a suffi-cient range of environmental variation in the sample of people being measured.

These requirements are very seldom satisfied in human popu-lations. There is a high degree of social stratification, which severely limits the range of environments experienced by the pairs of relatives. In other words, they are most likely to be drawn from the same social class, and therefore do not experience different environments.

From the equation on page 90 it can be seen that if there is no environmental variation, or when environmental variation is under-estimated, then all, or most, of the variation will be as a result of genetic variation, and one will get an artificially inflated heritability of 1 or close to 1. On the other hand, if there is no genetic variation within the sample, or when genetic variation is underestimated, then the heritability will be nil, or nearly so. There are, of course, more complicated genotype-environment interactions that are not taken into account.

> 'The fraud perpetrated by Burt, and unwittingly propagated by the scientific community, served important social purposes': to validate eugenicist policies that persecuted minority races and other politically dispossessed classes.

The psychologist Leon Kamin dropped a bombshell when he first called into question the authenticity of Burt's work in his presidential address to a meeting of the Eastern Psychological Association in the United States in 1972.

> The implausibility of Burt's claims should have been noticed at once by any reasonably alert and conscientious scientific reader. To begin with, he never provided the most elementary description of how, when or where his 'data' had been collected ... He never even identified the 'IQ test' he supposedly administered to untold thousands of pairs of relatives ... even the sizes of his supposed samples of relatives were not reported.[55]

And how did he manage to get the IQ scores of adults? Burt had written that he relied on personal interview; but in doubtful or borderline cases, an open or a camouflaged test was employed. 'The spectacle of Professor Burt administering "camouflaged" IQ tests while chatting with London grandparents is the stuff of farce, not of science.'[56] Numerous inconsistencies were found between successive reports on the same 'data'. By 1976 the medical correspondent of the *Sunday Times,* Oliver Gillie, was reporting that he could uncover no evidence that Burt's research associates, Miss Conway and Miss Howard, had ever existed.[57] He accused Burt of having perpetrated a systematic scientific fraud, a charge later supported by two of Burt's former students, Alan Clarke and Ann Clarke, now themselves prominent psychometricians. Later on Burt's biographer, Leslie Hearnshaw, also had to concur. A review of Hearnshaw's biography had this to say:

> Ignoring the question of fraud, the fact of the matter is that the crucial evidence that his data on IQ are scientifically unacceptable does not depend on any examination of Burt's diaries or correspondence. It is to be found in the data themselves. The evidence was there ... It is a sorry comment on the wider scientific community that 'numbers ... simply not worthy of our current scientific attention' should have entered nearly every psychological textbook.[58]

But as Rose, Kamin and Lewontin remark, it was not just a sorry comment on the wider scientific community. 'The fraud perpetrated by Burt, and unwittingly propagated by the scientific community, served important social purposes.'[59] These purposes are none other than the validation of eugenicist policies that persecuted minority races and all other politically dispossessed classes.

With Burt's heritability studies discredited, the few remaining twin studies all suffer to varying degrees from the limitations of small samples. For instance, some twins were not really separated; and the environments experienced by those twins who were separated may have been essentially similar. The most comprehensive studies so far have measured the correlation in IQ scores between parents and biological children, who share half their genes, and between parents and adopted children in the same families, who share none of their genes. No significant difference could be found, which suggests that the connection between genes and IQ is extremely tenuous, and even more so the connection between genes and intelligence. As we saw earlier, the brain development differs significantly between identical twins in accordance with the experience of each individual.

No-one doubts that genes are involved in intelligence, just as they are involved in every other aspect of the living being. However, *that does not mean that specific genes determine particular traits*. That is the reductionist fallacy that refuses to see the living being as an interconnected, entangled whole. To hunt for genes in the belief that organisms are a combination of traits, each attributable to particular genes, is to engage in Lewis Carroll's hunt for the snark, where the snark turns out to be a boojum.

Any project to hunt for intelligence genes, or genes for other equally dubious multigenic traits, is simply based on bad science that has already been thoroughly discredited, shown to be rotten to the core. It has no place in our society, for it can serve only to reinforce the genetic-determinist, eugenicist ideology that inspires it.

Twelve

THE MUTABLE GENE AND THE HUMAN CONDITION

The inherent mutability of genes in the human genome is associated with many 'genetic' and 'non-genetic' diseases. This dashes any hope eugenicists might have of 'purifying' human populations by ridding them of harmful or undesirable mutations. It also increases the uncertainty of genetic screening. Attempts at gene replacement therapy are uniformly unsuccessful and are already posing unacceptable hazards for patients. The design of more aggressive gene transfer vectors introduces further risks from the genetic recombination of vectors with viruses to generate new disease-causing viruses. Recombination between viruses coming from the environment and those in the organism is strongly implicated in many cancers in animals. Similar hazards also arise in the proposed use of modified viral DNA as vaccines and in the xenotransplantation of organs. Genetic-engineering biotechnology diverts attention and resources from the overwhelming causes of ill-health, which are environmental, and blames the victims. The key to genetic health is precisely the same as the key to physiological health: an unpolluted environment, wholesome organic foods free from agrochemicals, and sanitary, socially acceptable and aesthetically satisfying living conditions.

The clockwork cell

Somewhere in the pile of plans that describe how to make a man is a page with the heading: 'How to make eyes' ... In the short-sight gene this page has a misprint somewhere on it … Somewhere else there is a page on 'How to make hair' …[1]

So begins a popular book on genetic engineering, written by a molecular biologist. All the detailed plans for making an entire human being, we are told, are contained in the genes, which are like files in a filing-cabinet. We are then told that the cell, with its 'mass of complex machinery,' is like a factory, organised from a central office (the nucleus), where the files are kept.

> The author's image of the cell is a metaphor for the predominant social relationship in our society, with the boss ensconced in the central office, making decisions and forcing workers to do his will, in a strictly one-way information flow.

'DNA transmits its message to the cell, forcing it to listen,' the book continues; 'the nucleus [containing the DNA] is the ultimate source of all decisions and changes of direction in a cell's existence.'[2] It is clear that the author's image of the cell is a metaphor for the predominant social relationship in our society, with the boss ensconced in the central office, making decisions and forcing workers to do his will, in a strictly one-way information flow. This picture fits so comfortably, so reassuringly into the consciousness of those who are near the decision-making end of the social scale that it is very difficult to relinquish. And this is the picture largely held by genetic engineers, despite the fact that it is contrary to all the findings in molecular genetics that have accumulated over the past two decades.

There is no doubt that mainstream biologists are an anachronism. They have been left far behind as physicists, chemists and mathematicians have, one by one, ceased to see the world as one of static equilibria and linear, clockwork mechanisms. Biologists are stuck in the mechanistic era, refusing to see the reality of organisms as irreducible wholes within which genes (and genomes) are mutable and mobile as they respond to their cellular and physiological milieu, which is ultimately connected to the external ecological and social environment. Lewis Wolpert, a fellow of the Royal Society and prominent member of its Committee for the Public Understanding of Science, writes: 'Science is the best way to understand the world. By understand, I mean gain insight into the way all nature works in a causal and *mechanistic* sense [emphasis added].'[3] This effectively excludes all of quantum theory from his scientific world view.

Mainstream biologists are clearly unaware that the new key to living organisation—in place of linear, one-way genetic determination—is non-linear, multi-dimensional intercommunication. To assume otherwise in the face of the irrefutable mass of existing evidence, as genetic engineers are doing, is the stuff of bad science; it is to subject the public to unacceptable risks. Science itself must be placed under the closest scrutiny by ethical committees, alongside issues of eugenics and genetic discrimination.

In this chapter I shall review evidence for the high degree of mutability of genes in the human genome, which is associated with many 'genetic' and 'non-genetic' diseases. I shall then show how current attempts at gene replacement therapy are being frustrated by cellular and physiological reactions that already pose unacceptable hazards to patients. The design of more aggressive gene transfer vectors introduces yet further risks, because of the genetic recombination of vectors with resident viruses to generate new, disease-causing viruses. Recombination between external and resident viruses is strongly implicated in many cancers in animals; similar hazards may also arise in the proposed use of modified viral DNA as vaccines and in the xenotransplantation of organs.

> Science itself must be placed under the closest scrutiny by ethical committees, alongside issues of eugenics and genetic discrimination.

DNA callisthenics and histrionics

The usual textbook picture of the DNA double-helix, such as the one presented in chapter 6, gives the impression of a static molecule that, rather like a bad boss, issues memos to the 'work force' to do the work but does no work himself. In reality DNA is now known to be flexible and highly mobile. It has to be in order to work properly within the cell.[4] Stretches of DNA can adopt a variety of conformations or shapes, depending on the base sequence, the base composition, the immediate environment surrounding the DNA, and proteins that convey messages to the DNA from the cell as the cell responds and adjusts to its environment.

The DNA double-helix is usually right-handed, but a left-handed helix is also known. The many forms are in dynamic equilibrium with one another. DNA can be bent, kinked or unwound or can become supercoiled to form tertiary DNA structures. Even *triplexes*—consisting of three strands wound together—can be found. Many of the structures are formed as DNA interacts with enzymes that replicate DNA, that transcribe DNA or recombine with it by cutting and rejoining different stretches of it. Different DNA structures are also formed as it binds to the plethora of protein transcription factors (see chapter 7). Most surprisingly, a new DNA structure has been identified in which the bases, instead of being paired up inside the double-helix, are actually on the outside. This 'P form' may be involved in replication and transcription *in vivo*.[5] Replication and transcription are both very complicated processes (see chapter 7 for transcription). DNA replication requires at least eight different enzymes and proteins, and errors are invariably introduced, as the copying is not exact.

DNA in the genome is also subject to chemical modifications by stray ionising radiation (X-rays and gamma rays), ultra-violet light, and chemical mutagens from the environment. Damage or mistakes in DNA replication are repaired by many different DNA repair enzymes. In higher organisms, DNA is systematically modified by methylation—the addition of a methyl group ($-CH_3$) to the cytosine or the adenosine base, a reaction catalysed by DNA methylases. Methylation tends to silence genes, that is, prevent them from being expressed, and is part of the cell's armoury of defence mechanisms against foreign DNA, such as viruses, that become inserted in the genome. In addition DNA is subject to a host of fluid genome processes. These rearrange, delete, amplify, mutate and convert sequences as part of normal development, or in the course of gene expression, or because of environmental perturbations. Similarly, units of DNA—transposons and viruses—jump in and out of genomes, causing disturbances to gene activities and changing genome organisation in the process. (All these are described in some detail in chapter 7.)

So, most of the time, DNA is involved in rather mild exercises or callisthenics, but during crises it will also go into spectacular histrionics, giving large changes in organisation. The molecular and reproductive biologist Jeff Pollard, who in 1984 was one of the first to recognise the full implications of the new genetics, refers to DNA as a 'metabolic molecule'.[6] A high mutation rate is therefore expected, for mistakes can arise as a result of failures of repair, or as a result of hypermutation and other fluid genome processes, particularly when the environment is perturbed. DNA methylation itself is mutagenic, as methyl-cytosine is converted to adenine by deamination or removal of an amino group ($-NH_2$), and repair is less effective in this case. It is estimated that about a third of all point mutations in human diseases result from converting a methylated cytosine paired with guanosine, an mCG pair, by deamination to a TG pair.[7] Xeroderma pigmentosum is a particular human condition caused by the failure of one kind of DNA repair mechanism that removes defective dimers—two adjacent bases on the same strand joined together—caused by ultra-violet damage.[8] Patients with this disorder are hypersensitive to UV light and suffer from a high incidence of skin and eye lesions, including cancers, when exposed to sunlight. There are mutations in at least eight genes that can result in this condition.

Germ-line mutation rates

The overall mutation rates in germ-line genes estimated from mutations in known single genes that give rise to diseases are between seven and nine per thousand live births. Of these a third are recessive mutations in autosomes (non-sex chromosomes), a third are dominant mutations in autosomes, and a third are sex-linked mutations on the X chromosome.[9] These single genes are spread over the entire genome, associated with a wide variety of conditions, such as adenosine deaminase deficiency, Duchenne muscular dystrophy, cystic fibrosis, sickle-cell anaemia, haemophilia, and Huntington's chorea. These mutation rates are minimum estimates, because they already exclude those lethal mutations that kill the fetus before birth and also exclude others that do not lead to recognisable effects.

A comparable figure for mutation rates comes from 'DNA fingerprinting', which was discovered by the British geneticist Alec Jeffreys in 1985.[10] This is based on identifying variations in sections of DNA where certain short sequences are repeated a variable number of times in different individuals. These are known as variable-number tandem repeats, or VNTRs. The technique of DNA fingerprinting involves cutting the DNA with restriction enzymes, each recognising a specific sequence of several bases, running the fragments on electrophoresis, and probing the bands with the short repeats of interest. By means of different mixtures of cutting enzymes and probes, a very complicated pattern can be generated that is specific to each individual. The pattern can be used in identifying criminals and in assigning parentage. Children generally have a mixture of bands from both parents; however, up to 1 per cent show new bands that are not present in either parent, representing new mutations that have arisen in the germ cells of their parents. These mutations involve changes in the number of tandem repeats of short sequences—ten to fifteen base pairs long—interspersed throughout the genome, mostly in non-coding regions or 'junk DNA'.

Variable numbers of very short tandem repeats also occur in coding regions of genes.[11] The first example of these to be uncovered was the fragile X syndrome, which may be accompanied by severe mental retardation. The condition is named in reference to a distortion of the X chromosome in the patient, involving two small pieces that seem to be breaking away from the end of the long arms of the chromosome. Fragile X syndrome shows a strange pattern of inheritance, in that the severity of the disease can increase or decrease over two or three generations.

A gene has been discovered to be associated with fragile X syndrome, coding for a protein that binds RNA, and is particularly abundant in the nervous system. It is a complicated gene, 38 kb in length, with seventeen exons (see chapter 7 for details of the interrupted gene). A region within the first exon has repeats of the triplet CCG. Unaffected people have between six and sixty repeats, while those with fragile X syndrome have up to several thousand, and the greater the number of copies present the more severe the syndrome tends to be. The number of repeats tends to change in successive generations. Large numbers of repeats cause excessive methylation, and the gene is silenced.

Huntington's chorea is a similar disorder. It is a dominant nervous degenerative disease with variable age of onset and is a result of the multiplication of copies of a CAG repeat within the associated gene. Those with the disease have forty or more copies of the triplet; those with thirty-four copies or fewer show no symptoms. Again, the number of repeats can increase in successive generations, leading to earlier ages of onset. The number of repeats is more likely to increase if the gene is passed on by the father than by the mother. More than a third of all cases of the disease in which the gene is passed on by the father show an increase in copy number, sometimes up to forty copies. Mutations involving changes in tandem copy number repeats arise during DNA replication and are thought to be due to faults in recombination between chromosome pairs, so that one chromosome ends up with more copies and the other with fewer.

It is estimated that at least twenty-two new germ-line mutations arise in each person. This is a minimum estimate, as many mutations will go undetected if they do not have phenotypic effects.

In general, mutations arise with each round of DNA replication. As sperms take many more cell divisions to mature, and therefore more rounds of DNA replication, there are more opportunities for mutations to occur in the male germ cells. Most new mutations have been found in genes passed on from the father. The ratio of paternal to maternal germ-line mutation rate is about ten to one.

To estimate the rate of germ-line mutation, geneticists studied patients with haemophilia B, associated with mutations in factor IX, required for blood-clotting.[12] They found independent mutations in 95 per cent or more of all families with severe or moderate disease. There were 'hot spots' for multiple types of mutations. One of these was the dinucleotide sequence CG, which accounts for 25 per cent of the independent point mutations observed in this gene. Another hot spot accounts for 8 per cent of independent mutations, which are deletions or insertions of 20 bp or less. Larger deletions of 50 bp or more also occur and are associated with inversions of the gene sequence—the original sequence read backwards. In addition, other deletions are found within the coding regions where alternating purines and pyrimidines, such as GT or AC, occur. It is estimated that at least twenty-two new germ-line mutations arise in each person. This is a minimum estimate, as many mutations will go undetected if they do not have phenotypic effects.

A transposable element, called mariner, originally found in the fruit fly and since identified in many insects and other arthropods, is now found in primates, including humans, where it leads to a neurological wasting disease, Charcot-Marie-Tooth syndrome.

Mutations may also be caused by the integration of viruses, retrotranscripts (see chapter 7) or transposable elements into the genome. More than 500,000 separate integration events have been found in the human genome. Substantial sequence homology exists between external retroviruses and the retrotransposons found in the genome. Retroviruses, as you will recall, are RNA viruses that replicate by reverse transcription of their own RNA into complementary DNA, which is inserted into the host genome, where it directs the synthesis of many virus RNA genomes as well as the protein coat that packages the RNA into infectious virus particles. Howard Temin has suggested that retroviruses integrated themselves into the genome, gave up their independent existence, and evolved into transposable elements and other degenerate relics. On the other hand, it is also possible that the viruses had evolved from cellular transposable elements.[13] In general, retroviruses and transposable elements are specific to one host species.

A recent finding that gives cause for concern is that a transposable element, called *mariner*, originally found in the fruit fly and since identified in many insects and other arthropods,[14] is now found in primates, including humans, where it leads to a neurological wasting disease, Charcot-Marie-Tooth syndrome.[15] The gene containing the element, the CMT gene, has a large duplication of 1,500 kb, caused by unequal recombination between homologous chromosomes. This is thought to be due to the DNA-cutting enzyme encoded by the *mariner* cutting in the wrong place. Though the copy of the *mariner* in the CMT gene has been disabled, an active *mariner* element has been found in yet another gene, which could have helped the disabled copy do its damage.

How has *mariner* crossed so many species barriers? It is thought to have crossed the species barrier while integrated into the genome of a virus or some other pathogen. Each time *mariner* enters a new species it is thought to jump around wildly, disrupting many genes, until it loses its own genes for moving about; but at least one copy in the human genome remains active. Does that mean it is a recent acquisition? This same element has been experimented on by genetic engineers in an attempt to construct transgenic sterile mosquitoes for controlling malaria, a practice that has already been criticised as thoroughly ineffective and irrational.[16] For example, new batches have to be released, as sterile mosquitoes do not reproduce; they have to be kept alive during the dry seasons by providing ponds for them, which would encourage more mosquitoes to breed; and finally, the mosquitoes have to be kept alive by 'human volunteers' whom they bite and suck blood from! It is also highly hazardous. Has *mariner* spread from transgenic mosquitoes to human beings? If such transgenic mosquitoes are widely released, it is bound to result in the further spread of mariner elements to human subjects.

Geneticists are hoping to construct 'universal vectors' that can be used in all medically important insects.[17] This would have disastrous consequences for human health, of which the researchers are completely oblivious, being concerned solely with the way in which insects might be genetically engineered.

The high rate of germ-line mutation dashes any hopes eugenicists might have of 'purifying' human populations by ridding them of harmful or undesirable mutations. It also increases the uncertainty of screening tests and compromises their ability to predict the individual's risks of suffering from genetic diseases and other conditions. The present approach to health, which focuses entirely on genes, is seriously misplaced, particularly in view of the recent observations that defective genes associated with a range of hereditary diseases may regain normal functions by somatic mutations (see chapter 7).

Somatic mutations and cancer[18]

Somatic mutations are thought to be particularly associated with cancer, which is predominantly a non-genetic disease, in the sense that it is not inherited. Cancer manifests itself as uncontrolled cell multiplication, usually starting from a single cell that has undergone malignant transformation, after which its descendant cells proliferate as clones in the cancerous growth. However, many different genes can be involved in different cancers in different tissues, even in a single individual.[19] It is claimed that six to seven mutations may have to accumulate in the same cell before it becomes cancerous, as is consistent with the steep exponential increase in the incidence of cancer with age. The death rate from colon cancer in the United States rises from almost nil at age twenty to 100 per million at age sixty and to nearly 300 per million at age eighty-five.[20] However, somatic mutation rates do not show a sharp increase with age. As measured by the loss of an enzyme activity in leukocytes (white blood cells), the frequency of mutation increases linearly from an average of 1 in 10^5 cells at twenty years of age to 2 in 10^5 cells at age sixty. This increase in mutation rate is attributed to a decrease in the effectiveness of DNA repair.[21]

The genes related to cancer come in several categories. The two major ones are *oncogenes,* which promote cell growth, and *tumour-suppressor genes,* which constrain cell growth.[22] More recently three other groups have been identified: the *anti-apoptosis* genes, which prevent cell death, the *anti-metastasis* genes, which prevent the tumour from spreading, and the multi-drug-resistance genes responsible for resistance to drugs administered in chemotherapy (see chapter 7).[23]

Oncogenes are derived by mutation from normal cellular genes that promote cell growth, the *proto-oncogenes*. Mutations arise from many different mechanisms, including breaks and rearrangements in chromosomes caused by carcinogens and mutagens. A major cause of mutation is retroviral integration into or near any of the genes. These retroviruses can also carry oncogenes that they have originally captured from the cell. In some cancer cells the normal proto-oncogene is simply over-expressed, because of a strong viral promoter inserted near the gene. Tumour-suppressor genes block cell growth, and a tumour is thought to develop when both normal copies are inactivated by mutation. About twenty different tumour-suppressor genes have been identified so far. One cancer-related gene involved in cell death is p53, encoding a protein that normally brings the cell cycle to a halt when DNA damage is detected, so that the cell dies instead of progressing to the cancerous state. Mutations in p53 may allow the cell to continue with its damaged DNA, resulting in multiple mutations that eventually lead to cancer.

It is clear that many different kinds of somatic mutations can be associated with cancer. The question is often raised whether the mutations are the effect rather than the cause of cancer. Indeed, cancer cells accumulate mutations up to a thousand times faster than normal cells, and the mutations could have arisen after the crucial transforming event. There is now evidence that most

cancers are genetically unstable.[24] Most cancer cells show instability at the chromosomal level, involving loss and gains of
whole chromosomes or large portions of chromosomes. A minority
of cancers are unstable at the gene level, involving base
substitutions, deletions or insertions of a few nucleotides. While
genic instability is associated with defects in DNA repair, chromosomal instability is not, and its cause is completely unknown.

There is no doubt that environmental factors, such as X-rays,
gamma-rays, cigarette smoke and numerous other chemical
pollutants, increase the risk of cancer, though the increase in
mutation rates is not as clear-cut. Survivors of the nuclear bombs
in Hiroshima and Nagasaki showed an increased frequency of
cancers, including leukaemia, breast cancer and cancer of the
lungs and digestive system, compared with controls who had not
been exposed to the bomb. Since the war many people in the
armed forces and civilian populations have been exposed to
radioactive fall-out from nuclear tests as well as 'low-level'
radiation around nuclear installations. This exposure results in an
increased incidence of cancers over several generations.[25] In one
study a group of 1,068 children born to workers at the nuclear
processing plant at Sellafield, Cumberland, were compared with
another group of 1,546 children born outside the area but
attending the local schools. The leukaemia and cancer cases were
found only in the children born in Sellafield, suggesting that the
childhood cancers developed as the result of radioactive damage
to the parents' germ cells.

Similarly, death rates from lung cancer are five times higher for
asbestos workers and eleven times higher for smokers. For asbestos
workers who are also smokers the rate is fifty-three times higher,
resulting from the two risk factors being multiplied together.

> The overwhelming causes of ill-health are environmental, and
> not in our genes.

Cancer is second only to cardiovascular disease as a killer in
industrialised countries. Studies carried out since the last century

have documented the strong correlation between the incidence of cancer and the degree of industrialisation, measured by indicators such as gross national product (GNP).[26] In non-industrialised societies all over the world, cancer was either unknown or extremely rare. Apart from radioactive wastes from nuclear installations, the major culprits are the increasing amounts of industrial and agricultural chemicals discharged into the environment as landfills, waste streams, aerosols and fumes, and sprays and other applications to crops and farm animals. At least seventy thousand synthetic chemicals have been introduced into our environment since the industrial revolution.. Numerous studies have implicated pesticides, herbicides, heavy metals, synthetic chemicals, solvents and toxic fumes from town incinerators in damage to every organ system of our body, including the genes. This damage results in illnesses affecting the nervous system, the immune system, the hormonal system, and the liver and kidneys. They also cause birth defects, and cancers.[27] Recently weak electromagnetic fields near high-tension power lines and other electrical installations have emerged as contributory factors to cancer and cancer progression.[28]

The only environmental agents widely acknowledged by the establishment as causative factors in diseases are 'diet' and 'lifestyle', both supposed to depend on the individual victim. A diet high in saturated fats and a stressful life-style are found to increase risks of cancer. However, it is also known that carcinogens such as pesticides and pesticide residues accumulate in animal fat, increasing in concentration down the food-chain, so that 'toppredators' like human beings will be taking in dangerously high amounts of the carcinogens. What is becoming clear is that the overwhelming causes of ill-health are environmental, and not in our genes.

Gene dreams fade into nightmares

There have been over a hundred clinical trials in gene therapy since 1990, and 'not much of what has been trialed [tried] does work.'[29] 'Hundreds of people have been treated with gene therapy, but no one has been cured. Is it time for researchers to return to the lab?'[30] Harold Varmus, director of the US National Institute of Health, which has spent about $200 million a year on gene replacement therapy schemes, told a Congressional committee in May 1995: 'While there are several reports of convincing gene transfer and expression, there is still little or no evidence of therapeutic benefit in patients, even in animal models.'[31]

There are two forms of gene therapy. The first, *ex vivo* gene therapy, relies on taking cells—such as bone marrow cells—from patients, transforming them in culture with the missing gene carried in a suitable gene transfer vector, then returning the transformed cells to the patient. The other method, *in vivo* gene therapy, delivers the gene in the vector directly into the patient. Many of the problems come from the gene transfer vectors. For transforming cells in culture, retroviral vectors are used, as they infect cells that are multiplying and can insert themselves into the cell's genome. But because they insert at random they can easily cause cancer. For gene therapy *in vivo,* vectors made from adenovirus are used, which do not integrate into the chromosome and are less likely to disrupt the genome. An alternative is to use liposomes to deliver the genes without using vectors. This gets the genes into the cytoplasm but not the nucleus, so they cannot be transcribed and expressed.

However, patients were found to develop immune reactions against the vectors after the first dose. In clinical trials on cystic fibrosis, patients' airways became inflamed after breathing in aerosols of the adenovirus; one patient almost died. Later research in rats showed that injections of the adenovirus directly into the brain appeared to be harmless at first; but when the same animals were injected with the adenovirus in the foot two months later, they developed severe inflammation in the brain.[32] This was a surprise to the researchers, as conventional wisdom has it that the brain is protected from the immune system by the blood-brain barrier, which is not supposed to allow macromolecules to pass through.

It is clear that gene replacement therapy already poses unacceptable risks to patients, and threatens the survival of the schemes themselves.

> Contemplated schemes of gene replacement therapy are very likely to cause disease and to generate virulent viruses that can infect the population at large.

Desperate attempts are under way to salvage the gene replacement therapy schemes, as private companies have also invested heavily in developing this potential health care market The safety of gene therapy vectors is unproved, and there is a growing debate over the potential for generating infectious viruses and harmful effects caused by random insertion into the genome of the cell.[33] One candidate is the insect virus baculovirus, which has been found to invade mammalian cells (see chapter 8); the other is the AIDS virus, a retrovirus that can infect non-dividing cells. The vector constructed from the AIDS virus had all the genes that the virus needs to duplicate itself removed, so that it could be multiplied only with cell lines that harboured the endogenous helper virus. The possibility had been raised that the disabled AIDS virus could recombine into a virulent form and cause AIDS, but at least one of the authors of the research has been undeterred. The pressure is on to construct more and more aggressive gene transfer vectors, even though it is now well known that viruses can recombine, and that human genomes already harbour resident proviruses and related elements ready to help disabled viral vectors mobilise and to recombine with them. Furthermore, recombination between external and resident viruses is strongly implicated in cancers in animals, while the culturing of viruses can itself generate virulent variants from initially benign forms. In short, *contemplated schemes of gene replacement therapies are very likely to cause disease and to generate virulent viruses that can infect the population at large.*

Hazards from vector mobilisation and recombination

Retroviruses and retrovirus-like DNAs were first discovered in eukaryotic genomes in 1980 by Howard Temin, along with retro-transposons and other elements that are very similar to retroviruses (see above).[34] Because of their sequence homologies to viruses coming from the outside, it can be predicted that recombination will occur between the endogenous elements and the viruses. There is now experimental evidence of such recombination, which is directly involved in causing diseases.

Feline leukaemic viruses (FeLVs) of domestic cats are transmitted by infection. They are capable of inducing either acute disease or, after a prolonged incubation period, cancers in the lymphatic system. Up to three-quarters of the FeLV envelope glycoprotein gene may be replaced by sequences from a resident virus to produce biologically active recombinant viruses involved in generating malignant lymphomas in infected cats.[35] Because the envelope protein is replaced largely by the one encoded by the resident virus, these recombinant viruses are able to escape host immunity. Many other recombinant viruses are generated, some of them being implicated in diseases of the nervous system and of blood cells.

The mouse mammary tumour virus is transmitted to susceptible offspring by infection through milk, as exogenous virus, or through the germ-line, as resident provirus. Exogenously acquired and some resident mouse mammary tumour viruses are found to be expressed at high levels in lactating mammary glands, and the resident viral RNA is packaged together with the exogenous viral RNA in the same virus particles. This has given rise to a recombinant virus, found in the mammary tumours of infected mice, containing part of the gene coding for the envelope protein from the resident virus.[36]

Similar findings have been made in viruses infecting birds. A highly infectious avian leukaemic virus was isolated that was identical to the extensively characterised Rous sarcoma virus, except in one gene, *gag*. This difference accounts for its super-infectivity.[37] The new virus has been generated by recombination between the exogenous Rous sarcoma virus and resident viruses *in cultured cells*. This suggests that the culturing of viruses is already a hazard by itself. The researchers are developing this supervirus as a gene transfer vector for birds, in complete disregard of the potential dangers.

Recombination between an injected virus and resident viral genes has been demonstrated in strain AKR mice carrying a provirus.[38] These mice develop spontaneous cancers of the T-cells (leukocytes involved in the immune response) at between six and twelve months of age. The immediate cause is not the inherited provirus but requires recombination between the provirus AKv and two or more additional resident viruses. These recombinant viruses, called mink cell focus-inducing (MCF) viruses, were named for their ability to induce the abnormal growth of mink cells, indicating their expanded host range.

Recombination can also occur between different variants of an external virus in the course of viral proliferation. Drug-resistant HIV1 variants can be isolated from patients undergoing prolonged anti-viral chemotherapy, and can also arise in culture by passage through increasing concentrations of drugs. Viral recombination has now been shown to be responsible for generating multiple resistance to a single drug and also resistance to two different drugs, AZT and 3TC.[39]

These findings have enormous implications for the development of cancers, and also draw attention to the hazards inherent in gene transfer vectors and other naked DNA used in gene therapy that carry viral genes. I have already mentioned the transgenic DNA present in transgenic crops, all of which contain the cauliflower mosaic viral promoter. Because resident viruses and dormant proviral sequences are ubiquitous in all genomes, there are bound to be recombination events between the introduced vector or viral genes and resident viruses or proviral sequences. The findings also draw attention to the risks involved in culturing viruses for vector production, which can itself generate new viruses with increased host ranges.

The dangers of generating pathogens by viral recombination are real. Over a period of ten years, six scientists working on the genetic engineering of cancer-related oncogenes at the Pasteur Institutes in France have contracted cancer.[40] Further studies a year later revealed that the isolated DNA of a human oncogene applied to the skin on the back of mice gave rise to tumours in the blood vessels and lymphatic system within weeks.[41] These observations rang alarm bells among laboratory workers as well as the British Health and Safety Executive. In the course of culturing a human retrovirus (HTLV-II) associated with hairy-cell leukaemia in humans,[42] two infectious viruses with deletions and rearrangements of their genomes were generated that have increased abilities to transform normal cells into cancerous states.

I have mentioned the hazards from recombinant baculovirus, concurrently being developed for controlling insects in agriculture and as a gene transfer vector for human gene therapy (see chapter 8). Australian scientists have genetically engineered a virus that stops mice from becoming pregnant and hope to use similar viruses to control mouse plagues in the wild.[43] Critics point out that such contraceptive viruses could cause an ecological disaster by infecting and sterilising other species and should never be released.

A vaccinia-rabies recombinant virus was dropped in edible bait in Belgium a few years ago to vaccinate foxes against rabies. This was ostensibly to eradicate rabies in domestic animals that could infect human beings. As foxes and other wildlife ingesting the bait could carry another pox virus, such as the cowpox virus, which circulates among wildlife, recombination could occur between the two viruses. A survey in 1996 revealed that 63 per cent of bank voles and 7 per cent of wood mice species *do* carry antibodies against cowpox, indicating the presence of the cowpox virus. Nevertheless, *in direct contradiction of the evidence,* the researchers concluded that 'the risk of virus recombination in wildlife can therefore be considered to be extremely low.'[44]

A disturbing incident with a rabies vaccine in Tanzania ought to serve as a warning. An outbreak of rabies in the Serengeti Wildlife Park prompted a team of vets to give thirty-four animals a rabies vaccine. Within ten months four vaccinated dogs were dead, and since 1991 there have been no sightings of any of the dogs at all.[45] Did the vaccine regenerate live rabies viruses by recombination and kill the dogs?

Recombination between a viral vaccine against Aujeszky's disease and a co-infecting virus to regenerate infectious Aujeszky's disease virus has been demonstrated in cell cultures.[46]

Vaccines: prevention worse than the disease?

Another area of development likely to contribute to generating new viruses is that of recombinant DNA vaccines. The use of recombinant viral vaccines increases the likelihood of re-combination and also potentially broadens the host range of the new virus (or viruses) that may arise, as the viral genomes used in vaccines are often already chimeric in construction. As mentioned in chapter 9, the 'naked DNA' from viruses (viruses stripped of their protein coat) can have a wider host range than the viruses themselves. Therefore, DNA vaccines—those made from viral DNA—have the ability to infect hosts that are not susceptible to the intact viruses, thereby crossing wide species barriers, with many opportunities to recombine and generate new disease-causing viruses.[47] Recombinant DNA vaccines are worse, as even small modifications of viral DNA can have unpredictable effects on its host range and virulence.[48] Furthermore, recombinant viral DNA is generally more unstable than the original virus and more prone to recombine with other viruses and to pick up new genes from their hosts to turn them into pathogens.

Vaccines are notoriously ineffective against viruses that rapidly mutate and recombine. Even vaccines against bacterial pathogens perform erratically. The BCG vaccine against TB offers anything from 80 per cent protection to no protection against the disease. In the largest vaccination scheme in India, involving 350,000 people, the vaccine gave no protection whatsoever.[49]

> Over thirty years, the measles vaccine has caused vicious mutation of the disease, transformed it into a disease of adults and infants, and left us with inadequate immunity to pass on to our children.

Vaccines can cause the very diseases against which they are supposed to offer protection. An outbreak of measles occurred among a fully immunised secondary school population in Corpus Christi, Texas, in the mid-eighties.[50] In Britain there have been national campaigns since the fifties and sixties to mass-immunise children against infectious diseases, including whooping-cough, polio, diphtheria, measles, and tetanus. The efficacy of these vaccines has been seriously questioned. At the same time they have been linked to hundreds of deaths and cases of permanent brain damage and other illnesses well into the nineties. Attenuated (weakened) or killed viruses used as vaccines can give rise to mutant viruses or can encourage the growth of the viruses in the population at large. Three per cent of babies born to mothers given hepatitis B vaccine go on to develop a mutant form of the disease. In a large group of babies born to hepatitis-positive mothers and given full immunisation against the disease, one in sixty developed hepatitis B, and one in eighty had a mutant of the virus in the vaccine.[51]

The health journalist Lynne McTaggart, a long-time campaigner against iatrogenic diseases (diseases caused by prescription drugs and treatments), writes: 'Many vaccination programmes have left us far worse off than we were before. Over thirty years, the measles vaccine has caused vicious mutation of the disease, transformed it into a disease of adults and infants, and left us with inadequate immunity to pass on to our children. [And] we now have substantial numbers of children damaged by the vaccine.'[52]

> Vaccines produced in transgenic plants for use in humans and domestic livestock have an increased potential to generate new pathogenic viruses with extremely broad host ranges.

Current attempts to create vaccines against the AIDS virus have run into many difficulties. One made by deleting several genes from the related simian immunodeficiency virus (SIV) is found to cause AIDS in infant and adult macaques,[53] raising serious safety concerns over similar viral vaccines for humans.

Vaccines produced in transgenic plants[54] for use in humans and domestic livestock have an increased potential to generate new pathogenic viruses with extremely broad host ranges. There are two general strategies for producing vaccines. The first is to insert pieces of animal viral coat protein genes into plant viruses, such as the cow-pea mosaic virus. The chimeric virus is then multiplied in susceptible plants, which also synthesise the chimeric viral coat protein. The second strategy is to create transgenic plants, with the appropriate chimeric vector containing the animal viral coat protein, or those parts of it that are responsible for the immune reaction, so that the plant synthesises the protein continuously. The plant material is then fed directly to animals and human subjects for immunisation.

Both these practices are based on creating chimeric viruses or endogenous virus-like elements that already have broadened host ranges. Their ability to generate yet more viruses that attack a wide range of species should not be underestimated. As we saw in chapter 1, such cross-species viral pathogens with wide host ranges may already have evolved, some for the first time. There is no indication that researchers have taken this possibility into account. The release of these transgenic plants into the environment will contaminate our crops and has the potential to create ecological and health catastrophes. An acceptable alternative is to use plant tissue culture under strictly contained conditions. Some virologists, such as Terje Traavik, are coming around to the view that mass vaccinations are of dubious value under most circumstances, because of the inherent hazards involved in generating live recombinant viruses.

Xenotransplants: panacea or pandemic?

The debate continues over xenotransplantation—organs taken from animal species for transplanting into human beings. While ethics and risks have featured prominently in the debate, no-one has stressed the fact that it is commercially driven from the first. A lucrative international trade in human body parts has developed in the wake of the increasing privatisation of health care all over the world,[55] and supply has been far outstripping demand. David Sachs of Harvard University Medical School estimates that more than 400,000 people in the United States could benefit from heart transplants, even though the official waiting list for hearts in 1996 was 3,698.[56] This surely reflects the medical establishment's overenthusiastic subscription to the health market rather than an honest assessment of need. In 1988 a study by the Rand Corporation found that 25 per cent of all surgical operations in the United States are unnecessary, and cost a total of $132 billion a year.[57] The kind of estimate produced by Sachs would put the market for heart transplants alone at $2 billion a year. And the market for heart, lung, liver, kidney and other transplants is bound to increase, as organ failures, like cancer and many other diseases, are on the rise.[58]

> Human genes from transgenic pigs that suppress the 'hyperacute' rejection of transplanted organs also happen to suppress the body's defence against bacteria and viral infections, making much more likely the emergence and growth of recombinant, cross-species viruses.

The risks from xenotransplantation are well known and accepted by the mainstream scientific community. Robin Weiss, a professor at the Institute of Cancer Research in London, has shown that a pig retrovirus is capable of infecting human cells in the laboratory. And once the virus has gone through one life-cycle in human cells, it is then able to infect a wide range of other human cells.[59] That is why the Advisory Group on the Ethics of Xenotransplantation imposed a moratorium on clinical trials.[60] Proponents claim that 'pathogen-free' transgenic pigs can be raised for the purpose of transplantation;[61] but it will be impossible to get rid of the proviruses and related elements that are ubiquitous in eukaryotic genomes. It is these elements that will pose the greatest threats for recombination.

Sure enough, multiple copies of such resident retroviruses have since been found in the pig genome, dashing any hopes of breeding 'pathogen-free' pigs. What we must realise is that using body parts from so-called 'humanised pigs' genetically engineered for xenotransplants may actually be more dangerous than, say, using a pig heart-valve that has not been genetically engineered. (And I might add that it is less objectionable on ethical grounds to use pigs that have been farmed for food in the first place.) Transgenic pigs are now engineered with human genes that suppress the 'hyperacute' rejection of transplanted organ—the destruction of the donor organ within minutes of exposure to the body. This also happens to suppress the body's defence against bacteria and viral infections,[62] making much more likely the emergence and growth of recombinant, cross-species viruses.

The same problem, to a lesser though still significant extent, is inherent in the use of transgenic farm animals, such as sheep and cows engineered with human genes to produce pharmaceutically exploitable proteins, or in the armies of transgenic mice engineered with defective human genes to serve as models of human diseases. The exploitation of animals in this fashion has raised serious concerns about animal welfare (see chapter 10), particularly as any benefit that can be gained from such reductionist models of health and disease are questionable. As we saw in chapter 10, an acceptable alternative is now being developed by using the patient's own cells to regenerate the organ on an artificial scaffold in tissue culture, or in the patient's own body.

Gene technology will not improve the health of nations

Most recent developments of gene technology in human genetics and health are commercially driven. Far from improving the health of the people, they serve to *divert* attention from the overwhelming causes of ill-health, which are environmental, and to blame the victims instead. The same chemical and drug industries that have been major polluters of the environment, that have been causing increasing damage to all the organ systems of our body, including our genes, are now set to reap enormous profits from those made ill. Genuine genetic diseases that can be traced to single genes constitute less than 2 per cent of all diseases,[63] and even these have proved to be much more complicated than previously thought. In addition, at least 1 per cent of such genetic diseases are new mutations, most probably caused by environmental mutagens.

> Personalised medicine based on our genetic make-up is a pipe-dream. We have 100,000 genes, with hundreds of variants in each gene. Furthermore, up to 95 per cent of our genome may consist of so-called 'junk DNA', which has no known function.

Despite all the promises of gene therapy, there has not been a single documented success in twenty years. Yet it is still being aggressively pursued, with dangerous techniques that can cause cancer and create new viruses. Another promise, that of personalised medicine based on our genetic make-up, is a pipe-dream. We have 100,000 genes, with hundreds of variants in each gene. Furthermore, up to 95 per cent of our genome may consist of so-called 'junk DNA', which has no known function.

> The health care system is being rapidly replaced by a health market. At the same time, people who do become ill are stigmatised by their genes that 'predispose' them to be ill.

The health care system is being rapidly replaced by a health market. At the same time, people who do become ill are stigmatised by their genes that 'predispose' them to be ill. By extension, any other condition deemed to be undesirable will also be blamed on such 'predisposing' genes. Genetic discrimination and eugenics are taking insidious, privatised forms.

Since the nineteen-eighties, health care systems all over the world have been seriously undermined by 'free-market' imperatives. So-called 'structural adjustment programmes', supported by the World Bank, have forced Third World governments to impose charges on health care for the poor, to cut public spending by reducing services, and to promote private health businesses.[64] As a result, malnutrition and infant mortality rates have been increasing in many countries, reversing a long-term trend; and infectious diseases have re-emerged with a vengeance in immunologically compromised populations. It is doubtful whether genetic engineering can improve anyone's health, least of all the poor.

The plight of the Third World poor is almost invariably blamed on increase in population. While reproductive technologies are promoted to treat infertility among white Europeans and North Americans, women in racial minorities and in the South are being sterilised against their will, with drugs causing crippling side effects.[65] The Third World poor are routinely used as guinea-pigs for vaccines and drugs. A cholera vaccine tested on 85,000 Bangladeshi women and children by a Swedish company, beginning in 1985, was found to offer only fleeting protection, if any, and in any case is so expensive that no Bangladeshi would be able to afford it.[66] Have large vaccine trials like this one contributed to the re-emergence of new variants of old diseases? Third World governments should be on their guard against the new vaccines, especially those involving recombinant naked DNA.

Check-list of hazards in human genetics and medicine

The many and varied applications of genetic-engineering biotechnology in human genetics and medicine have special implications for ethics and health, for humans as well as animals. (In this check-list I have collected together issues raised in chapters 10, 11, and 12.)

Ethical implications

1. Genetic discrimination from diagnostic tests.
2. Negative eugenic practices in 'therapeutic' abortions.
3. Positive and negative eugenic practices in *in vitro* fertilisation and diagnostic techniques.
4. The marginalisation of women in the commercial control of reproductive technologies.
5. The possibility of the immoral use of human embryos in 'pharming' and in providing tissues and organs for transplantation.
6. The immoral use of humans and human embryos for experimentation.
7. Negative impacts on animal welfare in 'pharming' practices.

Hazards to human and animal health

1. The risk of cross-species epidemics as a result of facilitated recombination between animal and human viruses in xenotransplantation.
2. The risk of cross-species epidemics as a result of facilitated recombination between animal viruses and resident viruses in the human genome in 'pharm' animals, such as transgenic sheep.
3. The risk of severe immune reactions from vectors in gene replacement therapy.
4. The risk of cancer from facilitated recombination between gene replacement vectors and resident viruses.
5. The risk of superviruses arising from facilitated recombination between viruses and cells in culture.
6. The risk of cross-species superviruses arising from facilitated recombination between viral vaccines and resident viruses in plants, animals, and humans.
7. The risk of harmful mutations from cross-species transfer of transposable elements.
8. The risk of new iatrogenic diseases from new generations of genetically engineered drugs and vaccines.

Conclusion

Genetic-engineering biotechnology is neither going to feed the world nor improve our health—quite the opposite. In addition, it brings enormous risks. The real alternatives lie elsewhere.

Scientific findings accumulated over the past twenty years have invalidated every assumption of the genetic-determinist mentality that is driving and promoting genetic-engineering biotechnology. Scientific evidence is compelling us to an ecological, holistic perspective, especially where genes are concerned. Our destiny does not lie in the genes. Genes are not constant and unchanging, as previously supposed: instead, genes are found to respond to the physiology of the organism and require a stable, balanced ecology to maintain stability. Organic agriculture is predicated on a balanced ecology, which depends on a diverse community of healthy organisms free from agrochemicals. Similarly, the key to genetic health is precisely the same as the key to physiological health: unpolluted environment, wholesome organic foods free from agrochemicals, and sanitary, socially fulfilling and aesthetically satisfying living conditions.

Thirteen

THE NEW AGE OF THE ORGANISM

It is clear that we need a deep and sustained change of direction in all spheres of life before the dream of solving all the world's problems by genetic-engineering biotechnology turns into a nightmare. Contemporary scientific approaches that concentrate on the organism, on wholeness and complexity are more consistent with scientific findings in molecular genetics and other disciplines. Organic stability arises naturally as the result of a balanced ecology; this has large implications for health and disease, especially in the development of cancer and the emergence of new pathogens. Sustainable systems can similarly be understood in accordance with a theory of the organism, whose carrying capacity is not rigidly set by the physical limits imposed by the second law of thermodynamics but depends on its internal dynamic organisation. This holistic yet rigorous perspective in contemporary Western science is consonant with traditional indigenous sciences all over the world. Reductionist science has had its day. Let us reject the bad science that has served to exploit, to oppress, to obfuscate, and to destroy the earth and its inhabitants. Let us opt for a joyful and sustainable future—beyond genetic engineering.

Life beyond genetic determinism

Genetic determinism and capitalist economic theory stem from the same roots in nineteenth-century Britain, which they served remarkably well. The ideology of competition and exploitation validates and extols the social reality that gave it birth, and this social reality is in turn shaped and propagated by the ideology posing as science. Together they have succeeded only too well in conquering the world.

The ever-intensifying exploitation of human beings and of nature by the major economies of the world has far outstripped the rate at which renewable resources can be replaced and at which substitutes for non-renewable resources can be developed. This has resulted in widespread environmental degradation, the accumulation of toxic waste products, and consequently a downward spiral of ever-diminishing returns in production and poverty, misery and deteriorating health for the majority of the world's population.

'The main enemy of the open society, I believe, is no longer the communist but the capitalist threat.'[1] This statement is remarkable if only because its author is George Soros, a well-known capitalist who has himself benefited a great deal from the system. In the same article he criticises neo-liberal economic theory and social Darwinism and refers to the same mutually reinforcing relationship between mindset and reality that I have developed at length in this book. 'There is a two-way connection—between thinking and events ...'[2]

In this final chapter I shall outline some of the elements of alternative contemporary scientific approaches that concentrate on the organism, on wholeness and complexity, which are more consonant with scientific findings in molecular genetics and in other disciplines.

Richard Strohman, professor of molecular and cell biology at the University of California, Berkeley, has written a number of important critiques of genetic-engineering biotechnology for biotechnology journals. In one of them he describes the coming revolution in biology in terms not too unlike what I shall employ here.[3] He points out how anomalies within the genetic-determinist paradigm are being merely swept under the carpet by 'expert but conservative elements within the mainstream' in order to rescue the paradigm. But their explanations for the behaviour of complex systems become so contorted and convoluted, and invoke so many genetic agents with their 'interactive and co-dependent states,' that they serve only to obfuscate rather than contribute anything to furthering our understanding.

I start by considering the new view of organic stability and its implications for health and disease, especially for the development of cancer and for the emergence of new pathogens. I then introduce some new ideas on sustainability and biodiversity that have been developed in detail elsewhere. The object is to move science beyond reductionism to a holistic yet rigorous perspective that is consistent both with contemporary Western science and with traditional indigenous sciences all over the world.

The stability of organisms and species

How do organisms and species maintain their stability when genes and genomes are so mutable and fluid? The conventional, neo-Darwinian explanation is that natural selection is always at work, selecting out those that are unstable and hence 'unfit', so that only those that are sufficiently stable remain to propagate offspring like themselves.

This explanation fails to account for the *responsiveness* of genes and genomes to environmental and physiological changes (as described in chapter 7 and elsewhere throughout this book). The stability of organisms and species is dependent on the entire gamut of dynamic feedback relationships, extending from the social and ecological environment to the genes. Genes and genomes must also adjust, respond and, if necessary, change in order to maintain the stability of the whole. The key to living organisation is intercommunication and mutual responsiveness throughout the system.

The stability of organisms is diametrically opposite to the stability of mechanical systems. Mechanical stability—which applies also to so-called 'cybernetic' systems—is a closed, static equilibrium, maintained by the action of controllers, buffers or buttresses, which return the system to fixed or set points. A mechanical system works in a hierarchical manner, rather like most non-democratic institutions. Organic stability, on the other hand, is a state of dynamic balance that is attained in open systems far away from thermodynamic equilibrium. It has no controllers and no set points. It is radically democratic, as it works by inter-communication and mutual responsiveness of all the parts, so that control is distributed throughout the system.

> The dynamic stability of the organism depends on all parts of the system being able to adjust and respond appropriately in order to maintain the whole, including the genes.

The secret of the stability of living systems lies in a complex of dynamic *cycles* spanning a vast range of temporal (and spatial) domains. These cycles, which are most familiar to us as the spectrum of 'biological rhythms', are in effect coupled together in relationships of reciprocity and co-operation, so that balance is achieved over the system as a whole.[4] (This will be described in greater detail later.)

The dynamic stability of the organism depends therefore on all parts of the system being able to adjust and respond appropriately in order to maintain the whole, including the genes. When the system is well balanced within its socio-ecological environment, the entire range of dynamic cycles ensures that all parts of the system engage in a kind of perpetual return, and so genes and genomes are also dynamically maintained in constancy. As we have seen, a healthy system has various enzymes that 'proof-read' replicated DNA to correct errors and repair chemical and physical damage of DNA sequence (see chapter 12) in those genes that are in use (see chapter 7). On the other hand, when the system is stressed, mutational and other changes in genes and genomes will take place, which may alleviate the stress, as in the origins of so-called 'adaptive mutations' (chapter 7); but those changes in genes and genomes may also throw the system out of balance, resulting in its complete failure. Deleterious mutational changes, therefore, may be *symptomatic* of the breakdown of organic stability rather than its cause. This is becoming more and more evident in the development of cancer, as we shall see later.

> 'The body is actually *a social order of about 75 trillion cells* organised into different functional structures. Each functional structure provides its share in the maintenance of homeostatic conditions ... often called the *internal environment.*'

Some direct evidence for the importance of the system as a whole in the maintenance of the stability of its parts is seen in the enormous variability of isolated cells in culture, compared with their constancy and stability within the organism. This kind of 'somaclonal' variation is ubiquitous for plant cells in culture (see chapter 8). Similar variation exists for cultured animal cells. The cell biologist Harry Rubin spent nearly twenty years documenting the endless variation of mammalian cells arising in successive passages in culture, despite their supposed genetic uniformity. He has proposed a concept of 'progressive state selection' to account for the physiological stability of cells in the living organism, as opposed to their variability in culture. 'This concept assumes that physiological constraints can select among the ever-fluctuating physiological states in cells, and that repeated state selections result in heritability of those states. These considerations focus attention on the living cell and its neighbours which provide the immediate environment for selection, and ultimately on the whole organism.'[5] Rubin's explanation, of selection by the physiological environment, is not too dissimilar to my proposal that they are intercommunicating, so that in the ideal, 'each part is as much in control as it is sensitive and responsive.'[6] Each cell within the body will contribute to the physiological milieu of every other cell.

This state of affairs is best summarised by the medical physiologist Arthur Guyton:

> The body is actually *a social order of about 75 trillion cells* organised into different functional structures, some of which are called *organs.* Each functional structure provides its share in the maintenance of

homeostatic conditions ... which is often called the internal environment. As long as normal conditions are maintained in the *internal environment*, the cells of the body will continue to live and function properly. Thus, each cell benefits from homeostasis, and in turn each cell contributes its share towards the maintenance of homeostasis. This reciprocal interplay provides continuous automation of the body until one or more functional systems lose their ability to contribute their share of function. When this happens, all the cells of the body suffer. Extreme dysfunction leads to death, while moderate dysfunction leads to sickness.[8]

It will be instructive to examine how cancer can develop as a failure in the physiological ecology of cells, rather than as the result of random mutational events.

The epigenetic origin of cancer

There is increasing evidence that cancer is not a disease generated primarily by the accumulation of random somatic mutations, as is usually understood—though progression to an irreversible cancerous state may involve deleterious somatic mutations. The alternative explanation is that cancers have an *epigenetic* origin. ('Epigenetic' in the present context refers to physiological or developmental factors that are at least one remove from the 'genetic', which is anything that leads to changes in the base sequence of genes and genomes.)

The genetic theory of cancer first came into prominence in 1981, when three separate papers reported that DNA derived from long-term culture of a human bladder cancer could transform a mouse cell line, NIH 3T3. The responsible segment of the human DNA was similar to a gene carried by the Harvey rat sarcoma virus, and was named the *ras* gene. That was the first of the many oncogenes that were later discovered (see chapter 12). It turns out that NIH 3T3 cells are uniquely sensitive to transformation by the *ras* family of genes; moreover, this cell line readily undergoes 'spontaneous' transformation when it is subjected to moderate physiological stress. 'None of these findings proves that the alterations in tumour cell DNA actually caused the tumours; they simply show that genetic change is much more common in many, though not all, tumours than in normal tissue.[8]

Strong evidence against the genetic origin of cancer came from two studies, one of which used X-rays to induce malignant transformation, the other the carcinogen methyl-cholanthrene.[9] Both found that most, if not all, exposed cells were altered in some way, so that their progeny had a higher probability of transformation than untreated cells. In other words, the entire population of exposed cells showed an increased probability of transformation, and this increased probability was inherited in later cell generations. So, if one divides the exposed population into several sub-populations, each of them will show essentially the same frequency of transformation. Moreover, if these are further subdivided and propagated, the same frequency of transformed cells arises in all the sub-populations. Such high frequencies of transformation are also characteristic of spontaneous transformations induced by metabolic stress and are not caused by correspondingly high frequencies of mutations.

Still more suggestive is the observation that clones of cells transformed by X-rays or by metabolic stress revert to normal when placed under optimal growth conditions.[10] These results are reminiscent of the high rates of reversion in early stages of malignancies.

A team of Russian scientists has been studying spontaneous transformations of cells cultured from a number of inbred mouse and rat lines for several years. The cells produced sarcomas in the mice and rats from which the lines were established. On culturing cells from the tumours, colonies were obtained that were fully transformed, partly transformed, or not transformed at all. On six successive re-clonings of the transformed colonies the cells persisted in giving rise to all three kinds of colonies. The non-transformed cells, which had lost their ability to give rise to tumours in the animals, arose at high frequencies. Commenting on these results, Rubin writes: 'The question arises ... whether the underlying process in all tumours is fundamentally epigenetic in character. I know of no experiment that rules out this possibility.'[11]

The strong implication is that mutations are not the primary cause of transformation; instead they may arise after the crucial transformation of cellular state, in response to physiological stress. As we saw earlier, progression to the irreversible state may then be associated with somatic mutations.

Mutations may result from physiological stress

> We have to take seriously the possibility that mutations in human populations—both somatic and germ-line—may be the result of physiological imbalance and ecological stress, as has already been clearly shown for other organisms.

I believe we have to take seriously the possibility that deleterious mutations in human populations—both somatic and germ-line—may be the result of physiological imbalance and ecological stress, as has already been clearly shown for other organisms. Mammalian cells in culture, bacteria and yeast cells, as well as plants and insects, all show increased mutation rates under metabolic stress or stress from cytotoxic drugs and chemicals (see chapter 7). The results may be adaptive or corrective in some instances but deleterious, if not to the cell then certainly to the organism as a whole. This perspective has important implications for where we should concentrate intervention in health and disease. It is not in eliminating bad genes, or replacing bad genes with good ones in gene replacement therapy; nor is it in the development of more and more exotic specifically targeted drugs. There are already too many drugs on the market, causing a host of iatrogenic diseases (diseases induced by prescription drugs), which constitute a major problem in public health.[12] According to recent estimates, about 1.17 million people in Britain end up in hospital each year because of illnesses caused by drugs or treatment;[13] while in the United States, one million people are injured *in* hospitals, of whom up to 180,000 die.

As long as people's physiological states are compromised—by air pollutants, toxic wastes, pesticide residues and infectious bacteria in water and food, by malnutrition caused by poverty, by substance abuse, and by stress caused by social disintegration — high rates of mutation will occur, which may lead to further deterioration in health. It is time we redirected our efforts and resources to tackling the real problems facing our societies instead of creating more and more exotic and hazardous ways of exploiting the sick and the gullible. Health and disease are inextricably matters of social, ecological and physiological balance. They have no real reductionist solutions. Many enlightened physicians and members of the public are already practising a variety of holistic medicines based on treating the whole person in his or her socio-cultural milieu, and in stimulating the self-healing, regenerative powers of the organism even to the extent of repairing defective genes (see chapter 7). The Bristol Cancer Help Centre was among the first to adopt holistic health care in treating and preventing cancer and has had a successful history since the nineteen-eighties, despite recent efforts by the reductionist establishment to discredit its work.[14] But unless our governments act to curb radioactive and toxic discharges from industry, unless they act to reverse the increasing privatisation of health care, no amount of effort in holistic medicine can cope with the increasing deterioration in people's health from the environmental insults.

> Unless our governments act to curb radioactive and toxic discharges from industry, unless they act to reverse the increasing privatisation of health care, no amount of effort in holistic medicine can cope with the increasing deterioration in people's health.

The ecology of quiescent microbes

There is a strong parallel between the ecology of microbes in the environment and the physiology of cells within our body. The ecology of so-called quiescent microbes is a relatively new area of study but is already giving important insights into the factors that make microbes multiply out of control and become virulent.

The most interesting form in which quiescent microbes occur is in biofilms—thin layers of extracellular matrix secreted by the microbes which house a single species or multiple species of microbes. Biofilms are found coating solid surfaces in the environment—such as rocks and stones, gravel at the bottom of rivers, lakes and ponds, and the surfaces of aquatic plants. They may also be found coating the surfaces in our gut and our circulatory system. Until very recently biofilms were thought to be homogeneous layers in which dormant bacteria are entrapped. When they were eventually examined by non-destructive microscopic techniques, researchers discovered, to their surprise, that biofilms are structured communities of single species or of multiple species living together. The cells are disposed in aggregates around water channels, through which convection currents flow, so that nutrients and metabolites can circulate.[15] In multi-species biofilms, mixed-species micro-colonies are found where cells of metabolically co-operative species are juxtaposed so that they can benefit from exchanging substrates and end products. The term 'quiescent' is not appropriate, as chemical probes indicate that most of the cells are metabolically active. The cells in a biofilm are in effect enjoying a kind of multicellular life served by a circulatory system. They are metabolically active but non-proliferating, just like most of the cells in our body.

> The emergence of new virulent pathogens is strongly associated with the destruction of ecosystems by encroaching industrialisation. The strategy of controlling infectious diseases during the past fifty years may be entirely misdirected.

Further studies have revealed that the same bacteria can live within biofilms or in free-living plankton. But the two states are associated with the expression of different genes, as well as distinct morphologies. The physiology of biofilm bacteria is profoundly different from that of their planktonic counterparts. They live in large numbers of different micro-niches within multi-species communities forming stable colonies that persist indefinitely in the environment, where they are notably resistant to antibiotics. However, they also effectively prevent secondary colonisation by invading bacteria. This is particularly relevant for the normal complement of bacteria that live as biofilms in our gut. Studies have shown that biofilm species effectively prevent colonisation by invading pathogens.[16]

Observations on a wide variety of natural ecosystems have established that the vast majority of bacteria in most aquatic environments exist within biofilms in a non-proliferative but metabolically active phase, where the exchange of genetic materials continues to occur. These biofilms probably play a large role in recycling nutrients for higher organisms, and contribute to maintaining the stability of the ecosystem as a whole. It appears very likely, therefore, that the so-called quiescent state is the ecologically balanced state also for the microbial communities, and that they enter the proliferative phase only during times of stress. Stressful conditions may involve an influx of new pollutants or anti-microbials, of nutrients such as phosphates and nitrates, or some other major ecological disturbance. The emergence of new virulent pathogens is strongly associated with the destruction of ecosystems by encroaching industrialisation. Bacteria and viruses lose their natural hosts and become virulent in human populations whose physiological states are already compromised by mal-nutrition and poverty.[17] The ecological stress that gives rise to proliferating pathogens is analogous to the physiological stress that causes cancerous cells to proliferate out of control in the human body.

> The microbes do not compete, each against all the rest. On the contrary, they engage in unbridled co-operation, sharing even their most valuable assets for survival against the onslaught of selfish, myopic human beings. It is high time we put this 'warfare with nature' mentality behind us and started learning in earnest how to live sustainably and healthily with nature.

If that is the case, then the strategy of controlling infectious diseases during the past fifty years may be entirely misdirected. This was indeed the conclusion of the Harvard Working Group on

New and Resurgent Diseases (see chapter 3). Reductionist science has failed yet another reality test.

It is the 'warfare with nature' mentality as much as anything else that has brought about the present public health crisis in infectious diseases and antibiotic-resistance. There is an important moral in the way the microbes are winning the war over humans. They are telling us that it is wrong to see the world as isolated bits and pieces, to see linear chains of mechanical cause and effect. Nature is fluid and dynamic and thoroughly interconnected. The microbes do not compete, each against all the rest—on the contrary, they engage in unbridled co-operation, sharing even their most valuable assets for survival against the onslaught of selfish, myopic human beings.

I cannot help feeling that warfare with human beings is not what microbes want to engage in either. Virulence and antibiotic-resistance are signs of ecological stress, for them as for us. There is evidence, for instance, that bacteria that produce antibiotics also produce the enzyme for inactivating the antibiotic, and that what we call an antibiotic may actually be their sex hormone, which signals the bacterium's readiness to mate (see chapter 9). What we have done with our profligate use of antibiotics is to turn them into thoroughly promiscuous, sex-mad fiends. We have created, and continue to create, a horrendous array of rogue strains of microbes in their midst. I imagine that they too would much prefer that things were different and that they could live peaceably with us in a balanced ecological relationship, as they once did long ago. It is high time we put this 'warfare with nature' mentality behind us and started learning in earnest how to live sustainably and healthily with nature.

A theory of the organism and the sustainable system

The new genetics, in transcending the old reductionist paradigm, reaffirms the ecological wisdom of traditional indigenous peoples all over the world, who have practised sustainable agriculture on the understanding that the biological nature of each organism or species is inextricably linked to its environment and depends ultimately on the entire ecosystem, consisting of all other organisms. It is clear that intensive agriculture, in its new genetic engineering version, is just as unsustainable as the old, and carries new hazards inherent in the technology (see chapter 8). The alternative is not to abandon science, as some disillusioned environmentalists in the North seem to be advocating; nor is it a wholesale return to 'traditional' methods. It is important to stress that so-called traditional methods have also evolved through the ages as knowledge has accumulated, and it is simply Eurocentric arrogance to deny the existence of science in cultures other than the northern European.

I made it clear at the outset that Western science is also not the reductionist monolith that mainstream establishment scientists have been encouraged to project to the public. It is in the nature of all sciences to doubt, to explore and to evolve, in the light of new evidence, so that one can gain a reliable knowledge of Nature that will best enable us to live sustainably with her. It is on that basis that I wish to outline a theory of the organism, within the framework of contemporary Western science, and then to show how it may contribute to understanding sustainable systems.

Thermodynamic limits to growth

The notion of a sustainable system carries with it the idea that there are limits to growth and consumption. Goldsmith[18] and Rifkin and Howard[19] were among the first to draw attention to those limits, in particular the physical limits imposed by the second law of thermodynamics, which says that one can never get 100 per cent efficiency in natural processes—in other words, there are no free lunches in the world. To live, human beings extract energy and materials and transform them. In the process, useful energy invariably degrades into a disordered, unusable form, *entropy,* while materials turn into waste products. So there are physical limits to how fast these processes of extraction and transformation can take place before the system becomes overwhelmed by entropy and toxic wastes.

However, physical limits are simply ignored by mainstream neo-classical economic theories, which all begin with non-physical parameters—preferences, technologies, and distribution of incomes.[20] These non-physical parameters are taken as a given, while the physical variables of the quantity of goods produced and resources required are adjusted to fit an equilibrium or, more often, a constant rate of growth. Sustainable development, by contrast, treats physical parameters as given, setting limits to the size of the economic system that can be supported. That is the basis of the ecological concept of *carrying capacity*, which reflects the size of the economic system and some optimum rates of transformation of energy and resources compatible with sustaining the human beings within the system.

But how is the carrying capacity related to the rates of transformation of energy and resources? How is it related to the manner in which resources and energy are used, that is, to the mode of production?[21] How is it related to the complexity of the system, say, in terms of diversity of production, the division of labour, and so on? Which factors determine the carrying capacity of the system? Such questions are central to the issue of sustainability. And it seems to me that they are not sufficiently addressed by merely invoking the 'entropy law'.[22] I shall show how the physical limits are by no means static and given but are dependent on the way the system is organised, thus providing a basis for effective human intervention and choice.

A sustainable system is a kind of organism

A starting-point is to regard a sustainable system as a kind of organism. One can see that a healthy organism is the ideal sustainable system: an irreducible whole that develops, maintains and reproduces or renews itself by mobilising material and energy captured from the environment. The organism is sustainable precisely because of its anti-entropic tendencies. It is paradigmatic in the efficiency with which it uses energy and resources. In that respect at least it has no equal yet in any machines that our most advanced technologies can produce. So it is in understanding the thermodynamics of the living system that one may learn how to overcome and minimise entropic dissipation and decay.[23]

> Living systems have a dynamic structure that maximises energy storage and minimises energy dissipation.

The results of my studies over the past ten years or so suggest that the anti-entropic tendencies of the organism depend on its ability to *store* incoming energy, and to make this energy circulate effectively within the system to do work before it is dissipated; that it is the *intricate* structure of the system that determines how long the energy can remain in it, how efficiently work is done, and therefore how much energy is effectively stored within the system. It turns out that living systems have a dynamic structure that maximises energy storage and minimises energy dissipation. What does this dynamic structure consist of?

First of all, it consists of activities organised in cycles. Cycles involve perpetual return, and account for the dynamic stability of the system, as mentioned at the beginning of this chapter. Second, the activity cycles are nested one within another, like Russian dolls, spanning an enormous range of space-time from the very fast (nanoseconds) to the very slow (weeks or months) and from the very local to the increasingly global. In other words, the system has a deep space-time differentiation. Third, its activities are all coupled together in a *symmetrical, reciprocal* way. This is the most subtle relationship to appreciate. It entails both local autonomy *and* global cohesion. Energy-yielding activities are directly linked to energy-requiring ones, and they can readily exchange places. In other words, there is a co-operative give and take: parts in deficit can draw on those in surplus, and the roles can be reversed, so that energy is diverted to wherever it is most needed at all times. The net result is a dynamic balance, so the whole system is sustained.

This state of affairs is encapsulated in fig. 13.1, where the circle represents the entire life-cycle of the system, and the line represents the flow of energy that feeds the life-cycle. The life-cycle consists of the many subsidiary nested cycles of activity that enable it to achieve a net balance, especially of entropy production, represented by the equation $\Sigma\Delta S = 0$, while the necessary minimum dissipation is exported to the outside, as represented by the equation $\Sigma\Delta S > 0$. In this way the organism in effect sets itself free from the immediate constraints of the second law to become an autonomous system with a certain degree of independence from its environment. It is so organised that a full range of coupled cyclic, non-dissipative processes feeds off the dissipative flow. Consequently, the system maintains its organisation, and energy is always available within the system for all its vital activities.

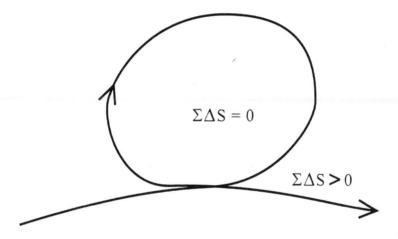

Fig. 13.1: The organism can be understood in terms of cyclic non-dissipative processes feeding off irreversible dissipative processes

The internal organisation or intricate dynamic structure of the living system, therefore, holds the key to its success. An intuitive representation of the intricate structure of the life-cycle is given in fig. 13.2. It consists of nested sub-cycles of different sizes, which are dynamically coupled together. As you can imagine, the more sub-cycles there are and the better they are coupled, the longer the energy is effectively stored within the system and the less is dissipated as entropy.

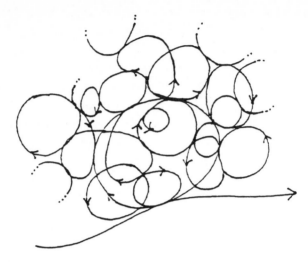

Fig. 13.2: The intricate structure of the life-cycle, consisting of many coupled sub-cycles

A model of a sustainable economic system

An economic system is first and foremost a society of people bonded by social contract to make their living together by using and transforming resources and has as its purpose achieving a good life for all. It is therefore in everyone's interest to have a healthy economy.

In modelling a sustainable economic system one has first to remember what an economic system is, and what it is for. An economic system is a society organised around a mode of production. There are many possible modes of production in diverse cultures of the world, which differ among themselves with respect to the distribution of resources and income and the degree of equity and emphasis on co-operation over competition.[24] Unfortunately, mainstream economic theories in the West are based exclusively on the capitalist mode of production, with its sole emphasis on competitiveness, and this can make one lose sight of the purpose of an economic system. An economic system is first and foremost a society of people bonded by social contract to make their living together by using and transforming resources, and has as its purpose achieving a good life for all. It is therefore in everyone's interest to have a healthy economy.

The economy is, to first approximation, an open system through which resources extracted from the 'source'—the ecological environment—flow to a 'sink'—the most immediate mental picture of which is the municipal dump, though it need not be so. Various commodities and services are exchanged or traded between 'source' and 'sink', and 'values' are added in processes of manufacture and in creative acts of art or artisanship, whose equivalence to energy or otherwise needs to be fully justified and explicated, along with such qualities of life as happiness, health, contentment, and well-being, not to mention clean air, nutritious food, comfortable shelter from inclement weather, and an unpolluted environment.

Like an organism, the economic system may be conceptualised as cyclic, non-dissipative exchanges or transformations of energy and resources, coupled with the dissipative flows or wastage due to death, depreciation, and other entropy-generating, irreversible processes. Because energy and resources come ultimately from the ecological environment, it makes sense to embed the economic system properly in its ecological setting (fig. 13.3). This is fully in accord with Hermann Daly's proposal to 'view the economy as a sub-system of the ecosystem' and to recognise that 'while it is not exempt from material laws, [neither] is it fully reducible to explanations by them.'[25]

> To be sustainable, the global economy must also have an intricate structure encompassing many local economic systems.

Fig. 13.3 makes it clear that the ecological environment is also conceptualised as a self-sustaining organic system of cyclic, non-dissipative processes coupled to the dissipative, one-way energy and material flow. To what extent is this justified? Lovelock's Gaia hypothesis proposes that the entire earth is a self-organising, self-regulating system maintained far away from thermodynamic equilibrium under energy flow.[26] In those respects it is indeed like an organism. The most conspicuous sign of the earth's self-regulating property is the constancy of its atmosphere, which is a highly non-equilibrium mixture of gases. The atmospheres of Mars and Venus, by contrast, are equilibrium mixtures of spent or exhaust gases that reflect their lifelessness.

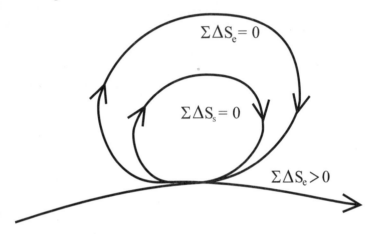

Fig. 13.3: The coupled flows of the economic and ecological cycles in a sustainable economic system

Let us say that the economic system depicted in fig. 13.3 is the global economy—which current WTO negotiations are aimed at establishing. To be sustainable, the global economy must also have an intricate structure encompassing many local economic systems. Ideally, the intricate structure of the global economy should look like the many-nested sub-cycles that make up the organism's life cycle (fig. 13.2). Each local economy in turn, say Britain or Malaysia, would have its own intricate structure of coupled cycles, similar to that of the global economy (again like fig. 13.2). (This is a property of *fractals*—dynamics generating space-time patterns that fall between the one, two or three dimensions we are used to—which characterise many living patterns and processes.) It is clear that local economies are coupled to the global through imports and exports of materials, human beings, and capital. If the entire global system is to be sustainable there has to be a proper balance between the local and the global, the same kind of reciprocal, symmetrically coupled relationships that one finds in organisms.

In the context of the planet's ecosystem, it is now generally recognised that human activity has had a far from benign effect. This has prompted the establishment of a Geophysiological Society for the study of planetary health.[27] In fact it can be argued that the deteriorating health of human beings is a direct consequence of the deteriorating health of our planet. For both cases, the present model of the organism may begin to offer some diagnostic criteria of health.

A healthy organism is one that maximises the non-dissipative cyclic processes and minimises the dissipative. This gives a set of criteria for recognising a healthy, sustainable system.

Diagnostic criteria for a sustainable system

Maximise non-dissipative cyclic flows

- Increase in energy storage capacity (carrying capacity, biomass)
- Increase in the efficiency of energy use (effective coupling in energy transfer)
- Increase in dynamic closure (cycles)
- Increase in space-time differentiation (energy residence time, diversity)
- Increase in balanced flows of resources and energy (symmetrical flows)
- Increase in reciprocal coupling of processes (free energy conservation)

Minimise dissipative non-cyclic flows

- Minimisation of entropy production (internal entropy balance)

The diagnostic criteria for sustainable systems are linked, so that once one is identified, the others are very likely to exist as well. Some support for these criteria is the fact that they are similar to those that Eric Schneider and James Kay have identified for mature, established ecosystems.[28] These authors have made significant progress in understanding the thermodynamics of ecosystems, though their conceptual framework differs from the one presented here. They compared the data collected for carbon energy flows in two aquatic marsh ecosystems adjacent to a large power station on the Crystal River in Florida. One of them ('stressed') was exposed to hot water effluent from the nuclear power station, which increased the temperature by 6°C; the other ('control'), not so exposed, was otherwise in similar environmental conditions. They found that the stressed system captured 20 per cent less energy, made 20 per cent less efficient use of the energy captured and had 50 per cent fewer cycles and 34 per cent less biomass than the controls. These findings suggest that the control system captures, stores and uses energy more effectively and has a greater carrying capacity in terms of biomass and a higher degree of dynamic closure (cycles), as consistent with the diagnostic criteria listed.

Schneider and Kay have also drawn attention to some interesting measurements made by Luvall and Holbo with a NASA thermal infra-red multi-spectral scanner, which assesses energy budgets of terrestrial landscapes.[29] Their data showed that the more developed the ecosystem, the colder its surface temperature. The interpretation by Schneider and Kay is that mature ecosystems are more effective in 'degrading energy'. An alternative interpretation, consistent with the model presented here, is that the mature ecosystems have a greater 'energy storage capacity', which is a well-defined thermodynamic concept. This greater energy storage capacity is related to its higher degree of space-time differentiation or intricate structure, greater dynamic closure (cycles), and more effective coupling of cyclic flows, achieving increased internal entropy balance, so that the system exports less entropy or heat. In other words, the dissipative branch is minimised while the non-dissipative cycle is maximised in a mature ecosystem.

This model can throw light on many aspects of an economic system, which are described in some detail elsewhere.[30] Here I wish to concentrate on certain essential features.

Money, energy, and entropy

> Money is by no means equivalent to energy. Perhaps a better analogy of energy in real-world economy is affection, trust, and good will, in return for which, originally, a gift was a token. The result is that all money is not equal, and today's economic difficulties arise from treating it as though it were. The flow of money can be associated with exchanges of real value, or it can be associated with sheer waste or dissipation. In the former case it is more like energy flow; in the latter case it is pure entropy.

The first thing that comes to mind whenever the word 'economics' is mentioned is money. It is indeed money that makes the economists' world go round; so it is all too easy to equate the circulation of money in the real-world economy with energy in the living system. It has even been fashionable in biochemistry textbooks to regard the universal energy-transducing intermediate ATP (adenosine triphosphate) as 'energy currency'. However, money is by no means equivalent to energy. Perhaps a better analogy of energy in real-world economy is affection, trust, and good will, in return for which, originally, a gift was a token. Later on, people traded goods or services, which again depend on trust and good will, if the equivalence in energy values is to be maintained. The big problem arose with the introduction of money, which is only arbitrarily related to the real value of things and services.

The result is that all money is not equal, and today's major economic difficulties arise from treating it as though it were. The flow of money can be associated with exchanges of real value, or it can be associated with sheer waste or dissipation. In the former case it is more like energy flow; in the latter case it is pure entropy.

Transactions in the financial or money market are purely for the purpose of extracting and concentrating 'wealth' away from real production. Money is thereby created, which is completely decoupled from the creation of value. As a result, as David Korten points out, 'the financial or buying power of those who control the newly created money expands, compared with other members of society who are creating value, but whose real and relative compensation is declining.'[31] It is estimated that for every dollar circulating in the productive world economies between twenty and fifty dollars circulate in the economy of pure finance. This money represents pure, uncompensated positive entropy or, in our scheme, pure dissipation.

> 'Instead of creating wealth, our money system is depleting our real wealth: our communities, ecosystems, and productive infrastructure.'

The other important source of uncompensated positive entropy is to be found in the unequal terms of trade consistently imposed by Northern powers on developing countries in the South. This has happened during both colonial and post-colonial times, with raw materials being extracted from the South with far too little compensation being paid, while at the same time manufactured goods are sold back to it at too high a price. Because the economic system depends ultimately on the flow of resources from the natural environment, which has its 'natural ecological economy', entropic costs can be incurred either in the economic system itself or in the ecosystem. Therefore, when the cost of valuable non-renewable ecological resources used up is not properly taken into account, or renewable resources are destroyed faster than they can regenerate, the entropic burdens fall on the ecological environment rather than on the economic system. But as the economic system is necessarily coupled to and dependent on input from the ecosystem (see fig. 13.3), the entropic burden in the latter will feed back to the economic system as diminished input, so the economic system becomes poorer as a result. In our model, poverty is absolute, as there is a finite optimum rate at which resources can be used and transformed. This also means that when individuals amass excessive resources and incomes, others become poorer in absolute terms. Poverty threatens the survival of the system as a whole. It represents an unbalanced, uncoupled, highly dissipative system (see below).

Evidence that money is both energetic and entropic is provided by the well-known unreliability of assessing the real wealth of countries from the gross national product (GNP)—the amount of spending on goods and services carried out by various sectors of the economy. Korten points out that the more environmentally burdensome ways of meeting a given need are generally those that contribute most to the GNP.[32] Driving a car contributes more than riding a bicycle; turning on an air-conditioner adds infinitely more than opening a window; relying on processed foods contributes more than eating natural foods in reusable containers. According to Daly and Cobb, if one reconstructs the GNP of the United States for 1960–86, counting only those increases in output that relate to improvements in well-being and adjusting for the depletion of human and environmental resources, the 'index of economic welfare' reveals that individual welfare peaked in 1969, then remained on a plateau before falling during the early and middle eighties.[33] Yet from 1969 to 1986, GNP per person went up by 35 per cent, and the consumption of fossil fuel increased by about 17 per cent. 'Instead of creating wealth, our money system is depleting our real wealth: our communities, ecosystems, and productive infrastructure.'[34]

Another suggestive estimate of energetic yield versus entropic costs comes from the comparison of twenty-five rice cultivation systems (see table 13.1), of which eight are 'pre-industrial', with low fossil fuel input (2–4 per cent) and high labour input (35–78 per cent), ten are 'semi-industrial', with moderate to high fossil fuel input (23–93 per cent) and low to moderate labour input (4–46 per cent), and seven are 'full-industrial', with 95 per cent fossil fuel input and extremely low labour input (of 0.04 to 0.2 per cent).[35] The total output per hectare (calculated in gigajoules, a unit of energy) in pre-industrial systems falls into low and high-output sub-groups; the output of the low sub-group is a twentieth to a fifth of the full-industrial yield. However, *the output of the high sub-group is two to three times that of the full-industrial systems.* The yield of semi-industrial systems is more homogeneous, with an average of 51.75 GJ, while the yield of full-industrial systems, even more uniform, averages 65.99 GJ. When the ratio of total energy output to total input is examined, however, pre-industrial systems range between 6.9 and 11.5, with the figures for the most productive systems being as high as 15.3 to 29.2. Semi-industrial systems give ratios of 2.1 to 9.7, whereas the ratios of full-industrial systems are not much better than 1.

These figures illustrate the law of diminishing returns remark-ably well. There is a plateau of output per hectare around 70–80 GJ, regardless of the total input, which is only exceeded in the three high-yielding pre-industrial systems of Yunnan. Intensifying energy input leads to a drop in efficiency—the ratio of output to input—which is particularly sharp as input approaches the output ceiling. The drop in efficiency reflects the increasing entropic costs of high rates of dissipation when the rate of energy input exceeds the capacity of the system to effectively store this input.

The exceptionally high output of the Chinese systems is also an indication that the energy-storing capacity or carrying capacity of a system *can* increase, depending, in particular, on the space-time differentiation and the dynamic closures introduced. For example, mixed cropping and crop rotation would increase space-time differentiation, while the use of farmyard and human manure as organic fertilisers, which has traditionally been practised in China, would increase dynamic closure.

The establishment of thriving microbial communities in the soil will also contribute to increased space-time differentiation for energy storage as well as improving dynamic closures by facilitating nutrient recycling. By contrast, monocultures destroy space-time differentiation and dynamic closures both in the larger ecological community and in the microbial ecology of the soil, leading to diminished energy storage capacity, despite the high levels of input.

	Input (I)	Fossil fuel (GJ)	Labour (%)	Output (%)	Output/ Input (GJ)
Pre-industrial					
1. Dayak, Sarawak (Malaysia), 1951	0.30	2	44	2.4	8.0
2. Dayak, Sarawak (Malaysia), 1951	0.63	2	51	5.7	9.0
3. Kilombero (Tanzania), 1967	0.42	2	39	3.8	9.0
4. Kilombero (Tanzania), 1967	1.44	3	35	9.9	6.9
5. Iban, Sarawak (Malaysia), 1951	0.27	3	36	3.1	11.5
6. Luts'un, Yunnan (China), 1938	8.04	3	70	166.9	20.8
7. Yits'un, Yunnan (China), 1938	10.66	2	78	163.3	15.3
8. Yut'sun, Yunnan (China), 1938	5.12	4	53	149.3	29.2
Semi-industrial					
9. Mandya, Karnataka (India), 1955	3.33	23	46	23.8	7.1
10. Mandya, Karnataka (India), 1975	16.73	74	16	80.0	4.8
11. Philippines, 1972	12.37	86	5	39.9	3.2
12. Philippines, 1972	16.01	89	4	51.8	3.2
13. Japan, 1963	30.04	90	5	73.3	2.4
14. Hongkong (China), 1971	31.27	83	12	64.8	2.1
15. Philippines, 1965	3.61	93	13	25.0	6.9
16. Philippines, 1979	5.48	33	16	52.9	9.7
17. Philippines, 1979	6.90	80	11	52.9	7.7
18. Philippines, 1979	8.72	86	7	52.9	6.1
Full-industrial					
19. Suriname, 1972	45.9	95	0.2	53.7	1.2
20. United States, 1974	70.2	95	0.02	52.9	0.8
21. Sacramento (United States), 1977	45.9	95	0.04	80.5	1.8
22. Grand Prairie (United States), 1977	52.5	95	0.04	58.6	1.1
23. South-west Louisiana (United States), 1977	48.0	95	0.04	50.8	1.1
24. Mississippi Delta (United States), 1977	53.8	95	0.05	55.4	1.0
25. Texas Gulf Coast (United States), 1977	55.1	95	0.04	74.7	1.4

Table 13.1: Balance sheet of energy costs and yields of rice cultivation systems

Dynamic closure, space-time differentiation, and co-operative reciprocity

As emphasised earlier, a sustainable system has two branches: the irreversible, dissipative branch, and the non-dissipative branch, which requires dynamic closure or cycles, space-time differentiation, and co-operative reciprocity. These principles have been well appreciated by traditional indigenous farmers in their 'internal input farming system', as Vandana Shiva points out.[36] This depends on a reciprocal, symbiotic relationship between individuals in the farming community and between farmers and their 'produce'. As human beings farm, tend and propagate animals and plants, the animals and plants provide sustenance for the human community.[37] Waste is minimised by the judicious recycling of nutrients and by diversification in the use of resources. By contrast, the so-called 'high-yielding varieties' introduced by the 'Green Revolution' are designed to destroy social relationships, break nutrient cycles, and dispense with recycling, so as to depend on intensified external input. This is the reason why fully industrialised intensive agricultural practices are so energy-inefficient, and ultimately non-sustainable.

In the global context, the current proposals of the World Trade Organisation and Multilateral Agreement on Investment to remove all barriers to trade, finance and investment threaten not only the survival of national economies but the survival of the global system as a whole.[38] One important reason is that they destroy the nested levels of dynamic closures and space-time differentiation that enable the system to store energy and to operate in the co-operative reciprocity that contributes to the sustainability of the whole system. Without effective barriers that can guarantee the co-operative reciprocity on which local autonomy depends, the aggressive multinational monopolies will further accelerate the extraction of cheap natural resources while inflating the price of goods. Both these measures will increase entropic costs, the one on the ecological environment, the other on the system itself, which will certainly spell the death of the global system.

The lack of barriers to finance and investment also leaves countries vulnerable to speculations on the world financial market, with disastrous consequences. The Asian financial crisis that occurred since the first edition of this book was precipitated by such speculations and in fact was predicted by eminent critics of the WTO and MAI, such as Martin Khor and Edward Goldsmith.

Enlightened sectors in business are already learning the lesson of sustainability from nature. Because of the dynamic closures involved in living cycles, there should really be no such thing as 'waste'. The most important species in the grand cycle of the earth's ecosystem are the scavengers that feed on waste, carcasses, and debris, thus releasing nutrients for green plants, which capture the energy of sunlight to pass on to animals and other plants in the food web. 'Everything that is excreted, exhaled, or exhausted from one organism is used by another.'[39]

Following this principle to its logical conclusion, industrial processes are now being designed to turn waste products into valuable inputs. A brewery in Namibia grows mushrooms on spent grain, then earthworms. The earthworms are fed to hens. The waste alkaline water from the brewery—which constitutes 80 per cent of the ground-water extracted—goes to cultivating *Spirulina,* an edible alga rich in protein, and is then channelled to fish ponds, where fish farming is introduced. Finally, the hen manure goes through a digester to produce methane for fuel. 'This integrated biosystem will produce seven times more food, fuel, and fertiliser than a conventional operation and four times as many jobs.'[40] This is none other than the minimisation of dissipation through increase in dynamic closure and space-time differentiation, so that the carrying capacity of the system is increased for a given rate of extraction of resources.

Conclusion

It is clear that we need a systematic change of direction in all spheres of life before the dream of solving all the world's problems by genetic-engineering biotechnology turns into a nightmare. In this final chapter I have given some indication of the sort of changes that are needed, and are already occurring. Fortunately for us, there is a substantial body of knowledge that goes beyond reductionist science to a deeper understanding of the organic whole. Some of this knowledge is already being put into practice in health, agriculture, and industrial processes.

Reductionist science has had its day. Let us reject the bad science that has served to exploit, to oppress, to obfuscate, and to destroy the earth and its inhabitants. Let us opt for a joyful and sustainable future—beyond genetic engineering.

Appendix

GLOBAL MORATORIUM ON
GE BIOTECHNOLOGY

NO TO PATENTS ON LIFE

Two statements are reproduced here, both calling for a global moratorium on GE biotechnology and a prohibition on patents on life.

The first is a relaunching of the Statement on Life and Evolution drafted during the 1997 State of the World Forum in San Francisco by Brian Goodwin, Fritjof Capra, Ervin Laszlo, and myself, which is intended for everyone. More than six thousand people from thirty-four countries have already signed it as this edition goes to press, thanks especially to all those who have collected signatures on our behalf and sent them in by post. The signed statement was presented to the 1998 State of the World Forum in San Francisco. We are still looking for our original target of 100,000 signatures and so will need all your help.

The second is the World Scientists' Statement, launched during the Biosafety Meeting in Cartagena, Colombia, in February 1999. More than a hundred scientists from twenty-four countries have signed it. You may like to sign both statements if you are a scientist; if you are a scientist who has already signed the Statement on Life and Evolution, please sign the World Scientists' Statement as well.

We shall be presenting both statements and signatures to

- the WTO — to get patents on life excluded from TRIPS,
- the UN Convention on Biological Diversity,
- our governments, and
- the WHO—to request an inquiry into genetic engineering and the recent resurgence of infectious diseases.

Send the signed statements to: Dr Mae-Wan Ho, Biology Department, Open University, Walton Hall, Milton Keynes, Buckinghamshire MK7 6AA, England. Alternatively, e-mail details to m.w.ho@open.ac.uk, stating which statement you agree to sign; or sign on at our web site: www.i-sis.dircon.co.uk.

Among the signatories to the Statement on Life and Evolution are:

Miguel A. Altieri, University of California, Berkeley, United States

Siti Aminah, Komphaslindo, Jakarta, Indonesia

Frappé Benoît, Parti de la Loi Naturelle, Montlignon, France

Beth Burrow, Edmonds Institute, United States

Fritjof Capra, Institute for Ecoliteracy, California, United States

Chee Yoke Ling, Nijar Gurdial, and Martin Khor, Third World Network, Malaysia

Victoria Corpuz, Indigenous Peoples' Centre for Policy and Education, Philippines

Ronnie Cummins, Pure Foods Campaign, United States

Kristin Dawkins and Yvette Flynn, Institute for Agricultural and Trade Policy, United States

Wytze de Lange, Dutch Coalition Against Patents on Life, Netherlands

Kristin Ebbert, Mothers and Others for a Livable Planet, New York, United States

Sue Edwards, Institute of Sustainable Agriculture, Ethiopia

Peter Fenwick and David Lorimer, Scientific and Medical Network, England

Khalsa Garcia, Aseed Europe, Netherlands

Benedikt Haerlin, Greenpeace International, Germany

Liz Hoskins and Helena Paul, Gaia Foundation, England

Florianne Koechlin, World Wildlife Fund, Switzerland

Dan Leskien, Friends of the Earth, Germany

Farhad Mazhar, UBINIG, Bangladesh

Tore Midtvedt, Karolinska Institut, Stockholm, Sweden

José A. Pascual, Friends of the Earth, Spain

Nicanor Perlas, Centre for Alternative Development Initiatives, Philippines

Bob Phelps, Australian GenEthics Network, Fitzroy, Australia
Darrell Posey, Oxford Centre for the Environment, Ethics and
    Society, Oxford, England
Marilyn Schlitz, Institute of Noetic Sciences, California, United
    States
Hernandez Sergio, Play Fair Europe, Germany
Nandas Bahhadur Siung, Global Research Carel for
    Ethnobiology, Nepal
Jaan Suurkula, Physicians for Responsible Genetics, Sweden
Beatrix Tappeser, Institute for Applied Ecology, Freiburg, Germany
Brian Tokar, Institute of Social Ecology, Vermont, United States
Etienne Vernet, Ecoropa, France
Christine von Weizsäcker, Ecoropa, Germany
Peter R. Wills, University of Auckland, Auckland, New Zealand
Vida Ogorelec Wagner, Slovenian Federation for Sustainable
    Development, Slovenia

Among the signatories to the World Scientists' Statement are:

Dr Michael Antoniou, molecular geneticist, Guy's Hospital,
    London, England
Dr Catherine Badley, biologist, University of Michigan, Ann
    Arbor, United States
Dr Susan Bardocz, geneticist, Aberdeen, Scotland
Prof. Phil Bereano, engineer, Council for Responsible Genetics,
    United States
Dr Javier Blasco, Aragonese Centre for Rural European
    Information, Aragón, Spain
Dr Christiane Boecker, MCommH, Community Health, Haïti
Dr Walter Bortz, physician, Stanford University, Stanford,
    California, United States
Dr Ignacio Capela, microbial ecologist, Berkeley, United States
Prof. Martha Crouch, biologist, Indiana University, Indiana,
    United States
Prof. Joe Cummins, geneticist, University of Western Ontario,
    Canada

Gordon Daly, PhD student, gene therapy, Kennedy Institute, England

Dr Bruno d'Udine, behavioural ecologist, Università degli Studi di Udine, Udine, Italy

Dr Tewolde Egziabher, agronomist, Ministry of the Environment, Addis Ababa, Ethiopia

Dr Ty Fitzmorris, ecologist, Hampshire College, United States

Prof. John Garderineer, biologist, University of Michigan, Ann Arbor, United States

Edward Goldsmith, ecologist, *The Ecologist,* London, England

Prof. Brian Goodwin, Schumacher College, England

Prof. Martha Herbert, pediatric neurologist, Massachusetts General Hospital, Massachusetts, United States

Dr Mae-Wan Ho, geneticist and biophysicist, Open University, Milton Keynes, England

Patrick Holden, organic agriculturist, Soil Association, England

Dr Vyvyan Howard, toxipathologist, University of Liverpool, Liverpool, England

Prof. Ruth Hubbard, biologist, Harvard University, Cambridge, United States

Prof. Tim Ingold, anthropologist, University of Manchester, Manchester, England

Dr Marijan Jost, plant geneticist, Agricultural College, Križevci, Croatia

Dr Jack Kloppenburg, rural sociologist, University of Wisconsin, United States

Prof. Richard Lacey, microbiologist, Leeds, England

Prof. Ervin Laszlo, Club of Budapest, Budapest, Hungary

Dr Herve Le Mear, biomathematician, University of Paris, Paris, France

Dr Katarina Leppanen, University of Sweden, Göteborg, Sweden

Dr Timothy Mann, geographer, Hampshire College, United States

Renata Menasche MSc, agronomist, Federal University of Rio Grande do Sul, Brazil

Prof. David Packham, material scientist, University of Bath, Bath, England

Dr Robert Poller, organic chemist, University of London, London, England

Dr Thomas R. Preston, University of Tropical Agriculture, Cambodia

Dr Arpad Pusztai, biochemical immunologist, formerly Rowett Institute, Scotland

Dr Carlos R. Ramirez, biologist, St Lawrence University, United States

Dr Peter M. Rosset, Institute of Food and Development Policy, United States

Angela Ryan, molecular biologist, Institute of Science in Society, England

Prof. Peter Saunders, biomathematician, King's College, London, England

Dr Nancy A. Schult, entomologist, University of Wisconsin at Madison, United States

Dr Brian Schultz, ecologist, Hampshire College, United States

Verena Soldati, biotechnologist, Basel Appell, Switzerland

Dr John Soluri, historian of science, Carnegie Mellon University, Pittsburgh, United States

Dr Vandana Shiva, Research Federation for Science and Ecology, New Delhi, India

Prof. Atuhiro Sibatani, molecular biologist, Osaka, Japan

Dr Gerald Smith, zoologist, University of Michigan, Ann Arbor, United States

Dr Ted Steele, molecular immunologist, University of Wollongong, Wollongong, Australia

Prof. Ian Stewart, biomathematician, University of Warwick, England

Prof. David Suzuki, geneticist, Sustainable Development Research Institute, UBC, Canada

Prof. Terje Traavik, Institute of Medical Microbiology, Tromsø, Norway

Rosa Vazquez, biology student, Ohio State University, Columbus, United States

Dr Oscar Zamora, agronomist, University of the Philippines, Philippines

Statement on Life and Evolution

Life is an intimate web of relations that evolves in its own right, interfacing and integrating its myriad diverse elements. The complexity and interdependence of all forms of life have the consequence that the process of evolution cannot be controlled, though it can be influenced. It involves an unpredictable creative unfolding that calls for sensitive participation from all the players, particularly from the youngest, most recent arrivals, human beings.

Life must not be treated as a commodity that can be owned, in whole or in part, by anyone, including those who wish to manipulate it in order to design new life forms for human convenience and profit. There should be no patents on organisms or their parts. We must also recognise the potential dangers of genetic engineering to health and biodiversity, and the ethical problems it poses for our responsibilities to life. We propose a moratorium on commercial releases of genetically engineered products and a comprehensive public inquiry into the legitimate and safe uses of genetic engineering. This inquiry should take account of the precautionary principle as a criterion of sensitive participation in living processes. Species should be respected for their intrinsic natures and valued for their unique qualities, on which the whole intricate network of life depends.

We recognise the validity of the different ways of knowing that have been developed in different cultures, and the equivalent value of the knowledge gained within these traditions. These add substantially to the set of alternative technologies that can be used for the sustainable use of natural resources that will allow us to preserve the diversity of species and to pass the precious gift of life in all its beauty and creativity to our children and their children, to the next century and beyond.

Name: _____

Title: _____

Affiliation (if any): _____

Address: _____

Signed: _____

World Scientists' Statement

We, the undersigned scientists, call upon our governments to

— impose an immediate moratorium on further environmental releases of transgenic crops, food and animal-feed products for at least five years;

— ban patents on living organisms, cell lines and genes;

— support a comprehensive, independent public inquiry into the future of agriculture and food security for all, taking account of the full range of scientific findings as well as socio-economic and ethical implications.

1. We are extremely concerned over the continued release and commercialisation of transgenic crops, food and animal-feed products in the face of growing scientific evidence of hazards to biodiversity, food safety, human and animal health, while neither the need nor the benefits of genetic engineering agriculture are yet proven.

   1.1. New scientific evidence has convinced us of the need for an immediate moratorium on releases.

   1.1.1. Herbicide resistant transgenes have spread to wild relatives by cross-pollination in both oilseed rape and sugar beet,[1] creating many species of potential super-weeds. One study shows that transgenes may be up to 30 times more likely to escape than the plant's own genes.[2]

   1.1.2. *Bt*-toxins engineered into a wide range of transgenic plants already released into the environment may build up in the soil and have devastating impacts on pollinators and other beneficial insects.[3]

   1.1.3. Serious doubts over the safety of transgenic foods are raised by new results of animal feeding experiments. Potatoes engineered with snowdrop lectin fed to rats caused highly significant reduction in weight of many organs, impairment of immunological responsiveness and signs suggestive of viral infection.[4]

   1.1.4. Research from the Netherlands shows that antibiotic resistant marker genes from genetically engineered bacteria can be transferred horizontally to indigenous bacteria in an artificial gut.[5]

1.1.5. Researchers in the United States found widespread horizontal transfer of a yeast genetic parasite to the mitochondrial genome of higher plants,[6] raising serious concerns over the uncontrollable horizontal spread of transgenes and marker genes from transgenic plants released into the environment.

2. The patenting of living organisms, cell lines and genes under the Trade Related Intellectual Property Rights agreement is sanctioning acts of piracy of intellectual and genetic resources from Third World nations,[7] and at the same time, increasing corporate monopoly on food production and distribution. Small farmers all over the world are being marginalised, threatening long term food security for all.[8]

3. The Governments of industrialised nations, by voting for patents on organisms, cell lines and genes, including human genes, are in danger of allowing corporations unrestricted exploitation of their citizens and natural resources through the treaties being negotiated in the WTO [World Trade Organisation] and the MAI [Multilateral Agreements on Investment]. Environmental standards, food safety standards and even basic human rights will be sacrificed to corporate financial imperatives.[9]

4. Governmental advisory committees lack sufficient representation from independent scientists not linked to the industry. The result is that an untried, inadequately researched technology has been rushed prematurely to the market, while existing scientific evidence of hazards are being downplayed, ignored, and even suppressed,[10] and little independent research on risks is being carried out.

5. The technology is driven by an outmoded, genetic determinist science that supposes [that] organisms are determined simply by constant, unchanging genes that can be arbitrarily manipulated to serve our needs; whereas scientific findings accumulated over the past twenty years have invalidated every assumption of genetic determinism.[11] The new genetics is compelling us to an ecological, holistic perspective, especially

where genes are concerned. The genes are not constant and unchanging, but fluid and dynamic, responding to the physiology of the organism and the external environment, and require a stable, balanced ecology to maintain stability.

In summary, we call upon our governments to

— impose an immediate moratorium on further environmental releases of transgenic crops, food and animal-feed products for at least five years;

— ban patents on living organisms, cell lines and genes;

— support a comprehensive, independent public inquiry into the future of agriculture and food security for all, taking account of the full range of scientific findings as well as socio-economic and ethical implications.

Signed: _____

Name:_____

Title: _____

Organisation:_____

Address:_____

_____

Telephone: _____

E-mail: _____

Area of expertise:_____

Are you willing to act as spokesperson for the moratorium?:

Comments: _____

_____

Send to:

Angela Ryan

Institute of Science in Society

Flat 3, 42 Manor Road

High Barnett EN5 2JJ

England

Telephone and fax: +44 181 4416480

E-mail: ryan@i-sis.dircon.co.uk

GLOSSARY

adaptive mutation or **directed mutation:** the phenomenon whereby bacteria and yeast cells in stationary (non-growing) phase have some way of producing (or selectively retaining) only the most appropriate mutations that enable them to make use of new substrates for growth.

allele: a particular variant of a gene.

allergen: a substance that causes the body to react hypersensitively to it.

amino acid: an organic acid carrying an amino acid group (–NH2). There are twenty different amino acids, which are joined together in a defined order to make up linear molecules of proteins, each of which contains hundreds of amino acids.

ATP (adenosine triphosphate): a chemical substance present in all organisms whose function is to act as an intermediate for energy transformation.

autosome: a chromosome other than the sex chromosome, or sex-determining chromosome.

bacteriophage: any virus that infects bacteria, also known as *phage*.

baculovirus: a virus that normally infects insects.

base: an organic base joined together with a sugar and a phosphate group to make a *nucleotide*. Many nucleotides—thousands to millions or more—are linked together through the sugar of one nucleotide to the phosphate of the next to make up long linear molecules called DNA or RNA. There are four different bases in DNA: *adenine, thymine, guanine,* and *cystosine*; in RNA, thymine is replaced by *uracil.*

biofilm: a layer of extracellular matrix containing quiescent, non-proliferating micro-organisms.

carcinogen: an agent, usually a chemical, that causes cancer.

carrying capacity: the quantity of organisms (number or total biomass) that an ecological system can support.

chromosome: a structural unit of genetic material consisting of a long molecule of DNA complexed with special proteins in eukaryotes, but not in prokaryotes.

clone: an identical copy of an individual or a gene, or the totality of all the identical copies made from an individual or a gene. In genetics, the clone is identical in genetic make-up to the original.

conjugation: the mating process in bacteria, which requires cell-to-cell contact to be established and in which genes are transferred between cells.

coupling of processes: links between processes so that effects on one affect the other; when coupling is symmetrical, the effect of process A on process B is exactly the same as that of B on A.

cytoplasm: the ground substance inside the cell, apart from the *organelles.*

directed mutation: see ADAPTIVE MUTATION.

DNA (deoxyribonucleic acid): the genetic material made up of a long chain of individual units called *nucleotides.* Each nucleotide consists of a base joined to a sugar and a phosphate group.

DNA methylation: a process in the cell that adds a methyl group, CH_3, to the base cytosine or adenosine, often resulting in gene silencing, or failure of the gene to become expressed.

DNA polymerase: an enzyme that makes DNA.

DNAse: an enzyme that breaks down DNA.

domain: part of a protein with a well-defined function, such as binding to a specific co-factor or to DNA.

dominant allele: an allele that is expressed when only one copy is present in an individual, that is, in heterozygous condition.

ecosystem: the totality of all plant and animal species that constitute an interdependent, inter-related community.

entropy: a measure of the disordered, degraded energy that is unavailable for work.

enzyme: a protein produced by living organisms that acts as a catalyst for a specific biochemical (metabolic) reaction.

epigenetic: developmental; any process not involving change in DNA base sequence in the genome.

epistasis: interaction between genes.

eukaryote: the major class of living things, including all multicellular, higher organisms and some single-celled organisms, which have a nucleus in their cells, containing the chromosomes.

exon: a coding region in an interrupted gene.

fractals: processes or patterns characteristic of living systems that fall between the usual one, two or three dimensions. Examples are the branching pattern of blood vessels, the repeated patterns of fern leaves, and so on.

gene: a unit of heredity, usually a stretch of DNA with a well-defined function, such as one coding for a protein, or one that promotes transcription of other proteins.

gene amplification: the process whereby genes or sequences of DNA in the genome are greatly increased in number of copies.

gene cloning: the technique of making many copies of a gene, isolating the gene, and identifying it.

gene conversion: the process whereby one sequence of a particular gene replaces another sequence in the genome.

gene expression: in molecular genetics, this usually means the eventual appearance of the polypeptide encoded by the gene.

gene silencing: the process (or processes) whereby certain genes in the genome are prevented from being expressed by chemical modifications and other means.

gene splicing: a process of modifying genetic material by cutting the DNA molecule (or molecules) and rejoining the cut ends so that different bits are now joined together, or some bits are removed from the original molecule. It is rather like what one does when editing magnetic tapes.

gene therapy: treating diseases by replacing the defective gene, either by incorporating a normal copy of the gene in the germ cells (egg or sperm) or in the embryo (*germ-line gene replacement therapy*) or by supplying copies of the normal gene to be taken up and incorporated in cells of the adult (*somatic cell gene replacement therapy*).

genetic code: the code establishing the correspondence between the sequence of bases in nucleic acids (DNA and the complementary RNA) and the sequence of amino acids in proteins.

genetic determinism: the doctrine that the organism is the inevitable consequence of its genetic make-up, or the sum of its genes.

genetic engineering: the manipulating of genetic material in the laboratory. It includes isolating, copying and multiplying genes, recombining genes or DNA from different species, and transferring genes from one species to another, bypassing the reproductive process.

genetic marker: any segment of DNA that can be identified, or whose chromosomal location is known, so that it can be used as a reference point to map or locate other genes; any gene that has an identifiable phenotype that can be used to track the presence or absence of other genes on the same piece of DNA transferred into a cell.

genome: the totality of the genetic material of a cell or organism.

genotype: the precise variant (or variants) of the gene (or genes) carried by an individual.

germ cell: a cell involved in reproduction, such as sperm cell and egg cell.

germ-line: the line of germ cells, assumed to be constant and unchanging, passed on from one generation to the next.

germplasm: the material in the germ cells that supposedly accounts for the unchanging hereditary influence that is passed on to subsequent generations.

Gram-positive, Gram-negative: traditional major divisions of bacteria. The Gram-positive bacteria are surrounded by a thick cell wall, which, however, is permeable to small molecules. Gram-negative bacteria, such as *Escherichia coli,* are surrounded by a second membrane, which functions as an effective barrier to small molecules.

heterozygote: an individual who has two different alleles of a gene.

heterozygous: a condition in which two different alleles of the gene are present in an individual.

homologous: similar; derived from a common ancestor.

homozygote: an individual who has two identical alleles of the gene.

horizontal gene transfer: the transfer of genes from one individual to another, of the same or different species, usually by means other than cross-breeding.

iatrogenic diseases: diseases caused by prescription drugs or treatments.

integron: a special kind of mobile genetic element that allows the insertion of antibiotic-resistant genes into specific sites, each of which is provided with a promoter for expression. Integrons can jump into and out of the bacterial chromosome and of plasmids and are particularly involved in the evolution of multiple resistance to drugs and antibiotics.

interrupted genes: genes whose coding sequence is interrupted at intervals by long stretches of non-coding sequences. The coding regions have come to be known as *exons* and the non-coding regions as *introns*. This structure is now found to be characteristic of most eukaryotic genes. The number and size of introns vary greatly, and they are often much longer than the coding sequences. After transcription, the intron regions are removed or spliced out from the RNA transcript before it is translated into protein.

intron: a non-coding region in a gene that comes between exons, the coding regions.

messenger RNA: the RNA intermediate in protein synthesis containing a transcribed copy of the gene sequence that specifies the amino acid sequence of the polypeptide it encodes.

metabolism: the totality of chemical processes that take place in living organisms, resulting in growth, development, and all energy transformation.

metabolite: one particular chemical intermediate generated in metabolism.

mitochondria: membrane-bound cellular organelles in which organic substrates derived from food are oxidised to provide energy for all kinds of vital activities. They carry their own complement of DNA and are replicated independently, so that when the cell divides, each daughter cell will receive half the mitochondria.

mobile genetic element, also called **transposon** or **transposable genetic element:** a sequence of DNA that can transpose (move) from one place to another in the genome of a cell.

multigene families: genes that exist in multiple copies in the genome, from several copies to many thousands or hundreds of thousands of copies.

mutagen: a substance or agent that causes genetic mutations by damaging or chemically modifying DNA.

nucleus: a structure in the eukaryote cell bounded by a membrane, which contains the genetic material, in the form of DNA organised into chromosomes.

oncogenes: genes associated with cancer.

origin of replication: a stretch of DNA that serves as a genetic signal for replication of a plasmid or vector, which is recognised by the host cell.

pathogen: any agent that can cause disease.

pathogenicity island: a large chromosomal region in pathogenic bacteria that codes for virulence genes and has been acquired by the bacteria from unrelated species by horizontal gene transfer.

phage: a bacterial virus.

phenotype: the expressed characteristics, or an expressed character, of an organism due to its genotype.

plasmid: a piece of parasitic genetic material found in a cell that can replicate using the cell's resources.

polygenes: the (hypothetical) many genes affecting a character, each having a small, additive effect on the character.

polypeptide or **protein:** a long chain of different amino acids joined together by special chemical (peptide) bonds.

prokaryote: the class of living things, including all bacteria, that do not have a nucleus in their cell.

promoter: a stretch of DNA or RNA preceding a gene, which is required for gene expression.

proto-oncogenes: cellular genes that, when mutated or overexpressed, become oncogenes.

provirus: a virus that has inserted its genome or a complementary copy of its genome into the host cell genome.

recessive allele: an allele that is not expressed unless two copies are present in the individual, that is, in homozygous condition.

recombination: the formation of new combinations of alleles or new genes that occurs when two pieces of DNA join up or exchange parts.

reductionism: the doctrine that a complex system can be completely understood in terms of its simplest parts; for example, an organism is to be completely understood in terms of its genes, a society in terms of its individuals, and so on.

regulator gene: a gene that acts to turn other genes on or off.

repressor: a protein that binds to an operator region of another gene to prevent it being expressed.

restriction: the process by which DNA is cut with restriction enzyme (or enzymes).

restriction enzyme: an enzyme that cuts DNA based on the recognition of a short specific base sequence in the DNA.

retrotransposon: a mobile genetic element that depends on reverse transcription to move and to duplicate.

retrovirus: an RNA virus that depends on reverse transcription for its replication. Retroviruses include many cancer viruses and the AIDS virus.

reverse transcription: the reverse of transcription—making a copy of complementary DNA (cDNA) from an RNA sequence—catalysed by the enzyme reverse transcriptase.

ribonuclease: an enzyme that breaks down RNA.

ribosomal RNA: RNA molecules that make up the ribosome.

ribosome: an organelle in the cell required for protein synthesis.

RNA (ribonucleic acid): similar to DNA except for the sugar in the nucleotide unit, which is ribose instead of deoxyribose, and the base, which is uracil instead of thymine. RNA is the genetic material for RNA viruses.

RNA editing: the process in which the base sequence of the RNA transcript is changed by the addition of bases to the RNA molecule or by chemical transformation of one base to another. This subverts the genetic information carried in the genes.

RNA polymerase: an enzyme that makes RNA.

self-similarity: the property of fractal structures, such as certain fern leaves and blood vessels in our body, that have similar patterns at different scales.

sequence homology: similarity in DNA sequence found in different species, indicating that they originated from some common ancestor.

shuttle vector: an artificially constructed vector that can replicate and transfer genes between two often distant species.

somaclonal variation: genetic variations of plant cells arising in cell culture as a result of increased genetic instability.

somatic: of the vegetative body, as opposed to *germ-line*.

substrate: a chemical substance that takes part in a chemical reaction catalysed by an enzyme.

thermodynamics: the branch of physics dealing with the transformation of energy, especially of heat and other forms of energy.

transcription: the process of making a complementary sequence of the gene sequence in the genome, which is either used directly, as in the case of ribosomal RNAs (rRNAs) and transfer RNAs (tRNAs) or is further processed into the messenger RNA, and translated into protein. The process is catalysed by the enzyme known as DNA-dependent RNA polymerase.

transcription factors: proteins in eukaryotes that regulate the transcription of other genes by binding to regulatory sequences of the gene, or by interacting with one another and with the RNA polymerase.

transduction: in genetics, the transfer of genes by viruses from one organism to another.

transfer RNA: RNA molecules that transfer specific amino acids to the messenger RNA so that the polypeptide it encodes can be synthesised.

transformation: in genetics, the uptake of genes by one organism of DNA belonging to another organism of the same or a different species.

transgenic organism: an organism created by genetic engineering, in which one or more foreign genes have been incorporated in its genome.

translation: the step in protein synthesis in which the messenger RNA directs the synthesis of a polypeptide of a particular amino acid sequence by 'translating' the genetic code.

transposable introns: transposons that move in and out of introns.

transposon: see MOBILE GENETIC ELEMENT.

vector: a carrier for transferring disease or genes; for example, the mosquito is a vector for malaria. Viruses, plasmids and transposons are vectors for genes. Aphids are vectors for transferring disease-causing viruses from one plant to another.

virulence: the ability (of pathogens) to infect organisms and cause disease

virus: a parasitic genetic element enclosed in a protein coat that can replicate in cells and form infectious particles, or remain dormant in the cell. Its genetic material can become integrated to the cell's genome to form *provirus*.

NOTES

Chapter 1 (p. 1–23)
1. Face-to-face debate, Oxford Centre for Environment, Ethics and Society, University of Oxford, 20 Feb. 1997.
2. 'Scientists scorn sci-fi fears over sheep clone', *Guardian,* 24 Feb. 1997, 7. Ian Wilmut, the senior scientist involved, was quoted as saying, 'It will enable us to study genetic diseases for which there is now no cure and track down the mechanisms involved. The next step is to use the cells in culture in the lab and target genetic changes into that culture.' In the same article Lewis Wolpert, a developmental biologist at University College, London, was reported as saying, 'It's a pretty risky technique, with lots of abnormalities.' Also report and interview on 'Eight o'Clock News', BBC Radio 4, 24 Feb. 1997.
3. Associated Press, 1998.
4. Marie Woolf, 'Ministers told to study GM health risks', *Independent on Sunday,* 2 May 1999.
5. As for instance Spallone, 1992.
6. George, 1988, 5.
7. My colleague Peter Saunders and I began working on an alternative approach to neo-Darwinian evolutionary theory in the seventies. Major collections of multi-author essays appeared in Ho and Saunders, 1984, Pollard, 1984, and Ho and Fox, 1988.
8. Wolpert, 1996.
9. See Hubbard and Wald, 1993.
10. Schumacher College, Totnes (Devon), 3–10 Feb. 1997.
11. See Korten, 1997.
12. Korten, 1997, 2.
13. See Perlas, 1994; also 'WTO: new setback for the South', *Third World Resurgence* 77–78, 1997, which contains many articles reporting on the meeting of the World Trade Organisation held in Singapore in December 1996.
14. Brown et al., 1993.
15. Udo and Grubb, 1990.
16. Michael Day, 'Superbug spectre haunts Japan', *New Scientist,* 3 May 1997, 5; R. Dobson, 'Rise of superbugs linked to antibiotics in animal feed', *Independent on Sunday,* 3 May 1998.

17. See Bik et al., 1995; Prager et al., 1995; Reidl and Mekalanos, 1995.

18. Whatmore et al., 1994; Kapur et al., 1995; Schnitzler et al., 1995; Upton et al., 1996.

19. Prof. Hugh Pennington on BBC Radio 4 news, Feb. 1997. He confirmed this to me in a personal interview on 2 July 1997.

20. Barinaga, 1996.

21. Reviewed by Davies, 1994.

22. Tschäpe, 1994.

23. See *World Health Report, 1996,* also Garrett, 1995, chap. 13, for an excellent account of the history of antibiotic-resistance in pathogens.

24. See Ho, 1999b.

25. See Davies, 1994.

26. *WHO Fact Sheet no. 139,* Jan. 1997.

27. Hoffmann et al., 1994; Schluter et al., 1995; de Vries and Wackernagel, 1998.

28. See Ho, 1996a.

29. Jager and Tappeser (1996) have extensively reviewed the literature on the survival of bacteria and DNA released into different environments.

30. See Lorenz and Wackernagel, 1994.

31. See Schubbert et al. 1994 and 1997; Doerfler et al., 1998. *New Scientist,* 4 Jan. 1997, 24, featured a short report on recent findings of the group that were presented at the International Congress on Cell Biology, San Francisco, December 1996.

32. Wahl et al., 1984; Doerfler et al., 1997. See also relevant entries in Kendrew, 1995, especially 'Slow transforming retroviruses' and 'Transgenic technologies'.

33. Debora MacKenzie, 'Killer virus piles on the misery in Zaïre', *New Scientist,* 19 Apr. 1997, 12.

34. 'Virus gets personal', *New Scientist,* 26 Apr. 1997, 13.

35. Heather Gardner, Knowles Kerry, and Martin Riddle, 'Poultry virus infection in Antarctic penguins', *Nature* 387 (15 May 1997), 245.

36. See Pain, 1997.

37. Briefing from Third World Network, April 1999; see also Ian Anderson, 'The pigs must die!', *New Scientist,* 3 Apr. 1999, 4.

38. I first drew attention to the dangers of horizontal gene transfer and related matters at a conference on food organised by the National Council of Women of Great Britain in April 1996 and again in a fully referenced paper presented at a Workshop on Capacity-Building in Biosafety for Developing Countries organised by the Stockholm Environmental Institute in May 1996 (see the volume edited by Virgin and Frederick, 1996, for a shortened version of the

paper), where I made it clear that capacity-building in biosafety is urgently needed for industrialised countries. Later I sent the full paper with detailed references to the Ministry of Agriculture, Fisheries and Food in London, with lists of hazards and information gaps for risk assessment that I believe ought to be directly addressed by the appropriate monitoring of field releases and specifically targeted research. I received a reply from the MAFF experts that stated that they could find little or no evidence for horizontal gene transfer by comparing gene sequences of organisms in existing data-bases. While dismissing some of the points I made as 'highly unlikely', they did state that they were addressing many existing information gaps by financing continuing research. The reply indicates that risk assessments are indeed being done in the absence of much necessary basic knowledge. I replied to the experts, challenging their interpretation on most of the points, but have yet to receive any further response. I have also given my papers to representatives of the Department of the Environment, and have had no reactions from them at all.

39. Quoted in 'The spectre of a human clone', *Independent,* 26 Feb. 1997, 1.

Chapter 2 (p. 24–47)

1. The Asilomar Declaration, drawing attention to the potential risks of recombinant DNA technology, was issued as the result of a conference held in Asilomar, California. This resulted in the first guidelines issued by the US National Institute of Health. The city of Cambridge, Massachusetts, debated recombinant DNA research and declared a moratorium pending the outcome of a citizens' review. In 1977 the first law regulating recombinant DNA research was enacted by the city.

2. See Ho, 1993, 1998a, 1995a, 1995b, 1997a.

3. Regal, 1994.

4. Snow, 1962, 138.

5. Hubbard and Wald, 1993.

6. 'When the price is wrong', *Guardian,* 27 Feb. 1997, 2.

7. From *Government Response to the Second Annual Report of the Government's Panel on Sustainable Development,* Jan. 1996, Mar. 1996, 16. Note that this is the government's response to its own panel, the reason being that it came up with a report recommending, among other things, a much more cautious approach to the commercialisation of genetic-engineering biotechnology than that taken by the government.

8. See Ho et al., 1998a, and references therein.

9. See Ronnie Cummins, *Food Bytes* 18; Greenpeace International press release, 29 Apr. 1999.

10. The Human Genome Initiative was established in 1988 by the US National Institute of Health, under the directorship of James Watson, joint Nobel Laureate for his discovery of the DNA double helix with Francis Crick in 1953.

11. John Moore's spleen was removed as part of the treatment for leukaemia. Unknown to him, the physician at the University of California, Los Angeles, developed and patented a permanent cell line from it, and two companies, Sandoz and Genetics Institute, took out licences. See Burrows, 1996.

12. Shiva, 1994.

13. See Nijar and Chee, 1994.

14. Egziabher, 1994.

15. Cropper, 1994.

16. Rob Edwards, 'Biotech firm "embarrassed" by leaked plant deal', *New Scientist,* 29 June 1996, 7.

17. See McNally and Wheale, 1996.

18. 'Patent threat to research', letter signed by nine scientists in Britain, *Nature* 384, 1997, 672.

19. 'Patents versus transplants', letter signed by sixteen scientists representing the Bone Marrow Transplant Services, Cord Blood Banks, and others, *Nature* 382, 1996, 108.

20. See 'Letter to Madeleine Albright', initiated by Kristin Dawkins and signed by numerous non-government organisations and individuals from all over the world, protesting that the United States has no right to use its commercial power to influence legislative processes in other countries.

21. See, for example, Aldridge, 1996, written by a science writer trained in genetic-engineering biotechnology.

22. Meister and Mayer, 1994.

23. Palca, 1986; also McNally, 1995.

24. See Ho and Steinbrecher, 1998.

25. See Belonga et al., 1990, and Mayeno and Gleich, 1994.

26. Nordlee et al., 1996.

27. Inose and Murata, 1995.

28. Skogsmyr, 1994.

29. Mikkelsen et al., 1996.

30. Holmes and Ingham, 1994.

31. United Nations Environmental Programme, *UNEP Cairo Expert Panel Report,* May 1995.

32. *Biosafety, Scientific Findings and Elements of a Protocol: Report of the Independent Group of Scientific and Legal Experts on Biosafety,* Third World Network 1996.

33. Third World Network has played a major role in informing UN delegates on many world issues throughout the nineties by providing powerful speakers, running seminars, and preparing briefing papers for circulation at UN conferences. Public-interest organisations in general are indispensable to the democratic process of the United Nations; that is because delegates from all countries, both North and South, are typically badly briefed and have little understanding of the issues, which makes it very easy for small groups with vested interests to take over the conferences. TWN is one of the most influential and knowledgeable public-interest organisations working at the United Nations. It also publishes a magazine, *Third World Resurgence,* which has a worldwide circulation of 100,000.

34. See Chee, 1996.

35. Letter to President Clinton from forty associations, including biotech companies, food growers, and farmers, 18 June 1997; reported by Reuters, 19 June. I am grateful to Phil Bereano of the Union of Concerned Scientists of the United States and Jaan Surkula of Sweden for bringing the news item to my attention.

36. See Burrow, 1995.

37. Mellon and Rissler, 1995.

38. Miller, 1995.

39. Personal communication, Beth Burrows of the Edmonds Institute.

40. Letter from Mae-Wan Ho to Department of the Environment, 14 Feb. 1997.

41. See Ho and Steinbrecher, 1998; also affidavits and reports produced by the author for the defence of civil society and responsible citizens, available from the Institute of Science in Society (www.i-sis.dircon.co.uk).

42. Hubbard, 1995.

43. See Hubbard and Wald, 1993.

44. *GenEthics News* 3, 1994, 6–7.

45. This was predicted by the Marxist geneticist Richard Lewontin of Harvard University in 1985 (see Lewontin, 1985).

46. Tom Wakefield, 'Too far, too fast?', *Guardian,* 5 Mar. 1997, 4.

47. Shiva et al., 1997.

48. Shiva, 1994.

49. Perlas, 1994, 1995.

50. Reganold et al., 1990.

51. Liebe Cavalieri, personal communication, 1995.
52. Shiva, 1993.

Chapter 3 (p. 48–66)

1. The distinction between transgenic agriculture and conventional breeding methods has been emphasised in many previous publications by the author; see in particular Ho and Tappeser, 1997, and Ho and Steinbrecher, 1998. For the special safety concerns see Ho, 1999b. For the link between foreign gene insertion and cancer see Wahl et al., 1984, and relevant entries in Kendrew, 1995.
2. Lin et al., 1994.
3. Hamilton and Carey, 1994.
4. Daniel Kadlec, 'Bearish on biotech', *Time,* 10 Mar. 1997, 52.
5. The British Biotech fiasco was reported in a series of articles in the *Times,* 20 April, 23 April and 26 May 1998. For a more recent assessment of the 'biotechnology bubble' see Ho et al., 1998a.
6. Quoted in *Genewatch* 9, 5, Nov. 1994.
7. Darwin, 1859.
8. See Strohman, 1994, for an excellent critique of reductionist, linear concepts in health and disease.
9. Mulvihill, 1995.
10. The evidence is extensively reviewed by a number of authors, beginning more than ten years ago: see Steele, 1979; Dover and Flavell, 1982; Pollard, 1984; Ho, 1987; Rennie, 1993; Jabonka and Lamb, 1995. See also chapter 7.
11. See Dover and Flavell, 1982.
12. Rennie, 1993.
13. Foster, 1992.
14. Rothenfluh and Steele, 1993.
15. Cullis, 1988.
16. Pollard, 1988.
17. See Foster, 1992; Symonds, 1994.
18. Pure Foods Campaign, information sheet.
19. *Bt Cotton Fiascos in the US and Australia* (Biotechnology Working Group Briefing Paper no. 2), BSWG, Montréal, May 1997.
20. 'Seeds of discontent: cotton growers say strain cuts yields', *New York Times,* 19 Nov. 1997.
21. See *Manitoba Co-Operator,* 24 Apr. 1997; also *Ram's Horn* 147, Apr. 1997.
22. Harvard Working Group on New and Resurgent Diseases, 1995.
23. See *Ecologist* 28 (2), Mar.–Apr. 1998, for excellent accounts of the links between cancer and radioactive and toxic wastes in the environment.

24. Natural Law Party briefing paper; see also Brennan et al., 1991.
25. This ideal is satisfied when the system is coherent. For the biophysics of coherence see Ho, 1993, 1995a, 1995b, 1997a, 1998a.
26. See Ho, 1988b.
27. Ho, 1993, 1998a.
28. Brian Goodwin, 'What's wrong with neo-Darwinism?', *Times Higher Education Supplement*, 19 May 1995, 18.
29. See Ho, 1993, 1996b and 1998a for a rigorous argument that participatory knowledge is the only rational knowledge, according to contemporary Western science.

Chapter 4 (p. 67–81)

1. Barzun, 1958, back cover.
2. Lamarck, 1809.
3. Darwin, 1859.
4. See Ho, 1995a, for more details on muscle energetics.
5. See Ho and Saunders, 1979, and Ho, 1984a, for a consistently epigenetic approach, as outlined here. Though other approaches (such as Goodwin, 1984, 1994, and Strohman, 1993, 1997) place much emphasis on development, they do not accept the actual feedback relationship between organism and environment as being crucial to the development and evolution of the organism itself.
6. A man actually gets more genes from his mother. Genes occur on chromosomes, which, like the genes they carry, occur in pairs. Humans have twenty-three pairs of chromosomes; the members of each pair are alike and of the same size (and differ from those of other pairs), except for the sex-determining chromosomes. Females have an equal pair, XX, which are both large; males, on the other hand, have an unequal pair, XY, the Y chromosome being a lot smaller. The father would have inherited his Y chromosome from his father and the X chromosome from his mother.
7. Olby, 1966.
8. Battacharyya et al., 1990.
9. See Olby, 1966.
10. See Ho, 1993.

Chapter 5 (p. 82–95)

1. See Ho, 1998c, for a recent review on evolution.
2. An important element in recent alternative approaches to evolution is the emphasis on the dynamics of developmental processes that generate non-random forms—so much so that a rational taxonomy of the forms could be derived: see Ho and Saunders, 1979, 1984,

1993, 1994; Goodwin, 1984, 1994; Webster and Goodwin, 1982, 1996; Saunders, 1984, 1997; Saunders and Ho, 1995; Ho, 1984b, 1988c, 1990, 1992.

3. See, for example, Turing, 1952; also Saunders, 1984, 1998, and Webster and Goodwin, 1997, and references therein.
4. The history of population genetics is told by Provine, 1971.
5. For an authoritative and detailed critique of heritability estimates see Lewontin, 1982. The treatment here differs in detail, though not in substance. Richard Lewontin has published extensively on the IQ debate and related issues.

Chapter 6 (p. 96–107)

1. Morgan, 1916, 187–90.
2. More details on the experiments performed, from the identification of DNA as the genetic material to the cracking of the genetic code, are to be found in Ho, 1976.
3. Schrödinger, 1944.
4. Dawkins, 1976.
5. Wilson, 1975.
6. See Kropotkin, 1914, also Ho, 1996c, for a more extended discussion of the point raised here.

Chapter 7 (p. 108–135)

1. Much of this account is based on Ho and Goodwin, 1987, and Ho, 1987a, 1987b; see also Jones and Taylor, 1995.
2. See Bjorklund et al., 1999, for a recent review.
3. See Ho, 1987b.
4. See Puttarju et al., 1999.
5. Holtorf et al., 1999.
6. See Landman, 1991; Jablonka and Lamb, 1995; also Ho, 1988b.
7. Blanc et al., 1996; Maier et al., 1996.
8. Lau et al., 1997; O'Connell et al., 1997.
9. Blanc et al., 1996.
10. O'Connell et al., 1997.
11. Lau et al., 1997.
12. See Ho, 1993, 1997c, 1998a; also Laszlo, 1994, 1996.
13. The account that follows is based on Ho, 1987b.
14. Dover and Flavell, 1982, back cover.
15. Gierl, 1990.
16. Temin, 1980.
17. Baltimore, 1985.
18. See Flavell, 1982.

19. Janetopoulos et al., 1999.
20. Temin and Engels, 1984.
21. See Rennie, 1994.
22. Gierl, 1990.
23. McClintock, 1984.
24. Temin and Engels, 1984.
25. Bostock and Tyler-Smith, 1982; Gudkov and Kopnin, 1985.
26. See Cullis, 1983, 1988; also Ho, 1987a, 1987b.
27. See Dover, 1982; also Ho, 1987b.
28. See Jablonka and Lamb, 1995; also Ho, 1996d.
29. Ho et al., 1983.
30. Temin, 1980.
31. Soares et al., 1985.
32. Hattori et al., 1986; see also Steele et al., 1998.
33. Rothenfluh and Steele, 1993; Rothenfluh et al., 1995; Steele et al., 1998.
34. Campbell et al., 1973; see also Ho, 1987a.
35. Hall and Hartl, 1974.
36. Cairns et al., 1988.
37. Riede, 1996.
38. See Foster, 1992; Longerich et al., 1995.
39. See Shapiro, 1997.
40. This is described in detail by Steele et al., 1998.
41. See Waisfisz, Morgan, Savino et al., 1999.

Chapter 8 (p. 136–167)

1. See *Food for Our Future: Food and Biotechnology,* London: Food and Drink Federation 1995.
2. Geoffrey Lean, 'And still the children go hungry', *Independent on Sunday,* 10 Nov. 1996, 12.
3. Hardy, 1994.
4. See A. Aslan, 'Food-population: experts want to break wheat's yield barrier', *Inter Press Service,* 18 Oct. 1996.
5. Pretty, 1995, 1998; Watkins, 1999.
6. Lester Brown of the World Watch Institute, quoted by Goldsmith and Hildyard, 1991.
7. Watkins, 1999.
8. Goldsmith, 1992.
9. N. Hildyard, 'An open letter to Edouard Saouma, Director-General of the Food and Agriculture Organization of the United Nations', *Ecologist* 21, 1991, 43–6.
10. See *Food for Our Future: Food and Biotechnology,* London: Food and Drink Federation 1995; Kendall et al. 1997; Brown, 1998.

11. See Goldsmith and Hildyard, 1984–92, for an authoritative account of the devastating effects of big dam projects on industrialising countries.
12. Cainglet, 1998.
13. Watkins, 1996.
14. E. Beringer, 'Seed action in Germany', *Landmark*, July–Aug. 1996, 13.
15. See Pretty, 1995.
16. Griffin, 1999.
17. Watkins, 1999.
18. Hildyard, 1996, 282.
19. Pretty, 1995.
20. See De Angelis, 1992; Pimm, 1991.
21. Moffat, 1996.
22. Raven, 1994.
23. Altieri, 1991.
24. C. Emerson, 'Throwing out the baby with the bathwater', *On the Ground*, 2 Sep. 1996.
25. Shiva, 1993.
26. See Goldsmith, 1992; Shiva, 1993.
27. ISAAA Report, 1998.
28. Cox, 1995.
29. Mikkelsen et al., 1996; see also Ho and Tappeser, 1997.
30. Perlas, 1994.
31. Altieri, 1991.
32. Pretty, 1995.
33. *Alternative Agriculture: Report of the National Academy of Sciences*, Washington 1989.
34. See Pretty, 1995.
35. Vazquez Vega, 1998.
36. Kothari, 1994.
37. 'Seed action in Brazil', *Landmark*, July–Aug. 1996, 10.
38. See Delta and Pine Land Company, press release, 3 Mar. 1998; 'Biotech activists oppose the "Terminator technology": new patent aims to prevent farmers from saving seed', RAFI press statement, 13 Mar. 1998.
39. Kendall et al., 1998.
40. See *Food for Our Future: Food and Biotechnology*, London: Food and Drink Federation 1995, 5.
41. Nordlee et al., 1996.
42. Frank and Keller, 1995.
43. Lemke and Taylor, 1994.
44. Inose and Murata, 1995.

45. Joint FAO-WHO Expert Consultation on Biotechnology and Food Safety, Rome 1996.
46. See Ho and Steinbrecher, 1998, for a detailed critique of the Joint FAO-WHO Food Safety Report.
47. International Center for Technology Assessment, 'Landmark lawsuit challenges FDA policy on genetically engineered foods', press statement, 27 May 1998.
48. 'Scientist in Frankenstein food alert is proved right', *Mail on Sunday,* 31 Jan. 1999; see also Goodwin, 1999.
49. Jorgensen and Anderson, 1994; Mikkelsen et al., 1996.
50. Eber et al., 1994; Damency, 1994.
51. Eber et al., 1994.
52. Rissler and Mellon, 1993.
53. See Holmes and Ingham, 1995.
54. 'Cotton used in medicine poses threat: genetically altered cotton may not be safe', *Bangkok Post,* 17 Nov. 1997; Hilbeck et al., 1998.
55. Hilbeck et al., 1998.
56. Florianne Koechlin, 'Risks from Bt crops', report of an international meeting of entomologists in Basel, Mar. 1999 (fkoechline@datacom.ch).
57. Crecchio and Stotzky, 1998.
58. Colman, 1996; Lee et al., 1995, and references therein. See also Parr, 1997; Steinbrecher 1997; Ho and Steinbrecher, 1998.
59. Benbrook, 1999.
60. See Ho et al., 1998a.
61. See Cooking, 1989.
62. Reported by Perlas, 1995.
63. Wahl et al., 1984; Walden et al., 1991.
64. Finnegan and McElroy, 1994; Holtorf et al., 1999.
65. Reynolds et al., 1996.
66. Johnston, 1989.
67. Hyrien and Buttin, 1986.
68. See review by Estruch et al., 1997.
69. Jeffrey Fox, 'Insecticide preservation policy: to be or not Bt', *Nature Biotechnology* 14, 1996, 687–8.
70. Estruch et al., 1997.
71. Traavik, 1998.
72. 'UK's on-off affair with Ciba-Geigy's Supermaize', *Splice of Life* 3 (1), 1996, 5–6.
73. Smirnov et al., 1994. I thank Jaan Suurkula for this information.
74. See Ho, 1999a.
75. Asante-Appiah and Skalka, 1997.

76. Bergelson et al., 1998.

77. Hoffmann et al., 1994; Schluter et al., 1995; Gebhard and Smalla, 1998; de Vries and Wackernagel, 1998.

78. Hoffmann et al., 1994.

79. De Vries and Wackernagel, 1998.

80. Schluter et al., 1995.

81. Gebhard and Smalla, 1999.

82. Cummins, 1998; courtesy of the author.

83. See Crouch, 1999.

84. Green and Allison, 1994.

85. Allison, 1995.

86. Lommel and Xiong, 1991.

87. Vaden and Melcher, 1990; Wintermantel and Schoelz, 1996.

88. Schoelz and Wintermantel, 1993.

89. Paulkaitis and Rossinck, 1996.

90. Cummins, 1994.

91. Cummins, 1994; Cann, 1997.

92. Xiong and Eikbush, 1990.

93. Smerdon et al., 1995; Vlack et al., 1990; Assad and Signer, 1990.

94. Heitman and Lopes-Pila, 1993.

95. See Ho, 1999 b.

96. Hoffmann et al., 1996.

97. Cummins, 1997. I thank the author for sending this article to me.

98. Schubbert et al., 1994, 1997; Philip Cohen, 'Can DNA in food find its way into cells?', *New Scientist,* 4 Jan. 1997, 14.

99. Doerfler et al., 1998.

100. Courvain et al., 1995, 1207.

101. Forbes et al., 1998..

102. Kendall et al., 1997.

Chapter 9 (p. 168–200)

1. *WHO Report, 1996,* Geneva: World Health Organisation 1996.

2. See Ho, 1998a, and Ho et al., 1998, for a detailed report on the possible contributions of genetic-engineering biotechnology to the recent resurgence of infectious diseases; also R. Dobson, 'Rise of superbugs linked to antibiotics in animal feed', *Independent on Sunday,* 3 May 1998.

3. See Lovelock, 1979, 1996, and references therein.

4. See Davies, 1994.

5. Udo and Grubb, 1990.

6. Garrett (1995) presents a detailed history of the rise of antibiotic-resistance in chapter 13 of her excellent monograph.

7. Riley et al., 1983.

8. WHO press statement 41, 21 May 1997.

9. See Knight, 1993.

10. See Mackey and Gibson, 1998.

11. See Garrett, 1995, 430.

12. Volk et al., 1995; also Hugh Pennington, 'Today', BBC Radio 4, Feb. 1997; confirmed by personal communication.

13. Brown et al., 1993.

14. See note 2.

15. The account given here is abstracted mainly from Davies, 1994, Nikaido, 1994, and Spratt, 1994. See Volk et al., 1995, 253–84, for a description of the classes of antibiotics and their mechanisms of action.

16. Levy and Novick, 1986, 79.

17. See Levy and Novick, 1986.

18. Trieu-Cuot et al., 1985.

19. See Sougakoff et al., 1987; Manavathu et al., 1988; Kell et al., 1993; Amabilecuevas and Chicurel, 1993; Coffey et al., 1995; Bootsma et al., 1996. Horizontal gene transfer is recently reviewed by Yin and Stotzky, 1997.

20. See Ho et al., 1998; Traavik, 1998.

21. Stachel et al., 1986.

22. Goussard et al., 1996.

23. See entries in Kendrew, 1995.

24. Lorenz and Wackernagel, 1994; Yin and Stotzky, 1997.

25. See Yin and Stotzky, 1997.

26. Bergh et al., 1989; Miller, 1998.

27. Ippen-Ihler and Skurray, 1993.

28. See Clewell, 1993; Yin and Stotzky, 1997.

29. Franke and Clewell, 1981; Clewell and Flannagan, 1993.

30. Stokes and Hall, 1989, 1992; Collis et al., 1993.

31. Roberts and Hillier, 1990; Speer, Shoemaker and Salyers, 1992.

32. Pang et al., 1994.

33. Pang et al., 1994, 1411.

34. Spratt, 1988.

35. Kehoe et al., 1996.

36. Upton et al., 1996.

37. Prager et al., 1995; Reidl and Mekalanos, 1995; Bik et al., 1995.

38. Reddy et al., 1995.

39. Baringa, 1996.

40. See Hacker et al., 1998; also Ho et al., 1998.

41. Martin, 1999

42. Hughes and Datta, 1983.

43. *WHO Fact Sheet no. 139,* Jan. 1997.

44. H. R. Smith, 'Vero cytotoxin-producing *Escherichia coli* O157: cause for concern', *SGM Quarterly,* May 1997, 54–5.

45. See Elegant, 1997.

46. See Neu, 1992.

47. J. Zepelin, 'US-Gesellschaft für Infektionskrankheiten warnt vor ausbreitung resistenter krankheitserreger/bessere hygiene', *Frankfurter Rundschau,* 12 Oct. 1997, a report on the annual conference of the Infectious Diseases Society of America.

48. Cornaglia et al., 1996.

49. See Davies, 1994; Mazodier and Davies, 1991; Torres et al., 1991.

50. Sandaa and Enger, 1994.

51. Mahy, 1997.

52. See Moens et al., 1996.

53. Pang et al., 1994.

54. Doerfler, 1991, 1992.

55. See Old and Primrose, 1994.

56. See Ho and Steinbrecher, 1997.

57. Frischer et al., 1994; Lebaron et al., 1994; Sandaa and Enger, 1994.

58. Ripp et al., 1994.

59. Neilson et al., 1994.

60. Goodman et al., 1994.

61. Mezrioui and Echab, 1995.

62. Doucet-Populaire, 1992; Guillot and Boucaud, 1992.

63. See Anderson, 1975, Freter, 1986, and, most recently, Mercer et al., 1999.

64. Roberts, 1989.

65. Mazodier and Davies, 1991, 148.

66. Khavari, 1997; Sandberg et al., 1994. This description is based on a letter by Joe Cummins, Terje Traavik, and myself, rejected by both *Nature* and the *New Scientist.* I thank my co-authors for allowing me to use the information here.

67. Spadafora, 1998.

68. 'Naked DNA raises cancer fears for researchers', *New Scientist,* 6 Oct. 1990, 17.

69. See Traavik, 1998.

70. Reviewed extensively by Jager and Tappeser, 1995.

71. Tschäpe, 1994.

72. Schrag and Perrot, 1996.

73. Tschäpe, 1994.

74. Costerton et al., 1994; Lewis and Gattie, 1991.

75. Coghlan, 1997.

76. According to the Novo Nordisk 1996 Environmental Report (kindly sent to me by their environment director), the Danish authority sets the following limits for untreated release of GMMs in terms of colony-forming units (roughly equivalent to live bacteria): waste water, 10,000/ml; air, 10,000/ml; solid waste, 10,000/g. Novo Nordisk also recycles inactivated GMMs as fertilisers for crops, under the trade name NovoGro.

77. I telephoned the Health and Safety Executive, London, in June 1997 to obtain information on the safety regulation of commercial-scale contained use. The person I spoke to told me that the agency had only a small leaflet, which he would send to me, and that if I required more detailed information I should ring another number for the health inspectors. I rang that number for the next two weeks, and never once was the telephone answered, nor was there an answering-machine to leave a message on. When the leaflet failed to arrive after a week I telephoned the HSE again. A different person assured me that the normal time it took for the leaflet to get to anyone was ten days; however, if I needed it right away I could pay £10, or £5 for delivery in the next two days. I protested that, as a public department, and for information of such vital importance to public health, they really ought to be more prompt and ought to provide it free of charge. He replied that the department received hundreds of enquiries every day, more than it could cope with, and that in any case the leaflet-provision service was privatised. What's more, the service he was providing—answering calls from members of the public—was also privatised, and if I needed to make a complaint I must do it elsewhere, as he was not the person responsible. When I finally received the information I discovered that the HSE, on the recommendation of the Advisory Committee on Genetic Modification, was circulating a document drafted by the ACGM (*Draft Guidance on Certificate of Exemption no. 1*) that would allow commercial and other contained users to release certain classes of live GMMs into the environment as liquid wastes on notification, without the need to monitor for the survival and subsequent evolution of the GMMs. I wrote to oppose the draft, spelling out the dangers and calling for a full reassessment of present safety regulations on contained use. I sent copies of the letter to several members of Parliament, who asked questions of the Departments of the Environment and Transport. The official line was reaffirmed in their reply, which I again challenged, quoting Stotsky's comments to me in an e-mail message. Since then

the Health and Safety Executive has admitted that I have raised some important issues and stated that it was commissioning an 'independent' critical review of the literature in 1998. However, no specific experimental research will be supported.

78. These reports are cited in a letter from N. Tomlinson, Ministry of Agriculture, Fisheries and Food, to the US Food and Drug Administration, 2 Dec. 1998.

Chapter 10 (p. 201–218)

1. Andrew Marr, *Independent,* 26 Feb. 1997, 17.
2. *Guardian,* 26 Feb. 1997, 6.
3. Andrew Marr, *Independent,* 26 Feb. 1997, 17.
4. 'Scientists scorn sci-fi fears over sheep clone', *Guardian,* 24 Feb. 1997, 7. Also in a report and interview on 'Eight o'Clock News', BBC Radio 4, 24 Feb. 1997.
5. Reported in the *Guardian,* 26 Feb. 1997, 6.
6. 'Roslin patents come under the spotlight', *Nature,* 15 May 1997, 217.
7. S. Conner and D. Cadbury, 'Headless frog opens way for human organ factory', *Sunday Times,* 19 Oct. 1997.
8. Quoted in the *Guardian,* 27 Feb. 1996, supplement, 5.
9. Tim Radford, '"Test-tube" thumb helps surgeons move towards own-body tissue', *Guardian,* 2 Nov. 1998.
10. Quoted in the *Guardian,* 26 Feb. 1997, 6.
11. Reported in the *Guardian,* 1 Mar. 1997, 7.
12. Quoted in the *Guardian,* 26 Feb. 1997, 6.
13. See Spallone, 1992, chap. 8, for an excellent critique of reproductive biotechnologies from a feminist's perspective.
14. Andrew Marr, *Independent,* 26 Feb. 1997, 17.
15. Quoted in 'Fearful symmetry', *Guardian,* 1 Mar. 1997, 1.
16. Quoted in 'Fearful symmetry', *Guardian,* 1 Mar. 1997, 1.
17. Andrew Marr, *Independent,* 26 Feb. 1997, 17.
18. Wilmut et al., 1997.
19. Gurdon, 1974.
20. Gurdon, 1974, 24.
21. King and Briggs, 1955.
22. Wilmut et al., 1997, 810.
23. See Edelman, 1992.
24. Moore, 1955.
25. See Doerfler et al., 1997.
26. 'And the cow jumped over the moon', *GenEthics News* 3, 1994, 6–7.
27. 'Alarm as cloned sheep develop abnormalities', *Independent,* 19 Jan. 1999, 1.

28. Wakayama et al., 1998.
29. Charles Arthus, 'The onco-mouse that didn't roar', *New Scientist,* 26 June 1993, 4.
30. See Lee et al., 1992, and Jacks et al., 1992, for 'retinoblastoma gene' effects, and Davies, 1992, for the effects of 'Lesch-Nyhan disease gene' and 'Gaucher's disease gene' in transgenic mice. See also Wirz, 1997, for a recent critique of gene-centred biology.
31. Kimbrell, 1993.
32. Denny Penman, 'Phoney life on animal pharm', *Guardian* (Society), 5 Mar. 1997, 4.
33. Wright et al., 1991.
34. Cited by Denny Penman, 'Phoney life on animal pharm', *Guardian* (Society), 5 Mar. 1997, 4.
35. See Wayne Kondro, 'Canadian government will revisit human cloning legislation', *Lancet* 353, 1999, 1599.
36. 'Human artificial chromosome constructed', *Nature Biotechnology,* 15 May 1997, 400.
37. Colman, 1996, 641S.
38. Colman. 1996, 6418.

Chapter 11 (p. 219–242)

1. See Alison Abbott, 'German physicians warn of genetics risks', *Nature (News)* 384, 1997, 5.
2. See 'China legalises eugenics', *GenEthics News* 4, 1995, 1.
3. See 'New guidelines for postal genetic testing', *GenEthics News* 15, 1996, 3–5.
4. House of Commons Science and Technology Committee, Third Report, *Human Genetics: The Science and Its Consequences,* vol. 5, *Report and Minutes of Proceedings,* London: HMSO 1995, xciii.
5. In the House of Commons human genetics report (see note 4 above), genetic science and industry rank sixth among the topics considered; human rights rank seventh.
6. See Spallone, 1992, chap. 7.
7. House of Commons human genetics report (see note 4), xxiii.
8. 'Survey finds high levels of genetic discrimination', *GenEthics News* 15, 1996, 5.
9. See the excellent critique of genetic determinism by Hubbard and Wald, 1993.
10. 'Controversy over genes and crime conference', *GenEthics News* 5, 1995, 3.
11. See Peter Montague, 'Pesticides and aggression', *Rachel's Weekly* (www.rachel.org).

12. Guillette et al., 1998, cited by Peter Montague, 'Pesticides and aggression', *Rachel's Weekly* (www.rachel.org).

13. For a detailed account of polymorphic gene markers and gene hunting see Jones and Taylor, 1995.

14. See Strohman, 1994.

15. See Jones and Taylor, 1995.

16. Kerem et al., 1989.

17. See Abbott, 1996, and Alper, 1996.

18. Mulvihill, 1995; van Heyningen, 1994.

19. Jones and Taylor, 1995, 126.

20. Brown and Kleiner, 1994.

21. Seitz et al., 1997.

22. Ji et al., 1997.

23. Bowcock, 1993.

24. Hoeksema and Law, 1996.

25. Lenoir et al., 1996.

26. Denotter et al., 1996.

27. R. Hubbard W. McGoodwin, 'An update on the "breast cancer gene"', *Genewatch* 10, 1996, 10.

28. National Cancer Institute, *Everything Doesn't Cause Cancer,* 1998.

29. See 'Cancer: are the experts lying?', *Ecologist* 28 (2) (special issue), 1998.

30. Abbott, 1996, 390.

31. See Summers, 1996.

32. See Hubbard and Wald, 1993.

33. S. Conner, 'Doctors test live embryos for cancer genes', *Independent on Sunday,* 28 June 1998.

34. See Augarten et al., 1994.

35. See note 23.

36. Offit et al., 1996.

37. See Friedman et al., 1997.

38. Strohman, 1994.

39. See House of Commons Science and Technology Committee, Third Report, *Human Genetics: The Science and Its Consequences,* vol. 5, *Report and Minutes of Proceedings,* London: HMSO, 1995, xci.

40. See Ho, 1987c.

41. Rose, 1995, 380.

42. See Lorenz, 1977.

43. Brunner et al., 1993.

44. Rose, 1995, 380.

45. See Rowe, 1987, cited by Spallone, 1992.

46. Spallone, 1992, 190.

47. Shihabuddin et al., 1996.
48. Lundstrom and Turpin, 1996.
49. Horrobin et al., 1996.
50. Marshall, 1984.
51. See Oliver Gillie, *Sunday Times,* 24 Oct. 1976.
52. Fernando, 1990, 24.
53. 'Campaigners vow to halt search for "intelligence genes"', *GenEthics News* 10, 1996, 1.
54. Binet, 1913, 41–2, cited by Rose, Kamin and Lewontin, 1984, chap. 6, which is an excellent account of the Cyril Burt affair.
55. Rose, Kamin and Lewontin, 1984, 102.
56. Rose, Kamin and Lewontin, 1984, 102.
57. Oliver Gillie, *Sunday Times,* 24 Oct. 1976, cited by Rose, Kamin and Lewontin, 1984, 104.
58. Review of *Cyril Burt: Psychologist* by J. S. Hearnshaw, *British Journal of Psychology* 71, 1980, 174–5.
59. Rose, Kamin and Lewontin, 1984, 106.

Chapter 12 (p. 243–269)

1. Bains, 1987, 15.
2. Bains, 1987, 26–7.
3. Lewis Wolpert, who heads the Royal Society's Committee on the Public Understanding of Science, states: 'Science is the best way to understand the world. By understand, I mean gain insight into the way all nature works in a causal and mechanistic sense ...' (Wolpert, 1996, 9).
4. See entries in Kendrew, 1995.
5. See Alison Mitchell, 'The A to Z of DNA', *Nature* 396, 1998, 524.
6. Jeff Pollard, cited in Rennie, 1993.
7. See entries in Kendrew, 1995.
8. See Cleaver and Kraemer, 1989, 2949–71.
9. See entries in Kendrew, 1995.
10. See Jeffreys et al., 1985. There is a great deal of controversy over the use of 'DNA fingerprinting' in evidence because of the technical difficulties involved, and also the size of the human populations from which individuals originate. For example, additional bands can arise from decomposition of the sample, just as a lack of bands can result from incomplete enzyme action. Individuals from small populations share many more genes than those from large populations, and their DNA 'fingerprint' may look very similar. See Thompson and Ford, 1990, for a detailed discussion of the problems involved.
11. Weatherall, 1993.

12. Sommer, 1995.
13. Temin, 1985.
14. See Warren and Crampton, 1994.
15. Philip Cohen, 'Doctor, there's a fly in my genome', *New Scientist,* 9 Mar. 1996, 16.
16. Spielman, 1994.
17. See Warren and Crampton, 1994.
18. See Jones and Taylor, 1996, 197–213, for a description that covers all aspects of cancer.
19. Elnatan et al., 1996.
20. Cairns, 1978.
21. Jones et al., 1994.
22. Thompson et al., 1991, chap. 16.
23. Leong et al., 1995.
24. See Lengauer et al., 1998.
25. See the excellent issue, 'Cancer: are the experts lying?', *Ecologist* 28, Mar.–Apr. 1998, for a collection of articles on cancer and environmental carcinogens.
26. See Z. Goldsmith, 1998.
27. See many articles in 'Cancer: are the experts lying?', *Ecologist* 28, Mar.–Apr 1998; also Christine Brewer, *No time to waste, no time to burn: Earthwatch briefing sheet on municipal waste incineration,* Earthwatch (Friends of the Earth Ireland) 1995; *Ban the Burn,* Greenpeace Ireland 1993.
28. This subject is dealt with in many papers in Ho et al., 1994.
29. John Hodgson, 'There's a whole lot of nothing going on', *Biotechnology* 13, 1995, 714.
30. Coghlan, 1995, 14.
31. Coghlan, 1995, 14.
32. Andy Coghlan, 'Gene shuttle virus could damage the brain', *New Scientist,* 11 May 1996, 6.
33. See Jane et al., 1998; Putnam, 1998.
34. See Temin, 1980.
35. Roy-Burman, 1996.
36. Golovkina et al., 1994.
37. Bieth and Darlix, 1993.
38. Di Fronzo and Holland, 1993.
39. Gu et al., 1995.
40. 'Cancer at Pasteur', *New Scientist,* 18 June 1987, 29.
41. 'Naked DNA raises cancer fears for researchers'. *New Scientist,* 17 Oct. 1990 .
42. Chen et al., 1983.

43. Ian Anderson, 'Alarm greets contraceptive virus', *New Scientist,* 26 Apr. 1997, 4.
44. Boulanger et al., 1996, 247; see also McNally, 1995.
45. See Pain, 1997.
46. Dangler et al., 1994.
47. See J. Cohen, 'Naked DNA points way to vaccines', *Science* 259, 1993, 1691–2.
48. See Traavik, 1998; also Ho et al., 1998.
49. See McKinney et al., 1998.
50. Gustafson et al., 1987. See Spleen, 1992, chap. 6, for an excellent account of the questionable benefits of vaccination.
51. Harridan, 1988; also 'Face the facts', BBC Radio 4, 19 June 1997; McTaggart, 1996.
52. McTaggart, 1996, 156.
53. Baba et al., 1999.
54. Charles Arntzen, 'High-tech herbal medicine: plant-based vaccines', *Nature Biotechnology* 15, 1997, 221–2; see also Dalsgaard et al., 1997.
55. See Kimbrell, 1993.
56. Quoted in 'Alternative ways of meeting demand', *Nature* 391, 1998, 325.
57. Quoted by Balasubramaniam, 1996.
58. See *Ecologist* 28, Mar.–Apr 1998.
59. Reported by David King, 'Pork that could give us the chop', *Times Higher Education Supplement,* 13 Sep. 1996, 17.
60. Barbara Nasto, 'Human xenotransplants banned in UK', *Nature Biotechnology* 15, 1997, 214.
61. Greenstein and Sachs, 1997.
62. Weiss, 1998.
63. See Strohman, 1993.
64. See Khor, 1996; Balasubramaniam, 1996.
65. See UBINIG and Asian Women's Human Rights Council, 1994.
66. See UBINIG, 1996.

Chapter 13 (p. 270–298)

1. Soros, 1997, 1.
2. Soros, 1997, 1.
3. Strohman (1997) describes a coming revolution in biology not too unlike the one I am putting forward here. He points out how anomalies within the genetic-determinist paradigm are being merely swept under the carpet by 'expert but conservative elements within the scientific mainstream,' in order to rescue the paradigm. But the

explanations for the behaviour of complex systems become so contorted and invoke so many genetic agents and their 'interactive and co-dependent states' that they are of questionable value.

4. See Ho, 1993, 1995a, 1995b, 1996b, 1997a.

5. See Rubin, 1992, 2.

6. Ho, 1996b, 263.

7. Guyton, 1980, 7.

8. Rubin, 1992, 1.

9. Kennedy et al., 1980; Mondal and Heidelberger, 1970.

10. Brouty-Boyé et al., 1979; Rubin et al., 1990.

11. Rubin, 1992, 1.

12. See Leape et al., 1991. Iatrogenic diseases may even be heritable, as shown by recent studies with rats and rabbits revealing that abnormalities induced by thalidomide may be passed on to the next generation. See Phillip Knightley, 'Thalidomide curse "may go on down generations"', *Independent on Sunday,* 20 Apr. 1997, 3.

13. See McTaggart, 1996.

14. See McTaggart, 1996.

15. See literature produced by Cancer Help Centre, Grove House, Cornwallis Grove, Bristol BS8 4PG, England.

16. Costerton et al., 1995.

17. Freter, 1986.

18. Edward Goldsmith started the *Ecologist* in 1970. Its famous manifesto, 'A Blueprint for Survival', appeared as a special issue of the *Ecologist* in 1971.

19. Rifkin and Howard, 1980.

20. Daly, 1996.

21. Martin Khor, seminar on globalisation and economics, Schumacher College, Totnes (Devon), Feb. 1997.

22. Rifkin and Howard, 1980.

23. This theory of the organism has been developed over a number of years: see Ho, 1993, 1994, 1995a, 1995b, 1996b, 1996e, 1997a. The description here is necessarily a very brief summary.

24. Martin Khor, seminar on globalisation and economics, Schumacher College, Totnes (Devon), Feb. 1997.

25. Daly, 1996.

26. Lovelock, 1979; see also Saunders, 1994.

27. Lee Kump, 'Geophysiological Society: Mission Statement', 1996.

28. Schneider and Kay, 1994.

29. Luvall and Holbo, 1991.

30. Ho, 1997d.

31. Daly, 1996.

32. Korten, 1995.
33. Daly and Cobb, 1989.
34. Korten, 1997, 14.
35. See Shiva, 1993.
36. Shiva, 1993.
37. The reciprocal, symmetrical relationship between human beings and nature is beautifully brought out in Grimaldo Rengifo Vasquez's description (1997) of the Peruvian farming communities that practise a sustainable agriculture so intimately integrated with the ecosystem that there is no separation between nature and culture. Peasants collect seeds from different places and grow them, adopting the plants as members of their family. In one of the oldest rituals celebrating the harvest of the new crop, last year's potato speaks to the new potato: 'As I bred these human beings, now I pass [this power] on to you.' 'The meaning of life', says Grimaldo, 'is not only to breed but to allow oneself to be bred.'
38. See many excellent chapters arguing against all aspects of the global economy in Mander and Goldsmith, 1996.
39. Mshigeni and Pauli, 1997, 41.
40. Mshigeni and Pauli, 1997, 42.

Appendix (p. 299–307)

1. M. Brookes, 'Running wild', *New Scientist,* 31 Oct. 1998; A. Snow and R. Jorgensen, 'Costs of transgenic glufosinate resistance introgressed from *Brassica napus* into weedy *Brassica rapa*' (abstract), Ecological Society of America, Baltimore, 6 Aug. 1998.
2. J. Bergelson, C. B. Purrington, and G. Wichmann, 'Promiscuity in transgenic plants', *Nature* 395, 1998, 25.
3. C. Crecchio and G. Stotzky, 'Insecticidal activity and biodegradation of the toxin from *Bacillus thuringiensis* subsp. *kurstaki* bound to humic acids from soil,' *Soil Biology and Biochemistry* 30, 1998, 463–70, and references therein.
4. C. Leake and L. Fraser, 'Scientist in Frankenstein food alert is proved right', *Mail on Sunday,* 31 Jan. 1999; B. C. Goodwin, Report on SOAEFD Flexible Fund Project RO818, 23 Jan. 1999.
5. D. MacKenzie, 'Gut reaction', *New Scientist,* 30 Jan. 1999, 4.
6. Y. Cho, Y.-L. Qiu, P. Kuhlman, and J. D. Palmer, 'Explosive invasion of plant mitochondria by a group I intron', *Proceedings of the National Academy of Sciences (USA)* 95, 1998, 14244–9.
7. See V. Shiva, *Biopiracy: The Plunder of Nature and Knowledge,* London: Green Books 1998; also Latin American Declaration on Transgenic Organisms, Quito, 22 Jan. 1999.

8. Corner House, *Food? Health? Hope?: Genetic Engineering and World Hunger, Briefing 10,* 1998.
9. See J. Mander and E. Goldsmith (eds.), *The Case Against the Global Economy and for a Turn toward the Local,* San Francisco: Sierra Club Books 1996.
10. See note 4.
11. See Ho, 1998a, 1999.

REFERENCES

Abbott, A. (1996), 'Complexity limits the powers of prediction', *Nature* 379, 390.

Allison, R. (1995), 'RNA plant virus recombination', *Proceedings of USDA-APHIS/AIBS Workshop on Transgenic Virus-Resistant Plants and New Plant Viruses,* Beltsville, Maryland, 20–21 April.

Allison, R. (1997), 'Update on virus recombination in transgenic crops' (22923mgr@msv.edu).

Alper, J. (1996), 'Genetic complexity in single-gene diseases', *British Medical Journal* 312, 196–7.

Altieri, M. A. (1991), 'Traditional farming in Latin America', *Ecologist* 21, 93–6.

Amabilecuevas, C. F., and Chicurel, M. E. (1993), 'Horizontal gene transfer', *American Scientist* 81, 332–41.

Anderson, E. S. (1975), 'Viability of and transfer of a plasmid from *E. coli* K12 in the human intestine', *Nature* 255, 502.

Asante-Appiah, D., and Skalka, A. M. (1997), 'Molecular mechanisms in retrovirus DNA integration', *Antiviral Research* 36, 139–56.

Assad, F. F. N., and Signer, E. R. (1990), 'Cauliflower mosaic virus P35S promoter activity in *E. coli*', *Molecular and General Genetics* 223, 517–20.

Atlas, M., Bennett, A. M., Colwell, R., van Elsas, J., Kjelleberg, S., Pedersen, J., and Wacker-Nagel, S. (1992), 'Persistence and survival of genetically modified micro-organisms released into the environment', in *The Release of Genetically Modified Micro-Organisms* (D. E. S. Stewart-Tull and M. Sussman, eds.), New York: Plenum Press, 117.

Augarten, A., Yahav, Y., Kerem, B. S., Halle, D., Laufer, J., and Szeinberg, A. (1994), *Lancet* 344, 1473–4.

Avery, O. T., MacLeod, C. M., and McCarty, M. (1944), 'Studies on the chemical nature of the substance inducing transformation in pneumococcal types', *Journal of Experimental Medicine* 79, 137–59.

Baba, T. W., Liska, V., Khiman, A. H., Ray, N. B., Dailey, P. J., Penninck, D., Bronson, R., Greene, M. F., McClure, H. M., Martin, L. N., Ruth, M., and Ruprecht, R. M. (1999), 'Live attenuated multiply deleted simian immunodeficiency virus causes AIDS in infant and adult macaques', *Nature Medicine* 5, 194, 203.

Bains, W. (1987), *Genetic Engineering for Almost Everybody,* London: Penguin.

Balasubramaniam, K. (1996), 'SAPs and the privatisation of health care: a recipe for disaster', *Third World Resurgence* 68, 13–16.

Baltimore, D. (1985), 'Retroviruses and retrotransposons: the role of reverse transcription in shaping the eukaryotic genome', *Cell* 40, 481–2.

Barinaga, M. (1996), 'A shared strategy for virulence', *Science* 272, 1261–3.

Barzun, J. (1958), *Darwin, Marx and Wagner,* New York: Doubleday Anchor.

Bauer, L. S. (1995), 'Resistance: a threat to the insecticidal crystal proteins of *Bacillus thuringiensis',* *Florida Entomologist* 78, 414–43.

Belonga, E. A., Hedberg, C. W., Gleich, G. J., White, K. E., Mayeno, A. R., Loegering, D. A., Dunnette, S. L., Pirie, P. L., MacDonald, K. L., and Osterholm, M. T. (1990), 'An investigation of the cause of the eosinophilia-myalgia syndrome associated with tryptophan use', *New England Journal of Medicine* 323, 347–65.

Benbrook, C. (1999), 'Evidence of the magnitude and consequences of the Roundup Ready soybean yield drag from university-based varietal trials in 1998', *Ag Biotech*, technical paper no. 1.

Bergelson, J., Pruuington, C. B., and Wichmann, G. (1998), 'Promiscuity in transgenic plants', *Nature* 395, 25.

Bergh, O., Borsheim, K. Y., Bratbak, G., and Heldal, M. (1989), 'High abundance of viruses found in aquatic environments', *Nature* 340, 467–8.

Bhattacharyya, M. K., Smith, A. M., Ellis, T. H. N., Hedley, C., and Martin, C. (1990), 'The wrinkled-seed character of pea described by Mendel is caused by a transposon-like insertion in a gene encoding starch-braching enzyme', *Cell* 80, 115–22.

Bieth, E., and Darlix, J.-L. (1993), 'Characterisation of a molecular clone of a highly infectious avian leukosis virus', *Comptes Rendus de l'Académie des Sciences, série III: Sciences de la Vie* 316, 754–62.

Bik, E. M., Bunschoten, A. E., Gouw, R. D., and Mooi, F. R. (1995), 'Genesis of novel epidemic vibrio-cholerae-O139 strain: evidence for horizontal transfer of genes involved in polysaccharide synthesis', *EMBO Journal* 14, 209–16.

Binet, A. (1913), *Les Idées Modernes sur les Enfants,* Paris: Flammarion.

Bjorklund, S., Almouzni, G., Davidson, I., Nightingale, K. P., and Weiss, K. (1999), 'Global transcription regulators of eukaryotes', *Cell* 96, 759–67.

Blanc, V., Jordana, X., Litvak, S., and Araya, A. (1996), 'Control of gene expression by base deamination: the case of RNA editing in wheat mitochondria', *Cell* 78, 511–17.

Bootsma, J. H., Vandijk, H., Verhoef, J., Fleer, A., and Mooi, F. (1996), 'Molecular characterization of the bro b-lactamase of *Moraxella (Branhamella) catarrhalis'*, *Antimicrobial Agents and Chemotherapy* 40, 966–72.

Bostock, C. J., and Tyler-Smith, C. (1982), 'Changes to genomic DNA in methotrexate-resistant cells', in *Genome Evolution* (G. A. Dover and R. B. Flavell, eds.), London: Academic Press, 69–94.

Boulanger, D., Crouch, A., Brochier, B., Bennett, M., Clement, J., Gaskell, R. M., Baxby, D., and Pastoret, P. P. (1996), 'Serological survey for orthopoxvirus infection of wild mammals in areas where a recombinant rabies virus is used to vaccinate foxes', *Veterinary Record* 138, 247–9.

Bowcock, A. M. (1993), 'Molecular cloning of BRCA1: a gene for early-onset familial breast and ovarian cancer', *Breast Cancer Research and Treatment* 28, 121–35.

Brennan, T. A., Leape, L. L., and Laird, N. M. (1991), 'Incidence of adverse events and negligence in hospitalized patients: results of the Harvard Medical Practice Study', *New England Journal of Medicine* 324, 370–6.

Brouty-Boyé, D., Gresser, I., and Baldwin, C. (1979), 'Reversion of the transformed phenotype to the parental phenotype by subcultivation of X-ray-transformed C3H/10T1/1 cells at low cell density', *International Journal of Cancer* 24, 253–60.

Brown, D. F. J., Farrington, M., and Warren, R. E. (1993), 'Imipene-resistant *Escherichia coli'*, *Lancet* 342, 177.

Brown, L. R. (1998), 'Struggling to raise cropland productivity', in *State of the World, 1998* (L. R. Brown, C. Flavin and H. French, eds.), London: Earthscan Publications, 79–95.

Brown, P., and Kleiner, K. (1994), 'Patent row splits breast cancer researchers', *New Scientist* 24 September, 4.

Brunner, H. G., Nelen, M. Breakefield, X. O., Ropers, H. H., and van Oost, B. A. (1993), 'Abnormal behavior associated with a point mutation in the structural gene for monoamine oxidas A', *Science* 262, 578–80.

Burrows, B. (1995), 'Scientists charge US agency with acting irresponsibly', *Third World Resurgence* 63, 2–3.

Burrows, B. (1996), 'Second thoughts about US patent #4,438,032', *Bulletin of Medical Ethics* 124, 11–14.

Cainglet, J. (1998), 'The politics of GE agriculture: a Filipino perspective', in *Global Genes,* Farmer's World Publications.

Cairns, J. (1978), *Cancer: Science and Society,* San Francisco: Freeman.

Cairns, J., Overbaugh, J., and Miller, S. (1988), 'The origin of mutants', *Nature* 335, 142–5.

Campbell, J. H., Lengyel, J. A., and Langridge, J. (1973), 'Evolution of a second gene for b-galactosidase in *E. coli', Proceedings of the National Academy of Sciences (USA)* 70, 1841–5.

Cann, A. J. (1997), *Principles of Molecular Virology* (second edition), London: Academic Press.

Chee, Y. L. (1996), 'Concerted moves to undermine a strong biosafety agreement', *Third World Resurgence* 74, 8–10.

Chen, I. S. Y., McLaughlin, J., Gasson, J. C., Clark, S. C., and Golde, D. W. (1983), 'Molecular characterization of genome of a novel human T-cell leukaemia virus', *Nature* 305, 502–5.

Cho, Y., Qiu, Y.-L., Kuhlman, P., and Palmer, J. D. (1998), 'Explosive invasion of plant mitochondria by a group I intron', *Proceedings of the National Academy of Sciences (USA)* 95, 14244–9.

Cleaver, J. E., and Kraemer, K. H. (1989), *The Metabolic Basis of Inherited Diseases,* New York: McGraw-Hill.

Clewell, D. B. (ed.) (1993), *Bacterial Conjugation,* New York: Plenum Press.

Clewell, D. B., and Flannagan, S. E. (1993), 'The conjugative transposons of Gram-positive bacteria', in *Bacterial Conjugation* (D. B. Clewell, ed.), New York: Plenum Press, 369–93.

Coffey, T. J., Dowson, C. G., Daniels, M., and Spratt, B. G. (1995), 'Genetics and molecular biology of b-lactam-resistant pneumococci', *Microbial Drug Resistance* 1, 29–34.

Coghlan, A. (1995), 'Gene dream fades away', *New Scientist* 25 November, 14–15.

Coghlan, A. (1996), 'Gene shuttle virus could damage the brain', *New Scientist* 11 May, 6.

Coghlan, A. (1997), 'Jet-setters send festering faeces around the world', *New Scientist* 17 May, 7.

Cohen, J. (1996), 'New role for HIV: a vehicle for moving genes into cells', *Science* 272, 195.

Cohen, P. (1996), 'Doctor, there's a fly in my genome', *New Scientist* 9 March, 6.

Collis, C. M., Grammaticopoulous, G., Briton, J., Stokes, H. W., and Hall, R. M. (1993), 'Site-specific insertion of gene cassettes into integrons', *Molecular Microbiology* 9, 41–52.

Colman, A. (1996), 'Production of proteins in the milk of transgenic livestock: problems, solutions and successes', *American Journal of Clinical Nutrition* 63, S639–45.

Commandeur, P., and Komen, J. (1992), 'Biopesticides: options for biological pest control increase', *Biotechnical Development Monitor* 13 (Dec.), 6–7.

Cooking, E. C. (1989), 'Plant cell and tissue culture', in *A Revolution in Biotechnology* (J. L Marx, ed.), Cambridge and New York: Cambridge University Press, 119–29.

Cornaglia, G., Ligozzi, M., Mazzarioli, A., Valentini, M., Orefici, G., and Fontana, R. (1996), 'Rapid increase of resistance to erythromycin and clindamycin in Streptococcus pyogenes in Italy, 1993–1995', *Emerging Infectious Diseases* 2 (4) (www.cdc.gov/ncidod/EID/eid.htm).

Costerton, J. W., Lewandowski, Z., De Beer, D., Caldwell, D., Korber, D., and James, G. (1994), 'Biofilms, the customized microniche', *Journal of Bacteriology* 176, 2137–42.

Courvain, P. S., and Grillot Courvain, C. (1995), 'Gene transfer from bacteria to mammalian cells', *Comptes Rendus de l'Académie des Sciences, série III: Sciences de la Vie* 318, 1207–12.

Cox, C. (1995), 'Glyphosate, part 2: Human exposure and ecological effects', *Journal of Pesticide Reform* 15 (4).

Creamer, R., and Falk, B. W. (1990), 'Direct detection of transcapsidated barley yellow dwarf luteoviruses in doubly infected plants', *Journal of General Virology* 71, 211–17.

Crecchio, C., and Stotzky, G. (1998), 'Insecticidal activity and biodegradation of the toxin from *Bacillus thuringiensis* subsp. *kurstaki* bound to humic acids from soil', *Soil Biology and Biochemistry* 30, 463–70.

Cropper, A. (1994), 'A novel approach', *Our Planet* 6.

Crouch, M. (1999), 'Terminator technology', *Nexus* 6 (1), 25–32.

Cullis, C. A. (1983), 'Environmentally induced DNA changes in plants', *CRC Critical Reviews in Plant Science* 1, 117–31.

Cullis, C. A. (1988), 'Control of variation in higher plants', in *Evolutionary Processes and Metaphors* (M.-W. Ho and S. W. Fox, eds.), London: Wiley.

Cummins, J. (1994), 'The use of cauliflower mosaic virus 35S promoter (CaMV) in Calgene's Flav Savr tomato creates hazard' (available from the author at jcummins@julian.uwo.ca).

Cummins, J. (1997), 'Insecticide viruses for insect control' (available from the author at jcummins@julian.uwo.ca).

Cummins, J. (1998a), 'Some new genetic toys' (available from the author at jcummins@julian.uwo.ca).

Cummins, J. (1998b), 'A virus promoter used in the majority of genetically engineered crops' (available from the author at jcummins@julian.uwo.ca).

Dalsgaard, K., Uttenthal, A., Jones, T. D., Xu, F., Merryweather, A., Hamilton, W. D. O., Langeveld, J. P. M., Boshuizen, R. X., Kamstrup, S., Lomonossoff, G. P., Porta, C., Vela, C., Casal, J. I., Eloen, R. H., and Rodgers, P. B. (1997), 'Plant-derived vaccine protects target animals against a viral disease', *Nature Biotechnology* 15, 248–52.

Daly, H. E. (1996), *Beyond Growth: The Economics of Sustainable Development,* Boston: Beacon.

Daly, H. E., and Cobb, J. B., Jr (1989), *For the Common Good: Redirecting the Economy toward Community, the Environment and a Sustainable Future,* Boston: Beacon.

Damency, E. (1994), 'The impact of hybrids between genetically modified crop plants and their related species: introgression and weediness', *Molecular Ecology* 3, 37–40.

Dangler, C. A., Deaver, R. E., and Koloziej, D. M. (1994), 'Measurement of Aujeszkys disease virus recombination in vitro under conditions of low multiplicity of infection', *Acta Veterinaria Hungarica* 42, 205–8.

Darwin, C. (1859), *On the Origin of Species by means of Natural Selection,* London: John Murray.

Davies, J. (1994), 'Inactivation of antibiotics and the dissemination of resistance genes', *Science* 264, 375–82.

Dawkins, R. (1976), *The Selfish Gene,* Oxford: Oxford University Press.

De Angelis, D. L. (1992), *Dynamics of Nutrient Cycling and Food Webs,* London: Chapman and Hall.

Denotter, W., Merchant, T. E., Beijerinck, D., and Koten, J. W. (1996), 'Breast cancer induction due to mammographic screening in hereditarily affected women', *Anticancer Research* 16, 3173–508.

de Vries, J., and Wackernagel, W. (1998), 'Detection of nptII (kanamycin-resistance) genes in genomes of transgenic plants by marker-rescue transformation', *Molecular and General Genetics* 257, 606–13.

Di Fronzo, N. L., and Holland, C. A. (1993), 'A direct demonstration of recombination between an injected virus and endogenous viral sequences, resulting in the generation of mink cell focus-inducing viruses in AKR mice', *Journal of Virology* 67, 3763–70.

Doerfler, W. (1991), 'Patterns of DNA methylation: evolutionary vestiges of foreign DNA inactivation as a host defence mechanism', *Biological Chemistry Hoppe-Seyler* 372, 557–64.

Doerfler, W. (1992), 'DNA methylation: eukaryotic defence against the transcription of foreign genes?', *Microbial Pathogenesis* 12, 1–8.

Doerfler, W., Schubbert, R., Heller, H., Kämmer, C., Hilger-Eversheim, K., Knoblauch, M., and Remus, R. (1997), 'Integration of foreign DNA and its consequences in mammalian systems', *Trends in Biotechnology* 15 (8), 297–301.

Doerfler, W., Schubbert, R., Heller, H., Hertz, J., Remus, R., Schrier, J., Kammer, C., Hilger-Eversheim, K., Gerhardt, U., Schmitz, B., Renz, D., and Schell, G. (1998), *APMIS Supplementum* 84, 62–8.

Doucet-Populaire, F. (1992), 'Conjugal transfer of genetic information in gnotobiotic mice', in *Microbial Releases* (M. J. Gauthier, ed.), Berlin: Springer Verlag.

Dover, G. A., and Flavell, R. B. (eds.) (1982), *Genome Evolution,* London: Academic Press.

Eber, G., Chevre, A. M., Baranger, A., Vallee, P., Tanfuy, X., and Renard, M. (1994), 'Spontaneous hybridisation between a male-sterile oilseed rape and two weeds', *Theoretical and Applied Genetics* 88, 362–8.

Edelman, G. (1992), *Bright Water, Brilliant Fire: On the Matter of Mind,* London: Penguin.

Egziabher, T. B. C. (1994), 'Where is the good will?', *Our Planet* 6, 17–19.

Elegant, S. (1997), 'Poor man's plague', *Far Eastern Economic Review* 17 April, 42–5.

Elnatan, J., Goh, H. S., and Smith, D. R. (1996), 'C-KI-RAS activation and the biological behaviour of proximal and distal colonic adenocarcinomas', *European Journal of Cancer* 32A, 491–7.

Estruch, J. J., Carozzi, N. B., Desai, N., Duck, N. B., Warren, G. W., and Doziel, M. G. (1997), 'Transgenic plants: an emerging approach to pest control', *Nature Biotechnology* 15, 137–41.

Fernando, S. (1990), 'The same difference', *New Internationalist,* July, 24–5.

Finnegan, H., and McElroy, D. (1994), 'Transgene inactivation plants fight back!', *Biotechnology* 12, 883–8.

Flavell, R. B. (1982), 'Sequence amplification, deletion and rearrangement: major sources of variation during species divergence', in *Genome Evolution* (G. A. Dover and R. B. Flavell, eds.), London: Academic Press, 301–23.

Forbes, J. M., Blair, D.E., Chiter, A. and Perks, S. (1998), *Effect of Feed Processing Conditions on DNA Fragmentation*, Section 5 — Scientific Report, MAFF.

Foster, P. L. (1992), 'Directed mutation: between unicorns and goats', *Journal of Bacteriology* 174, 1711–16.

Frank, S., and Keller, B. (1995), *Produktesicherheit von Krankheitsresistenten Nutzpflanzen: Toxikologie, Allergenes Potential, Sekundäreffekte und Markergene,* Zürich: Eidg. Forschungsanstalt für Landwirtschaftlichen Pflanzenbau.

Franke, A. E., and Clewell, D. B. (1981), 'Evidence for a chromosome-borne resistance transposon (Tn916) in *Streptococcus faecalis* that is capable of "conjugal" transfer in the absence of a conjugative plasmid', *Journal of Bacteriology* 145, 494–502.

Freter, R. (1986), 'The need for mathematical models in understanding colonisation and plasmid transfers in the mammalian intestine', in *Bacterial Conjugation* (D. B. Clewell, ed.), New York: Plenum Press, 81–93.

Friedman, L. S., Gayther, A., Kurosaki, T., Gordon, D., Noble, B., Casey, G., Ponder, B. A. J., and Culver, H. A. (1997), 'Mutation analysis of BRCA1 and BRCA2 in a male cancer population', *American Journal of Human Genetics* 60, 313–19.

Frischer, M. E., Stewart, G. J., and Paul, J. H. (1994), 'Plasmid transfer to indigenous marine bacterial populations', *FEMS Microbiology Ecology* 15, 127–35.

Garrett, L. (1995), *The Coming Plague: Newly Emerging Disease in a World Out of Balance,* New York: Penguin.

Gebhard, F., and Smalla, K. (1998), 'Transformation of *Acinetobacter* sp. strain BD413 by transgenic sugar beet DNA', *Applied and Environmental Microbiology* 64, 1550–4.

Gebhard, F., and Smalla, D. (1999), 'Monitoring field releases of genetically modified sugar beets for persistence of transgenic plant DNA and horizontal gene transfer', *FEMS Microbiology Ecology* 28, 261–72.

George, S. (1988), *A Fate Worse than Debt,* Harmondsworth (Middx): Penguin.

Gierl, A. (1990), 'How maize transposable elements escape negative selection', *Trends in Genetics* 6, 155–8.

Goldsmith, E. (1992), *Development: Fictions and Facts* (Ecoscript 35), Amsterdam: Foundation for Ecodevelopment.

Goldsmith, E., and Hildyard, N. (1984–92), *The Social and Environmental Effects of Large Dams,* vol. 1–3, Wadebridge (Cornwall): Wadebridge Ecological Centre.

Goldsmith, E., and Hildyard, N. (1991), 'World agriculture: toward 2000: FAO's plan to feed the world', *Ecologist* 21, 81–92.

Goldsmith, Z. (1998), 'Cancer: a disease of industrialisation', *Ecologist* 28, 93–9.

Golovkina, T. V., Jaffe, A. B., and Ross, S. R. (1994), 'Co-expression of exogenous and endogenous mouse mammary tumour virus RNA in vivo results in viral recombination and broadens the virus host range', *Journal of Virology* 68, 5019–26.

Goodman, A. E., Marshall, K. C., and Hermansson, M. (1994), 'Gene transfer among bacteria under conditions of nutrient depletion in simulated and natural aquatic environments', *FEMS Microbiology Ecology* 15, 55–60.

Goodwin, B. C. (1984), 'A relational or field theory of reproduction and its evolutionary implications', in *Beyond Neo-Darwinism: Introduction to the New Evolutionary Paradigm* (M.-W. Ho and P. T. Saunders, eds.), London: Academic Press, 219–41.

Goodwin, B. C. (1994), *How the Leopard Changed Its Spots: The Evolution of Complexity,* London: Weidenfeld and Nicolson.

Goodwin, B. C. (1999), 'Report on SOAEFD Flexible Fund Project R0818', Jan. (courtesy of author).

Goussard, S., Grillot-Courvalin, C., and Courvalin, P. (1996), 'Direct gene transfer from bacteria to mammalian cells by kamikazation, *96th General Meeting of the American Society of Microbiology,* H-84, 497.

Green, A. E., and Allison, R. F. (1994), 'Recombination between viral RNA and transgenic plant transcripts', *Science* 263, 1423.

Greenstein, J. L., and Sachs, D. H. (1997), 'The use of tolerance for transplantation across xenogenic barriers', *Nature Biotechnology* 15, 235–7.

Griffin, D. (1999), 'Agricultural globalization: a threat to food security?', *Third World Resurgence* 100–101, 38–40.

Gu, Z., Gao, Q., Fast, E. A., and Wainberg, M. A. (1995), 'Possible involvement of cell fusion and viral recombination in generation of human immunodeficiency virus variants that display dual resistance to AZT and 3TC', *Journal of General Virology* 76, 2601–5.

Gudkov, A., and Kopnin, B. (1985), 'Gene amplification in multidrug-resistant cells: molecular and karyotypic events', *Bioessays* 3, 68–71.

Guillot, J. F., and Boucaud, J. L. (1992), 'In vivo transfer of a conjugative plasmid between isogenic *Escherichia coli* strains in the gut of chickens in the presence and absence of selective pressure', in *Microbial Releases* (M. J. Gauthier, ed.), Berlin: Springer Verlag, 167–74.

Gurdon, J. B. (1974), *The Control of Gene Expression in Animal Development,* Oxford: Oxford University Press.

Gustafson, T. L., Lievens, A. W., Brunell, P. A., Moellenberg, R. G., Buttery, C. M. G., and Sehulster, L. M. (1987), 'Measles outbreak in a fully immunized secondary school population', *New England Journal of Medicine* 316, 771–4.

Guyton, A. C. (1980), *Circulatory Physiology,* Philadelphia: W. B. Saunders.

Hall, B. G., and Hartl, D. L. (1974), 'Regulation of newly evolved enzymes, I: Selection of a novel lactase regulated by lactose in *Escherichia coli',* *Genetics* 76, 391–400.

Hama, H., Suzuki, K., and Tanaka, H. (1992), 'Inheritance and stability of resistance to *Bacillus thuringiensis* formulations in diamondback moth, *Plutella xylostella* (Linnaeus) (Lepidoptera: Yponomeutidae)', *Applied Entomology and Zoology* 27, 355–62.

Hamilton, J. O'C., and Carey, J. (1994), 'Biotech: an industry crowded with players faces an ugly reckoning', *Business Week,* 26 September, 66–72.

Harding, K. (1996), 'The potential for horizontal gene transfer within the environment', *Agro-Food Industry Hi-Tech,* July–August, 31–5.

Hardy, R. W. F. (1994), 'Current and next-generation agricultural biotechnology products and processes considered from a public good perspective (NABC report 6)', in *Agricultural Biotechnology and the Public Good* (J. F. MacDonald, ed.), 43–50.

Harriman, E. (1988), 'The good old British jab', *New Statesman and Society,* 12 September, 10–12.

Heaton, M. P., and Handwerger, S. (1995), 'Conjugative mobilization of a vancomycin-resistance plasmid by a putative enterococcus-faecium sex-pheromone response plasmid', *Microbial Drug Resistance* 1, 177–83.

Heitman, D., and Lopes-Pila, J. M. (1993), 'Frequency and conditions of spontaneous plasmid transfer from *E. coli* to cultured mammalian cells', *Biosystems* 29, 37–48.

Hermansson, M., and Linberg, C. (1994), 'Gene transfer in the marine environment', *FEMS Microbiology Ecology* 15, 47–54.

Hilbeck, A., Baumgarner, M., Fried, P. M., and Bigler, F. (1998), 'Effects of transgenic *Bacillus thuringiensis*-corn-fed prey on mortality and development time of immature *Chrysoperla carnea* (Neuroptera: Chrysopidae)', *Environmental Entomology* 27, 480–7.

Hildyard, N. (1991), 'An open letter to Edouard Saouma, Director-General, the Food and Agriculture Organization of the United Nations', *Ecologist* 21, 43–6.

Hildyard, N. (1996), 'Too many for what?: the social generation of food "scarcity" and "overpopulation"', *Ecologist* 26, 282–9.

Ho, M.-W. (1976), *Molecular Genetics: S299 Genetics: A Second-Level Open University Course,* Milton Keynes: Open University Press.

Ho, M.-W. (1984a), 'Environment and heredity in development and evolution', in *Beyond Neo-Darwinism: Introduction to the New Evolutionary Paradigm* (M.-W. Ho and P. T. Saunders, eds.), London: Academic Press, 267–89.

Ho, M.-W. (1984b), 'Where does biological form come from?', *Rivista di Biologia* 77, 147–79.

Ho, M.-W. (1987a), 'Evolution by process, not by consequence: implications of the new molecular genetics for development and evolution', *International Journal of Comparative Psychology* 1, 3–27.

Ho, M.-W. (1987b), *Regulation of Gene Expression in Eukaryotes: S298 Genetics*, Milton Keynes: Open University Press.

Ho, M.-W. (1987c), *Genes in Populations: S298 Genetics*, Milton Keynes: Open University Press.

Ho, M.-W. (1988a), 'Evolution by process, not by consequence', in *Evolutionary Processes and Metaphors* (M.-W. Ho and S. W. Fox, eds.), London: Wiley, 117–44.

Ho, M.-W. (1988b), 'How rational can rational morphology be?', *Rivista di Biologia* 81, 11–55.

Ho, M.-W. (1988c), 'Genetic fitness and natural selection: myth or metaphor', in *Evolution of Social Behavior and Integrative Levels* (G. Greenberg and E. Tobach, eds.), Mahwah (NJ): Lawrence Erlbaum, 85–111.

Ho, M.-W. (1990), 'An exercise in rational taxonomy', *Journal of Theoretical Biology* 147, 43–57.

Ho, M.-W. (1992), 'Development, rational taxonomy and systematics', *Rivista di Biologia* 85, 193–211.

Ho, M.-W. (1993), *The Rainbow and the Worm: The Physics of Organisms*, Singapore: World Scientific.

Ho, M. W. (1994), 'What is Schrödinger's negentropy?', *Modern Trends in Biothermokinetics* 3, 50–61.

Ho, M.-W. (ed.) (1995a), *Bioenergetics: S327 Living Process*, Milton Keynes: Open University Press.

Ho, M.-W. (1995b), 'Bioenergetics and the coherence of organisms', *Neural Network World* 5, 733–50.

Ho, M.-W. (1996a), 'Are current transgenic technologies safe?: capacity building in biosafety urgently needed for developed countries', in *Biosafety Capacity Building: Evaluation Criteria Development* (I. Virgin and R. J. Frederick, eds.), Stockholm: Stockholm Environmental Institute, 75–80.

Ho, M.-W. (1996b), 'The biology of free will', *Journal of Consciousness Studies* 3, 231–44.

Ho, M.-W. (1996c), 'Natural being and coherent society', in *Gaia in Action: Science of the Living Earth* (P. Bunyard, ed.), Edinburgh: Floris Books, 286–307.

Ho, M.-W. (1996d), 'Why Lamarck won't go away', *Annals of Human Genetics* 60, 81–4.

Ho, M.-W. (1996e), 'Bioenergetics and biocommunication', in *Computation in Cellular and Molecular Biological Systems* (R. Cuthbertson, M. Holcombe and R. Paton, eds.), Singapore: World Scientific, 251–62.

Ho, M.-W. (1997a), 'Towards a theory of the organism', *Integrative Physiology and Behavioural Research* (in press).

Ho, M.-W. (1997b), 'Evolution', in *Handbook of Comparative Psychology* (G. Greenberg and M. Haraway, eds.), New York: Garland Publishing.

Ho, M.-W. (1997c), 'DNA and the new organicism', in *The Future of DNA* (J. Wirz and E. Lammerts van Bueren, eds.), Dordrecht: Kluwer Academic, 71–93.

Ho, M.-W. (1998a), *The Rainbow and the Worm: The Physics of Organisms* (second edition), Singapore: World Scientific.

Ho, M.-W. (1998b), 'On the nature of sustainable economic systems', *World Futures* 51, 199–221.

Ho, M. W. (1998c), 'Dangerous liaison—deadly gamble', *NABC Conference Proceedings* (in press).

Ho, M. W. (1998d), 'Evolution', in *Handbook of Comparative Psychology* (G. Greenberg and M. Haraway, eds.).

Ho, M. W. (1999a), 'Report on horizontal gene transfer: Director of Public Prosecutions [Ireland] v. Gavin Harte and Others, 22 March 1999' (www.i-sis.dircon.co.uk).

Ho, M. W. (1999b), 'Special Safety Concerns of Transgenic Agriculture and Related Issues' (briefing paper for Minister of State for the Environment), 6 April (www.i-sis.dircon.co.uk).

Ho, M.-W., and Fox, S. W. (eds.) (1988), *Evolutionary Processes and Metaphors*, London: Wiley.

Ho, M.-W., and Goodwin, B. C. (1987), *The Process of Heredity: Genetics S298*, Milton Keynes: Open University Press.

Ho, M.-W., and Saunders, P. T. (1979), 'Beyond neo-Darwinism: an epigenetic approach to evolution', *Journal of Theoretical Biology* 78, 573–91.

Ho, M.-W., and Saunders, P. T. (eds.) (1984), *'Beyond Neo-Darwinism: Introduction to the New Evolutionary Paradigm*, London: Academic Press.

Ho, M.-W., and Saunders, P. T. (1993), 'Rational taxonomy and the natural system, with particular reference to segmentation', *Acta Biotheoretica* 41, 298–304.

Ho, M.-W., and Saunders, P. T. (1994), 'Rational taxonomy and the natural system: segmentation and phyllotaxis', in *Models in Phylogeny Reconstruction* (R. W. Scotland, D. J. Siebert and D. M. Williams, eds.), Oxford: Oxford Science, 113–24.

Ho, M.-W., and Steinbrecher, R. (1998), 'Fatal flaws in food safety assessment: critique of the Joint FAO-WHO Biotechnology and Food Safety Report, *Environmental and Nutritional Interactions* 2, 51–84.

Ho, M.-W., and Tappeser, B. (1997), 'Potential contributions of horizontal gene transfer to the transboundary movement of living modified organisms resulting from modern biotechnology',

Proceedings of Workshop on Transboundary Movement of Living Modified Organisms Resulting from Modern Biotechnology: Issues and Opportunities for Policy-Makers (K. J. Mulongoy, ed.), Geneva: International Academy of the Environment, 171–93.

Ho, M.-W., Tucker, C., Keeley, D., and Saunders, P. T. (1983), 'Effects of successive generations of ether treatment on penetrance and expression of the bithorax phenocopy in *Drosophila melanogaster*', *Journal of Experimental Zoology* 225, 357–68.

Ho, M.-W., Popp, F. A., and Warnke, U. (eds.) (1994), *Bioelectrodynamics and Biocommunication,* Singapore: World Scientific.

Ho, M.-W., Meyer, H., and Cummins, J. (1998a), 'The biotechnology bubble', *Ecologist* 28 (3), 146–53.

Ho, M.-W., Traavik, T., Olsvik, R., Midtvedt, T., Tappeser, B., Howard, V., von Weizsacker, C., and McGavin, G. (1998b), *Gene Technology and Gene Ecology of Infectious Diseases,* Penang: Third World Network; *Microbial Ecology in Health and Disease* 10, 33–59.

Hoeksema, M. J., and Law, C. (1996), 'Cancer mortality rates fall: a turning point for the nation', *Journal of the National Cancer Institute* 88, 1706–7.

Hoffmann, T., Golz, C., and Schieder, O. (1994), 'Foreign DNA sequences are received by a wild-type strain of *Aspergillus niger* after co-culture with transgenic higher plants', *Current Genetics* 27, 70–6.

Höfle, M. G. (1994), 'Auswirkungen der freisetzung bakterieller monokulturen auf die natürliche mikroflora aquatischer ökosysteme', in *Biologische Sicherheit/Forschung Biotechnologie BMFT,* vol. 3, 795–820.

Holmes, T. M., and Ingham, E. R. (1995), 'The effects of genetically engineered microorganisms on soil foodwebs', in *Supplement to Bulletin of Ecological Society of America 75/2, Abstracts of the 79th Annual ESA Meeting: Science and Public Policy,* Knoxville, Tennessee, 2–7 August 1994.

Holtorf, H., Schob, H., Kunz, D., Waldvogel, R., and Meins, F. (1999), 'Stochastic and nonstochastic post-transcriptional silencing of chitinase and beta-1,3-glucanase genes involves increased RNA turnover: possible role for ribosome-independent RNA degradation', *Plant Cell* 11, 471–83.

Horrobin, D. F., Glen, A. I. M., and Hudson, C. J. (1995), 'Possible relevance of phospholipid abnormalities and genetic interactions in psychiatric disorders: the relationship between dyslexia and schizophrenia', *Medical Hypotheses* 45, 605–13.

Hubbard, R. (1995), 'Genomania and health', *American Scientist* 83, 8–10.

Hubbard, R., and Wald, E. (1993), *Exploding the Gene Myth,* Boston: Beacon Press.

Hughes, V. M., and Datta, N. (1983), 'Conjugative plasmids in bacteria of the "pre-antibiotic" era', *Nature* 302, 725–6.

Hyrien, O., and Buttin, G. (1986), 'Gene amplification in pesticide-resistant insects', *Trends in Genetics* 2, 275–6.

Inose, T., and Murata, K. (1995), 'Enhanced accumulation of toxic compounds in yeast cells having high glycolytic activity: a case study on the safety of genetically engineered yeast', *International Journal of Food Science and Technology* 30, 141–6.

Ippen-Ihler, K., and Skurray, R. A. (1993), 'Genetic organization of transfer-related determinants on the sex factor F and related plasmids', in *Bacterial Conjugation* (D. B. Clewell, ed.), New York: Plenum Press, 23–52.

Jablonka, E., and Lamb, M. (1995), *Epigenetic Inheritance and Evolution: The Lamarckian Dimension,* Oxford: Oxford University Press.

Jacks, T., Fazeli, A., Schmitt, E. M., Bronson, R. T., Goodell, M. A., and Weinberg, R. A. (1992), 'Effects of an Rb mutation in the mouse', *Nature* 359, 295–9.

Jager, M. J., and Tappeser, B. (1995), 'Risk assessment and scientific knowledge: current data relating to the survival of GMOs and the persistence of their nucleic acids: is a new debate on safeguards in genetic engineering required?: considerations from an ecological point of view', preprint presented to Third World Network Workshop on Biosafety, 10 April, New York.

James, C. (1998), *Global Review of Commercialized Transgenic Crops: 1998,* New York: ISAAA.

Jane, S. M., Cunningham, J. M., and Vanin, E. F. (1998), 'Vector development: a major obstacle in human gene therapy', *Annals of Medicine* 30, 413–15.

Janetopoulos, C., Cole, E., Smothers, J. F., Allis, C. D., and Aufderheide, K. J. (1999), 'The conjusome: a novel structure in Tetrahymena found only during sexual reorganization', *Journal of Cell Science* 112, 1003–11.

Jeffreys, A. J., Wilson, V., and Thein, S. L. (1985), 'Hypervariable "minisatellite" regions in human DNA', *Nature* 314, 67–73.

Ji, H. J., Liu, Y. L. E., Wang, M. S., Liu, J. W., Xiao, G. W., Joseph, B. D., Rosen, C., and Shi, Y. E. (1997), 'Identification of a breast cancer-specific gene, BCSG1, by direct differential cDNA sequencing', *Cancer Research* 57, 759–64.

Johnston, A. W. B. (1989), 'Biological nitrogen fixation', in *A Revolution in Biotechnology* (J. L. Marx, ed.), Cambridge: Cambridge University Press, 103–18.

Jones, S., and Taylor, K. (eds.) (1995), 'Processes of Heredity: S327 Living Processes, book 4, Milton Keynes: Open University Press.

Jones, S., Martin, R., and Pilbeam, D. (eds.) (1994), *The Cambridge Encyclopedia of Human Evolution,* Cambridge: Cambridge University Press.

Jorgensen, R. B., and Andersen, B. (1994), 'Spontaneous hybridization between oilseed rape (*Brassica napus*) and weedy *B. campestris* (Brassicaceae): a risk of growing genetically modified oilseed rape', *American Journal of Botany* 12, 1620–6.

Kado, C. I. (1993), 'Agrobacterium-mediated transfer and stable incorporation of foreign genes in plants', in *Bacterial Conjugation* (D. B. Clewell, ed.), New York: Plenum Press, 243–54.

Kapur, V., Kanjilal, S., Hamrick, M. R., Li, L. L., Whittam, T. A., Sawyer, S. A., and Musser, J. M. (1995), 'Molecular population genetic analysis of the streptokinase gene of *Streptococcus pyogenes*: mosaic alleles generated by recombination', *Molecular Microbiology* 16, 509–19.

Kehoe, M. A., Kapur, V., Whatmore, A., and Musser, J. M. (1996), 'Horizontal gene transfer among group A streptococci: implications for pathogenesis and epidemiology', *Trends in Microbiology* 4, 436–43.

Kell, C. M., Hordens, J. Z., Daniels, M., Coffey, T. J., Bates, J., Paul, J., Gilks, C., and Spratt, B. G. (1993), 'Molecular epidemiology of penicillin-resistant pneumococci isolated in Nairobi, Kenya', *Infection and Immunity* 61, 4382–91.

Kendall, H. W., Beachy, R., Eisener, T., Gould, F., Herdt, R., Ragen, P. H., Schell, J. S., and Swaminathan, M. S. (1997), *Bioenergineering of Crops: Report of the World Bank Panel on Transgenic Crops,* Washington: World Bank.

Kendrew, J. (ed.) (1995), *The Encyclopedia of Molecular Biology,* Oxford: Blackwell Science.

Kennedy, A. R., Fox, M., Murphy, G., and Little, J. B. (1980), 'Relationship between X-ray exposure and malignant transformation in C3H 10T1/2 cells', *Proceedings of the National Academy of Sciences (USA)* 77, 7262–6.

Kerem, B., Rommens, J. M., Buchanan, J. A., Markiewica, D., Cox, T. K., Chakravarte, A., Buchwald, M., and Tsui, L.-C. (1989), 'Identification of the cystic fibrosis gene: genetic analysis', *Science* 245, 1073–80.

Khavari, P. A. (1997), 'Cutaneous gene therapy', *Advances in Clinical Research* 15, 27–35.

Khor, M. (1996), 'Experts attack shift in global health strategy', *Third World Resurgence* 68, 7–9.

Kimbrell, A. (1993), *The Human Body Shop: The Engineering and Marketing of Life,* Penang: Third World Network.

King, J. L., and Briggs, R. (1955), 'Changes in the nuclei of differentiating gastrula cells, as demonstrated by nuclear transplantation', *Proceedings of the National Academy of Sciences (USA)* 41, 321–5.

Knight, P. (1993), 'Hemorrhagic *E. coli*: the danger increases', *ASM News* 59, 247–50.

Korten, D. C. (1995), *When Corporations Rule the World,* West Hartford (Conn.): Kumarian Press.

Korten, D. C. (1997), 'Civil Societies versus the Global Economy: A Struggle for Life', presentation to 22nd World Conference of the Society for International Development.

Kothari, A. (1994), 'The need for a protocol on farmers' rights and indigenous peoples', *Our Planet* 6, 39–40.

Krause, R. M. (ed.) (1998), *Emerging Infections,* San Diego: Academic Press.

Kropotkin, P. (1914), *Mutual Aid: A Factor of Evolution,* Boston: Extending Horizon Books.

Lamarck, J. B. (1809), *Philosophie Zoologique,* Paris.

Laszlo, E. (1995), *The Interconnected Universe,* Singapore: World Scientific.

Laszlo, E. (1996), *The Whispering Pond,* Rockport (Mass.): Element.

Lau, P. P., Zhu, H. J., Nakamuta, M., and Chan, L. (1997), 'Cloning of an Apobec-1-binding protein that also interacts with apolipoprotein B mRNA and evidence for its involvement in RNA editing', *Journal of Biological Chemistry* 272, 1452–5.

Leape, L. L., Brennan, T. A., Lair, N., Lawthers, A. G., Localio, A. R., Barnes, B. A., Hebert, L., Newhouse, J. P., Weiler, P. C., and Hiatt, H. (1991), 'The nature of adverse events in hospitalized patients: results of the Harvard medical practice study, II', *New England Journal of Medicine* 324, 377–84.

Lebaron, P., Batailler, N., and Baleux, B. (1994), 'Mobilization of a recombinant nonconjugative plasmid at the interface between waste water and the marine coastal environment', *FEMS Microbiology Ecology* 15, 61–70.

Lee, E. Y. H. P., Chang, C. Y., Hu, N., Wang, Y. C. J., Lai, C. C., Herrup, K., and Lee, W. H. (1992), 'Mice deficient for Rb are non-viable and show defects in neurogenesis and haematopoiesis', *Nature* 359, 288–94.

Lee, H. S., Kim, S. W., Lee, K. W., Ericksson, T., and Liu, J. R. (1995), 'Agrobacterium-mediated transformation of ginseng (*Panax ginseng*) and mitotic stability of the inserted beta-glucuronidase gene in regenerants from isolated protoplasts', *Plant Cell Reports* 14, 545–9.

Lemke, P. A., and Taylor, S. L. (1994), 'Allergic reactions and food intolerances', in *Nutritional Toxicology* (F. N. Kotsonis, M. Mackay and J. J. Hjelle, eds.), New York: Raven Press, 117–37.

Lengauer, C., Kinzler, K. W., and Vogelstein, B. (1998), 'Genetic instabilities in human cancers', *Nature* 396, 643–9.

Lenoir, G., Narod, S., Olopade, O., Plummer, S., Ponder, B., Serova, O., Simar, J., Stratton, M., and Warren, B. (1996), 'Mutations and polymorphs in the familial early-onset breast cancer (BRCA1) gene', *Human Mutation* 8, 8–18.

Leong, A. S. Y., Robbins, P., and Spagnolo, D. V. (1995), 'Tumor genes and their proteins in cytologic and surgical specimens: relevance and detection systems', *Diagnostic Cytopathology* 13, 411–22.

Levidow, L., Carr, S., von Schomberg, R., and Wield, D. (1996), 'Bounding the risk assessment of a herbicide–tolerant crop', in *Coping with Deliberate Release: The Limits of Risk Assessment* (A. van Doommelen, ed.), Tilburg: International Centre for Human and Public Affairs, 81–102.

Levy, S. B. (1984), 'Playing antibiotic pool: time to tally the score', *New England Journal of Medicine* 311, 663–4.

Levy, S. B., and Novick, R. P. (eds.) (1986), *Antibiotic Resistance Genes: Ecology, Transfer, and Expression* (Banbury Report 24), New York: Cold Spring Harbor Laboratory.

Lewis, D. L., and Gattie, D. K. (1991), 'The ecology of quiescent microbes', *ASM News* 57, 27–32.

Lewontin, R. C. (1982), *Human Diversity,* Freeman (New York): Scientific American Books.

Lewontin, R. C. (1985), 'Whatever happened to eugenics?', *Genewatch* Jan.–Apr., 8–10.

Lin, S., Gaiano, N., Culp, P., Burns, J. C., Friedmann, T., Yee, J.-K., and Hopkins, N. (1994), 'Integration and germ-line transmission of a pseudotyped retroviral vector in zebrafish', *Science* 265, 666–9.

Lommel, S. A., and Xiong, Z. (1991), 'Recombination of a functional red clover necrotic mosaic virus by recombination rescue of the cell-to-cell movement gene expressed in a transgenic plant', *Journal of Cell Biochemistry* 15A, 151.

Longerich, S., Galloway, A. M., Harris, R. S., Wong, C., and Rosenberg, S. M. (1995), 'Adaptive mutation sequences reproduced by mismatch repair deficiency', *Proceedings of the National Academy of Sciences (USA)* 92, 12017–20.

Lorenz, M. G., and Wackernagel, W. (1994), 'Bacterial gene transfer by natural genetic transformation in the environment', *Microbiological Reviews* 58, 563–602.

Losey, J. E., Rayor, L. D., and Carter, M. E. (1999), 'Transgenic pollen harms monarch larvae', *Nature* 399, 214.

Lovelock, J. (1979), *A New Look at Gaia,* Oxford: Oxford University Press.

Lovelock, J. (1996), 'The Gaia hypothesis', in *Gaia in Action, Science of the Living Earth* (P. Bunyard, ed.), Edinburgh: Floris Books, 15–33.

Lundstrom, K., and Turpin, M. P. (1996), 'Proposed schizophrenia-related gene polymorphism, expression of the ser9gly mutant human dopamine D-3 receptor with the semliki-forest-virus system', *Biochemical and Biophysical Research Communications* 225, 1068–72.

Luvall, J. C., and Holbo, H. R. (1991), 'Thermal remote sensing methods in landscape ecology', in *Quantitative Methods in Landscape Ecology* (M. Turner and R. H. Gardner, eds.), New York: Springer, chap. 6.

McClintock, B. (1984), 'The significance of responses of the genome to challenge', *Science* 226, 792–801.

Mackey, B. M., and Gibson, C. R. (1988), '*Escherichia coli* 0157: from farm to fork, and beyond', *SGM Quarterly,* May, 55–7.

McKinney, J. D., Jacobs, W. R., Jr, and Bloom, B. R. (1998), 'Persisting problems in tuberculosis', in *Emerging Infections* (R. M. Krause, ed.), San Diego: Academic Press.

McNally, R. (1995), 'Genetic madness: the European rabies eradication programme', *Ecologist* 24, 207–12.

McNally, R., and Wheale, P. (1996), 'Biopatenting and biodiversity: comparative advantages in the new global order', *Ecologist* 26, 5, 222–8.

McTaggart, L. (1996), *What Doctors Don't Tell You: The Truth about the Dangers of Modern Medicine,* London: Thorsons.

Mahy, B. W. J. (1997), 'Emerging virus infections', *Viral International* 48 (2), 1–2.

Maier, R. M., Zeltz, P., Kossel, H., Bonnard, G., Gualberto, J. M., and Grienenberger, J. M. (1996), 'RNA editing in plant mitochondria and chloroplasts', *Plant Molecular Biology* 32, 343–65.

Manavathu, E. K., Hiratsuka, K., and Taylor, D. E. (1988), 'Nucleotide sequence analysis and expression of a tetracycline-resistance gene from *Campylobacter jejuni*', *Gene* 62, 17–26.

Mander, J., and Goldsmith, E. (eds.) (1996), *The Case Against the Global Economy and for a Turn Toward the Local,* San Francisco: Sierra Club Books.

Marshall, R. J. (1984), 'The genetics of schizophrenia revisited', *Bulletin of the British Psychological Society* 37, 177–81.

Martin, W. J. (1999), 'Bacteria-related sequences in a simian cytomegalovirus-derived stealth virus culture', *Experimental and Molecular Pathology* 66, 8–14.

Mayeno, A. N., and Gleich, G. J. (1994), 'Eosinophilia: myalgia syndrome and tryptophan production: a cautionary tale', *Trends in Biotechnology* 12 (9), 346–52.

Mazodier, P., and Davies, J. (1991), 'Gene transfer between distantly related bacteria', *Annual Review of Genetics* 25, 147–71.

Meister, I., and Mayer, S. (1994), *Genetically Engineered Plants: Releases and Impacts on Less Developed Countries: A Greenpeace Inventory,* Greenpeace International.

Mellon, M., and Rissler, J. (1995), 'Transgenic crops: USDA data on small-scale tests contribute little to commercial risk assessment', *Biotechnology* 13, 96.

Mercer, D. K., Scott, K. P., Bruce-Johnson, W. A., Glover, L. A., and Flint, H. J. (1999), 'Fate of free DNA and transformation of the oral bacterium *Streptococcus gordonii* DL1 by plasmid DNA in human saliva', Applied and *Environmental Microbiology* 65, 6–10.

Mezrioui, N., and Echab, K. (1995), 'Drug resistance in *Salmonella* strains isolated from domestic waste water before and after treatment in stabilization ponds in an arid region (Marrakech, Morocco)', *World Journal of Microbiology and Biotechnology* 11, 287–90.

Mihill, C. (1996), 'Killer diseases making a comeback, says WHO', *Guardian,* 10 May 1996, 3.

Mikkelsen, T. R., Andersen, B., and Jorgensen, R. B. (1996), 'The risk of crop transgene spread', *Nature* 380, 31.

Miller, H. (1995) 'Don't need, don't look' (letter to the editor), *Biotechnology* 13, 201.

Miller, R. V. (1998), 'Bacterial gene swapping in nature', *Scientific American,* Jan., 67–71.

Moens, L., Vanfleteren, J., Vandepeer, Y., Peeters, K., Kapp, O., Czeluzniak, J., Goodman, M., Blaxter, M., and Vinogradov, S. (1996), 'Globins in nonvertebrate species: dispersal by horizontal gene transfer and evolution of the structure-function relationships', *Molecular Biology and Evolution* 13, 324–33.

Moffat, A. S. (1996), 'Biodiversity is a boon to ecosystems, not species', *Science* 271, 1497.

Mondal, S., and Heidelberger, C. (1970), 'In vitro malignant transformation by methylcholanthrene of the progeny of single cells derived from C3H mouse prostate', *Proceedings of the National Academy of Sciences (USA)* 65, 219–29.

Moore, J. A. (1955), 'Abnormal combinations of nuclear and cytoplasmic systems in frogs and toads', *Advances in Genetics* 7, 139–82.

Morgan, T. H. (1916), *A Critique of the Theory of Evolution,* Princeton: Princeton University Press, 187–90.

Morse, S. S. (ed.) (1993), *Emerging Viruses,* New York: Oxford University Press.

Mshigeni, K., and Pauli, G. (1997), 'Brewing and future', *Yes!': A Journal of Positive Futures,* spring, 41–3.

Mulvihill, J. J. (1995), 'Craniofacial syndromes: no such thing as a single-gene disease', *Nature Genetics* 9, 101–3.

Neilson, J. W., Josephson, K. L., Pepper, I. L., Arnold, R. B., Digiovanni, G. D., and Sinclair, N. A. (1994), 'Frequency of horizontal gene transfer of a large catabolic plasmid (PJP4) in soil', *Applied and Environmental Microbiology* 60, 4053–8.

Neu, H. C. (1992), 'The crisis in antibiotic resistance', *Science* 237, 1064–72.

Nijar, G. S., and Chee, Y. L. (1994), 'Intellectual property rights: the threat to farmers and biodiversity', *Third World Resurgence* 39, 8–10.

Nikaido, H. (1994), 'Prevention of drug access to bacterial targets: permeability barriers and active efflux', *Science* 264, 382–8.

Nordlee, J. A., Taylor, S. L., Townsend, J. A., Thomas, L. A., and Bush, R. K. (1996), 'Identification of a brazil nut allergen in transgenic soybeans', *New England Journal of Medicine,* 14 March, 688–728.

Offit, K., Gilewski, T., McGuire, P., Schluger, A., Hampel, H., Brown, K., Swensen, J., Neuhausen, S., Skolnick, M., Norton, L., and Goldgar, D. (1996), 'Germline BRCA1 185delAG mutations in Jewish women with breast cancer', *Lancet* 347, 1643–5.

Olby, R. C. (1966), *Origins of Mendelism,* London: Constable.

Old, R. W., and Primrose, S. B. (1994), *Principles of Gene Manipulation* (fifth edition), Oxford: Blackwell Science.

Oldroy, D. R. (1980), *Darwinian Impacts,* Milton Keynes: Open University Press.

Osbourn, J. K., Sarkar, S., and Wilson, M. A. (1990), 'Complementation of coat protein-defective TMV mutants in transgenic tobacco plants expressing TMV coat protein', *Virology* 179, 921–5.

Pain, S. (1997), 'The plague dogs', *New Scientist* 19 April, 32–7.

Palca, J. (1986), 'Living outside regulation', *Nature* 324, 202.

Pang, Y., Brown, B. A., Steingrube, V. A., Wallance, R. J., Jr, and Roberts, M. C. (1994), 'Tetracycline-resistance determinants in Mycobacterium and Streptomyces species', *Antimicrobial Agents and Chemotherapy* 38, 1408–12.

Parr, D. (1977), *Genetic Engineering: Too Good to Go Wrong?*, London: Greenpeace.

Paulkaitis, P., and Rossinck, M. J. (1996), 'Spontaneous change of a benign satellite RNA of cucumber mosaic virus to a pathogenic variant', *Nature Biotechnology* 14, 1264–8.

Perlas, N. (1994), *Overcoming Illusions about Biotechnology,* London: Zed Books, and Penang: Third World Network.

Perlas, N. (1995), 'Dangerous trends in agricultural biotechnology', *Third World Resurgence* 38, 15–16.

Pimm, S. L. (1991), *Balance of Nature: Ecological Issues in the Conservation of Species and Communities,* Chicago: University of Chicago Press.

Pollard, J. W. (1984), 'Is Weismann's barrier absolute?', in *Beyond Neo-Darwinism: Introduction to the New Evolutionary Paradigm* (M.-W. Ho and P. T. Saunders, eds.), London: Academic Press, 291–315.

Pollard, J. W. (ed.) (1984), *Evolution Theory: Paths into the Future,* London: Wiley.

Pollard, J. W. (1988), 'The fluid genome and evolution', in *Evolutionary Processes and Metaphors* (M.-W. Ho and S. W. Fox, eds.), London: Wiley, 63–84.

Prager, R., Beer, W., Voigt, W., Claus, H., Seltmann, G., Stephan, R., Bockemuehl, J., and Tschäpe, H. (1995), 'Genomic and biochemical relatedness between vibrio-cholerae', *Zentralblatt für Bakteriologie* 283 (1), 14–28.

Pretty, J. (1995), *Regenerating Agriculture: Policies and Practice for Sustainability and Self-Reliance,* London: Earthscan.

Pretty, J. (1998), 'Feeding the world?', *Splice* 4, 4–6.

Provine, W. B. (1971), *The Origins of Theoretical Population Genetics,* Chicago: University of Chicago Press.

Putnam, L. (1998), 'Debate grows on safety of gene-therapy vectors', *Lancet* 351, 808.

Puttarju, M., Jamison, S. F., Mansfield, S. G., Garcia-Blanco, M. A., and Mitchell, L. G. (1999), 'Spliceosome-mediated RNA trans-splicing as a tool for gene therapy', *Nature Biotechnology* 17, 246–52.

Raven, P. (1994), 'Why it matters', *Our Planet* 6, 5–8.

Reddy, S. P., Rasmussen, W. G., and Baseman, J. B. (1995), 'Molecular cloning and characterization of an adherence-related operon of myocplasma-genitalium', *Journal of Bacteriology* 177, 5943–51.

Redenbaugh, K., Hiatt, W., Martineau, B., Lindemann, J., and Emlay, D. (1994), 'Aminoglycoside 3¢-phosphotransferase-II (alph(3¢)II): review of its safety and use in the production of genetically engineered plants', *Food Biotechnology* 8, 137–65.

Regal, P. J. (1994), 'Scientific principles for ecologically based risk assessment of transgenic organisms', *Molecular Ecology* 3, 5–13.

Reganold, J. P., Papendick, R. J., and Parr, J. F. (1999), 'Sustainable agriculture', *Scientific American*, June, 72–8.

Reidl, J., and Mekalanos, J. J. (1995), 'Characterization of *Vibrio cholerae* bacteriophage-K139 and use of a novel mini-transposon to identify a phage-encoded virulence factor', *Molecular Microbiology* 18, 685–701.

Rennie, J. (1993), 'DNA's new twists', *Scientific American,* Mar., 88–96.

Reynolds, M. P., van Beem, J., van Ginkel, M., and Holsington, D. (1996), *Breaking the Yield Barriers to Wheat: A Brief Summary of the Outcomes of an International Consultation,* Centro Internacional para Mejoramiento de Maíz y Trigo [International Maize and Wheat Improvement Centre].

Riede, I. (1996), 'Three mutant genes co-operatively induce brain tumor formation in *Drosophila* malignant brain tumor', *Cancer Genetics and Cytogenetics* 90, 135–41.

Rifkin, J., and Howard, T. (1980), *Entropy: A New World View,* New York: Viking Press.

Riley, L. W., Remis, R. S., Helgerson, S. D., et al., (1983), 'Hemorrhagic colitis associated with a rare *Escherichia coli* serotype', *New England Journal of Medicine* 308, 681–85.

Ripp, S., Ogunseitan, O. A., and Miller, R. V. (1994), 'Transduction of a fresh-water microbial community by a new *Pseudomonas aeruginosa* generalized transducing phage, UT1', *Molecular Ecology* 3 (2), 121–6.

Rissler, J., and Mellon, M. (1993), *Perils Amidst the Promise: Ecological Risks of Transgenic Crops in a Global Market,* Washington: Union of Concerned Scientists.

Roberts, M. C. (1989), 'Gene transfer in the urogenital and respiratory tract', in *Gene Transfer in the Environment* (S. Levy and R. V. Miller, eds.), New York: McGraw-Hill, 347–75.

Roberts, M. C., and Hillier, S. L. (1990), 'Genetic basis of tetracycline-resistance in urogenital bacteria', *Antimicrobial Agents and Chemotherapy* 34, 261–4.

Rose, S., Kamin, L. J., and Lewontin, R. C. (1984), *Not in Our Genes,* Harmondsworth (Middx): Penguin.

Rothenfluh, H. S., Blanden, R. V., and Steele, E. J. (1995), 'Hypothesis: a memory lymphocyte-specific soma-to-germline genetic feedback loop', *Immunology and Cell Biology* 73, 174–80.

Rothenfluh, H. S., and Steele, E. J. (1993), 'Origin and maintenance of germ-line V genes', *Immunology and Cell Biology* 71, 227–32.

Rowe, D. (1987), *Beyond Fear,* London: Fontana.

Roy-Burman, P. (1996), 'Endogenous env elements: partners in generation of pathogenic feline leukemia viruses', *Virus Genes* 11, 157–61.

Rubin, H. (1992), 'Cancer development: the rise of epigenetics', *European Journal of Cancer* 28, 1–2.

Rubin, A. L., Arnstein, P., and Rubin, H. (1990), 'Physiological induction and reversal of focus formation and tumorigenicity in NIH-3T3 cells', *Proceedings of the National Academy of Sciences (USA)* 87, 482–6.

Salyers, A. A., and Shoemaker, J. B. (1994), 'Broadhost range gene transfer: plasmids and conjugative transposons', *FEMS Microbiology Ecology* 15, 15–22.

Sandaa, R. A., and Enger, Ø. (1994), 'Transfer in marine sediments of the naturally occurring plasmid pRAS1 encoding multiple antibiotic-resistance', *Applied and Environmental Microbiology* 60, 4243–48.

Sandberg, J. W., Lau, C., Jacomino, M., Finegold, M., and Henning, S. J. (1994), 'Improving access to intestinal stem cells as a route toward intestinal gene transfer', *Human Gene Therapy* 5, 323–9.

Sandmeier, H. (1994), 'Acquisition and rearrangement of sequence motifs in the evolution of bacteriophage tail fibers', *Molecular Microbiology* 12, 343–50.

Saunders, J. R., and Saunders, V. A. (1993), 'Genotypic and phenotypic methods for the detection of specific released microorganisms, in *Monitoring Genetically Manipulated Microorganisms in the Environment* (C. Edwards, ed.), New York: Wiley, 27–59.

Saunders, P. T. (1984), 'Development and evolution', in *Beyond Neo-Darwinism: Introduction to the New Evolutionary Paradigm* (M.-W. Ho and P. T. Saunders, eds.), London: Academic Press, 243–63.

Saunders, P. T. (1994), 'Evolution without natural selection: further implications of the Daisyworld parable', *Journal of Theoretical Biology* 166, 365–73.

Saunders, P. T., and Ho, M.-W. (1995), 'Reliable segmentation by successive bifurcation', *Bulletin of Mathematical Biology* 57, 539–56.

Schäfer, A., Kalinowski, J., and Pühler, A. (1994), 'Increased fertility of *Corynebacterium glutamicum* recipients in intergeneric matings with *Escherichia coli* after stress exposure', *Applied and Environmental Microbiology* 60, 756–9.

Schluter, K., Futterer, J., and Potrykus, I. (1995), 'Horizontal gene transfer from a transgenic potato line to a bacterial pathogen (*Erwinia chrysanthem*) occurs, if at all, at an extremely low frequency', *Biotechnology* 13, 1094–8.

Schneider, E. D., and Kay, J. J. (1994), 'Life as a manifestation of the Second Law of Thermodynamics', *Mathematical Computing and Modeling* 19, 25–48.

Schnitzler, N., Podbielski, A., Baumgarten, G., Mignon, M., and Kaufhold, A. (1995), 'M-protein or M-like protein gene polymorphisms in human group G Streptococci', *Journal of Clinical Microbiology* 33, 356–63.

Schoelz, J. E., and Wintermantel, W. M. (1993), 'Expansion of viral host range through complementation and recombination in transgenic plants', *Plant Cell* 5, 1669–79.

Schrag, S. J., and Perrot, V. (1996), 'Reducing antibiotic resistance', *Nature* 381, 120–1.

Schrödinger, E. (1944), *What is Life?*, Cambridge: Cambridge University Press.

Schubbert, R., Renz, D., Schmitz, B., and Doerrfler, W., (1977), 'Foreign (M13) DNA ingested by mice reaches peripheral leukocytes, spleen and liver via the intestinal wall mucosa and can be covalently linked to mouse DNA', *Proceedings of the National Academy of Sciences (USA)* 94, 961–6.

Schubbert, R., Lettmann, C., and Doerfler, W. (1994), 'Ingested foreign (phage M13) DNA survives transiently in the gastrointestinal tract and enters the bloodstream of mice', *Molecular and General Genetics* 242, 495–504.

Seitz, S., Rohde, K., Bender, E., Nothnagel, A., Kolble, K., Shlag, P. M., and Scherneck, S. (1997), 'Strong indication for a breast cancer susceptibility gene on chromosome 8, p12–p22: linkage analysis in German breast cancer families', *Oncogene* 14, 741–3.

Shihabuddin, L., Silverman, J. M., Buchsbaum, M. S., Seiver, L. J., Luu, C., Germans, M. K., Metzger, M., Mohs, R. C., Smith, C. J., Spiegelcohen, J., and Davis, K. L. (1996), 'Ventricular enlargement associated with linkage marker for schizophrenia-related disorders in one pedigree', *Molecular Psychiatry* 1, 215–22.

Shiva, V. (1993), *Monoculture of the Mind,* Penang: Third World Network.

Shiva, V. (1994), 'Why we should say "no" to GATT-TRIPS', *Third World Resurgence* 39, 3–5.

Shiva, V., Jafri, A. H., Bedi, G., and Holla-Bhar, R. (1997), *The Enclosure and Recovery of the Commons,* New Delhi: Research Foundation for Science, Technology and Ecology.

Skogsmyr, I. (1994), 'Gene dispersal from transgenic potatoes to conspecifics: a field trial', *Theoretical and Applied Genetics* 88, 770–4.

Smerdon, G., Aves, S., and Walton, E. (1995), 'Production of human gastric lipase in the fission yeast', *Gene* 165, 313–18.

Smirnov, V. V., Rudendo, A. V., Samgorodskaya, N. V., Sorokulova, I. B., Reznik, S. R., and Sergeichuk, T. M. (1994), 'Susceptibility to antimicrobial drugs of Bacilli used as basis for some probiotics', *Antibiotiki i Khimioterapiya* 39, 23–8.

Sommer, S. S. (1995), 'Recent human germ-line mutation: inferences from patients with hemophilia B', *Trends in Genetics* 11, 141–7.

Soros, G. (1997), 'Capital crimes', *Guardian,* 18 January, 1–3.

Sougakoff, N., Papadopoulou, B., Norman, P., and Courvalin, P. (1987), 'Nucleotide sequence and distribution of gene tetO encoding tetracycline-resistance in *Campylobacter coli'*, *FEMS Microbiological Letters* 44, 153–9.

Spadafora, C. (1998), 'Sperm cells and foreign DNA: a controversial relation', *Bioessays* 20, 955–64.

Spallone, P. (1993), *Generation Games, Genetic Engineering and the Future for our Lives,* London: Women's Press.

Speer, B. S., Shoemaker, N. B., and Salyers, A. A. (1992), 'Bacterial resistance to tetracycline: mechanisms, transfer and clinical significance', *Reviews in Microbiology* 5, 387–99.

Spielman, A. (1994), 'Why entomological antimalaria research should not focus on transgenic mosquitoes', *Parasitology Today* 10, 374–6.

Spratt, B. G. (1988), 'Hybrid penicillin-binding proteins in penicillin-resistant strains of *Neisseria gonorrhoeae'*, *Nature* 332, 173–6.

Spratt, B. G. (1994), 'Resistance to antibiotics mediated by target alterations', *Science* 264, 388.

Stachel, S. C., Timmerman, B., and Zambryski, P. (1986), 'Generation of single-stranded T-DNA molecules during the initial stages of T-DNA transfer from *Agrobacterium tumefaciens* to plant cells', *Nature* 322, 706–12.

Steele, E. J. (1979), *Somatic Selection and Adaptive Evolution,* Toronto: Williams and Wallace.

Steele, E. J., Lindley, R. A., and Blanden, R. V. (1998), *Lamarck's Signature: How Retrogenes are Changing Darwin's Natural Selection Paradigm,* Sydney: Allen and Unwin.

Steinbrecher, R. (1997), 'From green to gene revolution: the environmental risks of genetically engineered crops', *Ecologist* 26, 273–81.

Stephenson, J. R., and Warnes, A. (1996), 'Release of genetically modified microorganisms into the environment', *Journal of Chemical Technology and Biotechnology* 65, 5–16.

Stokes, H. W., and Hall, R. M. (1989), 'A novel family of potentially mobile DNA elements encoding site-specific gene-integration functions: integrons', *Molecular Microbiology* 3, 1669–83.

Stokes, H. W., and Hall, R. M. (1992), 'The integron in plasmid R46 includes two copies of the oxa2 gene cassette', *Plasmid* 28, 225–34.

Strohman, R. (1994), 'Epigenesis: the missing beat in biotechnology?', *Biotechnology* 12, 156–64.

Strohman, R. (1997), 'The coming Khunian revolution in biology', *Nature Biotechnology* 15, 194–200.

Summers, K. M. (1996), 'Relationship between genotype and phenotype in monogenic diseases: relevance to polygenic diseases', *Human Mutation* 7, 283–98.

Symonds, N. (1994), 'Directed mutation: a current perspective', *Journal of Theoretical Biology* 169, 317–22.

Temin, H. M. (1980), 'Origin of retroviruses from cellular moveable genetic elements', *Cell* 21, 599–600.

Temin, H. M. (1985), 'Reverse transcription in the eukaryotic genome: retroviruses, pararetroviruses, retrotransposons, and retrotranscripts', *Molecular Biology and Evolution* 2, 455–68.

Temin, H. M., and Engels, W. (1984), 'Movable genetic elements and evolution', in *Evolutionary Theory: Paths Into the Future* (J. W. Pollard, ed.), London: Wiley.

Thompson, W. C., and Ford, S. (1990), 'Is DNA fingerprinting ready for the courts?', *New Scientist* 31 March, 38–43.

Thompson, M. W., McInnes, R. R., and Willard, H. F. (1991), *Genetics in Medicine* (fifth edition), London: W. B. Saunders.

Torres, O. G., Korman, R. Z., Zahler, S. A., and Dunny, G. M. (1991), 'The conjugative transposon Tn925: enhancement of conjugal transfer by tetracycline in *Enterococcus faecalis* and mobilization of chromosomal genes in *Bacillus subtilis* and *E. faecalis*', *Molecular and General Genetics* 225, 395–400.

Traavik, T. (1998), 'Too Early May Be Too Late: Ecological Risks Associated with the Use of Naked DNA as a Biological Tool for Research, Production and Therapy: Report for the Directorate for Nature Research' [English translation], Trondheim.

Trieu-Cuot, P., Gerbaud, G., Lambert, T., and Courvalin, P. (1985), 'In vivo transfer of genetic information between Gram-positive and Gram-negative bacteria', *EMBO Journal* 4, 3583–7.

Tschäpe, H. (1994), 'The spread of plasmids as a function of bacterial adaptability', *FEMS Microbiology Ecology* 15, 23–32.).

Turing, A. M. (1952), 'The chemical basis of morphogenesis', *Philosophical Transactions of the Royal Society*, B.237, 37–72.

UBINIG, *Military Objectives of Cholera Research and Violation of Biomedical Ethics in the Research on Human Subjects: Women and*

Children of Bangladesh as Experimental Animals (UBINIG series on IGDDR, B, no. 1), Dhaka: Narigrantha Prabartana 1996.

UBINIG and Asian Women's Human Rights Council, *Report on International Public Hearing on Crimes Against Women Related to Population Policies, Cairo, September 1994.*

Udo, E. E., and Grubb, W. B. (1990), 'Transfer of resistance determinants from a multi-resistant *Staphylococcus aureus* isolate', *Journal of Medical Microbiology* 35, 72–9.

Upton, M., Carter, P. E., Organe, G., and Pennington, T. H. (1996), 'Genetic heterogeneity of M-type-3 G group A *Streptococci* causing severe infections in Tayside, Scotland', *Journal of Clinical Microbiology* 34, 196–8.

Vaden, V. S., and Melcher, U. (1990), 'Recombination sites in cauliflower mosaic virus DNAs: implications for mechanisms of recombination', *Virology* 177, 717–26.

van Heyningen, V. (1994), 'One gene—four syndromes, *Nature* 367, 319–20.

Vasquez, G. R. (1997), 'Protecting People's Rights to Productive Resources', presentation to Twenty-Second World Conference of SID, Santiago, Spain, May 1997.

Vazquez Vega, I. H. (1998), 'Situación de la Agricultura Biológica en Cuba', manuscript and personal communication, Vida Sana award ceremony, Barcelona, 9 June.

Virgin, I., and Federick, R. J. (eds.) (1996), *Biosafety Capacity Building: Evaluation Criteria Development,* Stockholm: Stockholm Environmental Institute.

Vlack, J., Scoulten, A., Usmany, M., Belsham, G., Klingeroode, E., Maule, A., Vanlent, M., and Zuideman, D. (1990), 'Expression of cauliflower mosaic virus gene I', *Virology* 1709, 312–20.

Volk, W. A., Gerbhardt, B. M., Hammarskjold, M. L., and Kadner, R. J. (1995), *Essentials of Medical Microbiology* (fifth edition), Philadelphia: Lippincott-Raven.

Wahl, G. M., de Saint Vincent, B. R., and De Rose, M. L. (1984), 'Effect of chromosomal position on amplification of transfected genes in animal cells', *Nature* 307, 516–20.

Waisfisz, Q., Morgan, N. V., Savino, M., et al. (1999), 'Spontaneous functional correction of homozygous Fanconi anaemia alleles reveals novel mechanistic basis for reverse mosaicism', *Nature Genetics* 22, 379–83.

Wakayama, T., Perry, A. C. G., Zuccotti, M., Johnson, K. R., and Yanagimachi, R. (1998), 'Full-term development of mice from enucleated oocytes injected with cumulus cell nuclei', *Nature* 394, 369–74.

Warren, A. M., and Crampton, J. M. (1994), 'Mariner: its prospects as a DNA vector for the genetic manipulation of medically important insects', *Parasitology Today* 10, 58–63.

Watkins, K. (1996), 'Free trade and farm fallacies', *Ecologist* 26, 244–55.

Watkins, K. (1999), 'Free trade and farm fallacies', *Third World Resurgence* 100–101, 33–7.

Weatherall, D. (1993), *The New Genetics and Clinical Practice,* Oxford: Oxford University Press.

Webster, G., and Goodwin, B. C. (1982), 'On the origin of species: a structuralist approach', *Journal of Social and Biological Structures* 5, 15–47.

Webster, G., and Goodwin, B. C. (1996), *Form and Transformation,* Cambridge: Cambridge University Press.

Weiss, R. (1998), 'Transgenic pigs and virus adaptation', *Nature* 391, 327–8.

Whatmore, A. M., Kapur, V., Musser, J. M., and Kehoe, M. A. (1995), 'Molecular population genetic analysis of the enn subdivision of group A Streptococcal emm-like genes: horizontal gene transfer and restricted variation among enn genes', *Molecular Microbiology* 15, 1039–48.

Whatmore, A. M., and Kehoe, M. A. (1994), 'Horizontal gene transfer in the evolution of group A Streptococcal emm-like genes: gene mosaics and variation in vir regulons', *Molecular Microbiology* 11, 363–74.

Wilmut, I., Schnieke, A. E., McWhir, J., Kind, A. J., and Campbell, K. H. S. (1997), 'Viable offspring derived from fetal and adult mammalian cells', *Nature* 385, 810–13.

Wilson, E. O. (1975), *Sociobiology,* Cambridge (Mass.): Belknap Press.

Winn, R. N., Vanbeneden, R. J., and Burkhart, J. G. (1995), 'Transfer, methylation and spontaneous mutation frequency of fX174am3cs70 sequences in medaka (*Oryzia latipies*) and mummichog (*Fundulus heteroclitus*): implications for gene transfer and environmental mutagenesis in aquatic species', *Journal of Marine Environmental Research* 40, 247–65.

Wintermantel, W. M., and Schoelz, J. E. (1996), 'Isolation of recombinant viruses between cauliflower mosaic virus and a viral gene in transgenic plants under conditions of moderate selection pressure', *Virology* 223, 156–64.

Wirz, J. (1997), 'DNA at the edge of contextual biology', in *The Future of DNA* (J. Wirz and E. Lammerts van Bueren, eds.), Dordrecht: Kluwer Academic, 94–103.

Wolfe, J. (1995), 'Cystic fibrosis', in *Processes of Heredity, S327: Living Processes, book 4* (S. Jones and K. Taylor, eds.), Milton Keynes: Open University Press.

Wolpert, L. (1996), 'In praise of science', in *Science Today: Problem or Crisis?* (R. Levinson and J. Thomas, eds.), London: Routledge, 9–21.

Wright, H., Carver, A., and Cottom, D. (1991), 'High-level expression of active human alpha-1 antitrypsin in the milk of transgenic sheep', *Biotechnology* 9, 830–4.

Xiong, Y., and Eikbush, T. (1990), 'Origin and evolution of retroelements based upon the reverse tramscrotase sequence', *EMBO Journal* 9, 3363–72.

Yin, X., and Stotzky, G. (1997), 'Gene transfer among bacteria in natural environment', *Applied Microbiology* 46, 153–212.

Young, R. M. (1985), *Darwin's Metaphor,* Cambridge: Cambridge University Press.

NOTE ON THE AUTHOR

Dr Mae-Wan Ho is a well-known and respected British scientist. She is reader in biology at the Open University, where she teaches and researches in genetics, evolution, and the physics of organisms and sustainable systems. She gained her PhD in biochemistry at Hong Kong University, became a postdoctoral research fellow at the University of California in San Diego, and was awarded a fellowship of the National Genetics Foundation. She went on to become a senior research fellow at the University of London before joining the Open University in 1976.

Mae-Wan Ho is a popular public lecturer and a frequent contributor to radio and television. Her awards include Chan Kai Ming Prize for Biological Sciences (Hong Kong), 1964, fellow of the National Genetics Foundation (United States), 1971–4, Vida Sana Award (Spain), 1998, and guest of honour at Women of the Year Luncheon and Assembly (England), 1998. She has written papers for the public and for policy-makers and debated with spokespersons of the biotech industry in Britain, the United States, and many other countries, and has debated issues in the United Nations, the World Bank, and the European Parliament. Since 1994 she has been scientific adviser on genetic-engineering biotechnology and biosafety to the Third World Network and other public interest organisations.

Mae-Wan Ho is also a prolific writer, with almost two hundred publications to her credit, covering human biochemical genetics, evolution, developmental biology, and biophysics. Her books include *Beyond Neo-Darwinism: Introduction to the New Evolutionary Paradigm* (1984), *Evolutionary Processes and Metaphors* (1988), *The Rainbow and the Worm: The Physics of Organisms* (1993 and 1998), *Bioelectrodynamics and Biocommunication* (1994), *Bioenergetics* (1995), *Gene Technology and the Etiology of Infectious Diseases* (1998), and *Love of the Magician* (forthcoming).

INDEX